FIELDWORK FOR SOCIAL RESEARCH

FIELDWORK FOR SOCIAL RESEARCH

A STUDENT'S GUIDE

RICHARD PHILLIPS
JENNIFER JOHNS

Sage

1 Oliver's Yard
55 City Road
London EC1Y 1SP

2455 Teller Road
Thousand Oaks, California 91320

Unit No 323-333, Third Floor, F-Block
International Trade Tower Nehru Place
New Delhi 110 019

8 Marina View Suite 43-053
Asia Square Tower 1
Singapore 018960

Editor: Jai Seaman
Editorial Assistant: Rhiannon Holt
Production Editor: Neelu Sahu and Tanya Kapoor
Copyeditor: Joy Tucker
Indexer: KnowledgeWorks Global Ltd
Marketing Manager: Ben Sherwood
Cover Design: Shaun Mercier
Typeset by KnowledgeWorks Global Ltd
Printed in the UK

© Richard Phillips & Jennifer Johns 2024

Apart from any fair dealing for the purposes of research, private study, or criticism or review, as permitted under the Copyright, Designs and Patents Act, 1988, this publication may not be reproduced, stored or transmitted in any form, or by any means, without the prior permission in writing of the publisher, or in the case of reprographic reproduction, in accordance with the terms of licences issued by the Copyright Licensing Agency. Enquiries concerning reproduction outside those terms should be sent to the publisher.

Library of Congress Control Number: 2023936481

British Library Cataloguing in Publication data

A catalogue record for this book is available from the British Library

ISBN 978-1-5297-6439-0
ISBN 978-1-5297-6438-3 (pbk)

At Sage we take sustainability seriously. Most of our products are printed in the UK using responsibly sourced papers and boards. When we print overseas we ensure sustainable papers are used as measured by the Paper Chain Project grading system. We undertake an annual audit to monitor our sustainability.

CONTENTS

List of Postcards vii
About the Authors and Contributors ix
Acknowledgements xiii

1. Introduction 1

Part I Getting Started 5

2. Fieldwork and the Field 7
3. Curiosity and Research Design 23

Part II Critical Fieldwork 37

4. Working Together 39
5. Ethical Fieldwork 55
6. Decolonising Fieldwork 75

Part III Methods in Context 91

7. Interviewing in the Field 93
8. Participant Observation and Participatory Fieldwork 115
9. Visual Fieldwork 133
10. Digital Fieldwork 153
11. Social Media for Fieldwork 173
12. Multisensory and Embodied Fieldwork 191
13. Exploring with Secondary Sources 209
14. Understanding and Handling Your Data 229
15. Takeaways: For Work and Life 245

Glossary 251
Bibliography 255
Index 289

LIST OF POSTCARDS

2.1	Why is fieldwork important? Notes from a chicken farm, by Peter A. Jackson	10
2.2	Unexpected events at an epilepsy clinic in Cape Town, by Mpoe Johannah Keikelame	17
3.1	Becoming curious: Korean students in Central Asia, by Su-Jeong Kim	25
3.2	Open-ended fieldwork, curiosity and learning in South India, by Matt Baillie Smith	30
4.1	Bodies uncomfortably close, by Michael R. Glass	43
4.2	Considering mobility, by Morag Rose	49
5.1	On the sleeper train to Austria, by Russell Hitchings	59
5.2	Drawing as an ethical research method, by Will Haynes	64
5.3	Is leaving ever possible? Some thoughts on fieldwork endings, by Sarah Marie Hall	70
6.1	What this day taught you, by Sarah de Leeuw	81
7.1	Conducting qualitative interviews with people who have life-limiting illness, by Geraldine Foley	104
7.2	Being present in an interview, by Jennifer Johns	108
8.1	Collecting and performing stories at a park in Lahore, by Sobia Zaidi	119
8.2	Students' recreational drug use, by Max Johnson	128
9.1	Observational sketches in Sheffield, by Richard Phillips	139
10.1	Renewing fieldwork traditions using digital techniques, by Minsung Kim	162
10.2	Using immersive technologies to explore digital fields, by Ana Javornick	165
11.1	Do no harm? Social media and the ethics of fieldwork, by Isabelle Côté	179
11.2	Digital storytelling: Building feminist solidarities through a women's WhatsApp story circle, by Pamela Richardson	187
12.1	Edmonton soundwalks, by Brett Lashua	202
12.2	Smells of a hospital, by Kate McLean	204

13.1 Beyond judgments: Using case files and court archives for empirical research, by Maayan Niezna — 212
13.2 Working with African political autobiographies, by Anaïs Angelo — 217
14.1 Critical judgements and qualitative data: Building and managing a corporate database in a research team, by Jennifer Johns, John R. Bryson and Vida Vanchan — 233
14.2 Managing sensitive interviews in Kuala Lumpur, by Kautsar Ramli — 237
14.3 Analysing images and texts in 'sustainable' supply chain research, by Lucy McCarthy and Anne Touboulic — 241

ABOUT THE AUTHORS AND CONTRIBUTORS

Authors

Jennifer Johns is Professor of Management at the University of Bristol Business School where she teaches on the global economy and digitalisation. Jennifer has led field classes in New York, Vancouver, France, Germany and within the UK to organisations and manufacturing locations. Her research and teaching activities focus on interdisciplinarity, striving to enrich research, and particularly fieldwork, through engagement and collaboration across disciplines. Jennifer has conducted her own fieldwork across Europe, Japan, Australia and the US.

Richard Phillips is Professor of Human Geography at Sheffield University, where he teaches cultural geography and creative research methods. Richard has led field classes in Vancouver, New York, Berlin, Paris, Liverpool and Glasgow, as well as closer to home in Sheffield and in the nearby Peak District. His books include *Creative Writing for Social Research* (with Helen Kara, 2021), *Storying Relationships* (with Claire Chambers, Nafhesa Ali, Indrani Karmakar and Kristina Diprose, 2021), *Sex, Politics and Empire: A Postcolonial Geography* (2006) and *Mapping Men and Empire: A Geography of Adventure* (1997).

Contributors

Anaïs Angelo is a Senior Researcher, Elise Richter Fellow, at the Department of African Studies, University of Vienna. Her work focuses on African postcolonial political history with a focus on biography writing, the history of African presidential powers and African women's political history.

Matt Baillie Smith is a Professor of Human Geography at Northumbria University. His research focuses on the relationships between civil society, citizenship and development in the Global South. His recent work has focused on volunteering in humanitarian and development settings, and on young people as development actors.

John R. Bryson is Professor of Enterprise and Economic Geography, University of Birmingham. His research focuses on exploring the complex ways in which production is organised in place and across space. His latest books include *Living with Pandemics: Places, People and Policy* (2021) and *Ordinary Cities, Extraordinary Geographies* (2022).

Isabelle Côté is an Associate Professor in Political Science at Memorial University of Newfoundland and Labrador, St John's, Canada. Her research examines the role of internal migration on intra-state conflict in Asia and beyond. She has co-edited *People Changing Places: New Perspectives on Demography, Migration, Conflict and the State* (2019) and *Resettlement: Uprooting and Rebuilding Communities* (2020).

Geraldine Foley is an Assistant Professor in Occupational Therapy, in the School of Medicine at Trinity College Dublin. Her research is situated in domains of life-limiting illness, focused primarily on patient, family and healthcare professional needs and preferences in palliative and supportive care.

Michael R. Glass is an Assistant Professor of Urban Sociology and Director of the Urban Studies Program at the University of Pittsburgh. Trained as a geographer, his research examines infrastructure, governance and regional change. His pedagogical focus is on reflexivity in community-based research and learning outcomes from urban fieldwork.

Sarah Marie Hall is Professor of Human Geography at the University of Manchester. Her research focuses on everyday life and the economy; social reproduction, care, ethics and consumption; and feminist methods and praxis.

Will Haynes is a Postdoctoral Researcher in the Department of Geography, University of Sheffield. He is interested in cities, visual methods and fieldwork in public spaces where we can meet people and learn from them. Will's doctoral research focuses on visibility and homelessness in Termini railway station in Rome.

Russell Hitchings is an Associate Professor in the Department of Geography at University College London. He has studied everyday life in a variety of contexts around the world and has published widely on qualitative methods, energy consumption, climate adaptation and nature experience. Russell is the author of *The Unsettling Outdoors: Environmental Estrangement in Everyday Life* (2021).

Peter A. Jackson is Professor of Human Geography at the University of Sheffield and Co-Director of the Institute for Sustainable Food. He leads the H3 project (Healthy soil, Healthy food, Healthy people) and has served on scientific advisory committees for Defra and the FSA. His teaching focuses on food consumption and sustainability.

Ana Javornick is a Senior Lecturer in Digital Marketing at the University of Bristol Business School. Her research focuses on consumer behaviour, digital technologies and well-being and she specialises in the use of immersive technologies in commercial contexts.

Mpoe Johannah Keikelame describes herself as an African woman holding a PhD in Psychology with a passion to share her experience as a qualitative researcher, health promotion practitioner and accredited facilitator. Her articles on health systems and epilepsy appear in journals including the *International Journal of Social Research Methodology* and *Epilepsy and Behavior*, and she has published on decolonising methodologies in *Global Health Action*.

Max Johnson carried out his research at the University of Sheffield as a human geography undergraduate. Having then read for a postgraduate degree in Sociology at the University of Bristol, he now works in the third sector, helping to drive the social change his academic career inspired him to believe was possible.

Minsung Kim is Associate Professor in the Department of Geography Education at Seoul National University, South Korea. His interests in fieldwork include teacher training – equipping school teachers and university lecturers to teach field classes – and conducting psychogeographic fieldwork in contemporary urban settings.

Su-Jeong Kim is Assistant Professor at Chonnam National University, South Korea. She loves to travel and is interested in issues of migration, migrant space and cities in developing countries.

Brett Lashua teaches Sociology of Media at University College London (UCL). He has worked with schools, community centres, musicians and arts organisations to address questions of youth inequalities, racialised borderlands and urban place-shaping. His research foregrounds collaborative participatory approaches including music-making, soundscapes, cultural mapping, documentary film-making and digital storytelling.

Sarah de Leeuw is a creative writer (poetry and literary non-fiction), critical human geographer and Professor in UBC's Faculty of Medicine. Her research, writing, teaching and activism focus on ways that place and coloniality work as determinants of health. She holds a Canada Research Chair in Humanities and Health Inequities and, in 2017, was appointed to the Royal Society of Canada's College of New Scholars, Artists and Scientists.

Lucy McCarthy is a Senior Lecturer at the University of Bristol Business School. She is a member of the Food Justice Network and ARCIO, the Action Research and Critical Inquiry in Organisations. Her background is in community and rural development, particularly around challenges of historically marginalised areas.

Kate McLean is Programme Director for Graphic Design at the University of Kent. Her art and design practice sits at the intersection of human-perceived smellscapes, cartography and the communication of 'eye-invisible' sensed data. She leads international public smellwalks and translates the resulting data using digital design, watercolour, animation, scent diffusion and sculpture into smellscape mappings. She is co-editor of *Designing with Smell: Practices, Techniques and Challenges* (2018).

Maayan Niezna is a Postdoctoral Research Fellow in Modern Slavery and Human Rights at the Bonavero Institute of Human Rights, University of Oxford. Her socio-legal research focuses on trafficking for labour exploitation, the regulation of labour migration and the rights of non-citizens.

Kautsar Ramli is a Lecturer in Enterprise and Innovation at Newcastle University Business School. Her research interests are mainly within the fields of business management and entrepreneurship, and their implications to policy and practice. Kautsar works on business resilience and other social aspects of entrepreneurship and its interdisciplinarity.

Pamela Richardson is a Research Fellow based in the Department of Geography at the University of Sheffield. She completed her doctorate at the University of Oxford in 2009 and followed with postdoctoral research in South Africa, Zimbabwe, Tanzania and Germany (2010–18). She has published work on agri-food systems, community-building, ethics, participatory and video methodologies.

Morag Rose is an artist-activist-academic interested in walking as a creative, political and social act. Research interests include access and equality in public space and the impact of urban regeneration. She is a Lecturer in Human Geography at the University of Liverpool and founder of psychogeographical collective the LRM (Loiterers Resistance Movement).

Anne Touboulic is Associate Professor at the University of Nottingham (UK) and a member of the leadership team of the Future Food Beacon, an interdisciplinary centre for food research. Anne has an interdisciplinary background in the social sciences and her research is inherently boundary-spanning.

Vida Vanchan is Professor of Geography and Political Science and Public Administration at the State University of New York (SUNY) Buffalo State. Her research focuses on development; global supply chains configuration and sustainability; manufacturing and industrial competitiveness; trade and investments (FDIs); cross-cultural management and negotiation; Southeast Asia and emerging economies.

Sobia Zaidi is an interdisciplinary artist, researcher and teacher. Using performance, installation and text as an instrument she explores the poetics and politics of bodies in space. She is interested in embodied ecologies, temporal geographies, homes and addresses. Sobia coordinates the Visual and Performing Arts programme at Forman Christian College in Lahore.

ACKNOWLEDGEMENTS

We led student field trips together when we were both lecturing in the Department of Geography at the University of Liverpool (around fifteen years ago now) and since this is our second book together our first acknowledgements go to each other – for the good humour, good ideas and understanding. We'd also thank the students who joined us then and the many students since. Together, in fields near and far, we've shared some wonderful adventures. We've learned from you – you're too many to mention but you know who you are – and for that we feel grateful and privileged.

Since Liverpool our paths have diverged, Richard working in geography at Sheffield University, Jennifer at the University of Bristol Business School, both of us continuing to lead field trips and contribute to fieldwork pedagogy and practice at all levels, from Richard's work in schools to Jennifer's at postgraduate level, and both of us supervising doctoral students whose own fieldwork renews and energises the fieldwork tradition. We are also grateful to those who have taught us, and to our friends and colleagues who we've worked and explored with over the years. We'd like to add our own personal acknowledgements to them here.

While we were completing this book – Richard writes – my former PhD supervisor, Cole Harris, died at his home in Vancouver. Like many of his students and colleagues, I treasure the memory of Cole's 'legendary field trips' – on Vancouver Island, up the Fraser Canyon, in the interior of British Columbia. These trips bemused me at the time – I rarely had much idea where we were going or why – but they opened my eyes and shaped me. I want to thank Cole and the others – including Yasmeen Quereshi, Katie Pickles, Graeme Wynn – who shared those adventures and helped plant the seeds that have grown into my contributions to this book. Since then, as I've taken my own field trips, I've learned from many students and colleagues, some of whom are featured in this book, and I've enjoyed working and travelling with you. Thanks especially to: Johanna Waters, Jess Dubow, Eric Olund, Rowan Jaines, Dan Hammett, Miguel Kanai, Pamela Richardson, Luke Temple, Peter Jackson, and Sophia Bezos. Thanks too to those who've joined in the fieldwork I never stop doing – the curious living and exploring – especially Alison Blunt, Gordon Pirie, Thom Sullivan, Charlotte Cory, Dave Featherstone. Special thanks to Helen Kara for your comments, suggestions, energy and inspiration. And to Ben Giles and Amanda Crawley Jackson for joining me and a group of students – with your cameras and field notebooks – in an unforgettable field trip in Sheffield in 2021, when Covid-19 restrictions eased and we were able to get out into the field together again. Finally, special thanks to Tom.

I also have some people I'd like to thank – Jennifer writes – from across several institutions and disciplines. My early fieldwork experiences were informed by Chris Perkins and Martin Evans at Manchester, including a memorable trip to Normandy (cut short due to mass food poisoning). Since that time I've enjoyed many trips and learned a great deal from students and staff in and beyond the field, including Johanna Waters, Trevor Barnes, Sarah Marie Hall, Adriana Nilsson, Kautsar Ramli, Ödül Bozkurt, Jon Swords and Alex Balch. My appreciation also for my colleagues at Bristol for their integrity, intelligence and humour. I would also like to thank my research collaborators in engineering, led by James Gopsill, who have led me to think more about what the 'field' is, and what it could be. I'd also like to acknowledge my personal network of family and friends, particularly my immediate family, Paul, Elea and Natalie for their enduring love and laughter. Also Samson and Frankie for providing the snoring Labrador soundtrack to our book meetings and my writing sessions.

We also both appreciate our editors at Sage – Jai Seaman and Rhiannon Holt – for their confidence in this project and formative insights, which have shaped this book and helped us to imagine and speak to our possible readers. We're also grateful to the anonymous readers who worked through entire drafts of this book and provided detailed and very helpful feedback.

Despite the happy tone of these acknowledgements, it also feels right to acknowledge that we have written this book during a strained time in many universities. We worked on this during and after the Covid-19 crisis, and through a period of unrest in which many university workers have been 'at breaking point' as one union banner rightly put it. We've persisted because this book – and the teaching that surrounds it – have felt like an antidote to what's become of university working life. In the field, with each other and with students, we rediscover the joy of discovery and learning, which we hope to share with you.

1
INTRODUCTION

This book is for you if you are a student or researcher, considering or taking a **field class** or planning independent **fieldwork**, perhaps for your dissertation or postgraduate research in the social sciences, arts or humanities.

Fieldwork involves study and research in material and virtual settings. Students sign up to field classes and plan fieldwork for a range of different reasons. Some like the idea of a break from the routine of lectures and seminars, and perhaps the sound of an exotic location. Others have more informed academic motives, recognising the scientific value or the creative possibilities of this form of research. Still others do fieldwork simply because they have to, as part of their courses. Whatever your reasons – and it is probably some combination of these – you will benefit from developing some clear, critical understandings of fieldwork, and from a practical introduction to field research methods. We have written this book because we love and value fieldwork and want to encourage others to do it well. We want to help you get the most out of your field trip or field research. We want it to orient, support, challenge, guide and inspire you as you leave the comfort zone of the classroom.

There are two sides to leaving our comfort zone, as we do in the **field**: opportunity and risk. First, this book explores opportunities and possibilities. We write to inspire and motivate you, encouraging your curiosity and **active learning**. In Part I: Getting Started, we explain what it means to 'start with curiosity' as you design research and plan what you will do in the field, developing detailed field research plans and conducting background literature reviews before you begin your fieldwork. Throughout the book, we highlight independent and innovative fieldwork, and encourage you to continue this tradition within your own work, engaging critically with fundamental questions such as: what is fieldwork? where is the field? and who is a field researcher? We hope that this book will help you to see how fieldwork can benefit you in your learning and life.

Venturing outside the classroom also brings risks and uncertainties. We explain some of these challenges, explaining and showing how it is possible to overcome intellectual and practical obstacles, turning these into opportunities for critical and active learning. One risk is that students – led into the field by instructors – may become passive, following a fieldwork leader around an unfamiliar location. This book encourages you to learn actively and suggests ways of doing this. Another risk in fieldwork that involves living and working with other people is that this will not always be harmonious, easy, effective or happy. We ask how students can learn from sometimes-difficult relationships, finding ways to work and live together. Relationships are also central to another risk, which is that fieldwork may be intrusive or clumsy. We explain some of the ways in which you can become sensitive and respectful towards the people you encounter and study in the field, and how you can ensure that your fieldwork is ethical, which means avoiding harm and actively benefitting others.

This book:

- explains how to approach and conduct fieldwork, and how to collect and organise **data** in the field;
- explains fieldwork methods that students are most likely to use, including observations, interviews and participatory methods;
- has most to say about qualitative methods, which are more central to fieldwork than their quantitative counterparts;
- encourages you to be innovative and shape your own fieldwork. To this end, the book explores innovative and emerging fieldwork methods including virtual and experimental fieldwork;
- speaks to students across disciplines in the social sciences, arts and humanities;
- speaks to students in different international contexts, reflecting diverse experiences;
- is inclusive and diverse in the voices it includes and the work it cites. This is in keeping with moves to decolonise the curriculum and embrace diverse student audiences (where diversity takes different forms including gender, sexuality, culture, religion, ethnicity, neurodiversity and corporeal diversity).

In Part II, we challenge you to think critically about fieldwork. Doing so will not only help you to avoid pitfalls; it will help you do better fieldwork. These challenges include thinking through the **ethics** of your proposed fieldwork, finding ways to work well with other students or researchers, and reflecting critically and creatively on field traditions. We explain what it means to decolonise fieldwork, and how you can play your part in this.

Complementing more general research methods literatures, we focus upon relationships between selected key methods and contexts in Part III. Reading through, you will need to decide which are most relevant to your own fieldwork. You won't generally need to choose between the methods we present, as you may be able to bring more than one technique to your own fieldwork. Doing so will enable you to spread your risk (in case one method doesn't work out or in case you're not very good at it), and it will enable you to triangulate findings (cross-checking the findings of various methods).

Researchers and field trip leaders have contributed case studies – we call these 'postcards' – to illustrate what fieldwork can do and the problems and challenges fieldworkers face. We include a wide range of authors – people from different parts of the world, with different identities and backgrounds, and at different stages of their careers – to ensure we provide diverse perspectives on fieldwork.

We want this book to be useful to you both practically and conceptually. In the final chapter we draw together some of these benefits including transferable skills such as the ability to solve problems and work in a team (employability attributes) and personal qualities and values such as a desire to find out for yourself and to make a positive difference in the world. We think of these as 'takeaways' for work and life. Throughout, we raise issues and questions that you should consider when you plan and conduct fieldwork. Rather than answering these questions for you – which would be impossible given the wide variation in field contexts – we help you answer them for yourselves. This is a pathway to conducting critical and imaginative fieldwork.

PART I
GETTING STARTED

Part contents
---

2 Fieldwork and the Field   7
3 Curiosity and Research Design   23

2
FIELDWORK AND THE FIELD

In this chapter you will learn

- what fieldwork is and why it is important to students and researchers across the social sciences and humanities;
- about the pros and cons of fieldwork and how to mitigate the latter;
- what and where the field is and what you can find there;
- how students can build on and renew fieldwork traditions, critically and creatively, to get the most out of their fieldwork.

Introduction

To appreciate and investigate the social world in all its complexity, social researchers conduct research in and through contexts and places. This is to say we do fieldwork.

Fieldwork takes many forms across the social sciences, arts and humanities. Student field classes range from short trips during scheduled class time through longer residential field courses, running to entire years abroad. Students also conduct independent fieldwork for undergraduate dissertations and honours, masters and doctoral theses. Some fieldwork involves close staff guidance and supervision; elsewhere students are expected and encouraged to create and run projects independently. Fieldwork is sometimes incorporated within study skills or substantive courses and sometimes delivered in freestanding modules. Field classes take place in a wide range of settings: local and non-local; domestic and foreign; public and private; urban, suburban, rural and rugged; bounded and relational; fixed and mobile; physical and virtual. On a field course you may be assigned specific tasks or expected to devise and conduct your own project. Most often students do a mixture of directed and independent research.

What do these different forms of fieldwork have in common? One thing stands out: they all involve learning and enquiry through first-hand experience and observation of and in the world beyond the classroom. These include the tangible outside world – the subject of conventional definitions of fieldwork (Lonergan and Andersen, 1988; Livingstone et al., 1998) – and also digital spaces.

We begin this chapter by taking a step back, saying why we have written this book and what it offers to researchers and students. Then we explain the power of fieldwork, which enables us to appreciate the complexity and messiness of the social world. We go on to explain the terms that will be important in the course of this book, beginning with fieldwork and the field. We survey fieldwork traditions across academic disciplines and across the world, and then explain what holds them together and what you can gain from thinking about your own fieldwork as part of this bigger tradition.

For Fieldwork

We decided to write this book when we were leading a field trip together. We had noticed that students were getting involved and engaging more than they had in the classroom. It wasn't just the glamour and novelty, though there was some of each on this particular trip – which happened to be in Vancouver and included visits to film production studios, community gardens and social enterprises. It was that students were taking an active role in their learning, discovering things for themselves, finding or rediscovering abilities, developing new kinds of confidence and returning each day with new ideas and experiences. Later, leading trips in less obviously beautiful places closer to home, most recently in the waste grounds and derelict sites of post-industrial Sheffield (on Richard's urban exploration field class) and advanced manufacturing units in Bristol (on Jennifer's industrial site visits), we have found fieldwork just as rewarding. We have also found that the magic of the field works for different kinds of students: those of different ages, backgrounds and disciplines. So, we continue to believe in fieldwork, leading field courses in our respective disciplines, geography and management studies, and conducting our own fieldwork too.

Fieldwork is where teaching, learning and enquiry really come alive. This is true not only in undergraduate and graduate study, but also in academic and professional research. Jennifer's research has involved extensive fieldwork in different geographical contexts and digital spaces to investigate how things – like films or jet aircraft – are manufactured. Richard's collaborative research exploring the relationship attitudes and practices of young British Muslims is equally contextual, conducted and situated within particular sites such as the Glasgow Women's Library and within broader relational contexts such as the Pakistani diaspora (Phillips et al., 2021).

We begin, then, with a passion for fieldwork. We are not alone in this. When providing feedback on their courses students often describe field trips as the high points of their degrees. Some report that time in the field brought their book learning to life, 'seeing how it mattered' (Hope, 2009: 175). Some academics identify fieldwork as the emotional and intellectual high points of their professional work. Cole Harris, a Canadian geographer, wrote of 'exhilarating experiences in the field' (Harris, 2001: 329). We share this passion, though we do not idealise fieldwork or gloss over its difficulties.

It is important you are aware not only of the pros of fieldwork but also the cons, the benefits but also the potential risks. This can help you make informed decisions about whether and how to approach the field, and to assess and mitigate potential risks. The latter includes conflict between students, which we have witnessed in our field trips, and the marginalisation and exclusion of some students (including those with disabilities, non-drinkers and women), which we have tried to guard against. Other challenges include the necessity of negotiating problematic field traditions in which, as geographer David Stoddart blithely put it, some people and places have been framed as if they were 'waiting for exploration' (Stoddart, 1986: x). Some critical intellectuals regard these issues as insurmountable, feminist geographer Gillian Rose dismissing this 'initiation ritual of the discipline' (Rose, 1993: 69) as masculinist, **ableist**, heavy-drinking and imperialist. Others argue that problems with fieldwork can be addressed, to some extent solved, and this is where we stand. Getting the most out of fieldwork means learning from all aspects of fieldwork, not just the thing you are studying but also the ways in which you are studying.

Fieldwork means finding out for yourself. We believe that fieldwork can encourage students to become active learners, not simply passive recipients of second-hand knowledge. Through fieldwork, we hope to give students permission to be academically curious about the social world and we offer some guidance on how to do this. We encourage a particular form of **curiosity** as a driver of active learning – one that is critical and empathetic and balances an appropriate interest in others with a respectful attitude towards them. So we want to encourage and guide fieldwork that is: ethical, inclusive, inspiring and geared to how students learn effectively and, we hope, happily. We approach fieldwork – to quote Michael Schrage (1999), a professor of management studies – as a form of 'serious play': activity that can be pleasurable, while also searching and insightful.

One qualification is important here. Fieldwork can feel exciting, perhaps adventurous (Gerber and Chuan, 2000), sometimes joyful, but we need to handle this with care. Adventure has colonial overtones, which we can trace to histories in which white, male, Western protagonists travelled to and clashed with people in colonial settings (Phillips, 1997). Some of these traditions continue in the form of tourism, another form of pleasure-seeking travel (Sarmento and Brito-Henriques, 2013; Urry and Larsen, 2011). So, though fieldwork can be outwardly reminiscent of adventure and tourism, it is important not to get too carried away with this. As we go on to explain in Chapter 6, Decolonising Fieldwork, it is possible to embrace the intellectual excitements and the pleasures of fieldwork while guarding against colonial traditions and actively maintaining a critical frame of mind.

This book is not just about fieldwork; it is *for* fieldwork, or rather for a particular approach to fieldwork and the field. To illustrate the value of fieldwork, we turn now to a postcard from food and farming researcher Peter Jackson, who explains why it was important for him to visit a field site in person. In this example, fieldwork involves observation, as Jackson and colleague Polly Russell walk around a farm, noticing the sounds and smells of the place, asking questions and listening to what they are told. Through this particular form of fieldwork – observation, which we explain in detail in Chapter 8 on Participant Observation and Chapter 12 on Multisensory and Embodied Fieldwork – we make the more general point that fieldwork in all its forms, contextual research involving a range of methods, can be a source of unique and powerful insights.

Postcard 2.1

Why is fieldwork important? Notes from a chicken farm, by Peter A. Jackson

My first visit to a broiler house, where intensively reared chickens are 'grown' to their full slaughter weight in around 40 days from hatching, was a revelation. I was studying the development of the modern British chicken industry, tracing all the links in the supply chain 'from farm to fork'. Having interviewed the retailers and done some consumer focus groups, it was time to visit the broiler sheds.

I went with my colleague Polly Russell to visit a farm in Dorset where Polly already knew the farmer quite well, having recorded her life history over a number of previous visits. From this and other interviews I knew that the farmer was well regarded in the industry as someone whose animal husbandry was considered a model of good practice. As we entered the first shed, I was taken aback by the number of chickens, lined up in neat rows, with several thousand in each shed. I didn't find the conditions as shocking as old-fashioned battery farming, where chickens are kept in cages for their eggs, though animal rights campaigners object to the high stocking densities at which many broiler chickens are kept. What impressed me most was the matter-of-fact way that the farmer 'walked the sheds', using her expert eye to detect any problems with the heating, lighting and water supply, stopping to pick up any animals that were injured and, occasionally and abruptly, wringing the neck of any birds that were suffering and needed putting out of their misery. When we stepped outside, the dead birds were disposed of in a large metal incinerator.

The farmer clearly cared about the welfare of her birds, even though they were, to some extent, just a source of income. She said it was hard to feel emotionally attached to chickens, compared to the way she cared for her pet dog, for example. There were so many of them and the turnover was so rapid. But she could immediately sense when something was wrong as she walked the sheds several times a day: were they listless or flighty, noisy or unusually quiet?

It was hard to come away from the sheds without some sympathy for the modern-day chicken grower as well as greater insight into the lives of the chickens themselves. Many of the consumers we talked to expressed a nostalgic longing for a lost 'golden age' of farming, wanting chicken to taste like it used to in some imagined past. This may be understandable, given the rapid intensification of agriculture in recent years, but it ignores the fact that mass consumption of chicken only became a reality in the last couple of generations (since the 1960s). Before then, chicken was a treat, to be enjoyed on high days and holidays, rather than the cheap and ubiquitous source of protein that it has become today.

Visiting the farm was a good 'reality check' for when consumers talked fondly of times past and when retailers employed rose-tinted images to sell intensively reared birds. Being 'in the field' also served as a reminder, as one of our other informants told us, that there's a living thing at the end of the supply chain. We saw at first hand the way that nature can fight back, with chickens developing hock burn and other unsightly conditions when they are kept at too high a density or when the ratio of breast meat to leg strength means that they 'come off their legs'. Visiting the farm raised all kinds of issues that might have escaped me had I stayed in the office and simply read the focus group and interview transcripts that Polly was recording. While our project focused on the way food is 'sold with a story', it was vitally important to combine our narrative methods with some direct observation 'in the field'.

What is Fieldwork? Research in Context

Fieldwork needs defining at this point in the book, although as it means different things to different people there is no single definition. As a starting point, we asked researchers in a range of social science and humanities disciplines: what does fieldwork mean to you? Their answers – some of which are shown in Table 2.1 – show that fieldwork is a varied tradition, which varies across disciplines, times and places. That said, these definitions have much in common, converging around an understanding that fieldwork involves finding out for yourself through contextual research.

Table 2.1 Perspectives on fieldwork. We asked the authors of postcards, featured in this book, what fieldwork means to them. Here are some of their answers

What does fieldwork mean to you?	Author
Fieldwork is getting out and collecting data (words, numbers, recordings, observations, feelings etc.) that help answer your research questions. It's exploratory, reflexive and (hopefully) illuminating, sometimes frustrating, exhilarating, exhausting, fun.	Morag Rose, Artist-activist-academic, University of Liverpool, UK
Fieldwork is the practice of testing theories and concepts. Urban sociology is innately field based. The field can include many settings, from your college campus to streets, suburbs, or streams.	Michael Glass, Urban Sociology, University of Pittsburgh, USA
A fiction, of the imagination; also a fact-finding effort, both transformative and exploitative; a sometimes harshly disciplining project of an often-transdisciplinary nature; always an 'and/both' phenomenon that can too frequently be oppressive while at the same time being remarkably full of astonishment and wonder.	Sarah de Leeuw, Faculty of Medicine, University of Northern British Columbia, Canada
I think fieldwork is movement, encounters, relationships.	Su-Jeong Kim, Geographer, Chonnam National University, South Korea
Work that is conducted in different spaces in a field that is natural or artificial that seeks immersion of all senses and that is affected by external or internal control.	Mpoe Johannah Keikelame, PhD in Psychology, South Africa
Fieldwork is a misnomer. Neither does it have to take place in a field, nor does it have to feel like 'work'. 'Engaging with/learning from strangers' are, I would argue, better depictions.	Isabelle Côté, Political Scientist, Memorial University of Newfoundland, Canada
If research includes processes for moving from unknowing to knowing, fieldwork involves gathering information to create a kind of mapping, moving from being 'lost' towards places of knowledge.	Brett Lashua, Sociology of Media, University College London (UCL), UK
Fieldwork emphasises first-hand research including direct observation of people and places. In my work it has included interviews and focus groups as well as visual methods such as photography and film.	Peter Jackson, Geography, University of Sheffield, UK

Continued

Table 2.1 Perspectives on fieldwork. We asked the authors of postcards, featured in this book, what fieldwork means to them. Here are some of their answers (Continued)

What does fieldwork mean to you?	Author
Fieldwork for me is interacting with other bodies in a contested space with genuine curiosity. This interaction starts with acknowledging and recognising other bodies and can result in building co-created narratives and temporal geographies of interplay, exchange, dialogue and collective presence.	Sobia Zaidi, Interdisciplinary performance artist, researcher and teacher, Forman Christian College, Lahore, Pakistan
Fieldwork is how we carry out scientific research in the real world outside an academic sphere in order to gain answers and insight into the research questions and/or problems. It is conducted via direct observations and/or interactions with the subject matters.	Vida Vanchan, Geography and Political Science, State University of New York (SUNY), USA
Fieldwork is the point where learning in the classroom meets the real world and creative academic enquiry can be initiated through exploration and discovery in the real world.	Minsung Kim, Geography Education, Seoul National University, South Korea
Fieldwork for me means looking for information and insights that cannot be accessed from my office. Accessing primary sources, talking to people and getting an impression of the real world: everyday occurrences, big events, and interactions between people and institutions. It is a way to understand law in its social context.	Maayan Niezna, Bonavero Institute of Human Rights, University of Oxford, UK
Active, purposeful engagement and planned (at least to some degree) encounters with people, places, or other specifically defined socio-materialities. Seeks to learn something new. Takes place within a framework of knowledge that shapes particular lines of enquiry, methods of experimentation and mode of engagement. The 'work' works towards, cultivates and anticipates that there will be an outcome.	Pamela Richardson, Geography, University of Sheffield, UK
Fieldwork is the process by which researchers collect data from or about their target population(s) in the naturalistic setting. It includes a spectrum of approaches including interviewing and observation, but in essence it encompasses all forms of data collection which help the researcher understand and contextualise participant interactions and behaviour.	Geraldine Foley, Occupational Therapy, Trinity College Dublin, Ireland
Fieldwork is the opportunity to creatively explore and interpret the beautifully complex world we live in, and also one of the most important tools we possess to create positive change.	Max Johnson, Works in third sector in Bristol, UK, where he sees his role as 'helping to drive social change'

Through fieldwork, students and researchers seek to appreciate social life in context, where its complications, juxtapositions and contradictions are revealed. Cole Harris, an expert in the historical geographies of colonialism, contrasted his own investigations – his own ramblings in the towns and villages, historical landscapes and archives of Quebec and British Columbia – with the rarefied statistical tables and charts, compiled by a colleague at the University of Toronto:

> One of my colleagues in the late 1960s, an eminent spatial theorist, could not abide the world as it presented itself to the senses. It was too cluttered. He liked to be driven,

and he would sit in the back seat of a large car with the blinds down. At home he watched gangster films and adjusted his equations. But most of us are not such purists. We are more inclined to take the world as it is – or as it seems to be – to get out into it, look hard at it, ask questions about it, and grapple with the conundrums so presented. This usually means fieldwork ... (Harris, 2001: 329)

Harris writes with a lightness of touch but makes a serious point: through unstructured fieldwork it is possible to appreciate the complexity of the social world, which distilled data and elegant theories can miss. Jane Jacobs, the influential urbanist, made a similar point about the importance of fieldwork in cities. Critical of urban planners who (she said) devised regeneration plans from the comfort of their offices, Jacobs went out into urban neighbourhoods, walking, chatting and watching. She participated in the street life of places like Hudson Street, where she lived in New York. 'I put out the garbage can, surely a prosaic occupation, but I enjoy my part, my little clang, as the droves of junior high school students walk by the centre of the stage dropping candy wrappers.' Through these small observations, Jacobs drew broader conclusions:

Under the seeming disorder of the old city, wherever the old city is working successfully, is a marvellous order for maintaining the safety of the streets and the freedom of the city. It is a complex order. Its essence is intricacy of sidewalk use, bringing with it a constant succession of eyes. (Jacobs, 1962: 50)

Now, for a more contemporary illustration of the power of fieldwork to investigate the contextual complexity of social life in context, we turn to the work of critical race scholar Azeezat Johnson, who researched intersections of race, gender and religion through a study of the clothing practices of black Muslim women in Britain. Johnson adapted the work of law professor Kimberlé Williams Crenshaw, who compared the discrimination experienced by black women to a pile-up in a traffic junction. 'If an accident happens in an intersection, it can be caused by cars travelling from any number of directions and, sometimes, from all of them' (Crenshaw, 1989: 149). The analogy of the intersection points to the contextual complexity in which social life is lived. Working with this concept, Johnson investigated 'the interplay of social relations within particular locations' (Johnson, 2017: 5). Investigating 'how bodies are produced and shift across different spaces' (Johnson, 2017: iii), she considered everyday spaces such as cafés, homes and prayer rooms (see also Warren, 2016), and explored a range of spatial scales from the global geographies of diaspora through the space of the body. For Johnson, as for Harris and Jacobs in their very different ways, these settings are both a subject and also a locus of research. We frame this fundamentally contextual research as fieldwork.

Helen Kara, a creative research methods expert, locates fieldwork 'between method and methodology' and distinguishes fieldwork through its attention to research in and through 'place and space' (Kara, 2020: 6). Kara explains that methodology is a contextual framework – 'a coherent and logical scheme, based on views, beliefs and values, that guides the choices that researchers make' (Kara, 2020: 6; drawing upon Grierson and Brearley, 2009: 5). 'Within a methodological framework,' she continues, 'methods are the tools that researchers use to gather and analyse data, write and present their findings' (Kara, 2020: 6). Similarly, we can understand fieldwork as a framework within which methods for data collection and analysis data are situated or contextualised. Though some of the methods discussed in this book are also explained in more general research methods books, we approach them in a distinctive way in this book: as methods in context. For example, Chapter 7, on **interviewing**, focuses upon interviews about and within particular contexts, such as where the interviewer and interviewee can walk and talk within a location that is relevant to their conversation.

Since space and place are fundamental to fieldwork, it is important to be clear about these terms. Place is where people and things come together, intersecting in ways that are variously unique and universal, an 'endless series of specificities' (Massey, 1991; Booth, 2015). Space is more open ended, encompassing the 'dimension of the world in which we all live' (see Massey, 2005). Fieldworkers engage with places in two contrasting ways. Some, having already identified a theme to research, seek out places in which to do so, based on *a priori* knowledge or groundwork. Others, including students taking structured field courses, begin with a field site and then identify a theme to study there. However you get there, you ultimately end up researching a phenomenon in a particular field context.

Where is the Field?

We define fieldwork as research in context – study and research in and through material and digital settings – and we have begun to think of these settings as places where human lives converge in complex and sometimes messy ways. But what or where are these places? The following bullet points illustrate some of the different forms that these places – the field in fieldwork – can take.

- Some scholars have investigated exceptional locations that seem uniquely revealing and important, but it can be just as illuminating to study ordinary and 'common places' (Pratt, 1986; Gold et al., 1991: 29). For example, while the urban planning researcher Ed Soja (1989) justified his geographical focus by arguing that 'it all comes together in Los Angeles', others have argued the case for conducting research in less celebrated, lower-profile locations, which tend to be understudied (Neal et al., 2016).
- Whereas unfamiliar places are easily stimulating, seemingly familiar places are also important sites for fieldwork. Eric Pawson and Elizabeth Teather (2002: 282), teaching a fieldwork class in Canterbury, Aotearoa New Zealand, found that some of the greatest insights came in everyday locations, which the students learned to see afresh, paying attention to people and things they had previously overlooked: 'One student did not have to travel far in order to gain an excellent mark; he and his group analysed the tiny area around the petrol station where he worked part time,' exploring changes in the landscape and the penetration of global brands in local life.

- While fieldwork is often conducted in faraway locations (Nairn et al., 2000), it is also possible closer to home and even at home (Blunt and Dowling, 2022; Munthali, 2001). And, though fieldwork does generally take place in 'the world beyond the classroom' (as we put it above), it is also possible to conduct fieldwork within and about the classroom, as educational researchers have shown (e.g., Willis, 1977). There is much to see in our local areas and daily lives, if only we know how to look. There are also political reasons for shifting focus from the faraway to the local, particularly where the former is constructed as exotic, as some fieldwork destinations tend to be seen, to the 'endotic' (Phillips, 2018). The renewed focus upon endotic fieldwork has political as well as practical and intellectual advantages, breaking from a colonial tradition in which fieldwork traditionally led to rural and less developed parts of the world, far from the students' personal, social, cultural and economic homes (Munthali, 2001). Endotic fieldwork can represent a break with these colonial traditions.
- Another reason for choosing endotic fieldwork, for travelling vertically rather than horizontally, drilling down into the detail and texture of the local and easily accessible, is environmental. Fieldwork closer to home – especially when reached by train rather than plane or on foot rather than in a vehicle – tends to have a smaller carbon footprint.
- Field sites also assume a range of scales: ranging from the global through the national, regional, local, down through a series of more intimate spaces – including streets, schools (Thomson and Hall, 2016), offices, farms, homes (Blunt and Dowling, 2022) and bodies (Nast and Pile, 2005). We develop the last of these themes in Chapter 12, Multisensory and Embodied Fieldwork.
- Though they may be bounded, singular and fixed, field sites also include relational spaces (within and between locations) (Katz, 1994) and networks, overlapping with moving or mobile spaces (Davies, 2009). This means that you can do fieldwork across multiple sites, sequentially or simultaneously.
- The field can be a physical site, of course, but it can also be a virtual space: such as a website (Dodge and Kitchin, 2006), **secondary data** collected from the internet, an interview conducted online or research conducted within a wholly digital context like a video game or virtual world. **Digital fieldwork** has been expanding at a pace and assuming a significance that merits a chapter of its own in this book (Chapter 10).

So the field is where we do fieldwork, but this begs another question: what is fieldwork? We answer this question in two ways: first by exploring a series of practices that count as fieldwork; second by questioning the scope of these practices and inviting you to do the same. Recognised fieldwork practices include ethnographic work (explained in Chapter 8, Participant Observation and Participatory Fieldwork) and practices of looking and listening to other people and things (explained in Chapter 9, Visual Fieldwork, and Chapter 12, Multisensory and Embodied Fieldwork). But the scope of these practices – what counts as fieldwork – remains open and debatable. In the past, fieldwork has been conceived as a stage in research which revolves around data collection (Fuller et al., 2006). This understanding is problematic for two reasons. First, it echoes colonial traditions in which fieldwork was fundamentally extractive, a form of data mining

(Munthali, 2001; Nhemachena et al., 2016). Second, where fieldwork is understood merely as data collection, opportunities are missed to create, explore and interpret the data *in situ*, involving the people who may be represented in that data. Conversely, where we think of field data as something we make rather than collect, we stand to develop more collaborative and reciprocal relationships with people we encounter in the field, while also developing more realistic understandings of the knowledge we produce (Ellingson and Sotirin, 2020). We develop these themes in Chapter 6, Decolonising Fieldwork, and Chapter 14, Understanding and Handling Your Data.

The field is also defined by its distinctive 'temporality'. Unlike most other classes, fieldwork tends to be concentrated in a single block of days or weeks in which learning is particularly intense. The co-presence of a particular group of students and field course leaders over a period of time in a particular place all establish the conditions of possibility for 'transformative' learning (Herrick, 2010: 114). For undergraduates, field courses are typically away from home, involving immersion in a setting. This cultivates a distinctive way of being and working in which the distractions and multitasking of everyday life are set aside and those on the field trip are fully present, doing just one thing and doing it together (Glass, 2015).

Active Learning

Fieldwork is a form of active learning, distinguished from more passive ways of encountering the world.

Since field classes can take students to holiday destinations, they are sometimes mistaken for pleasure trips and tourism. (We use the term 'field class' to denote a course component that includes fieldwork.) A manual on teaching geography in higher education warned, perhaps a little too sternly, against confusing field trips with 'picnics, outings or senior class excursions' (*Field Training in Geography*, by P. F. Lewis, quoted by Gold et al., 1991: 21). Some critics have dismissed fieldwork as 'academic tourism' (Mowforth and Munt, 1998: 101) and condemned fieldwork that smacks of tourism, which is often presumed to be uncritical and neo-colonial. Student fieldwork may sometimes be guilty of this. Dina Abbott (2006) felt uneasy about a field trip to Gambia, in which British students were taken on a tour, which introduced the small West African country's history as a slave trading post. Tourists, students among them, 'are welcomed with a potted history of enslavement and after they feel they have "done Gambia", return to the boat' (Abbott, 2006: 330). Abbott concludes that these students are 'indistinguishable by local people from another set of "white" tourists' (Abbott, 2006: 335).

Some students and course leaders reply to these charges by distinguishing themselves from tourists. We asked students who had been with us on a field trip if this was the right thing to do. Was there a difference between fieldwork and tourism and, if so, what? Here are some of their answers:

> Fieldwork incorporates a different level of interaction as we studied areas and issues that most tourists would not fully understand or even want to engage with. (Hannah)

You have to make sure that although you can have fun on the field trip, the primary reason is to work and gain skills. (Anthony)

Tourism is visiting a destination for recreational, leisure or business purposes and creates money for that destination whereas fieldwork is research in that particular destination with a goal for a project in which study in this area is necessary. (Soraya)

I visited areas (of Vancouver) I wouldn't have on a tourist holiday. (Elizabeth)

Another thing these students might have added is that fieldwork can be very hard work. This is particularly true of long-haul trips, in which long flights cause fatigue and jet lag can limit the ability of both staff and students to hit the ground running (Nairn et al., 2000).

Field course leaders make similar points, insisting that 'this is not a Cook's Tour' and they are not tour guides. Geographers Neil Coe and Fiona Smyth (2010: 126) distance their own field classes from 'field teaching in which the teacher/lecturer assumes the familiar role of knowledgeable expert' who provides commentary, explanation and interpretation, sometimes enrolling local experts, but relegating students to 'passive recipients' of knowledge. The active learner, in contrast, needs the freedom to do more than answer direct questions and hear what course leaders and experts are saying. This message is important but not new. Previous generations of fieldworkers also tried to design fieldwork that was exciting and engaging for students, inviting them to learn actively. As far back as 1955, geographer Sidney William Wooldridge argued that 'proper fieldwork' was about 'doing' and not about students being told (Wooldridge, 1955: 79; quoted by Marsden, 2000: 31). Active fieldwork continues within longer traditions of student-centred, enquiry-based (Roberts, 2013) and progressive (Marsden, 2000: 33) educational philosophy and practice.

So a field trip is not a holiday. It is an opportunity for active learning. But what is active learning and how is the field a catalyst for this engaged form of study and research?

Active learning means finding out for yourself, making your own decisions about what to study and how. These include decisions about the kind of fieldwork you wish to do. This means taking responsibility for your own fieldwork, engaging critically with field traditions and practices.

To illustrate the power of active learning in the field – whether by a student or an academic or professional researcher – we now turn to a postcard by Mpoe Johannah Keikelame, a health researcher with a doctorate in psychology. This postcard illustrates the importance of keeping an open mind in the field and learning from surprising circumstances and events.

―――― **Postcard 2.2** ――――

Unexpected events at an epilepsy clinic in Cape Town, by Mpoe Johannah Keikelame

This postcard comes from a community health centre in an urban township in Cape Town, South Africa. I was there to conduct research on the perspectives and experiences of patients with epilepsy, and their interactions with carers.

Continued

With the consent of patients and carers, I constructed an observation guide which I used to make observations and collect data. This guided me in using my eyes and ears – to document what I saw, heard and touched in the course of my observations.

I went to the patients' waiting area and unexpectedly saw a health educator who was preparing to give a health talk on epilepsy. The waiting area was being used by patients who would sit and wait to get their medical files from the clerks before their consultation with the healthcare practitioners. I decided to observe the educator's talk.

I began by noting the date, time, place and length of the observed health talk. I recorded: details of the person who was giving the health talk; the content that was covered; the language through which the health talk was given; the questions that were asked and by whom; the type of answers that were given and by whom; the kind of epilepsy information that was on the poster and the language; the physical layout and structure of the waiting area; the position of the health educator; the area from which the health educator gave the health talk and the area in which I sat to conduct the observations.

I then drew a diagram (Figure 2.1) of the physical set-up of the waiting area; the patients' and clerks' seating arrangement, the intercom through which clerks call out patients to collect their medical files; the benches on which patients sat; the open rows through which patients moved around in the waiting area and the main entrance of the waiting area.

From the drawing of the physical set-up of the health talk venue and the detailed reflective notes of this unexpected observation, I was able to gain a contextual understanding of the health systems factors that affect promotion of health literacy of patients with epilepsy and their carers. This unexpected event enabled me to realise the importance of embracing such unpredicted events in fieldwork as they can provide insightful information to enrich the data.

This fieldwork reminded me of Anne Mulhall's reflection that 'It is sometimes important that we use our eyes and ears to gain an understanding of how social settings in which healthcare is provided

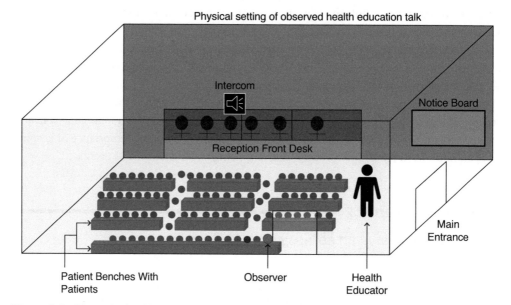

Figure 2.1 Venue for health talk on epilepsy: setting and layout. Sketched by Mpoe Johannah Keikelame

are constructed' (Mulhall, 2003: 307). These settings have a strong bearing upon patients' access to appropriate healthcare services, as I saw from my work in this epilepsy clinic.

This postcard illustrates that, however well you plan your fieldwork, you never know what will happen. I had not anticipated the guest speaker, present at the epilepsy clinic in the township that day, but I adapted to the unexpected and gained some valuable insights.

Fieldwork Tradition and Innovation

An active approach to fieldwork also involves the freedom to experiment and innovate, working within field traditions where it is helpful to do so, but reaching beyond them and adapting them where that is appropriate.

Students in some social science and arts and humanities disciplines learn that fieldwork is central to their heritage and tradition. Others enter the field without preconceived ideas about why they may be doing it and how. Wherever you stand on this – whether or not you follow in the footsteps of previous generations in your discipline – fieldwork is yours to make what you will. It is helpful to know about field traditions, but then it is important to feel free to renew and reshape these understandings and practices, critically and creatively.

Disciplines with strong field traditions include anthropology, urban sociology, geography, cultural studies and development studies (Lunn, 2014; Patel, 2015). Most students in these disciplines are required to attend residential field classes or conduct independent fieldwork. Anthropologists, maintaining a tradition laid down by field researchers, theorists and writers including Claude Lèvi-Strauss and Clifford Geertz (Pratt, 1986), are typically expected to demonstrate that they have conducted sustained and competent fieldwork – by which they generally mean **ethnography** (Blommaert and Jie, 2020; Pole and Hillyard, 2016). Some cognate disciplines – from urban sociology to cultural studies – have adopted and adapted anthropological methods and traditions. Robert E. Park and E.W. Burgess, working in Chicago in the early part of the twentieth century, established an ethnographic urban fieldwork tradition that has remained influential since (Becker, 1999).

Human geographers, though more methodologically eclectic, have an equally strong field tradition. As geographer Robin Kearns has observed, 'The field is to geography what the dig is to archaeology, or the archive to history: both a literal place and a key imaginary' (Kearns, 2002: 76; see also Powell, 2002). This tradition reaches back through the work of influential academics such as Berkeley geographer Carl Sauer (1956), intellectual predecessors such as the polymath Alexander von Humboldt (1769–1859) (Mathewson, 2001; West, 1979; Wulf, 2015) and institutions such as the American Association of Geographers (AAG) and Royal Geographical Society (RGS) (Livingstone, 1992). It is helpful to know something of these traditions – without following them too closely – in order to understand some of the implications of doing fieldwork today.

One thing that it is particularly important to know – when deciding where you stand in relation to field traditions – is where those traditions come from. Some, particularly those of anthropology and geography, began in former colonial powers and in the Global North and involved fieldwork (there and) in the colonised world and the Global South. These traditions have been contested and criticised, not least by postcolonial and feminist critics and historiographers (e.g., Desai and Potter, 2006; Hammett et al., 2014; Rodrigues, 2019; Rose, 1993; Scheyvens, 2014). Still, these asymmetries live on, through trips that criss-cross the Global North and reach into the Global South. This tradition of fieldwork, in which people from wealthier countries fan out across the world, sometimes into poorer regions, now includes researchers from ascendent economies including Singapore, South Korea and Hong Kong (Chuan and Poh, 2000; Ostuni, 2000; Kwan, 2000). This presents a challenge to decolonising fieldwork, interrogating and transforming power relations, rooting out colonial legacies and reinventing field traditions and practices. We take up these challenges throughout this book, especially in Chapter 6, Decolonising Fieldwork. We invite you to continue this critical project by learning from fieldwork traditions and precedents, playing your own part in contesting and jettisoning them where you decide it is necessary, making informed decisions about your own fieldwork and your relationships with field traditions.

In disciplines without such clearly articulated fieldwork traditions – including health studies, education, law, business and management studies, religious studies, modern languages and sociology – many students and researchers do fieldwork but do not always call it that (though some do). Modern language degrees generally involve a year abroad, in which students practise and extend their language skills and immerse themselves in the culture, in a form of ethnographic fieldwork (Wells et al., 2019). One sociologist – with expertise in gender and class, and a track record of empirical research – put it this way to Richard, a geographer: 'You do fieldwork; we do research.' If your discipline does not have a strong field tradition, it may not be so troubled by the intellectual and political baggage that goes with it, especially the baggage associated with colonialism. That said, researchers in your discipline may also be working with field methods that originated in colonial settings, so it is important for you to know something about the lineage of those methods and traditions.

Conclusion

At best fieldwork offers something distinctive and valuable to students and researchers: the opportunity to appreciate and investigate the social world in all its complexity and messiness through study in and about particular contexts and places. In order to get the most out of fieldwork, it is important you are aware not only of the pros of this form of learning and enquiry, but also the cons. Forewarned of potential pitfalls, you will be in a position to decide whether fieldwork is for you and, if it is, to mitigate the risks to ensure that your own fieldwork is constructive and critical.

Fieldwork takes many forms, some of which contradict stereotypes about students travelling from rich countries to field sites, near and far, physical and virtual, and complicate assumptions and expectations about what students do when they get there: what fieldwork entails.

There are different ways of understanding and doing fieldwork, with contrasts between – as well as within – disciplines and parts of the world. These different approaches remind us that fieldwork is varied and dynamic, open to criticism, creativity and innovation. One of our motivations to write this book was to encourage greater appreciation of, and learning about, fieldwork across different disciplines.

In the field there are pitfalls to avoid and sensitivities to understand and navigate. Field traditions can be constraining and problematic. While it is important to know how others have conceived and practised fieldwork in the past, you should not be bound by what they have done, nor do you have to follow the patterns and apparent rules they have set. Elements of fieldwork tradition – including implicitly colonial and patriarchal, asymmetric power relations – are particularly problematic. That said, fieldwork traditions are constantly changing. By understanding concerns about and criticisms of fieldwork, it is possible for you to develop a critical, robust approach to your own fieldwork: to insist on getting the most out of the experience while optimising your impact on others.

After reading this chapter you should have a clearer picture of how and why fieldwork is an important component in your education and research. It may have given you pause for thought regarding your own motivations for conducting fieldwork and should encourage you to think critically about your engagement with the field.

Key terms

Active learning means finding out for yourself, making your own decisions and about what to study and how. Active fieldwork involves learning and enquiry through first-hand experience and observation in and of the social world.

The **field** is the site, place, time or context in which fieldwork takes place. The field may be real or virtual, material or representational, bounded or relational, singular or plural, far away or close to home. A **field class** is a course component (known in some places as a module or unit) which includes fieldwork.

Fieldwork means finding out for yourself through contextual research. Fieldwork can involve one or more of a range of methods of data collection, analysis and communication.

Further Reading

Nhemachena, Artwell, Mlambo, Nelson & Kaundjua, Maria (2016) The notion of the 'field' and the practices of researching and writing Africa: Towards decolonial praxis. *Africology: The Journal of Pan African Studies*, 9(7): 15–36.

Artwell Nhemachena, Nelson Mlambo and Maria Kaundjua, all at the University of Namibia, Windhoek, make the case for decolonising fundamental notions of fieldwork and the field, particularly where this is conducted in Africa.

Pole, Chris & Hillyard, Sam (2016) *Doing Fieldwork*. Sage.
According to this book, fieldwork is 'about getting involved with what and who you are researching'. Using the terms 'fieldwork' and (a form of) 'ethnography' interchangeably, the authors advance a fieldwork tradition that originates in anthropology and is also closely associated with urban sociology.

Scheyvens, Regina (ed.) (2014) *Development Fieldwork: A Practical Guide*, 2nd ed. Sage.
Challenges of fieldwork – including ethical concerns about negotiating unequal power relations between research practitioners and participants – assume heightened forms in the Global South. This book builds upon postcolonial criticism of fieldwork traditions and power relations.

3
CURIOSITY AND RESEARCH DESIGN

In this chapter you will learn

- how to find a topic that interests you, or become interested in a topic you've been assigned;
- how to channel your curiosity into a focused research idea and, from there, a feasible research design.

Introduction

If you have signed up for a field class or are planning some fieldwork of your own, there is a good chance you have done so out of curiosity about a subject or place you would like to know more about, or a problem you think is important and would like to address. This desire to see or know and then 'to know why, and how' – in other words, this curiosity – is important because it can motivate you to learn and begin to make enquiries in the field (Inan, 2012: 6). Curiosity can also help if you are assigned a topic or problem you did not come up with yourself. The more interested you are in your field research – or the more interested you become – the easier it will be to stay motivated and energised. And, when you start with curiosity, there is a good chance you will find and develop a field project that is both interesting and original. Originality is the 'holy grail' of research – a sought-after, highly valued and yet elusive quality – that can bring your work to life and make it stand out. There is no simple formula for doing original fieldwork but curiosity can help.

What if you don't feel curious? How can you find or deepen interest in your fieldwork? This chapter suggests ways of awakening and deepening your curiosity. What can you do with this desire for knowledge? How can you channel it? This chapter suggests ways to focus your curiosity by identifying research aims and objectives, designing field research, identifying methods, anticipating and navigating risks, and remaining interested from start to finish.

Being or Becoming Curious

Throughout this book we encourage you to approach fieldwork actively, bringing your own ideas and energies forward, starting with your own curiosity. The freedom to follow your interest – coupled with the expectation that you will do so – can be a mixed blessing. Left to get on with it, albeit with support from a field course leader, even the most confident student can feel daunted as well as excited. Clare Herrick, a geographer who has led field trips in Santa Cruz, California, has noticed that some students enjoy 'the freedom to enjoy and experience a new place in their own time'. She observes that 'students may actively reject the necessarily "over-organised" nature of some field trips, calling for more free time in a schedule dictated by the need to conduct relevant and pedagogically valuable research projects in a limited time period' (Herrick, 2010: 111). But not everyone enjoys this freedom or the uncertainty it brings. As Jennifer observed when leading a field trip to Frankfurt for International Business students, many students expressed their uncertainty about the time allocated to their own research. They felt disoriented and asked 'exactly what are we supposed to *do*?' Some students feel more comfortable with structured learning, and with more guidance and direction. This reflects different ways of learning about and knowing the world – neurodiversity – as well as differences in personality and style. So we do not take your curiosity for granted or expect you to be immediately at ease with curiosity-driven fieldwork. Instead, we begin by explaining what curiosity is, before suggesting ways of stimulating and channelling it.

Curiosity is often portrayed as a natural drive or instinct, which we feel most keenly in childhood, but sometimes lose or repress as adults. But some kinds of curiosity can be taught and learned, then channelled as a catalyst for education and enquiry, innovation and creativity. An influential work on the philosophy of teaching and learning – *Émile: Or, Concerning Education* by Jean Jacques Rousseau (1762) – illustrates how we can cultivate curiosity in ourselves and encourage it in others. According to Rousseau, experience of the world – picking up and holding an object, or encountering another person – can prompt us to wonder, ask questions, define problems and then seek answers. This presents a powerful vision for fieldwork: which begins with experience and with paying attention to the sounds, sights, smells, tastes and textures of particular field sites, to the emotions and feelings that arise through field experiences and encounters (Phillips, 2015; Payne, 2014). In this way, curiosity becomes an incentive for learning, inspiring us to explore and enquire (Zuss, 2012).

Rousseau's image of a child, touching and asking questions about a stone, illustrates how exposure to a field site might awaken our curiosity. This is particularly apparent when we are working with others, with whom we may be able to discuss our new experiences and begin to ask questions. A contemporary example of the ways in which field experiences can ignite curiosity is provided by Su-Jeong Kim, who is based in South Korea and leads fieldwork in Central Asia (Postcard 3.1).

Postcard 3.1

Becoming curious: Korean students in Central Asia, by Su-Jeong Kim

This postcard tells how a group of students, initially tired, hot and hungry, went in search of familiar food but found themselves learning and exploring, curious about an unfamiliar setting and the people who live there.

The students did not know much about the place, and neither did I, as the leader of the group. I had planned a two-week field trip to Uzbekistan and Kazakhstan with Korean university students to study the arid landscapes, environmental issues and cultural geographies of the Korean diaspora in Central Asia.

We struggled with language: most people there spoke Russian and communicating in English, our second language, was rarely possible. We found other ways of getting by. Students found it helpful to install and use translation apps. The challenges of weather and food were more persistent. Even though Korea has a hot and humid summer climate, the daytime temperature in Uzbekistan and Kazakhstan in July reaches 46 degrees Celsius. And the students struggled with unfamiliar food, most of which was prepared with lamb and mutton oil. Some suffered stomach pain, diarrhoea, fever and food-poisoning symptoms. At times like this, familiarity can be comforting so the students went in search of Korean food.

But there was little information about Korean restaurants on Google Maps or the internet. This was probably because Kyzylorda – in Kazakhstan – is not a tourist destination. Koreans rarely go there for travel or business. This forced us to find our own accommodation and restaurants. We had no choice but to wander the streets in the hot sun, read the Russian signboards and look for a restaurant.

At this point, the problem of food turned into an opportunity, sparking encounters and curiosity in unexpected ways. Some people who heard us speak wanted to know if we were from Korea. We said we were college students from Korea, looking for a Korean restaurant. They took us to a restaurant called Gooksi, a place where summer food is eaten by Koryoin, the Korean diaspora in Central Asia. We sat down in the restaurant and chatted; the people we met on the way were the president of the Koryoin Association of Kyzylorda and her party. While our food was served, we listened to stories about the history and present life of the Koryoin who migrated and settled in Central Asia.

This sparked our interest in the details of the food. This Gooksi differed from the usual noodle dishes we know. While Korean noodles are mainly eaten with two or three garnishes in a hot broth, Central Asian Gooksi consists of cold broth topped with meat, tomatoes, Koryoin-style Kimchi, cucumber, egg, and many other garnishes (Figure 3.1). The president of the Koryoin Association explained that Gooksi is fusion food prepared by the Koreans who were forcibly taken to Central Asia during the Japanese colonial period. They used the ingredients that were to hand: locally sourced tomatoes and, in the absence of Koryoin-style Kimchi, cabbage or carrots as a garnish substitute. In the heat, they preferred their broth cold.

We had set out in search of familiar and comforting food. We ended up finding some of what we had wanted but with a twist, and with stories and conversations we had not expected. Thanks to the kindness of the Koryoin we met unexpectedly on the street, we learned about cultural hybridity and became interested in the local and diaspora communities. We ended the day less hungry but more curious.

Continued

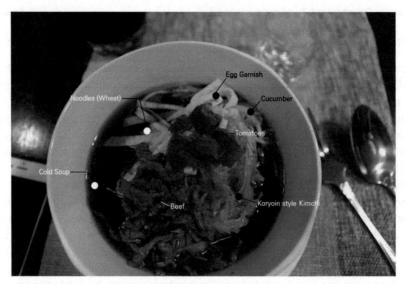

Figure 3.1 Gooksi in Kyzylord, photographed and annotated by Su-Jeong Kim

Su-Jeong Kim's postcard illustrates how encounters with others – including fellow students and other people you meet in the field – can spark curiosity. These encounters need not – and often cannot – be planned. This postcard shows that it helps to try to be open to opportunities that may arise when you least expect them to. Other examples of serendipitous fieldwork – in which unexpected experiences and encounters spark curiosity – include Mpoe Johannah Keikelame's postcard from the epilepsy clinic in Cape Town (Postcard 2.2) as well as more sustained research projects such as a study of the gig economy by cultural geographers Elizabeth Straughan and David Bissell (2021). Straughan and Bissell were in a taxi in Melbourne on their way to conduct an interview when they sensed that their real story began within the taxi itself, and in their encounters with the driver, an employee of the precarious gig economy. Their experience in the cab got them thinking and asking questions about 'technologically mediated encounters' and led to a project on 'affirmative sociality associated with curiosity'. In this example, the researchers' curiosity prompted questions about curiosity itself. The researchers' curiosity, once ignited, sparked more sustained research.

Ways of Cultivating Curiosity

It is inspiring to read about serendipitous curiosity in which lucky encounters open new questions and research directions. But what if this does not happen to you? It can be stressful to rely upon luck. It helps to know that most of us need assistance if we are to cultivate our curiosity and begin to use it as a starting point for our fieldwork. You may have been encouraged to become and stay curious when you were a child (Mazrui, 2003: 140) but, if not, it is never too late to start. Recognising the value of curiosity in a range of professions and pursuits, educators and organisations have established workshops and seminars to teach curiosity in settings as diverse as public administration (Hatcher, 2019), nursing (Kedge and Appleby, 2009), dementia care and befriending (Phillips and Evans, 2018).

Here are some things you can do to induce and train your curiosity. These begin with immersing yourself in the field, using initial moments to notice as much as you can, then move towards observing how you observe and, finally, training your gaze to see more critically and insightfully.

First, and most generally, immerse yourself in the field you plan to study and see what you notice. As we explained in the previous chapter, the field can take many forms: physical and digital – from a city street to a hospital waiting room, an office to a forest, a social media site or a digital archive. Whatever or wherever your field is, we encourage you to use your initial moments there to really look around and notice as much as you can. The postcards in this chapter – in which students on international field classes begin fieldwork in Central and South Asia respectively – illustrate how other students have done this. In their initial moments – before they had settled on a project – the students had a window of opportunity in which they were noticing many different things. This can be an equally stimulating and exciting part of your fieldwork too, a time to open your eyes and your mind, finding new interests and opening up lines of enquiry. You need to know a little about what we don't know before you can frame and begin to answer research questions and define research interests (Inan, 2012: 67), and this is the time to find out a little about a lot of different things. During the first moments in an unfamiliar place, you can gain a little of this awareness – a sense of what you might like to know more about – and this can be a starting point for your fieldwork.

Second, we can be curious about our own curiosity, observing how we observe. Your initially free-ranging observations may seem unfocused and in a sense they are. This is not a bad thing according to the psychoanalyst Adam Phillips (2019). He advises that, rather than always trying to concentrate and worrying when we fail to do so, we should pay attention to our own flickering attention, to the things we notice and the things that occur to us. One way of noticing what we notice is to fill our field notebooks with observations; another is to look at and read through these notebooks. Because these notes are assembled quickly without the usual filters and constraints – the discipline we imposed upon our more polished writing – they speak truths about what we are really interested in. They are, as creative writing instructors put it, a form of 'free writing' (Phillips and Kara, 2021), possibly scrappy but often telling, bringing our preoccupations to the surface. Some of our noticing is triggered by the interests we bring to the field. If we are interested in weeds, we will notice weeds in the field. If we are interested in clothing, we will notice what people wear and the contexts in which they dress in particular ways. Because we are curious about things we care about, there is no such thing as 'sheer' or 'mere' curiosity (Inan, 2012: 126), which means that, however distracted they may be, our initial observations will be valuable.

A third way in which to cultivate your curiosity is to train your gaze to see more fully and critically. In familiar settings we tend to wear blinkers, seeing the same things, travelling the same paths, only noticing what is out of the ordinary or out of place. This means that, if your fieldwork is in a familiar or local setting, closer to home or even at home, you may find it harder to open your eyes and your mind to its possibilities. You may need to learn or relearn how to notice the things, places and people around you. Georges Perec, the French experimental writer, provides some useful tips for noticing, 'training the gaze' (Perec, 1997: 50) to see more and see differently:

> Observe the street, from time to time, with some concern for system perhaps.
>
> Apply yourself. Take your time.
>
> Note down the place: the terrace of a café near the junction of
>
> the Rue de Bac and the Boulevard
>
> Saint-Germain
>
> the time: seven o'clock in the evening
>
> the date: 15 May 1973
>
> the weather: set fair
>
> Note down what you can see. Anything worthy of note going on.
>
> Do you know how to see what's worthy of note? Is there anything
>
> that strikes you?
>
> Nothing strikes you. You don't know how to see.
>
> You must see it more slowly, almost stupidly. Force yourself to write down what is of no interest, what is most obvious, most common, most colourless.

Some other methods, influenced by Perec's experimental fieldwork (Phillips, 2018), are illustrated in the 'Try This' box below and in Figure 3.2. These activities are borrowed from and inspired by a series of books about creative and experimental fieldwork including *The Art of Noticing* by Rob Walker (2019), *How to be an Explorer of the World* by Keri Smith (2008: 64), *Mission:Explore* (Geography Collective, 2010) and *The Lonely Planet Guide to Experimental Travel* (Antony and Henry, 2005). Some of these activities – such as letting a dog take you for a walk (Figure 3.2) – might seem frivolous, even silly, but they make serious points. First, being playful can open your eyes, other senses and minds to the world and the people around you. Though it can be childish, play can also be 'serious' (Schrage, 1999), both for children and adults, who stand to learn and develop as they play. Second, being playful is not always easy; we may need some help in getting started.

CURIOSITY AND RESEARCH DESIGN | 29

Figure 3.2 Let a dog take you for a walk
Source: Geography Collective (2010: 56–57)

━━━━━━━ **Try this** ━━━━━━━

The following activities, borrowed from some experimental field guides and explorers' manuals, can help you to notice things around you, becoming more curious.

1. 'Go to a shopping centre and play hide-and-seek. Which are the best three shops to hide in?' (Geography Collective, 2010: 145). What do you notice when you are playing rather than shopping?
2. Travel around a town or city. This can be somewhere you know well, or think you do, or somewhere new to you. Each time you reach an intersection, flip a coin, turning left for a head, right for a tail. Where does this take you? What do you notice?
3. 'Notice something you always notice; now notice something you've never noticed' (Walker, 2019: 85). This exercise is based on an idea by the artist Nina Katchadourian.
4. Let a dog take you for a walk (see Figure 3.2).

To illustrate how curiosity can initiate fieldwork, we now turn to a more detailed example, in the form of a postcard from a field class in South India. Matt Baillie Smith, a development specialist, explains how he encouraged students on a field trip to be curious: both about the setting (previously unfamiliar to the students) and also about themselves and their reactions to the people and happenings there (Postcard 3.2). Initially curious about other people, the students also begin to question their own reactions, their own curiosity.

Postcard 3.2

Open-ended fieldwork, curiosity and learning in South India, by Matt Baillie Smith

The silence of students on the minibus as it pulls out of Thiruvananthapuram airport in South India and onto the highway always seems a sharp contrast to my excitement at arriving. Curious about what has or hasn't changed since last time (from the road surface to mobile phone billboards), wondering when we will stop for a dosa (a South Indian pancake), considering whether it is going to be a hot day for the journey, I sense I am spared some of the students' anxiety about what they are seeing and what is to come. These often bewildering early experiences are not the bit before the field visit starts, but the very stuff of the fieldwork.

Our approach worked to encourage a curiosity that works through, and against, powerful imaginaries of place, space and identity that mediate understandings of India. There is a lot more baggage to be dealt with than the endlessly debated rucksack contents collected at the airport. Development discourses can produce Orientalising imaginaries which privilege the agency of the outsider, while popular imaginaries of the extremes of the Himalayas and steam of the tropical jungle invoke spaces to play in, erasing the social. Colonial and postcolonial histories of exploration can become entangled with 'helping', shaping a circumscribed curiosity predicated on assumed 'rights' to mobility and fantasies of 'discovery' and 'making a difference'. This all rubs up against critiques of the 'white saviour', the climate impacts from air travel and the need to decolonise the thinking and practices of development. Curiosity risks becoming focused on India as an 'object', or being paralysed by the challenge of navigating these entanglements, and the contradictions inherent in how we ended up together on a bus travelling from Thiruvananthapuram to Madurai.

We allowed time for reflection, exploring emotional reactions, learning, re-imagining project ideas and possibilities and changing minds. This is the key 'cultural work' that is essential to the fieldwork, an 'open-ended' and relational approach that produces expected and unexpected conversations to trouble imaginaries and provoke curiosities. We worked closely with Indian academics, NGO colleagues and students to facilitate exchanges that make the familiarity of popular imaginaries 'strange', but, for the visiting students, also make the strangeness first encountered as we leave the airport seem more 'familiar'. Sometimes students are sent off around the city in an auto-rickshaw for an hour with no planned itinerary and, on return, share reflections with Indian partners, asking questions and reflecting on why particular things are 'noticed'. These experiences can help unsettle powerful imaginaries, fostering curiosities less framed by instrumentalised approaches to knowledge. They can also begin connections to, among others, urban geographies, geographies of religion, of youth, of gender and geographies of development.

Our approach is as much about understanding the significance of positionality in shaping the creation of knowledge as it is about enhancing understanding of South India. Through this, students begin to see the contours, contradictions, nuances and relationalities of the places and spaces they encounter. They can begin to think more critically, reflexively and relationally about caste or about child labour, for example, mindful of the baggage they might have brought, but now able to understand where they might be asking from. The collapse of comfortable 'helper' narratives or the difficulty of putting a decolonising agenda into practice can destabilise students' sense of themselves. This needs care, and an inclusive approach to what counts as a project. One participant chose, as their 'field project', to keep a reflexive diary and to narrate not only their experiences, but also those of the group's processes of change. Another, when in India, began to see commonalities with their Christianity and the experiences of young Christians in South India, and went on to construct their project around exploring those experiences. Others stuck to more conventional 'development' themes, such as analysing the impact of NGO education projects. For some, a project may emerge on return home, when learning around positionality and difference provides a new lens on what was previously just 'familiar'. The key in this is providing a way for participants not simply to develop their understanding of South India, but to do so by developing curiosity about themselves and the relationships they are entangled in.

Ethical Curiosity

These students from a British university visiting India – starting with curiosity about the people and places around them but then becoming curious about their own curiosity – raise questions about the ethics and power relations of curiosity, which include some uncomfortable colonial overtones. Curiosity-driven enquiry can lead to casual intrusion into other people's lives, as for example when it is directed at their bodies or private lives, and when it involves extractive data gathering. But, as we argue in more detail in Chapter 5, Ethical Fieldwork, and Chapter 6, Decolonising Fieldwork, the curious impulses behind some fieldwork can be mobilised in other ways, which are actively ethical and decolonising. For example, a fieldwork method in which 'openness and curiosity' converge with colonial traditions – ethnography (explained in Chapter 8, Participant Observation and Participatory Fieldwork) – exemplifies the risks but also the possibilities of curiosity-driven fieldwork. Reflecting on the ethnographic tradition within their own discipline – modern languages – Naomi Wells and colleagues argue that this approach cannot just be extricated from its colonial roots; it can be mobilised against them. They argue that 'an ethnographic sensitivity encourages an openness to less hierarchical forms of knowledge, particularly when consciously seeking to invert the traditional colonial ethnographic project and envision instead more participatory and collaborative models of engagement' (Wells et al., 2019). Similarly, in an essay on 're-Africanising African universities', Mazrui (2003) argues that curiosity is fundamental to creative and critical scholarship. We develop these points in Chapter 6, Decolonising Fieldwork.

To ensure your curiosity-driven fieldwork is ethical and critical, it is important to cultivate a second kind of curiosity: 'curiosity about one's own curiosity' (Rabinow, 1996: 170–171). This means asking what consequences your curiosity might have for other people and yourself, and considering who and what your curiosity is for. Is your interest in others intrusive? Exploitative? Self-indulgent? Prurient? Empathetic? Caring? Curiosity has the potential to be all of these things, so it is important to be self-reflexive about the particular characteristics of the curiosity you are experiencing, cultivating and expressing. Beyond this ethical distinction, we can also differentiate between kinds of curiosity in fieldwork and in academic research more generally.

Scholars sometimes advocate 'focused curiosity', distinguishing this from distracted, gossipy and childlike counterparts. Advocating scientific curiosity, geographer John K. Wright (1947: 4) distanced himself from the 'nosy, impertinent' curiosity of 'monkeys, small children, and gossips'. Similarly and more recently, philosopher Ilhan Inan distinguished between 'novelty seeking, sensation seeking' curiosity and its more august, conceptual counterparts requiring particular cognitive and linguistic competences (Inan, 2012: 125). Again, it is important to be self-reflexive about your curiosity, asking what kind of curiosity it is, whether it belongs in fieldwork and, if so, where. You are likely to find open-ended curiosity most helpful in the early stages of fieldwork when you are identifying a topic, finding interest in it and beginning to develop it into a project.

Having cultivated your curiosity about fieldwork problems, you may have begun to develop some ideas for your own fieldwork. Now that you have a sense of what you would like to know more about, it is time to begin to focus your ideas and develop a field project, complete with a **research design** including aims, questions, objectives and methods.

How can I translate my ideas into a field research project?

Once you have an inspirational thought – a sense that you are onto something that could be interesting – you need to develop this further and translate it into the environment where you plan to research. Colin Robson and Kieran McCartan (2015) – professors of childhood studies and criminology respectively – liken research design to crossing a river. With each step you move between stepping-stones which represent your focus, questions, strategy and methods. Step one is your research focus. Gaining this focus and clarity can involve a fair amount of exploration of the academic literature on your topic. You must move from having an idea, or problem, to identifying a tightly focused and practical research agenda. Reviewing the existing literature is important as it helps you to see what existing knowledge there is, as well as spotting gaps in that knowledge (some of which you might be able to fill).

It can help to make connections between your initial fieldwork ideas – the problems and topics that arouse your curiosity – and things you already know. However responsive you may be to things you notice as you anticipate and then enter the field, you will not be starting from zero in terms of your knowledge. All researchers, however 'unstructured or inductive', bring 'orienting ideas, foci and tools' to the field (Miles and Huberman, 1994: 27), and it can be helpful to reflect on what these may be. The first step is to work out how to build on your existing knowledge and combine it with your thoughts on what you find interesting about your field site(s). Do you want to build on a previous learning experience/topic? Or do you want to expand your horizons and engage with a topic that inspires you? What contemporary issues are you interested in? How do you know if these initial ideas relate to your field location(s)? Where does your tentative research idea fit into the wider research field? To begin to explore these questions and situate your preliminary ideas, see Figure 3.3.

Having started with curiosity, identifying topics you are curious about and locating these within the research literature and within wider fields of knowledge (by working through

- It appears nobody has investigated this topic…I'll have a go.
- A key paper investigated this topic and raised questions regarding the role of X… I'll investigate X.
- A key paper investigated this topic and found that X was occurring….but they ignored the possible effects of Y. I'll investigate the effects of Y.
- A key paper investigated this topic at location Z and found that X was occurring….I'll see if the same is true for location W.
- A key paper investigated this topic and demonstrated that the dominant effects on X were Y and Z. This may be wrong…I'll investigate this.
- A key paper investigated this topic several years ago….I'll investigate and see if this is still true.
- A key paper investigated this topic and found that X was happening. A different key paper found that Y was happening….I'll investigate and see which is right (or if both are incorrect).
- A key paper investigated this topic using method A….I'll use different methods and compare my results.
- A key paper was written over fifteen years ago using physical fieldwork….I'll investigate using digital fieldwork and compare my results.
- Since a key paper was written, a new dataset has become available….I'll investigate to see if the new data supports their conclusions.

Figure 3.3 Developing your idea within its academic context

Figure 3.3), the next step is to specify the problems you want to solve or questions you want to answer. In this way, curiosity forms a crucial first step in a cycle of problem finding and problem solving. The sociologist Richard Sennett (2008) argues that this cycle is seen in practical settings – from construction sites to domestic kitchens – and also in research and development, including pure and applied scholarship. One expression of this is found in problem-based learning (PBL), in which students are provoked by exposure to circumstances and problems, then come up with questions that drive their own learning (Pawson et al., 2006; Spronken-Smith, 2005). Most closely associated with medical training, PBL is also advanced in other disciplines and learning spaces including fieldwork (Bradbeer et al., 2004). Defining problems or questions means asking what precisely you would like to know more about, or what you need to know. Questions and problems are best kept simple and direct, clear and answerable. At the end of this chapter, we suggest a reading on research design that includes useful tips on defining research questions, aims and objectives: *Qualitative Research* by David Silverman (2020).

Once you have a broad set of research questions or themes, you will be ready to consider what data to collect and to begin to think forward about how you will interpret your data. These are methodological questions.

How do I choose my field research methods?

You may already know and be experienced in using some research methods. You may need to learn about other methods which are relevant to your fieldwork interests. In Part III – Methods in Context – we introduce a range of useful and inspiring field research methods. In some cases, this is likely to build upon what you already know and feel confident about. In others, it will expose you to methods and ideas that may be new to you. Remember that research methods require different skillsets so we advise that you think through the most appropriate methods for your research topic alongside the practical constraints you face: these include the time and resources you have to hand, as well as your own abilities, strengths and weaknesses.

You should select fieldwork method(s) on the basis of their ability to generate the data you need, combined with consideration of the specific demands of your field site. For example, if you want to investigate a community's memories of a particular event, in-depth interviews combined with archival research may be most appropriate. You could speak to community members to research their recollections, and you could look at community and media resources generated at the time of the event to capture contemporary views. The number of interviews you conduct and volume of secondary sources you collect will be influenced by the amount of time you are in the field (this also applies to digital fieldwork as your time is not limitless). You will need to be very clear why you have chosen a particular method (or combination of methods). All too often researchers do not make explicit links between their research objectives, the theories they are trying to access and the research methods they have chosen.

Try this

Choose one of the following fieldwork challenges or questions:

- investigate modern farming practices through a chicken farm;
- explore how entrepreneurs use social media to build new markets;
- investigate a migrant community through the food they cook and eat.

For the project you have chosen, identify three fieldwork methods you could use to investigate this issue. What are the advantages and disadvantages of each method? How might you choose between or combine these methods? (It is often helpful to have more than one method in a project.) Which method(s) are likely to be most feasible in your fieldwork context? Can you anticipate areas where you might face challenges?

Each research context requires us to consider which methods are most appropriate. We also need to anticipate that we may need to adapt our methodology while in the field. This flexible and adaptable approach to fieldwork is illustrated in a study of women who gamble. Sociologist Jun Li planned mixed methods fieldwork including covert participant observation and interviews with women in casinos in Ontario (these methods are explained in Part III). She played slot machines and watched while other women gambled, and also interacted with them, taking field notes later on (Li, 2008: 104). But Li changed course when she became uncomfortable with acting covertly, something she felt had 'unintentionally infringed their right to privacy' and subjected her as a researcher to 'psychological pressure and inner conflicts' (Li, 2008: 106). Adapting her methodology, Li decided to conduct observations overtly and used these more open encounters to recruit interviewees. This example illustrates a more general point: it is advisable to continually evaluate the research methods we have chosen, adapting and amending them as we go.

Fieldwork is dynamic, unfolding in ways that cannot always be planned or predicted, and yielding unexpected data. Research design can – and often should – change as we experience the field and learn about the context and the research methods. Good research design is not linear. We can rethink, rework and redesign our research before and during our fieldwork, with our data collection re-informing our research design as needed. The same applies to analysis and our data collection – a feedback loop that we discuss in Chapter 14, Understanding and Handling Your Data.

Another example of the translation of curiosity and questions to research design is provided by feminist geographer Emily Frazier, who conducted research with refugees and resettlement actors in the United States. Doing so, she used semi-structured interviews, participant observation, participant-driven photography and photo elicitation (all of which are explained in Part III of this book). Frazier opted for participatory methods because this approach can enable participants to explore and document their own experiences (Frazier, 2020). Things didn't go as smoothly as Frazier had hoped and expected. One person declined her invitation to participate because his full-time work left little time. Another agreed to participate but struggled to find time to take photos, sending rushed 'selfies' instead. Like Li, who changed the course of her study of gambling (described above), Frazier learned from her 'fieldwork failure', which was revealing in its own way (Frazier, 2020: 142). From this, we can see that it is important to translate research questions into research methods, but then to be flexible about the latter, seeing research design as a work in progress.

We encourage you to think creatively about your research design. Don't default to what seems like the obvious research method – it may not be appropriate. Do consider what resources are available and think about the different perspectives you can gain from using particular methods (and combinations of methods). Part III takes you through many qualitative fieldwork methods. Think about reading through them all *before* you make your research design decisions and revisit again when you want more in-depth knowledge of the specific methods you have chosen.

Conclusion

Whether you have *carte blanche* to define your own project, or more limited freedom to complete an assignment, curiosity will help: by directing you towards questions, problems and themes that can really interest you.

Some students are naturally comfortable with curiosity-driven fieldwork. Others prefer more structure and appreciate clear guidance. Wherever you stand on this spectrum – from open-ended to structured fieldwork – we encourage you to follow your curiosity and set your own agenda at least some of the time. This could be exciting and productive because it is the point where you really begin to take ownership of your fieldwork. At best, curiosity can be a starting point for critical, self-possessed fieldwork.

Once you have made a start, ideally by finding a topic that interests you or interest in a topic you have been assigned, your challenge is to translate this into a feasible research idea. At this point, your task is to define and refine curiosity-driven questions, then to develop these into a research design (these steps are set out in Figure 3.3). Your research design will situate your questions in the academic literature on your subject, identify and bound a field site in which to conduct research and specify methods for data collection and analysis. At this point, the inspiration of initial curiosity turns to the perspiration of actual fieldwork where our research experiences may give us cause to revisit our methodological choices. We therefore need to remain open and adaptable in order to maximise our time in the field.

Key terms

Curiosity is the desire to know, see or learn something.
Research design is the strategy you develop to answer your research question or problem. It includes the data you collect, the methods you choose and the ways in which you analyse your data.

Further Reading

Kara, Helen (2020) *Creative Research Methods: A Practical Guide*, 2nd ed. Policy Press.
This book is filled with creative and challenging ideas, which encourage curiosity and then provide inspiration for what to do with it.

Silverman, David (2020) *Qualitative Research*, 5th ed. Sage.
Qualitative methods expert David Silverman's book provides clear guidance on how to go from the ideas of research to the practicalities of designing, conducting and writing about your research.

Smith, Keri (2008) *How to be an Explorer of the World*. Penguin.
For inspiration and practical tips, which can help you discover (or rediscover) your curiosity, variously finding things that interest you, and interest in things around you, we recommend this lively illustrated manual. There are useful suggestions for further reading, and many ideas for 'explorations' you can try out yourself.

PART II
CRITICAL
FIELDWORK

Part contents
---

4 Working Together	39
5 Ethical Fieldwork	55
6 Decolonising Fieldwork	75

PART II

4
WORKING TOGETHER

In this chapter you will learn

- how to travel and work effectively with others;
- why you might be required to travel and work in a group rather than alone;
- what problems you might face when working with others and how you can overcome and learn from them;
- how you can help ensure that all students – regardless of differences such as gender, age, sexuality, class and physical capabilities – are included and valued in fieldwork.

Introduction

Fieldwork is often a shared experience. This is not the case for everyone – Masters and PhD students are more likely to work alone and this can bring problems including loneliness and personal risk – but undergraduates tend to conduct fieldwork in groups, travelling and working with others. This is also true of digital fieldwork, a subject we explore in more detail in chapters on digital fieldwork, secondary sources and social media.

Some people find collective fieldwork enjoyable, a chance to make friends, deepen relationships and put aside the individualism of their university experience. Others struggle with reduced personal space and the sustained presence of others, some of whom bring different work ethics, personalities and attitudes. Most of us experience a mix of these positives and negatives. When we conduct fieldwork together, we all confront ethical issues and challenges, revolving around how we treat each other and behave together. These issues are discussed in more detail in chapters on ethical fieldwork and decolonising fieldwork. Here, we provide some guidance on how to survive and prosper in a group setting, and how to ensure that your fieldwork is as inclusive as possible.

This chapter explores what it means to work together, travelling and living in close proximity to other students, sometimes sharing bathrooms and bedrooms, and sometimes sharing marks for group work. This raises moral questions about how to be respectful and considerate of others as well as practical questions about how to ensure that when working together you do so effectively and productively. We begin by asking why fieldwork tends to be conducted collaboratively – in groups – before moving on to explore the implications of this for equality, diversity and **inclusion** and the part you can play in all this.

Collaborative Fieldwork

Since university education can be individualistic you may find fieldwork challenging, revolving as it does around travelling and working together. It is common for fieldwork to involve elements of group work. You may be put into a group with people you don't already know, and might not think you like, at least not at first. You may worry about this at first; many students do. Will other group members drag down your marks? Will they press you to work all the time? Or might they keep you up at night?

But there are good reasons why field trip leaders favour groups, and why some intentionally break up pre-formed alliances and friendship groups, creating groups for the purposes of fieldwork. Eric Pawson, an advocate of 'problem-based learning' in which students work together to solve problems, reports that students tend to find group work difficult at first, but later see its advantages. 'My skill base has changed considerably,' one veteran of group fieldwork told Pawson. 'I'm more of a free thinker. I'm more open to hearing other people's opinions,' said another (Pawson and Teather, 2002: 280). A third reflected that they had 'gained skills about group work and dynamics' that helped them feel ready for 'entering the working world' (Pawson and Teather, 2002: 281). Talking through projects, students are pushed to 'negotiate meanings' and 'to express themselves in the language of the subject' (Jacques and Salmon, 2007: 1). To put this in less business-like terms, you can learn, notice and understand more together than you might alone. Learning together can be effective, opening doors that lone scholarship leaves closed.

Collaborative work is often incorporated in field courses for practical reasons which include ensuring personal safety, providing practical support and providing for a division of labour which can promote greater empirical depth and breadth in the relatively short space of time that most field trips allow. And, of equal importance, working together is a way of building up valuable skills. A study commissioned by the UK government identified a demand for skills that can be acquired through group fieldwork as employers highlighted shortages in team, communication and management skills (DfES, 1999). Developing and being able to demonstrate such skills can provide graduates with a way of distinguishing themselves from others in increasingly competitive graduate labour markets. These skills and attributes don't just make you more employable; as we explain in the final chapter on the 'takeaways' of fieldwork, they can also be important in life.

Becoming a Team

The challenge for any group is to grow into a team. This involves getting to know each other – perhaps through a combination of informal social time together and more structured group conversations – then identifying roles, agreeing ground rules and beginning to work together (Tuckman, 1965; Tuckman and Jensen, 1977; Pawson and Teather, 2002).

The first stage – getting to know each other – also involves getting to know oneself. This means identifying characteristics and personality traits and asking what each individual might bring to the group. This is an established practice in business and management recruitment and planning, which profiles individuals and matches them to roles (Belbin, 1981). A simple way of doing this is to have a group discussion, reflecting on the skills and strengths of members of a team. Teaching at the University of Otago in Aotearoa New Zealand, Rachel Spronken-Smith (2005) facilitates workshops in which students working in groups of five or six begin by identifying their skills and complementarities. Doing so, they pinpoint strengths and weaknesses, reflecting on the skills they have and those they would like to develop, and the ways in which they might contribute to the group. Groups then discuss how they would like to operate and what roles – such as chair and secretary – need filling. This enables group members to better manage their expectations of each other. The following 'Try This' exercise will help group members find and agree on roles that are right for each of you (see Levin, 2005).

Try this

1. Looking at Table 4.1, match yourself to one or more of the team roles.
2. Invite others in your group to identify the roles they might play, based on their characteristics.
3. As a group, discuss the roles you would each like to play, and see if you can agree who will be the team leader, secretary and who will lead in areas such as contacting and liaising with participants, delivering presentations and producing written work. Make sure that everyone knows what is expected of their chosen role.
4. The group leader – not necessarily you – should then lead a discussion to find ground rules that everyone will be happy to sign up to. For example, you might agree on communication practices, such as not interrupting others when they are speaking and responding to messages within a certain period of time, and you might discuss what to do when something goes wrong.

Table 4.1 Roles for project team members

Team roles	Strengths	Potential contribution to fieldwork
Innovator	Produces ideas, is ready to challenge inertia and complacency.	May be invaluable if you are developing your own group research idea.
Investigator	Can bring contacts and information to the team, and work well with challenges.	Effective in planning data collection, and contacting potential research participants.
Chair/coordinator	Self-confident, positive.	Good at guiding a team and making decisions.
Implementer	Makes things happen, changes ideas into plans.	'Can do' attitude will be valuable in the field.
Team worker	Shows an interest in others' ideas, listens, concerned with social interaction, places teams above personal concerns.	Aims to have a happy team and will work to achieve this.
Plant	Creative and imaginative, unorthodox.	May provide a novel solution if research problems arise.
Completer/finisher	Follows through, conscientious, works hard to finish things properly.	Will not run out of enthusiasm so role in writing up may be valuable.

Source: Adapted from Jacques and Salmon (2007: Table 6.1) and Belbin (1981).

Challenges, conflicts and solutions

Working together is challenging. Thrown together in the field, individuals do not always find it easy to get along or end up liking each other, nor do we always know how to address these issues, or how to talk through difficulties and explore solutions. But we don't have to like someone to be able to work well with them; and we may not always work well with people we do like. If you acknowledge conflicts where they arise, you may find ways to resolve these issues and even to benefit from them. You may learn to work with people from outside your friendship groups – something you will probably have to do in later life.

It is difficult to talk about conflict, though it is possible to try. One way to broach difficult issues is to start a conversation about the roles and rules you have agreed and about your goals and priorities. Here, from our own field teaching, is an example of where group members have faced up to problems and found solutions. On one field trip, tensions arose when two members of a group seemed reluctant to conduct interviews in the evenings, when informants were available. When pressed, they revealed that they had obtained tickets for several sporting events – we were in Vancouver and the Canucks (the local ice hockey team) were playing! They had not realised that this could interfere with their project work. To the rest of the group they seemed to be prioritising their social activities and treating the field trip as a holiday. A compromise was reached when the two students expressed their commitment to the project and offered to compensate for their absence by collecting data on their scheduled day off. A different scenario arose when a group decided to separate into two teams, each working on opposite sides of a city. Feeling confident, they did not arrange a group meeting for three days. When they finally met, it became clear that the teams had been working differently, one team taking written notes, the other relying solely on recordings of interviews they were conducting. The students agreed that they should have met more often, though it was not too late to make some decisions about how to use their last few days in the field.

While some problems arise out of misunderstandings and disorganisation – where everyone is still trying to do their best – others stem from differences in attitudes, ambitions and abilities. Some want to work harder than others; others are content to let them; still others struggle to keep up. The reasons for these differences are complex, involving more than simply bossiness on one part and laziness on another, though that may be part of the story. More complex drivers of group dynamics include issues with confidence (Levin, 2005) and differences in brain function and associated behavioural traits – known as neurodiversity – which correspond to different ways of learning. Where individuals are floundering and groups are failing to cohere, it may be helpful to attempt an open and constructive discussion with the group about how to bring the individual back and help them to flourish, and how everyone can learn from the group diversity, but this needs to be handled gently. This may help the individual feel supported rather than persecuted by the group, and it may also help others to see their own part in the problem, given that the problem may not be the so-called free-rider, but the group dynamic. Though conflict is difficult, everyone can learn and even benefit from (what they learn from) it. Conflict is not limited to university projects; it can recur after graduation in the world of work. Potential employers value candidates with experience of how to cope with this, who may also have learned important lessons about working with diverse teams.

The second half of this chapter is devoted to another aspect of travelling and working together in the field – ensuring that everyone feels included and welcome, regardless of any differences or variations in physical abilities. This opens up a discussion of the ways in which fieldwork is embodied – something we do through our bodies – and therefore the ways in which the differences between our bodies shape the fieldwork we might do. (For a more detailed explanation of these terms, see Chapter 12, Multisensory and Embodied Fieldwork.) These themes come together in the following postcard, in which Michael Glass, an urban sociologist based in Pittsburgh, shares moments from the field trip he led in Asia.

Postcard 4.1

Bodies uncomfortably close, by Michael R. Glass

The humid tropical heat embraced us as we exited our extremely air-conditioned Western-style hotel in Kuala Lumpur. Our study group had arrived two days earlier from the United States, and our bodies were still adjusting to the time zone and the local climate. The day's itinerary focused on a visit to the Batu Caves – a Hindu temple cave complex within limestone hills in the city's metropolitan limits. The Batu Caves are the culminating point for the annual Thaipusam festival and hence a significant cultural site well-connected by the city's transportation infrastructure. The excitement about a day's excursion was palpable, and the jetlagged students were keen to stretch their legs at the start of a week's intensive fieldwork. Although we had prepared by wearing sensible lightweight fabrics and comfortable shoes, our excitement would be tempered by our discomfort and fatigue, brought on by the heat and humidity.

We piled into a shuttle van, bodies uncomfortably close together and the windows open as we were driven to the site. The drive took 30 minutes, and we spent the commute comparing the city's highways to those we were more familiar with in Pittsburgh. Upon arrival we unfolded ourselves stiffly from the van onto a sun-scorched concrete plaza where numerous other vans and buses parked. The cave entrance is barely visible from the plaza; what dominates the landscape is a 140-foot tall golden statue of Lord Murugan, the Hindu god of war that stands adjacent to the steep 272-step staircase that each tourist and pilgrim must climb. The limestone hills are even more impressive, covered by native vegetation and home to wildlife including precocious monkeys that are accustomed to the presence of human visitors. We paused at the base of the staircase to recall details about the site's cultural and geographic significance. We then began to climb.

The thrill of group fieldwork is that each participant experiences a research site in a different fashion. Our own physical, social and cultural attributes shaped how we encountered the site. Ascending with different rhythms, some stopped and started, others determined to climb without pause. We had read classic critiques of ableism in fieldwork and ensured that slower walkers weren't subject to undue peer pressure. Pauses for photos with monkeys and to look out at the city skyline helped

Continued

muster the group, but by the top of the stairs all of us were feeling a measure of bodily fatigue. Entering the cool, damp caves gave relief that faded once we exited and began our descent. Returning to the plaza we found that the temperatures had increased, and our exhaustion was amplified by a walk to the nearby train station. Hot, sticky and tired, conversations waned and we all struggled to muster the same enthusiasm that had marked the start of the day. We boarded the train and were again immersed in artificial air-conditioned comfort. The students gradually began to talk again, sharing insights from the cave visit and the train itself – including the discovery of gender-specific carriages that prompted new lines of enquiry for the rest of the trip.

Embodiment is part of fieldwork, since our bodies become part of the site. This means we will experience punctuated rhythms of comfort and discomfort as we enter unfamiliar environments. I learned that it's okay for us to embrace these different sensations, since multisensory encounters can generate new perspectives on research sites. This works even better in group settings because our research partners encounter sites in different ways, and they can support us when our attention or energy lapses.

Being Included and Including Others

Whoever you are – whatever your physical and mental abilities and disabilities, talents and needs may be, and whatever your background and heritage, gender and sexuality – there is a place for you in fieldwork. Inclusion, diversity and equality in fieldwork is everyone's responsibility. Universities, colleges and academic staff in some – but not all – parts of the world have legal responsibilities to ensure that reasonable adjustments are made for particular groups of students (those with 'protected' characteristics such as sexual orientation, gender, religion, race and disability), and moral responsibility to be sensitive towards differences. Students also have important parts to play in inclusion: claiming your place in the field, and including and valuing others. This is fundamental. The United Nations (UN) Convention on the Rights of Persons with Disabilities – now ratified by over 160 countries – seeks to 'ensure an inclusive education system at all levels' (United Nations, 2006: Article 24).

Everyone benefits from more inclusive fieldwork, where we all feel welcome and involved. Inclusion involves openness to, and respect for, all forms of difference including gender, sexuality, religion, ethnicity, culture, heritage, race, bodily differences and ages. The pursuit of inclusion is often grouped together with that of equality and diversity within institutional equality, diversity and inclusion strategies, which take different forms and have reached different stages in different countries and parts of the world, but generally begin with recognising differences and also involve making alterations and adjustments to teaching and learning and the institutional settings in which they take place (Ahmed, 2012). Inclusion is not just a matter of fairness. Diverse and inclusive field trips also have educational benefits. They provide opportunities for students to contribute in different ways and to learn from each other.

Figure 4.1 *Flying While Fat.* Still from animation by Stacy Bias, who identifies as an artist and queer activist

Exclusion and Inclusion

Inclusive fieldwork begins with awareness of the issues and challenges. This means recognising that fieldwork has not always been inclusive. Some students and staff have been left out of activities or entire trips or made to feel awkward. And some belong to groups that are underrepresented in the wider student population. These include people with physical and/or mental disabilities, those experiencing socio-economic hardship and others who are minoritised through their culture, religion, sexuality or gender. For Muslims, for example, alcoholic drinks are haram (forbidden), as are some foods, and body modesty is valued; these practices clash with some field traditions including nights out and shared bathrooms. For LGBT+ students, fieldwork can mean crossing into jurisdictions with different laws and customs, which can feel uncomfortable at best, and at worst can put individuals in great danger. Fieldwork can also be uncomfortable for women. Women's rights and freedoms vary between countries, potentially to the exclusion or disadvantage of female staff and students. Women are also much more likely to have to modify their fieldwork to stay safe – for example, avoiding particular locations – and are less likely to be able to work alone. More generally, fieldwork can reinforce and reproduce hierarchies, typically privileging able-bodied male students over others, in what feminist geographer Gillian Rose (1993) argues is a masculinist tradition (Datta, 2008; Vanderbeck, 2005).

But, with care and empathy we can find solutions, many of which are inexpensive and simple but effective. Some easy but important suggestions are provided in Table 4.2. Some of these solutions are the responsibility of field trip leaders, but students also have important parts to play. As a student, you have a right to expect your university or college to be doing its best to provide inclusive fieldwork, following the rules of thumb set out in the table. Many

Table 4.2 Exclusion and inclusion: problems and solutions

Issues	Problems	What students can do	What field trip leaders can do
Mobility	Some people may be left behind or left out of fieldwork that involves walking. Fieldwork often involves unspoken but unrealistic assumptions about how far and how fast others can walk.	Let your field trip leaders know if your ability to walk is limited, for example by health conditions or fitness. Be tolerant and accommodating if others on your trip cannot walk as far or as fast as you can. Try to ensure your plans are fair to all.	Think about how far, fast and long you plan to walk. Build in options for different abilities and endurance: faster and slower, longer and shorter walks. Provide alternatives such as taxis for those less able to walk.
Accessibility: physical and face-to-face	Uneven surfaces and stairs, barely noticed by one student, form a real barrier to another (Simmons, 1994). Some places are more accessible than others (Fuller et al., 2004; Borland and James, 1999).	When you are planning social activities and independent fieldwork, remember everyone's needs for access. Tell field trip leaders about your needs regarding accessibility, and help them plan fieldwork you can participate in.	Consider the accessibility of all travel and learning spaces including classrooms, laboratories, libraries, museums and field sites such as streets, markets and museums. Work within more accessible sites, and make these spaces as accessible as possible.
Accessibility: virtual	Not everyone can sit at a desk for a long time, those with visual impairment will struggle and some people cannot tolerate particular digital environments or programs because of epilepsy, brain injury, neurodiversity.	Take advantage of reasonable adjustments that may be available, which may involve providing information to field trip leaders and working with occupational health providers to ensure equipment and expectations meet your needs and those of fellow students. Be understanding of other students who cannot spend long periods in front of a screen or on a mobile device.	Set limits on time spent in front of a visual display unit, provide alternatives for those who cannot do so, and those who are visually impaired. Explore technological alternatives and provide where possible, considering the costs of data and equipment.
Travel	A journey that one person enjoys may be stressful or uncomfortable for another. Some students may be anxious about flying. Economy airline seats are unsuited to some people with larger bodies (Evans et al., 2021).	Let leaders know if you have concerns about travel or specific needs such as for seats that meet your needs.	Ensure that travel arrangements are consistent with your equality, diversity and inclusion commitments. This may mean providing specific travel facilities such as larger seats and exempting some students from some travel.

Continued

Table 4.2 Exclusion and inclusion: problems and solutions (Continued)

Issues	Problems	What students can do	What field trip leaders can do
Accommodation	On residential fieldwork, students are commonly assigned to shared, single-sex bedrooms, and expected to share bathrooms. Not everyone is comfortable with these shared intimacies.	If you need a larger bed, a single room and/or private time and space, don't be afraid to say so. Legitimate reasons include mental and physical health conditions, and cultural and religious customs regarding ablution and body modesty.	Be flexible with accommodation provisions, and make provisions for students with particular needs.
Toilets	Toilet access limits where we can go and for how long. Some students can wait longer than others, who need regular and more private facilities. Others need bathrooms for ablution before prayer.	If you feel able, explain your needs to the field trip leaders and also to fellow students. If you are an able-bodied man, remember that not everyone can disappear behind a tree when they need to relieve themself.	Make it easy for members of the group to explain their needs. Find out where and when toilets will be available, plan toilet breaks and announce these in advance.
Schedules	The intensity of fieldwork – involving long periods with others – demands social skills and resilience that not everyone has. The sensory stimulation of fieldwork can be exciting and inspiring to some, but leave others feeling overloaded and anxious.	If you have particular needs for rest and privacy – for example, for prayer, attending to menstruation, taking medication and breastfeeding try to tell the field trip leader. If you just find it easier to know where you will be and when, please let the field trip leader know that too.	Provide detailed itineraries in advance (Greene et al., 2020). These should include regular breaks with private space and time for rest and self-care. Inform students and teaching staff in advance.
Eating	Fieldwork often involves eating together. Food may be provided or there may be visits to cafés and restaurants. There is a risk that some students may not be able to access the food they need when they need it.	Let field trip leaders know about your dietary needs: your intolerances, allergies, religious and cultural requirements, and medical requirements that may dictate the timing of eating and drinking.	Consult members of a group about their dietary needs: what they can and cannot eat, and when. Remember that disrupted routines present challenges for those with specific requirements to eat – and sometimes fast – depending on faith and health conditions.

Continued

Table 4.2 Exclusion and inclusion: problems and solutions (Continued)

Issues	Problems	What students can do	What field trip leaders can do
Drinking	Social activities, from wind-down drinks to nights out in the course of a field trip, often involve alcohol. Students who drink tend to bond with each other while marginalising and excluding some others (Gillen, 2015; Rose, 1993). Those who don't drink – whether for cultural or religious reasons, personal preference, or medical conditions including addictions – can be excluded and made to feel uncomfortable.	Don't pressure anyone to drink alcohol, and ensure that people can participate fully in social activities without drinking. Everyone should be aware of the ways in which their drinking may affect others, and take responsibility for this.	Field trip leaders may need to set rules about alcohol, depending on the circumstances of the trip. There may be people in the group whose needs take precedence. The field trip may be in a location that is either illegal for students in a particular age group, or where alcoholic drinks are illegal or offensive (Gillen, 2015). Where judgement is involved, it may be best to ask the group to discuss and agree their own approach to alcoholic drinks.
Costs	For some students the costs of fieldwork are prohibitive. The field trip may also interrupt regular paid work, which some students rely upon to pay their fees and living expenses. Field trips can also interrupt unpaid work including care that some students give to family members. Their absence – if it can be arranged – will have knock-on effects on family members.	If you have free time and are planning social activities, remember that your fellow students have different means, so try to plan activities that others can afford. It is not always easy to talk about money, so this requires tact and care.	Find out about financial assistance that may be available to students who need it. Share this information with students and encourage them to apply. This can be sensitive and raise concerns about fairness, so has to be handled with care. Since most students have limited means, it is best to work on the assumption that costs should be kept to a minimum throughout.

Note: This table introduces difference, exclusion and inclusion but is illustrative rather than comprehensive.

universities are working to become more inclusive but most have important work left to do (for some international case studies see: Sandoval et al., 2021; Cameron et al., 2019), and this applies to fieldwork as to other forms of teaching and learning. Students can play a part in this unfinished project, prompting and informing your institutions to change.

Adjustments to make fieldwork more accessible range from logistical considerations to choices of destinations and sites. They range from ensuring that activities are not too physically demanding and that students have access to toilets when needed, to considering the safety and needs of particular groups. For example, to check risks posed to LGBT+ students, field trip leaders should consult sources that provide information on relevant laws and customs, freedoms and dangers (e.g., https://ilga.org/maps-sexual-orientation-laws). You should expect field trip leaders to have made such checks when planning fieldwork destinations and assessing risks, though it can sometimes be necessary to remind them. You may also need to communicate any specific needs you may have, which your university will need to know about in order to make reasonable adjustments or other provisions for you. This kind of communication is not always easy. Few of us like to talk to colleagues and fellow students about our toilet needs or sexualities, our limited budgets or family responsibilities, our medical conditions or anxieties. But it is important to try, since an understanding of everyone's needs is fundamental. This can sometimes mean busting taboos and confronting initial embarrassment, though you should be able to provide this information confidentially and anonymously, enabling field trip leaders to provide for your needs. In addition to informing others about your needs, it is also important to consider theirs, whether or not they have explained them directly. The following postcard illustrates the need to consider the mobility of other students, remembering that they may have a different range and speed to your own.

Postcard 4.2

Considering mobility, by Morag Rose

My fieldwork explores walking as a creative, social and political act. Walking is often taken for granted, dismissed as merely pedestrian. However, the everyday is fascinating and our bodies can be a powerful research tool: immersion in space is a fantastic way to explore and understand. I'm not alone in this. Walking – whether guided tours or simply getting from A to B – is integral to most field trips. For my own research I have often joined tours organised by artists, creative walkers, tourist guides and others; I feel very lucky to be able to take part in such fun activities for work.

Sadly, though, my postcard is not a simple 'wish you were here'. I am a Disabled person and I have a mobility impairment which means my walking is sometimes slow and painful. I can struggle with steep steps and other physical barriers. Disabled activists, academics and Disabled Peoples Organisations (DPOs) talk about the social model of disability which explains how the environment limits our ability to participate equally. This is a political and structural issue not just a personal one and if we want to make fieldwork open and welcoming to all we need to consider equality of access.

My worst fieldwork experiences have been on tours that did not consider diverse bodies in their planning and promotion. For example, I recently went on a public walk organised by an artist and promoted through a well-respected venue. I chose to attend partly because the booking information said the event was fully accessible. This was very helpful as often this information is difficult and time consuming to find. Unfortunately, it was not true. The tour included two flights of stairs! This should have been an obvious indication the tour wasn't accessible for everyone – for example, there is no way a wheelchair user could get up the steps. There were also several busy road crossings without

Continued

drop curbs or safe places to cross. Additionally large parts of the tour were over cobblestones. These can be painful and potentially dangerous for people with sensory or mobility impairments and some **neurodiverse** people. Other tours have been challenging for me because they lasted much longer than advertised or the pace was very fast and the guide did not check in with participants. All of these events caused me physical discomfort and made me feel awkward and embarrassed. I don't think this was intentional but it could have been easily avoided.

I believe one of the most important aspects of creating a better experience is clear, honest, open communications. When organising or publicising an event give as much information about the venue and activities as possible – and, of course, make sure this information is correct. This allows people the dignity of making an informed choice about the risks and rewards of joining you. Be open to questions about the specific needs of individuals, make space for them to ask and be listened to in advance of your event. Remember 'Disabled People' are a heterogeneous group with diverse individual and intersectional identities. Create a culture of care where access is the default not the exception. When you are on your expedition be alert and reflexive to the needs of everyone, including issues that may emerge as your trip progresses. There are many excellent resources to support you making sure everyone can feel welcome and able to join you.

Disability

To illustrate ways of making fieldwork more inclusive, we now turn to the specific example of how to include students with disabilities (John and Khan, 2018; Kingsbury et al., 2020). Disability takes many different forms, both mental and physical, visible and invisible (Fuller et al., 2004). It has been defined as 'a physical or mental impairment that has a "substantial" and "long-term" negative effect on [a person's] ability to do normal daily activities' (UK Equality Act, 2010).

We provide some suggestions for including students with disabilities in fieldwork. These ideas are gleaned from our own experiences, from the growing literature on this subject (e.g. Adams and Brown, 2006; Fuller et al., 2009; Geography Disability Network, 2004; Bhakta et al., 2015; John and Khan, 2018) and also from field trip leaders who responded to a survey we posted online. For their responses to the survey, we are grateful to Melanie Bickerton, Stephen Lane, Gerry Kearns, Faith Tucker, Sarah Davies, Kate Spencer, Greg Holland, Ann Rowan, Jen Dickinson, Caroline Upton and others who chose to remain anonymous. We have also gleaned advice to staff and students posted online by institutions and organisations including the University of Minnesota, whose website we acknowledge. All this advice revolves around enabling students and supporting their learning (Chiarella and Vurro, 2020; Giles et al., 2020) and ensuring that everyone is included to the extent they can be. These tips are for everyone – staff and students, those with disabilities and those without. These tips supplement more general provisions such as the need for regular rest breaks and for clarity about access to toilet facilities, which make fieldwork more accessible to everyone (Table 4.2).

If you don't have a disability, remember that some staff and students do, and may be facing barriers to travelling and participating in the field. Consider them in everything from your walking speed to your evening plans. Whether or not you have a disability, you will find it helps to review Table 4.2 to help make the trip more inclusive and enjoyable for everyone. The key to this is preparation and good communication – finding out what you can in advance, expressing your needs (to the extent that you feel able) and listening when others express their needs. You will also find it helpful to find out as much as you can about your host culture. The more you know, the better prepared you will be. You may also find it helpful to find out about grants or allowances that may be used to cover additional costs such as insurance, individual transport and one-to-one carers or tutors (such as sign language interpreters and mobility supporters). Table 4.2 is also helpful to staff members leading field trips.

Finally, here is an example of how everyone – including staff and students – can help to make fieldwork more inclusive. This takes the form of feedback from a student who experiences anxiety and who appreciated reasonable adjustments that the field trip leader had made but still struggled, and later reflected on how things could have been better:

> The main thing is the idea of knowing what we are doing. [The field trip leader] sent the timetable and information documents to us in advance but within those there was some ambiguity. For example, a lot of the timetable said 'group project work' but I didn't know what that was. I think for people like me if they knew exactly what was meant by 'group project work' then they could plan what they were doing and who they would be with a little better. Also, I think another area of anxiety for me personally was not knowing who I would be sitting with on the plane and just being given a random seat number once at the airport. A lot of anxiety I think comes from the idea of the unknown and by minimising the areas of ambiguity as much as possible it provides more certainty for the anxious mind. I think in terms of carrying this out effectively – maybe on the questionnaire in which we listed medical conditions there could be a section for things like anxiety and worries or concerns so [the leader can reassure] those more likely to need extra support. That understanding may be all it takes to get those people who would otherwise feel unable to go to think that a field class is something they could actually do!

Conclusion

It is common for students taking field classes to be asked to work together. Working together can be difficult. Some students find it stressful, struggling with conflict and resenting apparent free-riders. But, at best, collective fieldwork can be productive and enjoyable, a chance for each person to find new skills and ways of contributing, while learning to value others and respect differences, and enjoying the companionship and benefitting from the safety of numbers. We tend to work together more happily and effectively when we are self-reflexive and empathetic, acting on the tips provided in this chapter. Working through the tensions and difficulties that can sometimes arise, it is possible to aim for something more than damage limitation and problem solving; at best, it is possible to gain skills for employment and life, while enjoying each other's company and making new friends.

In this chapter, we have also seen that there can be a place in the field for everyone (who wants it). For this to be possible, fieldwork sometimes needs to change; sometimes plans and traditions need to be tweaked and adjusted. In some cases, fieldwork traditions need to be radically overhauled – for example, where it is assumed that participants can walk a certain distance, manage for hours without toilet facilities, cope with uncertainty and spend extended periods in the presence of others. Some people are excluded by these traditions. Students can play a part in making changes and adjustments. Those doing fieldwork may need to be flexible about how things are done, and sensitive and empathetic enough to find out what changes are needed.

Everyone – not just those who may have been left out – has something to gain from more inclusive fieldwork. Different students bring different abilities and talents to the field trip. Some may struggle with things you find easy, but they may also be able to contribute in ways you had never imagined. Be open to what others can bring to the field trip, especially if you are working together as a group, where a range of strengths and characters can be productive and there is no need for everyone to be or do the same thing. We all have something to learn from recognising the diversity of human experiences, the differences between our bodies and minds and the worlds we inhabit. Exploring these differences, we may not just make fieldwork more inclusive – we may also begin to see new dimensions of human life.

Key terms

Ableism is a form of discrimination, which favours able-bodied people. In fieldwork, ableism can take the form of assumptions about students' bodily capabilities, ranging from how far they can walk to how long they can manage away from a toilet, with the effect that some students are excluded from some activities, even from entire trips.

Inclusion involves openness to, and respect for, forms of difference including gender, sexuality, religion, ethnicity, culture, heritage, race, bodily differences, neurodiversity and age. The pursuit of inclusion is often grouped together with that of equality and diversity within institutional equality, diversity and inclusion strategies, which are geared towards recognising differences and making alterations and reasonable adjustments. In educational settings, this means adjusting teaching and learning practices and the institutional settings in which they take place, ranging from classrooms to virtual learning environments to field sites (Ahmed, 2012).

Neurodivergent refers to an individual or group of people who is/are not neurotypical (autistic, ADHD etc.). A **neurodiverse** group includes people who are variously neurodivergent and neurotypical.

Teamwork skills are important for fieldwork and can be acquired through fieldwork. Teamwork skills take various forms, ranging from leadership (the role played by a project leader or chair) to supportive team membership (listening to others, cooperating with them, prioritising the needs of the group above personal concerns and so on). These skills can be valuable in future employment and also in life.

Further Reading

Ahmed, Sara (2012) *On Being Included: Racism and Diversity in Institutional Life*. Duke University Press.
This book critically examines the discourses and practices of equality, diversity and inclusion in institutional settings.

Chilisa, Bagele (2019) *Indigenous Research Methodologies*. Sage.
Group work goes against the grain for many students, brought up in universities and societies dominated by competitive individualism. And yet, this is not the only way of relating to other students. From a postcolonial and indigenous standpoint, Bagele Chilisa argues for an alternative, more 'relational' approach to working together.

Hall, Tim Healey, Mick & Harrison, Margaret (2002) Fieldwork and Disabled students: Discourses of exclusion and inclusion. *Transactions of the Institute of British Geographers*, 27(2): 213–231.
Advocates of sensory research tend to make assumptions about the bodies of researchers – their abilities to see, hear, touch, taste, smell or move around – which are not always right and are often exclusionary and discriminatory. This article acknowledges that different students have different bodies and bodily capabilities. The authors encourage us all to recognise the diversity of students' bodies and capabilities, and work with the possibilities that everyone brings.

Levin, Peter (2005) *Successful Teamwork! For Undergraduates and Taught Postgraduates Working on Group Projects*. Open University Press/McGraw Hill.
A short, accessible book for students, which covers the challenges of group work and provides practical suggestions and solutions.

5
ETHICAL FIELDWORK

In this chapter you will learn

- to ensure that your fieldwork does not harm anyone or anything;
- to consider ways in which your fieldwork could benefit other people;
- to navigate ethical review and get the most out of it;
- to frame your entire project ethically – from planning, through data collection in the field, through your eventual departure and what happens after you leave;
- to reflect upon your relationships and positionality.

Introduction

Your fieldwork is likely to affect other people: in particular, the individuals and communities you encounter in your research. Some of these people may give their time to answer your questions, allow you into their lives or help you out in other ways. Others may just see you around their neighbourhood or lurking around their social media sites and wonder, perhaps worry, about what you are up to. This raises ethical questions and challenges. In research and, more specifically, in fieldwork, ethics are concerned with the researcher's intentions and/or impacts. Ethical responsibilities begin before you enter the field and continue while you are there and after you leave.

What does this mean for you and the research you will be doing? Ethical considerations apply not only to all stages but also to all forms of fieldwork. Whether you are conducting face-to-face research such as interviews and ethnographic observations, working with secondary sources such as statistical records and community archives, and whether you are doing fieldwork in person or online (Agbebiyi, 2013), it is essential to anticipate and negotiate ethical risks and opportunities, and to be attentive to those that emerge in the course of your fieldwork.

Because it is often presented as a box-ticking exercise, a hurdle to be cleared before the interesting work can begin, ethics can seem a little dry on first inspection. The reality is quite different, or should be. Fieldwork presents ethical challenges, which are more than obstacles to avoid. If we approach these challenges constructively, we can find they drive our research forward and make for better research.

You will find that the starting point for thinking about ethics is the formal ethical processes that your institution will likely ask you to think about before you enter the field. While it is important to understand how to navigate these, there are bigger, more fundamental issues to consider that are about how and why we do research. Ethics should be much more – and much more productive – than compliance with **ethical review** procedures (Schrag, 2011). It is also important to design and conduct research that not only avoids harm but more positively stands to benefit others, and enhances your own understanding of your encounters in the field and the knowledge they produce.

Before going any further, it is important to clarify the terminology we shall use when framing ethics. Thinking of ethical responsibility, we distinguish between participants and others. First, there are the people who directly and knowingly participate in your fieldwork. These participants – the generic term we use here – include interviewees, informants who directly provide data and respondents who respond to your questions. Then there are people whom you encounter in other ways, who may not know they feature in your fieldwork. These 'non-consenting others' (Mannay, 2016) include people you may encounter in a public place, physical or virtual, as well as people whom you may hear about second hand – for example when an interviewee mentions them, or when they appear in a secondary source.

We begin this chapter by explaining the ethical minimum – ensuring that you avoid harm – before reaching towards a more ambitious ethical agenda. This leads, towards the end of the chapter, to a discussion of **positionality**. There, we explain what it means to become conscious of our positions in the field and the power dynamics that shape our encounters there.

First, Do No Harm

The most important ethical questions you must ask are concerned with risk. Could your fieldwork harm anyone? How? What steps can you take to prevent or mitigate this harm? These concerns are particularly acute where more vulnerable groups are involved, so researchers interested in groups with known risk factors such as street children, political dissidents and homeless people tend to devote more attention to ethical questions – and to be subjected to closer scrutiny by ethics committees – than others whose research involves less sensitive groups such as business leaders and people in public office. (Note, however, that while some groups are known to be more vulnerable than others, we cannot prejudge the vulnerability of an individual. Ethical reflection and review are concerned with estimating and mitigating risks, and this involves probability rather than certainty.)

Imagine, for example, that you are interested in observing and/or interviewing undocumented workers. Might this cause anxiety to these individuals, who may worry that you are working for the immigration authorities or police? Could it put them in danger, perhaps if their employers see them cooperating with you? Furthermore, you may not only risk the safety or well-being of individuals, but also their families and communities and possibly yourself. To avoid harming people, you may have to rethink your project completely, or it may be enough to modify your data collection methods or the ways in which you write up and circulate findings.

It is also important to consider your own safety, recognising and mitigating any risks that fieldwork poses to you as a researcher and other people you encounter in the field. If you are on a group field trip, it is possible that someone else may have completed this risk assessment on your behalf; your responsibility then will be to understand the risks and mitigation that has been put in place. This is likely to include familiarising yourself with emergency numbers and procedures, which may include working in groups rather than alone, and making provisions for your physical, mental and emotional safety.

Ethical Review

For most students, ethical review begins with their university or college's ethics procedure. Our advice is to assume you need to gain ethical clearance unless told otherwise. Institutional ethical codes vary between organisations, also between countries and over time, but they typically revolve around several checkpoints, designed to safeguard people (human participants) and places (including natural or historic environments). Ethical responsibilities apply not only to data collection but also to how you manage, store and use your data, all of which we return to in Chapter 13 on secondary data and Chapter 14 on data handling.

Ethical clearance, though sometimes viewed as a tick box exercise, is important. It is there to protect people – those you encounter in the field, as well as yourself and other students – so you must gain ethical approval before you can do any research. If you start your fieldwork without first gaining ethical clearance, you may have to discard the data you have collected, and you may face other penalties.

Some researchers are required or encouraged to go through more than one ethical review, and/or gain other forms of clearance before starting work. This is because ethical procedures and safeguards are formalised and enforced by institutions, funding bodies, publishers, disciplinary organisations and associations, national research governance bodies and governments. For example, the British Sociological Association (BSA) and American Sociological Association (ASA) have both published ethical codes that are easily found and accessed online, and the same is true of the organisations representing other disciplines and practitioners. For example, the Association of Internet Researchers (AoIR) provides ethical guidelines for internet research (see: https://aoir.org/ethics/).

Safeguards also exist, designed to protect particular, potentially vulnerable groups. For example, if you want to work with children in the UK, you have to obtain 'DBS clearance' (DBS stands for Disclosure and Barring Service) – based on legal checks – and similar provisions exist in other jurisdictions. It is increasingly common for countries and communities to want a say in the governance of research that involves them. Following similar moves in Aotearoa New Zealand, the San people of South Africa issued a code of ethics in 2017 (Callaway, 2017; South African San Institute, 2017; Schroeder et al., 2019). Aboriginal peoples around the world are moving in similar directions, issuing ethical codes that they ask researchers to understand and respect (Castellano, 2004).

While some countries have yet to regulate foreign researchers in their jurisdiction, others are introducing means of doing so, as are supra-national authorities and regulators such as the European Union's PRO-RES Framework (https://prores-project.eu/). (PRO-RES supersedes the EU's previous voluntary ethical Code of Practice for Socio-Economic Research, namely RESPECT, which is still worth consulting because it is more accessible to student audiences. The guidelines include sections on avoiding personal and social harm, complying with the law and upholding scientific standards.) Depending on where in the world you are planning fieldwork, and with whom, you may also have to seek permission from national or local research governance bodies, or you may voluntarily do so (Brydon, 2006). Illustrating this point, Rachel Ayrton, a research student based in the UK who wanted to conduct fieldwork in Uganda, had to gain ethical approval from two sets of research committees: one in the UK, the other in Uganda. She also felt responsible to other, more personal ethics, defined by her Christianity and her commitment to social justice (for a more sustained discussion of her ethical reflections, see Kara, 2018: 11–14).

Formal ethical reviews tend to focus upon anticipating and avoiding harm to human participants. Researchers are generally required to demonstrate that they have a plan for securing informed consent, that they will only go ahead with fieldwork when this consent is forthcoming, and with participants who are capable of understanding and consenting to their involvement (Tindana et al., 2006). Ethical clearance procedures typically use screening questions to identify projects for detailed scrutiny and possible rejection or modification. Some commonly asked screening questions are shown in Figure 5.1.

- Does the study involve participants who are particularly vulnerable or unable to give informed consent?
- Will the study require the cooperation of a gatekeeper for initial access to participants? Who might this be?
- Will it be necessary for participants to take part without their knowledge at the time?
- Does the study involve deliberately misleading participants?
- Will the study require discussion of sensitive topics that may cause distress or embarrassment to the participant?
- Is there a chance that criminal activity or child protection issues will be raised?
- Could the study induce psychological stress or anxiety or cause harm or negative consequences beyond the risks encountered in normal life?
- What will you do with data you collect? How will you communicate this to participants?

Figure 5.1 Ethics screening questions

The collection and analysis of secondary data raises another set of ethical concerns. In some cases, you simply have to follow rules about the material you can access and what you can do with it. Using **archives**, for example, you may be required to specify what you wish to do with the data you collect, and you may be prevented from quoting and reproducing what you find. Some organisations do this to protect themselves, fearful of what you might uncover; troubling examples of this are provided by churches and children's homes with histories of abuses and cover-ups. Others limit access to data in order to protect people in their care or power. You will not be able to access very localised ('small area') census data where there is a risk that individual households may be identifiable.

The minimal research ethic – do no harm – also points to other spheres including the physical environment and **artefacts**, both natural and cultural. Researchers who want to study the natural environment – perhaps by digging soil pits or removing samples of rock or water – have to address the ethics and possible consequences of their actions (Maskall and Stokes, 2009: 28–29). How might fieldwork affect a human setting, for example when a large group of students descends upon a small community, or when successive year groups repeatedly return to the same place? These actions can disrupt local life. They can also saturate the research environment as potential respondents become reluctant to participate or conditioned to respond in particular ways. You may not have much control over these things if, as a student, you are required to participate in a field class that has been planned for you. Still, you do have the power to reflect on the ethical implications of these choices, maybe to question your course leaders, and perhaps to make choices of your own within these constrained circumstances. Conscious of the climate crisis, students are challenging universities to come up with more sustainable fieldwork, which may mean working locally (rather than travelling long distances) or travelling differently, with a lower carbon footprint. Ethics extend to taking responsibilities for the environmental impacts of our work. This means asking difficult questions. What is the carbon footprint of a field trip you are planning? How do you know? To find out how some universities – spurred on by students – are making fieldwork more sustainable, read the following postcard by Russell Hitchings, a geographer based in London who leads field trips in Vienna (Postcard 5.1).

Postcard 5.1

On the sleeper train to Austria, by Russell Hitchings

You find me on a sleeper train where, accompanied by a colleague and a group of twenty third-year geography undergraduates, I'm just starting the second leg of a rail journey from London to Vienna. I can hear some students sniggering in the adjacent cabin as they figure out how to pull down the beds without hitting classmates they don't yet know well on the head. We've not gone by train before. Our module is all about everyday life in cities and how various techniques can help us to examine certain easily overlooked aspects of how people rub along together there. Because of our focus on

Continued

methods, more than specific places, we can go anywhere really. For the last few years, we've flown from London to have a look at what people were doing in Stockholm.

We thought we'd try the train because we felt that we should, as they say, 'practise what we preach' in our teaching. You'll have no doubt come across arguments about cutting carbon emissions in response to the climate emergency. Given that most of those in our home discipline have a lot of time for them, it's perhaps surprising that geographers so often set off on trips with their students that entail significant emissions. Part of the issue is that geographers collect their evidence from places all around the world and that can mean that we want to take our students to the most insightful spots. In that sense, I'll admit that we are particularly well placed in our module to question that practice. It's also connected to the idea that going to new places means that we learn in an intense and immersive way about cultures and contexts with which we were often unfamiliar before. That is something they'll say much more about elsewhere in this book, I'm sure. It's also occasionally about enticing students onto our degree courses with the promise of exciting trips. Whichever argument is the most dominant, all of these reasonable reasons put us in a potentially hypocritical position regarding student field trips in geography, which is something that some of my colleagues have been increasingly determined to address.

Anyway, that is why we are on the sleeper train to Vienna. The students seemed excited about this new feature at the start (or they knew that we were and deemed it wise to mirror that back). This was partly because many hadn't travelled in this way before. In that sense, we are feeling quite pleased with ourselves because we also seem to be delivering on the idea that geography degrees encourage you to learn from a range of new experiences. Perhaps this could be a double win for us – we get to do the right thing by the environment, and our students get to learn in a fun new way too. Still, none of them has said very much so far about our underlying reason for choosing the sleeper train this year. No one has yet mentioned how relieved they are to be travelling to see how Austrians share public space in a more sustainable way. Conversations have more often been about the breakfast options on the train tomorrow morning. And that, I think, asks some quite searching questions about the role of university studies. To what extent do our students see the essays they sometimes write about the urgency of tackling global warming as a merely intellectual exercise in evaluating evidence and making arguments? If it's more than that, when and how do the discussions that we have together embolden us all to push for lower impact living?

Getting Started

Whether or not you are required to gain formal ethical approval, the following guidance will help you ensure that your fieldwork respects basic ethical standards. These are starting points.

First, plan how to communicate clearly and appropriately with participants. This means using plain language and ensuring that you are working within the correct language(s). You may need to translate your information sheets and consent forms and if you are explaining your project verbally you may need to ensure that you or a fellow student are able to work within those languages. This will be important throughout, but especially when you explain your project and invite people to get involved. If you need a written statement, varying from a few sentences you can include in an email to a longer and more formal document, the template provided in Figure 5.2 may help you get started. Your college or university may have its own templates for information sheets and other documentation, which you may need to distribute to participants. Printed information sheets might seem formal or official for some audiences. It may be enough for you to explain your project verbally. If so, you will still need to tailor your statement to your audience, considering, for example, their age and literacy. We discuss in more detail the options open to you when you are conducting research online and cannot exchange physical documents in Chapter 10, Digital Fieldwork. Reflecting on fieldwork in settings where not everyone is literate, development studies scholar Regina Scheyvens and colleagues advise researchers to explain 'fully and honestly' what projects are about and provide opportunities for participants to ask questions (Scheyvens et al., 2003: 142). Ethics committees sometimes require evidence of these conversations, for example in the form of a taped conversation (Scheyvens, 2014: 144; see also Banks and Scheyvens, 2014), though this can be too formal, and recording requires permission of its own, which participants must have the right to refuse.

Keep this to one page if possible. Write clearly and simply, avoiding technical terms, jargon and acronyms.

Title of Study

1. Introduce yourself. What is your name and where are you studying or working?
2. Invite the person to take part in the study. Explain that there is no pressure to accept.
3. Purpose: explain why you are doing this research.
4. Why have I been chosen to take part? Explain who is involved in the project and why they have been chosen.
5. What will happen if I take part? In plain language, explain what you will ask of the participant and what will happen during the research. (Think: what would you want to know if you were to take part in a research study?)
6. Personal data. Unless you have been granted ethical approval to do so, explain that you will not collect personal data such as names and addresses, and that participants will remain anonymous in the data you collect and findings you share.
7. If you would like to take photographs or make sound recordings, explain why and ask the participant for permission. Explain what you plan to do with the images or recordings.
8. What are the risks of taking part? Explain any risks involved. Reassure the participant that they can withdraw their involvement and the data they have provided, should they have second thoughts or feel uncomfortable. (You will need to have decided how to manage this, and what promises you can make.)
9. Are there any benefits in taking part? Are you paying participants? Will they benefit in other ways? If not, make this clear too.
10. Will I be named, or anonymous? Explain how you will record and use data. Will it be confidential? How will it be attributed?
11. What will happen to the results of the study? How will the findings be shared with participants and will they be published?
12. Who can I contact if I have further questions? Give a name and institutional contact (your supervisor or Chair of the relevant ethics committee) for participants to contact if they have questions.

Figure 5.2 Participant information sheet

Though many researchers stress the importance of honesty with participants, there are some exceptions. There may be instances in which it is ethically defensible to conduct covert research in which researchers either do not explain or actively conceal the nature and purpose of their research. In Chapter 9, on visual methods, we meet the artist and freelance illustrator Lynne Chapman, who sketches people in public places without asking their permission (Heath and Chapman, 2020). She explains: 'if you do that, you're stuck drawing a portrait' which can constrain and impair the encounter. Chapman advises that it is possible to draw people without being voyeuristic or otherwise unethical. In a book about 'the art, politics and ethics of undercover fieldwork' sociologist David Calvey (2017) presents a broader argument for covert research, demonstrating that covert fieldwork requires extra care and justification, but that it can be insightful and ethical.

Second, make reasonable efforts to ensure that participants are happy to be involved. Formal ethics procedures typically require researchers to gain written proof of 'informed consent', stating that they understand the project and have agreed to participate. A printed consent form may be most helpful alongside a conversation. Asking participants to sign seemingly legalistic documents can be too formal though, and few people actually read them. A common response is 'OK, where do I sign so we can do this thing?' So you have to ask who a consent form is really for. Social scientist Elizabeth Chaplin, whose research involves taking pictures of people, explains that in her experience it is enough simply to ask people whether they are willing to be photographed, then to seek written permission before publishing the photograph (Chaplin, 2004: 45). Lucy Bray (2007), a Professor in Child Health Literacy whose research explores children's experiences of healthcare, explains that informed consent must be tailored to participants, and must often involve the spoken rather than written word. Gaining informed consent may also involve more than one person. Where children are concerned, parents and other adults such as teachers and nurses may need to be involved (Bray, 2007). Where organisations or communities are concerned – from industrial corporations to Indigenous peoples – it may be necessary to gain consent at different levels: including the individual, community, group and collective (Chilisa, 2019).

It is not always necessary or reasonable to gain consent. Principles of informed consent are most straightforward where you plan to work with individuals. It may not be appropriate to gain the consent of individuals for ethnographic projects involving groups or gatherings. Imagine, if you were researching a music festival, football match or street demonstration, trying to explain your project to everyone you might encounter at the event. At best, the conversation might come across as unnatural and awkward; at worst, it might interrupt the event and people's enjoyment (Davies et al., 2014). It might be appropriate to seek the consent of a gatekeeper or community leader, who may then explain the project and if necessary provide you with an introduction. If in the course of those events you decide you want to take some photographs or conduct interviews, you may seek permission from the individuals concerned.

Third, respect the anonymity and privacy of participants. This is the default position for social research. Exceptions to this rule apply, such as where participants ask to be named, or explicitly waive their right to anonymity (Scarth, 2016). In her research with business leaders across several industry sectors, Jennifer has encountered the occasional – often very passionate and opinionated – interviewee who is keen to have their quotes attributed to them. This is not typical and most research participants feel more comfortable sharing their thoughts with the assurance of anonymity. However, true anonymity is not always feasible, since it may sometimes be possible to guess the names of participants, particularly where the community you are researching is small and the background information is revealing. If you say you interviewed the chief of police in a particular city, for example, it may be necessary to warn participants that their anonymity may not be watertight (Gabb, 2010). You should then only proceed if they consent to participation once aware of this risk.

Fourth, respect participants' confidentiality. Ethical review boards like to seek assurances of confidentiality, for example in clarification of how private information will be handled and used (Scheyvens et al., 2003: 146). In practice, confidentiality involves judgement and commitment. You may need to make decisions about what to include in a report and what to withhold, sometimes leaving out information that an ethics committee might not have forbidden. Garth Myers, a Professor of Urban International Studies who conducts ethnographic research in East Africa, has reflected that writing was 'a delicate matter' of differentiating 'anybody's business' from 'nobody's business' (Myers, 2001: 198). He suggests that, where sensitive or personal information is involved, it is a good idea to involve the research participants in making decisions about what to include and how.

Finally, ensure that your ethical reflections do not end when you (hopefully) receive ethical approval, but continue throughout your time in the field and after that. In the 'real world', research ethics is or should be an ongoing and iterative process (Kara, 2018). Rather than speculating once-and-for-all about the harm you may do in the future, ethical research demands that you monitor and mitigate issues that emerge in the course of your work. You may have to think on your feet and make decisions as you go. We can learn from geographer Kim England's research on lesbian-owned businesses in Toronto. In the course of her fieldwork, England began to see that her findings risked harming participants and their communities, should these findings fall into the wrong hands, so she made the difficult decision not to publish (England, 1994; see also: Nast, 1994; Staeheli and Lawson, 1994).

But, while it is sometimes necessary to withhold or destroy your data (Johnsen et al., 2008), there may be other ways around this ethical challenge. It may be enough to anonymise findings and use pseudonyms (made-up names) and generic identities (for example, age, gender or occupation). Other solutions include creating composite pieces, drawing together findings from different participants through distilled and potentially fictionalised sketches, case studies and stories (Phillips and Kara, 2021: 126). Geographers Hester Parr and Olivia Stevenson provide a powerful example of this from their work on missing persons. Rather than compromising confidentiality by retelling stories of individuals, whom some readers might recognise, they distilled stories in fictionalised form, altering details of time, place and circumstance while communicating the essence of the stories they had gathered from across Scotland (Parr and Stevenson, 2014). Another example of how creative research methods can be used for ethical reasons is provided in

Postcard 5.2. Working with field sketching – a method we explain in more detail in Chapter 9 on visual methods – Will Haynes makes the ethical decision to leave his camera at home and use a sketchbook in fieldwork involving homeless migrants in Rome (Haynes, 2021).

Postcard 5.2

Drawing as an ethical research method, by Will Haynes

Drawing, or sketching, can be a practical fieldwork tool, but it is also interesting to think of it through a lens of research ethics. My PhD explores how homeless migrants are made (and make themselves) visible and invisible at Termini railway station in Rome. Visual sources are therefore an important

Figure 5.3 *Migrants hanging out above Via Marsala, Rome.* Field sketch by Will Haynes

part of my research. However, many of the people I am writing about are vulnerable: they are living on the street without residence permits or they are working informally or engaged in illegal activity, perhaps dealing drugs etc.

Putting a camera in the faces of homeless people I barely know, or undocumented migrants who don't want to be photographed (or identified by the authorities), is unethical and might endanger their safety. Drawing enabled me to hang out in and around the station, drawing little attention to myself, while observing and documenting how different people lived. I was not aiming to capture exact likeness, but more to conjure an atmosphere, and depict how certain spaces were being used and inhabited by certain people throughout the day and night.

During my fieldwork, I would sit down somewhere (a café or a bench, for example), pull out my notebook and pencil, and sketch while making observations. To avoid being obvious or outstaying my welcome, I would sometimes finish the drawing at home, like polishing off a diary entry. Of course, ethical questions remained. As a researcher, how am I choosing to frame this image? What kind of representation is the drawing giving? How long can I sit drawing the person opposite me, without them noticing or becoming irritated? It is worth noting that, while taking photographs of people's faces requires their consent, I think the same principles should apply to drawing. If you sketch someone's recognisable likeness (and intend on using their image in your work), you should still ask for consent. However, I tried to keep my drawings as abstract and anonymising as possible. I usually drew people as silhouettes, situated around

Figure 5.4 *Police officers in Termini station.* Field sketch by Will Haynes

Continued

Figure 5.5 *Migrants sitting in the sunshine on the Dogali monument.* Field sketch by Will Haynes

more well-defined places in the urban landscape. I never drew faces, wrote down names, or detailed anyone's identity.

It was not just ethical issues of working with marginalised people that I had to consider. I wanted to include the police in my visual data because of the way they enforce rules in the station and interact with the homeless migrants in interesting ways. But the police don't like being photographed (and the same ethical principles apply to them too) – so I drew them too.

Drawing was also a practical and ethical solution to basic access issues in the field, particularly for researcher safety. Public places like stations often aren't 'public' at all – private security might come and tell you off (or worse) if they catch you taking photographs. Drawings might also be used as an ethical way of supplementing other data collected in the field. A drawing has room for interpretation – it could be used as some sort of visual prompt in a future interview.

I think drawings can capture and suggest processes that are in flux, like movement or speech. For a railway station – a place where people, goods, vehicles, are rushing by – a drawing can keep this mobile and multisensory nature alive. I recommend drawing to other researchers who want to conduct ethically driven visual research methodologies. Admittedly I wasn't very good at drawing initially, but I improved the more I tried.

Proactively Ethical Fieldwork

Who is your fieldwork for? Who stands to gain from the work you do in the field? (Posel and Ross, 2014). 'What is at stake when a group, a place or a topic is researched?' (Jazeel and McFarlane, 2007: 782). These questions are points of departure for proactively ethical fieldwork, driven by the desire to do more than simply anticipate and avoid harm – an important but minimal ethical standard derived from biomedical research – and to think more ambitiously about who and what fieldwork can be for (Millora et al., 2020). You may want to design and conduct fieldwork that not only avoids harm but more positively stands to benefit participants and their communities.

To answer honestly the question of who your fieldwork is for, you may need to acknowledge that it is at least partly for you. You stand to gain academic and employment skills; to obtain grades and credits towards your degree; to satisfy your curiosity; and possibly generate intellectual property with commercial value. Reflecting on her own motives and interests in conducting fieldwork in Sudan and New York, geographer Cindi Katz admits that career interests have shaped the ways in which she has worked and published. She acknowledges that her 'field projects all have probably been more beneficial to [her] than to [the participants]' (Katz, 1994: 71–72). But, in acknowledging this, Katz pursues a different kind of fieldwork, shaped by a more ambitious ethical agenda. She challenges us all to ask who is likely to benefit from our fieldwork (Keane et al., 2017) and who else could benefit from it? This means reflecting on each aspect of fieldwork, not only your relationships with participants but also with others who support your work – for example, by cooking for you and driving you around (Powell, 2008).

A growing number of researchers are exploring ways to benefit participants and their communities. As an undergraduate conducting a small field project, you may feel sceptical about whether you can really give anything back. It is wise to be realistic rather than overly ambitious about this, and it is better not to make promises you may not be able to keep. Other researchers have shared these concerns. Stan Stevens, a geographer who has been privileged to spend many years conducting sustained fieldwork among Indigenous peoples in Nepal, suggests that 'short-term researchers may get away with carrying out grab-and-run research, taking what they can and clearing out with little regard for reciprocity and responsibility,' whereas those with longer-term fieldwork interests tend to be more responsible, if only initially out of necessity. This involves 'listening to and responding to what indigenous people think is important and working on behalf of their interests and concerns' (all quotations from Stevens, 2001: 72). It is not only ethically desirable to give something back to participants; promising to do so can also pay off by attracting people to get involved (Scott et al., 2006: 35).

How can you give back during your fieldwork? There are many different ways to do so; the simplest begin with compensating participants for their time and sharing research findings. Payments may be appropriate but they require care, and must be culturally and economically appropriate, in keeping with local norms of gift giving and hospitality, and measured to avoid insult, irrelevance, tokenism and other potential pitfalls (Hammett et al., 2019; Hammett and Sporton, 2012). It may be simpler and more appropriate to share findings, perhaps by sending copies of your field report or a digest of findings in appropriate language. Or you may give something more immediate and tangible. Conducting fieldwork with children in Sudan, Cindi Katz tried to balance her own self-interest in conducting research with the interests of participants and their families and communities by providing information they might find useful in their farming and planning (Katz, 1994; Brydon, 2006). Geographer Elizabeth Chacko, whose fieldwork involved interviews with villagers in India, noticed that few people (then) had access to cameras. She thanked participants with photographs, which many 'cherished' (Chacko, 2004: 60). Chacko also explored deeper forms of reciprocity in an attempt to make her interviews less one-sided. 'Women also asked me questions during the interview itself,' she explains, 'and in the spirit of reciprocity and equalising the power balance, I often let the respondent take on the role of interviewer' (Chacko, 2004: 60). Others suggest that fieldwork should ideally involve reciprocal learning processes: 'research partnerships' involving 'mutually beneficial opportunities for shared learning, exchange of ideas and the advancement of knowledge' (Scott et al., 2006: 31).

When we start to think about mutually beneficial fieldwork, we move beyond the unilateral language of 'giving back' and to think instead of co-production. The latter is more equal, each side saying what they want from research from the start, agreeing what the benefits should be, and working towards these. This approach corresponds to a form of action research, which we explain in more detail in Chapter 8, Participant Observation and Participatory Fieldwork, which includes words of caution against over-promising and conversely of promising only what you can actually deliver in what may be a short-term fieldwork project.

Ultimately, the ethical dilemmas you face and your scope for both avoiding harm and giving something back will reflect the methods you are using and your circumstances, including how long you are able to stay in the field and the resources at your disposal. For example, as we go on to discuss in Chapter 9, Visual Fieldwork, it can be harmful to point a camera or stare at someone, and also to post or publish images of them, though both forms of visual contact also present opportunities. Similarly, online research presents its own ethical challenges. For example, if you are using social media as a means of gathering data, discussed in Chapter 11 on social media, you may need to decide whether to follow or friend a participant, whether to comment, like or share the material they post, and whether to simply observe their online presence by 'lurking' (Bryman, 2016; Kara, 2018). We discuss these specific ethical challenges in Part III, where we reflect on the ethical issues associated with particular fieldwork methods. This is fitting because ethics cannot be raised and resolved within a single chapter; they permeate fieldwork as a whole and run right through this book about it.

Try this

You receive a phone call from an older person, whose voice you struggle to place. 'I liked you as soon as we met,' she tells you. Then you remember: you interviewed her last year as part of fieldwork. You've moved on from the project, and though you enjoyed meeting her too, you're not sure what should happen next. What do you do?

Relationships, Positionalities and Exit Strategies

It is never too early to start thinking about how and when you may leave the field. In other words, it is important to have an exit strategy. This is recognised by researchers across the social sciences: including in management and marketing studies (Franco and Yang, 2021; Michailova et al., 2014), medical sociology (Watts, 2008; Morrison et al., 2012) and human geography (Hall, 2009).

With a good exit strategy, you will be able to anticipate and mitigate potential harm or hurt, considering all the relationships you initiate in the course of your research. Some participants may interpret your approaches and interest in them as a genuine friendship (Walton and Hassreiter, 2015), and in some cases something deeper, more lasting than a professional information-gathering exercise. Some of the participants and other people you meet in the field may expect something back, even if you have not explicitly promised it, and even if they do not say what they are hoping for. So it is important for you to reflect on these relationships, what you want from them, and what you would like to give. Will they be temporary or longer lasting? Will they be reciprocal? Will you be explicit about what you are – and are not – looking for and prepared to put into these relationships? Will you explain your eventual departure in advance and will you tell participants whether or not you plan to stay in touch? It is important to consider these things before you share phone numbers and connect with others through social media. We know of students who, having handed out contact details, were contacted with requests for money and assistance. They might have avoided this if they had been clearer about the nature and scope of their interest in the other person or if they had used a university rather than a personal phone number or email. Of course, it is always possible to block a caller or unfriend a contact, but it is far better to avoid the circumstances in which doing so might seem necessary.

Reflecting on her fieldwork in Central America, geographer Julie Cupples (2002) provides an example of the complexity of relationships that can emerge in the course of fieldwork and the ethical dilemmas that can follow. Cupples sensed a 'heightened state of awareness and stimulation' including 'intellectual stimulation but also sexual desire' (Cupples, 2002: 385). 'At times, men feigned interest in my research project in an attempt to spend time with me.' For her part, Cupples did 'sometimes take advantage of such interest' – as she put it – to 'further my research and make connections with places and people'. This example illustrates the complexity and ambiguity of relationships that can arise in the field, and reminds us that the researcher is not necessarily in a position to dictate the terms of such relationships. Whether we like it or not, 'we are also positioned by those whom we research' (Cupples, 2002: 383). So, though a simple rule of thumb might be to clarify relationships, to avoid 'flirting in the field' (Kaspar and Landolt, 2016) and to abstain from sexual encounters that might complicate working relationships and might also be risky and potentially exploitative (Coffey, 2018), the reality may not be so straightforward. Sociologist Amanda Coffey argues that we have much to learn, through sexualised encounters in the field, about social and power dynamics there, the relational nature of the research process and the possible emotions of fieldwork: ranging from love and hate to excitement and alienation (Coffey, 2018).

Departure doesn't necessarily happen at a single point of time. It can be gradual and is a process that should be considered right from the initial stages of planning our research. Departure can also be more complex where researchers have developed closer relationships with participants. Departure can be emotionally complex for you as a researcher, 'much more than saying goodbye' (Michailova et al., 2014: 143). Some researchers carry the field with them in the form of personal histories, memories and concerns (Coffey, 1999). Looking back on her time with Somali immigrant women in Finland, sociologist Marja Tiilikainen reflected that when she was in the field she was not entirely there, and when she was back home she found it difficult to leave the field completely behind (Tiilikainen, 2002). Other researchers make a more decisive break with the field and the people they encounter there when their fieldwork ends. All this can be confusing. A well-managed exit can include elements of self-care, enabling the researcher to leave their work behind and redefine (or sever) relationships and ties with research participants (Cohen, 2015; Hirvi and Snellman, 2012).

Your departure is not all about you or your own feelings. The way in which you leave the field also impacts upon your research participants. It is important to acknowledge and mitigate the risk that participants may feel abandoned or used when the researcher leaves the field and their lives (Franco and Yang, 2021). Where relationships are ambiguous, some participants may feel they have been dropped, having been led to expect continued contact (Hall, 2009). Participants may also have unspoken expectations surrounding the uses of the data they provided, including through dissemination and publication (Knott, 2019). Students are not always able to publish or otherwise share results, while professional researchers are not always able to do so as soon as participants might expect. For all these reasons, ethical complications can develop after the researcher leaves, though these can be anticipated and mitigated with careful planning.

Postcard 5.3

Is leaving ever possible? Some thoughts on fieldwork endings, by Sarah Marie Hall

My first experience of 'leaving' the field related to my PhD research. I spent two years from 2007–2009 with six families across the North West of England, exploring everyday consumption practices and family relationships. Ethnographic research is known to rely on rapport, trust and connection, and my project was no exception. I had developed especially deep social bonds with two of the families, partly as a result of us sharing working-class experiences and backgrounds.

After around six months, it became clearer to me that I needed a disengagement strategy, a way to round off the research to enable me to start analysing data and writing up. While I felt close to and deeply connected to the families, I knew that I needed some 'distance' (by which I mean mental and emotional, rather than simply physical) to be able to make sense of what I had observed and needed time to write. I was concerned, however, about how to go about this 'leaving' when I wasn't really going anywhere, for I would be staying living in the area and would still be working on the project.

I also knew that just because the fieldwork phase was going to end, it did not mean that my care about participants would, could or should be terminated so easily.

After some consideration, my approach consisted of a mixture of gentle signposting and reminders about my plans, and more overt measures such as what are termed 'ending rituals' such as holding a 'thank you' lunch and giving a small gift and card. I also spoke to participants multiple times about whether they wanted to keep in touch, making sure they knew how to contact me but being clear that the ball was in their court, as it were. I was mindful of the ethics of leaving, and that not everyone might want to keep in touch with me. This was something I felt comfortable with then, and still to this day. It places the ultimate decision with participants and gives them agency in how and if they communicated with me outside traditional research project parameters.

I have since used similar techniques for 'leaving' ethnographic and engaged research 'on my doorstep' on multiple occasions over the years since that first ethnographic study; when, as is the case for many researchers, the empirical element of my project came to a close, but I have stayed living and working nearby. In recent times I have also experienced returning to the field; having moved away from a place where I had carried out research (due to a house relocation), and then coming back again years later. This has led me to question, as per the title of this postcard, whether leaving is ever possible. Not only might we stay in places to carry out fieldwork for short or extended periods, but we might also return to them after having left. While I am no longer in regular contact with participants from my initial ethnography, they have never really 'left' me. Over the intervening period I have thought about them often. Furthermore, as I have returned to live in the area, I frequently take bus journeys past their former homes, walk by bus stops we had been waiting at together, or enjoy a cup of tea at the same cafés. Fieldwork relations can be long lasting and can include our relationships to people and place as researchers, as well as them with us.

The aspiration to leave fieldwork may be well-intentioned, and can be for personal, professional and practical reasons alike. However, I consider questions of ending, staying and leaving the field and fieldwork to be absolutely crucial in any research project planning, including my own experience and the ethics of leaving for participants and myself alike.

Given the need to anticipate and plan for your departure, from the moment you begin to develop and do your fieldwork, we have some tips.

1. Include an exit plan as part of your research design (Morrison et al., 2012). Think about when the fieldwork may end (do you have a set end-date?), how you will manage the process of returning to the field and reconnecting with participants if this is necessary.
2. Provide participants with an idea of how long you expect them to be involved in the research, explaining that this is just an estimate (Franco and Yang, 2021).
3. Consider how you will signal to participants that your research relationship is coming to an end. This could be a thank you letter or email and/or gift (if appropriate).
4. Remember not to make any assumptions about how research participants may perceive your relationship. 'Researchers are often unaware of how the members regard them until they are either about to leave or are actually out the door' (Altheide, 1980: 303).

5   Think about how you will conclude the research process and then include your research participants in the dissemination of research findings. Providing feedback is the 'give' ingredient after a long 'take' period of generating field data (Michailova et al., 2014). Feedback to participants may not be the same as other types of dissemination – your participants are unlikely to want to read your essay or dissertation. But a short summary, noting the valuable contribution of the participants and the key findings is more accessible.

Understanding your fieldwork as a series of encounters between yourself and other people in the field, you can begin to think more explicitly and critically about your own presence there: how you behave and are perceived, and how this affects the kinds of encounters you have and what you find out. As geographer Linda McDowell put it, 'we must recognize and take account of our position, as well as that of our research participants, and write this into our research practice' (McDowell, 1992: 409). In fieldwork, our circumstances shape what we can find out and know. Acknowledging our 'positionality', it is possible to be explicit about the limits of what we know – since 'all knowledge is produced in specific circumstances and that those circumstances shape it in some way' (Rose, 1997: 305). In other words, we all make our own knowledge, produce our own findings, which can never be objective or neutral, but can nevertheless be rigorous. This is partly a matter of intellectual rigour – understanding the limits of our knowledge, while maintaining high standards of scholarship and consciously avoiding bias (Croskerry et al., 2013) – and also of ethics, since it allows us to interrogate the unequal power relations through which knowledge is generally produced. We develop this discussion in the next chapter, Decolonising Fieldwork, where we acknowledge that students and academic researchers, particularly those affiliated to universities in Western countries, tend to approach the field from positions of relative power. This presents a fundamentally ethical challenge: to understand our privilege and bring this understanding to the field.

Conclusion

Fieldwork always presents ethical challenges. This is why we have suggested a series of ethical problems, then guided you as you begin to address them, but we have not provided answers. There are rarely any 'right' answers' to ethical challenges. In most cases, ethical issues are matters of judgement, which you will need to resolve for yourself by identifying the issues at stake and making informed decisions through discussion with other students and field leaders. In some cases, particularly those involving at-risk groups, these decisions may be taken out of your hands as you are forced to rethink your research by university ethics committees, but these cases are the exceptions.

So, the onus is (partly) on you. Though we can guide you through systems of ethical scrutiny and explain the ethical standards that researchers are now required to follow, we must ultimately turn the important ethical questions back to you, and to your own ethical judgements and values. Linda McDowell concludes simply that 'you must hold on to your own standards of ethical behaviour and decency and to treat others as you would prefer to be treated yourself if the relationship between the researcher and the reverse were to be reversed' (McDowell, 1997: 393). There is no simple rule book for this; ethical fieldwork means 'learning to think and act ethically' (Kara, 2018: 38).

Advancing an ethical project should be a reward in itself, and it is certainly a responsibility. But an understanding of ethical issues can also deepen our understanding of broader issues concerned with the knowledge we produce, its form and content, purpose and consequence.

Key terms

Ethical review is the process that researchers are required to successfully complete before they are permitted to start fieldwork. Ethical review is administered by institutions – such as the college or university in which the researcher is studying or working – and also by funding bodies and regulators by organisations governing research within a disciplinary or national framework.

Ethics is a branch of philosophy, also known as moral philosophy, concerned with questions of right and wrong (Singer, 2016). Moral philosophers distinguish a series of ethical dimensions: the intrinsic virtues of individuals or acts, the values that lead them to behave that way and the consequences of their actions. The latter – the ways in which research affects people – are particularly important considerations for those undertaking fieldwork for social research.

Positionality refers to the circumstances in which knowledge is produced and shaped, and where we stand in relation to the people or topic we are investigating. By acknowledging our positionality, it is possible to be explicit about the origins, content and limits of what we know. Understanding our positionality, it is also possible to become more aware of our responsibilities to other people.

Further Reading

Franco, Paolo & Yang, Ye (2021) Exiting fieldwork 'with Grace': Reflections on the unintended consequences of participant observation and researcher–participant relationships. *Qualitative Market Research: An International Journal*, 24(2): 358–374.
An accessible reflection on exiting the field based on doing marketing research. It emphasises the methodological importance of how researchers exit fieldwork to draw attention to implications for participant and researcher well-being.

Hall, S. M. (2009) Private life and work life: Difficulties and dilemmas when making and maintaining friendships with ethnographic participants. *Area*, 41(3): 263–272.
Insightful and personal reflections by human geographer Sarah Marie Hall on her experiences researching her PhD using ethnography with families.

Kara, Helen (2018) *Research Ethics in the Real World: Euro-Western and Indigenous Perspectives*. Policy Press.
This book explains the what and the how of research ethics. Helen Kara writes directly to students and researchers, communicating an understanding of research ethics that is at once practical and intellectually challenging. Distinguishing between Euro-Western and Indigenous research ethics, Kara encourages researchers to be curious about and respectful towards other peoples' ethics.

6
DECOLONISING FIELDWORK

In this chapter you will learn

- why it is important to decolonise fieldwork;
- how you can play a part in decolonising fieldwork;
- to identify and break with fieldwork's colonial, Eurocentric roots and traditions;
- to learn from an increasingly diverse body of fieldwork and practitioners, reaching beyond the canon of work by Western, white men to include people in different parts of the world, particularly those with different racial and cultural backgrounds.

Introduction

Fieldwork is embroiled with **colonialism**, past and present. Everyone who teaches or practices fieldwork has a part to play in decolonising fieldwork. The first step is to be clear about the brutal realities of colonialism – which extended to genocide in its darkest hours – and the parts that field researchers have played as agents of colonialism and servants of empires. Research was, and is, a useful lever in the colonisers' toolbox, helping to justify land grabs, family separations and all sorts of enormously abusive deeds. The abuse of research by colonisers is not consigned to history; it continues today. Other researchers, who may be well intentioned, can also reproduce colonial approaches through their words and methods (Crane, 2017). The Australian census is extractive and abusive to Aboriginal and Torres Strait Islander peoples (Walter and Andersen, 2016). In the US, the human remains of millions of native Americans are held by universities and health authorities as 'data', despite the tribes concerned wanting their relatives back so they can dispose of their remains in appropriate ceremonial ways, and laws having been passed to enable this back in the 1990s – but it's still not happening (Dunbar-Ortiz, 2014).

However, not all those who have conducted fieldwork or field research have been equally complicit with this historical wrong. Inspiring examples of those who have tried to ensure that their fieldwork has been anti-colonial reach as far back as the turn of the eighteenth century, when Alexander von Humboldt, the European explorer, made himself *persona non grata* throughout the Spanish Empire for his outspoken criticisms of racists and empire builders (Wulf, 2015). Humboldt, a white man who started out with privileges of personal wealth, professional training, sustained education and personal connections, showed that it is not only possible to (at least try to) extricate fieldwork from colonialism, but also to use fieldwork against colonialism. Doing so, we can not only make fieldwork more ethical and equitable, and help to make the world a better place; we also stand to learn, opening our minds and eyes to the possibilities and diversity of the world. So, while fieldwork has been embroiled in colonialism as part of the Euro-Western research paradigm, it is not necessarily or essentially colonial. It is our responsibility and opportunity to ensure that it is not.

Before going any further, we need to pick up a point we explain more fully in Chapter 5 on fieldwork ethics, namely the need to acknowledge our positionality. We have introduced ourselves as academics, teaching and conducting research at universities in the UK, in departments of Geography (Richard) and Management Studies (Jennifer). This means that many people will see us as middle-class professionals, whether or not we see ourselves and our backgrounds that way. These are just some aspects of our positionality. Others, relevant to this chapter, include race and nationality. Both of us are white and hold British passports. We make these points, not because we expect you to be interested in us as individuals, but because our positionality shapes our work as fieldwork leaders and teachers. For the purposes of this chapter, it is relevant that we have not personally suffered colonial dispossession and that, on the contrary, we have benefitted from various forms of white privilege. Colonialism is our problem too, and as educators and field trip leaders we seek to use some of our privilege against colonialism and in the interests of decolonising fieldwork. We encourage you, as you conduct your own fieldwork, to reflect upon your own positionality, particularly with respect to colonialism, past and present.

Students Calling for Change

Students can sometimes feel that they are at the bottom of a hierarchy in which other people – instructors and leading authors in their subjects – decide and control what can be studied and how. But you can challenge these decisions and practices. One way in which students have done so – starting a revolution that has begun to unsettle academic hierarchies and assumptions across the world – is by demanding that their curriculum be decolonised. Students in South Africa have been particularly vocal. Their protests have erupted several times, most notably in 2015 and 2016 when activists brought the University of Cape Town to a standstill. What had begun as a protest against student fees morphed into something broader: from #FeesMustFall to #RhodesMustFall. Their targets included a statue of the former colonial governor of the Western Cape (where Cape Town is located), Cecil Rhodes, though the students also built a bonfire of books and paintings that they identified as relics of colonialism (Murris, 2016). This movement spread across South Africa and around the world (Moncrieffe et al., 2020; Prinsloo, 2016), where memorials to Rhodes came to represent something more general and pervasive, in the form of a campaign to decolonise the curriculum and the academy (Joseph Mbembe, 2016). Toppling Rhodes and decolonising the curriculum are connected – both contesting the elevated place of white, Western men, whether as statues and figureheads, or as academic authorities. These calls for change in South Africa built upon a wider movement with origins in other parts of the Global South (or 'majority world') and among other colonised peoples. Intellectually, this movement took inspiration from Paulo Freire's foundational work, *Pedagogy of the Oppressed* (first published in 1970), which questioned the values underpinning education and research, and advocated emancipatory learning (Freire, 2020) in which participants have more control over the research process (Warwick-Booth et al., 2021: 8).

Like the protests at the University of Cape Town, the wider movement to decolonise the curriculum is controversial and radical, with far-reaching implications for schools, colleges and universities (Meda, 2020). Interviewed about their motivations, some student protesters spoke of clear and ambitious goals – to challenge the dominance of Western knowledge, which originated in and served colonialism and apartheid, and to accord greater respect and status to ways of knowing that have been devalued and marginalised (Le Grange, 2020). This means accommodating and respecting the voices and knowledge of Indigenous and colonised peoples. At stake, in this struggle over reading lists and research methods, is nothing less than intellectual or 'epistemic' freedom (Ndlovu-Gatsheni, 2018). Rather than just learning about other people's cultures and ways of knowing the world, African students are demanding an education that (also) teaches African scholars, Indigenous Knowledge (Joseph Mbembe, 2016) and African languages (wa Thiong'o, 1992), and works with African sources and textbooks (Mawere and Mubaya, 2016; Mawere, 2015). This means identifying and dismantling legacies of colonialism within the curriculum (Le Grange, 2020) and according greater respect to Indigenous ways of knowing and seeing the world (e.g. Chilisa, 2019; McGregor et al., 2018; Smith, 2021; Windchief and San Pedro, 2019).

South African demands for the **decolonisation** of education – of the curriculum and the ways in which universities are organised – have counterparts in other continents including Latin America (DeCarvalho and Flórez-Flórez, 2014) and among Indigenous peoples across the world (Smith, 2021). They also resonate among students in the Global North, particularly among those with minority ethnic backgrounds and those with heritage in former colonies, who can struggle to recognise themselves and their experiences in the curriculum. Many others, without such personal experiences of colonialism and marginalisation, support this movement to decolonise the curriculum, whether out of a shared rejection of the injustices of colonialism or simply out of a desire to receive as broad and inclusive an education as possible, learning from many different ways of seeing and knowing, both 'Euro-Western' and Indigenous, and everything in between (Kara, 2018: 21).

Why does (some) fieldwork need decolonising?

Dina Abbott, a geography professor at the University of Derby in England, had deep misgivings about a field trip she had been asked to lead in the small West African state of Gambia.

> How can I, as a non-white person, reinforce a geographical tradition of fieldwork that exposes myself and students (mostly white) to the 'history of slavery' re-enacted within a framework of skewed power relations? (Abbott, 2006: 331).

Reflecting on this particular field class, in which students from a British university, most of whom were white, would visit African former slave trading stations (or 'forts'), and that their visit echoed tropes of 'dark tourism' (see also McMorran, 2015), Abbott raised broader questions about the colonial dimensions of fieldwork.

The problems with fieldwork resonate with those of cross-cultural social research more generally (Liamputtong, 2010). Speaking as a Maori scholar, with personal and professional experience of research involving Indigenous communities, education scholar Linda Tuhiwai Smith (2021: 1) explains the problem:

> From the vantage point of the colonised, a position from which I write, and choose to privilege, the term 'research' is inextricably linked to European imperialism and colonialism. The world itself, 'research', is probably one of the dirtiest words in the Indigenous world's vocabulary.

In *Decolonizing Methodologies* (2021), Smith encourages Indigenous peoples to conduct their own research, rather than deferring to the expertise of visiting researchers. That said, she also speaks to students and scholars from other backgrounds, encouraging them to try to study the colonial issues and sensitivities surrounding their fieldwork before deciding whether and how to conduct research among Indigenous people and in colonial settings.

By bringing the colonial past and present into focus and asking challenging questions about the colonial overtones of contemporary fieldwork, we can begin to think critically about – and then change – the power relations inherent in these practices. The following points identify ways in which fieldwork was and is colonial, anticipating ways in which it may be decolonised. It is important to understand these charges while differentiating between and critically evaluating them. It will be important to be measured, distinguishing between more and less colonial fieldwork, and between colonial and anti-colonial fieldwork, past and present. First, though, it is important to understand why the wider fieldwork tradition has been closely associated with colonialism. Here are some of the issues.

1. A picture of fieldwork that many people carry around is one in which white students travel from their homes in the Global North to sites in the Global South, where most people are black or brown (Hughes, 2016). This picture, all too often unexamined and

unchallenged, jars for those who cannot see themselves within it. Dina Abbott (2006: 331), speaking 'as a non-white person' about the whiteness of fieldwork traditions, makes the case for change. This presents a challenge: to recognise the 'normative whiteness' of fieldwork (Hughes, 2016: 1), also to seriously reflect on whether it is appropriate for white researchers from the Global North to conduct fieldwork in black majority parts of the Global South, and then (if such fieldwork can be justified) to consciously navigate these racial dimensions.

2. The field, visited by white, Western students and researchers, is widely regarded as an exotic locale: distant and exciting to visit and see. Fieldworkers tend to seek out 'the exotic, spectacular and remote' (Rose, 1993: 70, quoting Stoddart, 1986: 55). There is not necessarily anything wrong with getting excited about fieldwork but it is important to think critically about why some places may be regarded as more exciting than others. Reaching beyond the narrowly etymological definition of the exotic – as 'outside' and at some remove from the familiar and domesticated – the exotic imaginary 'oscillates between the hackneyed foreignness of a far-flung cliché, understood in Eurocentric terms, and radical otherness' (Kapor, 2019: 87). Field sites and the people who live there, constructed as variously natural, colourful, exciting, interesting, primitive, picturesque and as bearing little relation to the visitors' homes and the society from which they come, echo forms of colonial exoticism. Similarly, when teachers and researchers try to explain what fieldwork is and why they continue to do it, many speak of exploration and discovery. These terms are closely associated with colonialism. The most famous explorers have been white, Western men, heroic figures adventuring in places they called *terra incognita* (unknown land, a term that appeared on maps) or *terra nullius* (nobody's land, a legal term used to justify land appropriation or theft) and others called home. This raises questions about what terms such as 'exploration' and 'discovery' should mean outside the colonial tradition.

3. Fieldwork – particularly where it involves travel from Western to non-Western settings, and from Global North to South – has been criticised for elevating the knowledge and findings of the researcher above the knowledge and experiences of local people (Keikelame and Swartz, 2019). This 'encounter between the West and the Other' has produced a one-sided picture of the world, which is not only unbalanced but also impoverished (Smith, 2021: 8). This assumption of superiority, manifest in deference to Western authorities and publications, compounded by a tendency to ignore and remain ignorant of local sources and knowledge, is a form of Eurocentrism or, more precisely, an unfounded assumption of Euro-American or global northern superiority.

4. Two other colonial echoes, perpetuated in international fieldwork, are the tendency to approach the field as a kind of mine, the spoils of which implicitly benefit the researcher or their society, and a real-world laboratory, a vehicle for education and research by privileged outsiders (Le Grange, 2020; Tilley, 2011: 2). Indeed, fieldwork is widely regarded as a data-gathering exercise – the part of research that involves the collection and extraction

of data – distinct from the analysis and interpretation that may take place closer to home. Where this work takes place in African and other Global South settings, it echoes one-sided colonial encounters in which researchers extract items of value to them and their employers and governments, including lucrative forms of data. Anthropologists Artwell Nhemachena, with University of Namibia in Windhoek colleagues Nelson Mlambo and Maria Kaundjua, compare this fieldwork tradition to resource extraction, which comes at the expense of deeper engagement with people and place. They argue that Africa's creativity, culture and civility are overlooked, just as colonial traditions and excuses are perpetuated (Nhemachena et al., 2016; see also Ndlovu-Gatsheni, 2011: 7). Some white, Western researchers acknowledge that their fieldwork may benefit them more than their participants, prompting practical questions about how to respond and reform fieldwork (e.g., LaRocco et al., 2020). In Chapter 14, on handling data, we explore some of the ways that doing more analysis and dissemination while in the field can help move from 'taking' data to 'giving back' in various ways.

5   Specific fieldwork methods – such as ethnography (which we explain in Chapter 8, Participant Observation and Participatory Fieldwork) – are also embroiled within colonial traditions and relations (Asad, 1973; Wells et al., 2019). We can trace ethnography to a fundamentally colonial tradition, conceived by Europeans as the study of 'uncivilised others' (Uddin, 2011, p. 455). Ethnographers have interrogated this colonial inheritance theoretically – with powerful postcolonial and decolonial critiques (Chabram, 1990; Gonzales, 2016). Doing so, they have recovered a field tradition with greater 'openness to less hierarchical and hegemonic forms of knowledge, particularly when consciously seeking to invert the traditional colonial ethnographic project and envision instead more participatory and collaborative models of engagement' (Wells et al., 2019). The challenge for those practising ethnographic field research is to follow through on this critical reformulation of ethnography.

6   Fieldwork is typically subjected to the ethical codes and scrutiny of the institution, professional body, scholarly society and/or funding body of the researcher's country of origin. Though scrutiny may be rigorous and though the researcher may take ethics seriously, this remains an asymmetrical arrangement. Where – as is so often the case – the researchers originate in a Western country in the Global North, this leads to an ethical approach which, however well intended, is Euro-Western and possibly colonial (Kara, 2018).

We go on in the second half of this chapter to show how it is possible to work through each of these concerns about the colonial underpinnings of fieldwork. Before doing that we take a step back, to hear from a researcher whose fieldwork brings colonialism to the fore. We turn to a postcard by Sarah de Leeuw, a professor in the University of British Columbia's Faculty of Medicine, who reflects upon and tries to shift the colonial power relations and histories that underpin her fieldwork. Here, she explores the possibilities of creative writing in her research (and in her life). She writes a letter to her younger self, suggesting how she might learn from what initially seemed a disappointing day in the field.

Postcard 6.1

What this day taught you, by Sarah de Leeuw

Dear Me of My Past,

You'll be thinking you know something.
You'll be feeling pretty sure-footed.
Like, as you father would say, you've 'got the world by its short and curlies'.

It'll be an October morning, that time of year when daylight is waning in north-central so-called British Columbia ('so-called' because by this time in your PhD you'll be woke enough, savvy enough, to always add 'so-called' to British Columbia, a sign of your enlightened decolonising gaze).

Birch and cottonwood leaves are golden, drifting down to rest on frost-whitened ground. Blue sky. Crisp wind. You'll have a feeling of elation. You've just secured a research grant for your PhD research. You come from a family with no PhDs, so this means something to you, a stamp of approval, a statement that your ideas have worth to those you want to impress – namely big-name professors and those with a high impact-factor.

You've got the enlightened lingo down. It's shone through in your applications. You're expressly not an Indigenous researcher. You don't do 'Indigenous research' – instead, you show up committed to allyship, vulnerable and authentic in your claiming of White-Euro-Colonial positionality. You know the words. You're anti-colonial. Sometimes you deliver guest-lectures about it.

This week, this bright cool autumnal week, you sing out loud in your car as you drive the three hours to the small northern First Nations community you've been invited into – it's important that you were invited. You remind yourself of this. The community neighbours one of the largest Residential Schools in north-central BC, Canada. You avoid affixing 'Indian' to Residential Schools because you know what a problematic word it is. You've even presented a conference paper tackling the racist lexicon of the term. You're here, in 'the field', in a community, to talk to people about residential schooling, about education as colonial violence. You're here to do good. You're holding tight to your achievements, your goodness. The Annual General Assembly of the First Nations community you've been invited to engage (that's the word you used in your grant proposals … engage …) is slated to begin at 1.30. You arrive early. You want to show you care.

The hall is empty.

You push your disappointment down, wishing you weren't, actually, craving to be eagerly met by all the people you're here to engage. You wander around the community hall, writing imaginary academic papers in your head about anti-colonial Indigenous resistance to settler white space. In your head, the paper is lauded for its ground-breaking, yet humble and creative, contribution to human geography. You admonish yourself for your ego. But you continue to sketch introductory paragraphs in your head. It's now 2.00pm. No one has shown up to the community hall. You wander over to the band office, which doubles as a nursing station, feeling a sharp sense of uncertainty. The door is locked. You notice a handwritten note pinned to the peeling and greying cork board beside the entry way: 'Closed for Funeral.'

Why didn't anyone tell you? You've driven three hours to get here! You have a three-hour drive back! You had a talk prepared! You wanted to meet people! Your grant included this community engagement event. Today was a deliverable.

Continued

You feel confused.
Let down.
Utterly deflated and disappointed.

It will not be until many years later that you realise what this day, this cold golden October day in the field, taught you. Gifted you. Because of this day, you will carry with you an understanding of the world, and your tiny part in it, for the rest of your career. The rest of your life.

With kindness to yourself and all your mistakes,
from You of Your Future.

Having heard from Sarah de Leeuw about her reflections on conducting fieldwork in northern British Columbia – a part of the world where colonialism can often feel recent and raw, and where researchers cannot ignore it, we move on to identify some practical steps that students can take to decolonise fieldwork. Here, we revisit the themes introduced above, each distinguishing a dimension of colonial fieldwork.

Decolonising: Practical Steps

Students can play leading parts in decolonising the curriculum. You don't have to wait for course leaders or institutions to lead on this subject. This is a challenge for everyone, not something white students can leave to classmates who are black or brown, or those who live in the Global South. The following paragraphs, summarised in Table 6.1, suggest some of the things you can do to help decolonise fieldwork, exploring possible responses to each of the issues introduced above.

First, if you are white, start by recognising your privilege (LaRocco et al., 2020). You may not feel very privileged, particularly if you are working your way through university and building up debts to study, so this can be challenging at first. Still, it is important to understand that on some level many undergraduates conduct fieldwork in the context of unequal power relations – an uneven field – in which they encounter others from positions of relative power. To reach this understanding, it may help to take a race awareness workshop, whether or not this is compulsory in your course of study.

Notice whose work you are reading and paying attention to. Try to make sure that the books and articles you read and cite are by authors with a range of racial backgrounds. Reach beyond the canon of work by Western, white men to include people in different parts of the world and from other genders, particularly those with different racial and cultural backgrounds. If your own university's library holdings or reading lists do not contain such material – or do not contain enough – then request suitable additions. This form of decolonisation involves reading widely and respecting different forms of knowledge; it also involves something more complicated and fundamental: 'removing the barriers that have silenced non-Western voices'

DECOLONISING FIELDWORK | 83

Table 6.1 Decolonising fieldwork: what you can do, and what you can ask staff to do

Colonial fieldwork	Problem	What students can do	What students can expect course leaders to do
Whiteness	White privilege of (some) students conducting fieldwork. White privilege of (some) course leaders Fieldwork in the footsteps of white colonial explorers Reading lists dominated by white authors	Recognise white privilege Reading widely: not just white Western authors	Diversify reading lists Contest barriers to exclusion of non-white authors
Exoticism	Fieldwork conceived as research in a non-local or unfamiliar setting, as a form of exploration and/or discovery Field sites regarded through a tourist/colonial gaze	Disrupt tourist/colonial gaze Question your choice of destination and your desire to go there	Develop local fieldwork alternatives Teach students about the colonial origins and implications of terms such as 'exploration', 'discovery' and 'exoticism', encouraging critical engagement with such terms
Eurocentrism	Western science or scholarship assumed superior to worldviews and cultural values of local people Fieldwork conducted in language of visiting students Behaviour conforms to norms of origin countries, e.g., clothing and alcohol	Invest in learning (about) local languages and cultures Respect local cultural values Actively consider how you dress and behave	Engage with local ethical values, e.g., Indigenous Ethics Explain local cultural norms, e.g., clothing, drinking, sex
Extractive fieldwork	Fieldwork conceived as data collection phase of research Field site conceived instrumentally as a data mine and/or laboratory Exploitation of field sites and people who live there	Try to make sure that fieldwork benefits others – not just you Consider ways to involve local people as participants and researchers	Train students in participatory and action research Learn about Indigenous research methods and consider what you can learn from them, even if it is not appropriate or possible for you to adopt them directly yourself
Colonial methods	Field traditions with colonial histories, e.g., ethnography	Read criticism of fieldwork methods, e.g., ethnography Learn from postcolonial reformulations of field methods	Critique fieldwork methods and traditions Attempt fieldwork methods that break with colonial traditions
Colonial ethics	Fieldwork framed within ethical codes and scrutiny of the researcher's home country, culture and institution, rather than those of the research environment	Allow ethical considerations to shape your research design Think laterally and creatively about research ethics, going beyond your university's minimum requirements	Allow time to teach fieldwork ethics; do not leave until last Provide feedback on students' ethical documentation, rather than simply approving or rejecting

in higher education that has been 'dominated by Western thought' (Harvey and Russell-Mundine, 2019: 789; Sabati, 2018). This requires us to put down our 'epistemic privilege' (Ndlovu-Gatsheni, 2018) – rejecting or unlearning things we may have been taught, perhaps by people we respect – to open our minds to other ways of knowing and seeing the world. But how? We can start by learning from others who have tried this. Vaibhav Kaul, an independent scholar and film-maker based in the Himalayas, contrasts two ways of understanding environmental change and glacial and hydrometeorological hazards in a mountain village. His fieldwork, which involved filming and storytelling, explored local understandings and interpretations of floods, respecting these explanations and narratives as much as their Western and scientific counterparts. Kaul shared his findings in conventional academic forms including his doctoral thesis and publications (Kaul and Thornton, 2014), but also through other media including his award-winning documentary film – *Mountain, Priest, Son* (2018). Kaul's film explores a community's own 'understanding of its own vulnerability and resilience in the face of dramatic environmental change' (see https://mountainpriestson.wordpress.com/).

We have tried to learn from the spirit of Kaul's fieldwork and film-making practice so that, reading this book, you will hear a range of voices, including some that have previously been neglected. You will encounter fieldwork by a wide range of students and researchers. We have tried to read widely and acknowledge work by those who live, work and publish in many different parts of the world, with a range of backgrounds and identities in terms of their gender and sexuality, ethnic, racial, religious and national identification. We did not want this to be another book in which white, Western men would dominate, as they have often done in the past. In this way, we respond to the more general argument that the wider academic curriculum – what is taught and how – remains too close to its origins in the Western academy and the 'usual suspects' who have dominated it – and therefore needs to be decolonised (Tooth and Viles, 2021).

Second, what can you do to ensure that your fieldwork does not become another example of exotic travel? The first step is to question where you are planning to go, why it appeals to you and what you think you know about it. A team of environmental researchers, heading to the tropics, stopped to ask themselves challenging questions. 'Why were we doing this research anyway? Whom were we really trying to help? Were we just research tourists on a "tropical jolly"?' (Mistry et al., 2009: 86). Decolonisation need not mean that white student groups should no longer travel from their homes in the Global North to sites in the Global South, though it should mean that you question whether such travel is appropriate and, if you do decide to go ahead, then how you do so. If you do travel a significant distance to conduct fieldwork, you should critically examine the ways in which you understand and see your field sites. Question and challenge the tourist gaze with its tendency to render unfamiliar people and places as other and exotic (Kapor, 2019; Masson and Mata, 1998).

Whether you are taking or planning a field course, don't assume that fieldwork destinations should be distant or superficially 'exciting'. Consider possibilities for fieldwork closer to home: in 'endotic' settings (Phillips, 2018), reached through vertical rather than horizontal travel

(Forsdick et al., 2019). More local fieldwork may also be consistent with efforts to reduce carbon footprints and increase inclusion of students with disabilities (Munthali, 2001).

The idea of the exotic fieldwork destination cuts deeper than simply the choice of destination. As discussed above, exoticism and related terms such as exploration and discovery pervade the language of fieldwork, importing colonial legacies and tropes. This raises practical questions about how first to recognise, then avoid, then improve upon the colonial tropes that are often used to define fieldwork. Those who love fieldwork often speak of exploration and discovery, terms and practices that are closely associated with colonialism. Despite their colonial overtones, exploration and discovery are not always or intrinsically colonial, and some of those who identify with these terms and practices have consciously modelled themselves as anti-colonial. The Geography Collective – the 'guerilla geographers' introduced in Chapter 3, Curiosity and Research Design – argue that 'it's really fun and important to get exploring and questioning the world' (Geography Collective, 2010: 196).

Third, to ensure that your fieldwork is not Eurocentric it is important to respect and recognise the local knowledge and experiences of the people you encounter in the field, those who live in the places you are visiting (Keikelame and Swartz, 2019). Do not think you know better or that Western science or scholarship is superior to the worldviews and cultural values of local people. This means learning local languages and steeping yourself in the stories, arts and other traditions of those who live locally (Khupe and Keane, 2017: 26). As you study their knowledge and culture, and ideally learn something of their language, you may become better informed about your own behaviour among them. You may decide to conform to some cultural values, such as refraining from drinking alcohol in places where doing so is offensive or frowned upon (Gillen, 2015) or covering your body in places where some Western clothes are seen as immodest or inappropriate. On other subjects, you may decide to be less compliant, finding ways to resist norms you disagree with, which may include heteronormative values and ableist attitudes. These decisions, involving matters of principle, are best handled with care and respect because they can be complicated by colonial traditions in which people from Western countries have a history of assuming they know best (Massad, 2015; Phillips, 2007).

Fourth, how do you ensure that your fieldwork is neither extractive nor exploitative? Explore possibilities for mutually beneficial fieldwork. Where possible, share ownership of the fieldwork and involve local people – particularly those with experiences of colonisation – as participants rather than merely informants or subjects. Always share your findings with participants (see Chapter 11 on social media and Chapter 14 on data handling). When Indigenous people and colonial subjects become researchers rather than merely researched, everything changes: the project begins with different questions, priorities, problems, ethics and dynamics (Smith, 2021). The field is no longer merely a means to an end – a kind of data mine or laboratory – as participants have a deeper stake in it. Independent researcher Helen Kara (2018) frames this as a matter of ethics, contrasting the extractive ethics of Euro-Western fieldwork with the reciprocity of Indigenous ethics (see also Warwick-Booth et al., 2021: 71). As with all aspects of fieldwork, the ways in which you 'give back' need to be tailored to your time and resources. Don't make promises you can't keep. As we explain in Chapter 8, Participant Observation and Participatory Fieldwork, action research – in which you co-produce research with participants and share all the benefits – may not be feasible within the time-scale of your project, or within the resources at your disposal. Allowing and enabling participants to share the ownership, control and benefits of the research are fundamental to decolonising fieldwork (Keikelame and Swartz, 2019: 47). The principles of mutually beneficial rather than extractive fieldwork can spill over from the research itself to the wider sets of relationships, which fieldwork typically entails. In the course of fieldwork, you may find yourself buying things from other people, chatting to them, striking up friendships, sharing hot drinks and everyday tasks. As we explain in Chapter 5 on research ethics, the challenge for those seeking to ensure that fieldwork is neither extractive nor exploitative is to navigate these complex relationships ethically.

Fifth, how do we decolonise fieldwork methods? Here, it is important to recognise the colonial origins of, and perspectives within, particular methods and fieldwork practices, then to interrogate and reshape these. By understanding what has come before, you can seek to tread a different path. We can learn from researchers who identify as Indigenous and those with experiences of colonisation, such as Linda Tuhiwai Smith (2021), who invites everyone including white people to get involved in the much bigger project of decolonisation (see Further Reading list at the end of this chapter). We can also learn from critical researchers in disciplines with particularly problematic histories and those working with methods that have been embroiled in colonial encounters. Critical anthropologists and geographers, for example, have worked hard to extricate their disciplines and research tradition from their colonial roots. Doing so, they have consciously rejected a model of research in which the white Western researcher sees all and knows best (Wells et al., 2019; Asad, 1973: 163) and they have attempted to share and co-produce research with participants (Bejarano et al., 2019; Dutta, 2021).

Finally, how do you decolonise the ethics of fieldwork, such that the work you conduct meets the ethical standards of everyone involved, and not just you and your home country and institution? A starting point for students is to think laterally and ambitiously about the ethics of the fieldwork you are planning. As we explain in Chapter 5 on ethics, it may not be enough to satisfy your institutional ethics committee, though this is an essential start. You may also need to gain approval from the people most affected. This may mean consulting national officials and/or appropriate individuals within communities and cultural groups, and this may include studying their ethical codes, which may be written or unwritten (Keikelame and Swartz, 2019). It is good practice to find out about Indigenous and other contextual ethical concerns and perspectives that are relevant to the fieldwork you are doing rather than working with mainstream understandings of ethics, which are drawn from Western sources including biomedical research (Kara, 2018). Rather than just thinking of ethics as a box-ticking exercise to complete before entering the field, we encourage you to reflect on ethics from the beginning of your project to the end. By doing so you can take ownership and make sure you embed your own decolonial principles into your fieldwork.

Reflexivity

When – as is common in fieldwork – you travel to a place or social or cultural setting in which you are an outsider (Mullings, 1999), where your language, manners, clothing, education, skin colour, hair style or some other characteristic sets you apart (Krzywoszynska, 2015), it is best to be aware of this, and curious about its implications. When these encounters cut across lines of power and differences in privilege, it is even more important to recognise and carefully navigate them. These are not just matters of personality; they also involve broad differences, structured around race, ethnicity, gender, sexuality, nationality and other dimensions, which interact and intersect, as we discussed in Chapter 2, Fieldwork and the Field (Crenshaw, 1989). Sensitive to the differences between yourself and others, you may be able to negotiate these differences, avoiding the pitfalls of colonial fieldwork and exploring the possibilities of decolonised fieldwork. This critical awareness is termed **reflexivity**.

Reflexivity means turning the research focus inward, examining your own approach and methods and being curious about how you are seen by others in the field (Desai and Potter, 2006; Lunn, 2014; Scheyvens, 2014). It involves curiosity about the power relations between yourself and others in the field (Chacko, 2004; Dowling, 2005). As feminist geographer Linda McDowell (1992: 409) put it, 'we must recognize and take account of our position, as well as that of our research participants, and write this into our research practice'.

By first turning some of your focus inward, it is ultimately possible to reflect on how your fieldwork may affect other people (Schuermans and Newton, 2012). Illustrating what this reflexivity entails, LaRocco, Shinn and Madise (2020) reveal their positionality as white, Western, professional women, conducting fieldwork in Botswana. Doing so, they confront the 'disparity in benefits and return on research investment' between themselves, their research participants and research assistants in what, they recognise, is an impoverished region. Their study illustrates a broader point: that academic researchers tend to approach the field from positions of relative power. Sarah McLafferty argues that, 'except in rare cases, the researcher holds a "privileged" position – by deciding what questions to ask' and how (quoted by Rose, 1997: 307). This privilege may be compounded by the researcher's relative wealth: Tariq Jazeel and Colin McFarlane (2010: 110) recognise that 'metropolitan privilege' shapes their research in the Global South, while others refer to the privilege associated with professional status and class (Dowling, 2005). As we've acknowledged, you may not feel very privileged, especially if you are a young person without financial security, running up debts in order to take a field trip, but many undergraduates nevertheless conduct fieldwork from positions of relative power. This extends to encounters in which you may be asking the questions and shaping the research agenda. So it is best to begin by acknowledging – being reflexive about – the power relations you may encounter in the field. Reflexivity means asking how our circumstances and positionality shape what we can find out and know (Rose, 1997: 305). Being explicit about our positionality, we can see the limits of our knowledge and understand how our knowledge is relational, shaped by relationships and uneven power relations. Thus, while reflexivity is an important foundation for decolonising fieldwork, it is also fundamental to understanding the nature and limitations of the knowledge produced through the research you do.

Reflexivity is crucial as a springboard for changing behaviour: changing how you engage with people and places in the field. Reflexive fieldwork begins with the question posed by Australian feminist geographer Robyn Dowling – 'what sort of power dynamics do you expect between yourself and your informants?' (Dowling, 2005: 27) – and moves on to ask further questions about the power dynamics you or they might want and be able to achieve. These questions can be extended to reflect on everyone affected by your fieldwork – not just informants but participants too, and a range of stakeholders – and others too: non-human lives, things and places.

Conclusion

Decolonising fieldwork begins with troubleshooting – recognising and addressing its colonial underpinnings – and then reaches towards something productive and positive.

In terms of troubleshooting, this chapter has introduced a number of things to look out for and guard against: colonial overtones and patterns in fieldwork, which need reform. We focused upon six issues: racial dynamics (whiteness), exoticism, Eurocentrism, extractive fieldwork and a continuation of methods and imaginative tropes inherited from the colonial past. We then went on to suggest ways in which students and researchers are addressing these issues, pointing to things that students have done and can do to help decolonise fieldwork. These actions revolve around reflexivity: reflecting on field relationships and, where necessary, reshaping them. With decolonisation in mind, reflexive fieldwork begins with acknowledging the realities of power in the field, the ways in which historical events and entrenched ways of seeing can shape the ways in which people may see you and experience your fieldwork.

Decolonisation may not always be capable of undoing the wrongs of the colonial past and present, but it can lead towards new and more enlightening ways of knowing and seeing the world. When we read more widely – recognising and removing barriers to the inclusion of non-Western and non-white authors and publications – and when we learn from the widest possible range of sources and media, we will all benefit. When, rather than assuming we know best or that our understandings are superior, we listen carefully to others, we all have lots to gain. When we conduct relational fieldwork – involving others as partners and participants rather than merely as sources – we have opportunities for research that is not only ethical, but also more insightful and proactively responsible to others.

Key terms

Colonialism begins with the appropriation of land, labour and resources, and often involves the establishment of settlements and governments in distant lands. Colonial empires have declined and have been succeeded by less overt and tangible configurations of power, but colonialism lives on, in a range of forms: including resilient forms of racism, colonial discourse, domination and subordination.

Decolonisation is one of a number of related terms – others including anti-colonialism and postcolonialism – that refer to activist and critical practices, concerned with dismantling and fighting contemporary colonialism in all its forms. Ngugi wa Thiong'o – the African scholar and writer – coined a term that helps to explain what it might mean to decolonise fieldwork and the wider curriculum: 'decolonising the mind' (wa Thiong'o, 1992).

Reflexivity turns the focus inward upon the researcher, their positionality and practice. Being reflexive means being curious about how you are seen by others in the field, and about the power relations behind those perceptions and relationships. Being reflexive means reflecting critically upon your work and encounters in the field.

Further Reading

Abbott, Dina (2006) Disrupting the 'whiteness' of fieldwork in geography. *Singapore Journal of Tropical Geography*, 27(3): 326–341.
Reflecting on the author's sense of unease about a field trip to Gambia, this paper finds colonial and racial dimensions in contemporary student fieldwork, identifying dilemmas of whether and where to go to do fieldwork.

Chilisa, Bagele (2019) *Indigenous Research Methodologies*. Sage.
This book provides a foundation in Indigenous methods, methodologies and epistemologies. It illuminates the perspectives of Indigenous people and historically oppressed communities, and intersections with other dimensions of difference and oppression encompassing gender, sexuality and disability.

Smith, Linda Tuhiwai (2021) *Decolonizing Methodologies: Research and Indigenous Peoples*, 3rd ed. Zed/Bloomsbury.
We recommend this foundational work on decolonising methodologies, which will help you to see why methods need to be decolonised, gives useful tips for going about this and shares examples of fieldwork by Indigenous and colonised researchers.

PART III
METHODS IN CONTEXT

Part contents

7 Interviewing in the Field	93
8 Participant Observation and Participatory Fieldwork	115
9 Visual Fieldwork	133
10 Digital Fieldwork	153
11 Social Media for Fieldwork	173
12 Multisensory and Embodied Fieldwork	191
13 Exploring with Secondary Sources	209
14 Understanding and Handling Your Data	229
15 Takeaways: For Work and Life	245

7
INTERVIEWING IN THE FIELD

In this chapter you will learn

- why you might use interviewing in fieldwork;
- what to consider when you design your interview research;
- how and why to look beyond standard semi-structured interviews in your fieldwork;
- how to select the most appropriate type of interview for your project;
- to think openly about where and how to interview, whether interviews should be static or mobile, and virtual and physical interviewing.

Introduction

Interviewing is a well-established qualitative research method across the social sciences and humanities as it suits many situations. Semi-structured interviewing is often considered the 'go-to' method in fieldwork due to the flexibility of the method and our natural inclination to find things out by conversing with others. Interviewing is used to research a wide range of topics: recent examples range from urban highway development in Lima, Peru (Stiglich, 2021), work and belonging in Helsinki airport, Finland (Vieno, 2021), oral histories of Japanese women living in the UK (Burton, 2015) to the sharing practices of users of a Makerspace in Manchester, UK (Johns and Hall, 2020). The popularity of interviewing method means that it is extensively discussed in the literature on research methods. Rather than repeat the existing guidance offered in methods texts on the how and why of interviewing, this chapter challenges you to think more creatively about interviewing in the field. We re-examine interviewing, both in the context of fieldwork and pushing the boundaries of what we consider interviewing to be and how to use the method.

When we picture an interview, we likely see two people facing each other across a desk in an indoor office space. This is a common research context, but many other possibilities exist (see Hammersley, 2008). One such possibility, which we focus upon in this chapter, is the field interview. Being 'in the field' means that you can grasp the opportunity to speak to people while they are inhabiting spaces and doing things you are interested in. Since the spaces that people use in their work, recreation, social and other activities are constantly changing, the settings in which you may want to conduct interviews may also need to adapt. Rather than interviewing a worker in their office, for example, you may do so in a co-working space or a café near their home office. This chapter talks through the ways in which interviewing can maximise the opportunities, afforded by particular physical or virtual environments, for generating rich data and meaningful research.

Insights

Interviewing is essentially the act of asking questions of research respondents but there are many aspects of this seemingly simple method that we need to consider, particularly when we use it during fieldwork, and whether it is the right method to use. Put simply, interviewing is the process of finding, contacting and meeting with research participants with the purpose of asking questions about their experiences and knowledges, and the listening – in open and non-judgemental ways – to what they say.

The act of listening to, and often probing, research respondents can be an excellent way of collecting information. In some situations, interviews are the best method as they allow you to ask direct questions and explore subjects in depth. For example, Jennifer was able to ask direct questions in interviews with representatives of 3D printing firms (Postcard 7.2).

In other interviews, less direct questions are more suitable. For example, Richard's research on young peoples' friendships and relationships during the COVID-19 pandemic broached some challenging topics including loneliness, which most people find difficult and stressful to open up about (Phillips et al., 2022). Rather than asking direct questions, Richard's team invited participants to select objects that reminded them of their experiences of lockdown, and to talk about their objects. This provided insights into compex emotions without probing or pressuring anyone to speak.

In other situations, even indirect questions are better avoided. One reason why interviews are not always suitable is that, for some people, they can feel like interrogations. Sociologist Bev Skeggs (see Skeggs and Wood, 2008) argues that some groups including benefit claimants and migrants are routinely forced to account for themselves to middle-class professionals. If you have ever been assessed for a disability or housing or unemployment benefit, or quizzed at length by a border or immigration official, you may see Skeggs' point: that interviews can be stressful encounters where the interviewee is or feels powerless, the stakes are high and the risks real. For some interviewees – such as politicians and business leaders – this will not be an issue. But for others, an interview may be a potential ordeal, to be avoided.

Interviews can be an intense experience, particularly if the topic of the research is personal and/or sensitive. There can be issues around finding the right people to interview, gaining access and identifying potential language issues and more. In new field environments we may feel these challenges more acutely. In consequence, there are many questions to consider in the planning and execution of interviewing, particularly during fieldwork. We have summarised four key questions in Figure 7.1.

INTERVIEWING IN THE FIELD | 95

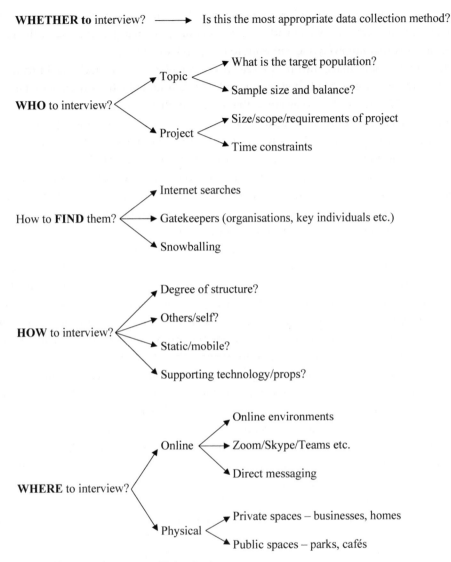

Figure 7.1 Key questions around interviewing

Ethics

As researchers we have to be sensitive to the ethical considerations raised by interviewing, beginning with questions about who to approach or how to recruit interviewees, how to explain and then conduct the interview and then managing the data you collect.

When you are designing your research methodology, think carefully about how you recruit participants. How do you approach them? How do you make sure they don't feel coerced (by you or someone else like their boss or family member) into participating in the research? Participation must come freely *and* with an understanding of what you will ask in the interview. Remember that not everyone will want to be interviewed by you.

Might your questions make the interviewee uncomfortable? If you are tackling difficult topics, such as the interviews conducted by psychologist Paul Rosenblatt with grieving families (Rosenblatt, 2007), we need to be aware of the possibility that your interview might provoke discomfort or pain. Asking individuals to recall past events or to share some types of knowledge can cause hurt and distress. The ways in which you ask questions need to be sensitive, and you need to be clear in advance if a difficult topic is going to be discussed. It is important to let the interviewee know that you will be prepared to stop the interview at any point, should they become uncomfortable or concerned, and that they need not provide a reason if they wish to stop the interview for any reason. Then, of course, it is your responsibility to be attentive to the interviewee's feelings and follow through on this promise.

A further set of ethical issues are raised by the ways in which you store and use the information you collect in an interview. What do you do if individuals in a community share secrets with you? Can you use that in subsequent interviews? There must be clear guidelines about what you can do with information. Typically, the answer is no, we should not share information between participants. There may be instances where we are ethically (and sometimes legally) obliged to share information outside the interview. This can relate to criminal activities where there is a moral obligation to protect others from harm. For example, if you are conducting research on modern slavery, what do you do if an interviewee tells you they (or another person) are trapped in slavery? The one-to-one nature of interviews can sometimes yield information that we are not prepared for. We therefore need to make sure we consider as many of these possibilities as possible and be prepared for them. In the modern slavery example it would be appropriate to pass on information to the individual about how to get help, including details of a national telephone hotline for reporting modern slavery.

Another form of ethics underpinning interview research are ethics of care, encompassing care towards others and care of the self – yourself. Wherever you interview you need to stay safe – make sure you understand the risks, limitations and opportunities that interviewing offers. Consider the risks. Sustainable business researchers Gail Whiteman and William Cooper (2011) conducted fieldwork in subarctic Canada to study the management practices of Cree hunters. They spent eighteen months visiting villages and conducting in-depth interviews with the Cree community. During the research, Gail Whiteman slipped down a rock face above rapids and nearly died. This raises an important point about keeping safe in the field, but also can lead us to take a different perspective on the field environment, to understand how our research participants view and engage with those spaces. For Whiteman, this experience illustrated the ways in which those who live in this context (subarctic Canada) use spatial and temporary cues from topography and ecological processes, which affect their resilience and survival (Whiteman and Cooper, 2011). As discussed in Chapter 3, Curiosity and Research Design and Chapter 5, Ethical Fieldwork, when you plan your research you will have to risk assess your activities, but try to avoid any dangerous situations during your fieldwork.

Interviewing in the Field

There are many forms of interviewing. The semi-structured interview has become the default method of interviewing – for good reasons related to its flexibility and accessibility – but there are other forms that we can consider in the field. Take time to think about the demands of your particular research topic and the kinds of data you would like to generate with your interviews. How far will you need to interrogate the topic? How will you gain access? How much will you need to probe interviewees? The more in-depth the research, the less structured your interviews need to be. Don't assume you will do conventional sit-down face-to-face interviews. We encourage you to consider more dynamic interviewing. Would some of the conversations benefit from being conducted *during* the practice you seek to understand? Mobility can be incorporated into your interviewing. Also consider ways in which you can combine different forms of interviewing. You do not have to choose just one method of interviewing; in fact you can mix and match to suit your research topic, the time you have for your research and your field location. Remember too that you can incorporate virtual and physical interviewing together.

Accessing interviewees and getting started

As you begin the interview research process you will need to identify potential respondents and negotiate access. The degree of difficulty you experience in completing these tasks can vary according to your topic. Generally speaking, the more formal the organisations or institutions you are approaching, the harder it may be to identify the right people to approach and to gain access to them. Conducting research on a local community of crafters will be easier than seeking to interview senior politicians, for example.

To date, comparatively little has been written on gaining access to interviewees. A recent exception is a contribution by John R. Bryson and his collaborators (Bryson et al., 2022) in which they offer guidance based on their collective research experiences interviewing over 300 British and international manufacturing firms. The team advises us to consider several aspects of gaining access, including how we find the right people to approach, when to time our approaches and how to persuade individuals to participate in our research. Remember that the working patterns of organisations and individuals can vary. Approaching a potential interviewee during particularly busy times is likely not to be productive. In the case of businesses, identify if there are seasonal variations in their activities, and avoid the end of the tax year. You are advised to create a positive, professional impression. Draw on any points of connection you might have – for example, a shared university affiliation – and think about how to persuade interviewees that they will benefit from participating in your research. You won't always get it right but remember 'accessing firms is both an art (persuading individuals to participate in the study) and a science (identifying firms and developing robust survey instruments). Many academics learn this art by a process of trial and error' (Bryson et al., 2022: 204). The message therefore for students is to take some time to think about the right strategy for your research and ask for advice wherever you are able.

When you have negotiated access, what should the interview contain? When you are in the field you may want to place particular emphasis on asking questions that can help you understand this new environment. Even if it is a place, situation or debate you are relatively familiar with, asking respondents questions can produce some fascinating insights into your topic and field location. Try to include a few questions that place the topic in broader context. For example, are there any local issues that impact on your topic? These could be new local or national policies impacting on how the place is developing, or particular organisations that the individual is connected to. These may not seem relevant to your topic but bear in mind that part of being in the field is learning about that place in general terms as well as your specific research topic.

Consider not only the information you want to gain from the interviewee, but also the different ways you can go about achieving this data collection. This means translating your own research interests and questions into conversational gambits. Begin by putting the interviewee at ease, and then exploring how to get the best out of them and your exchange. Try to develop rapport with the interviewee, perhaps by allowing time for 'warm-up' questions that will be easy to answer and allow you and your respondent to chat and get to know each other a little. In this way, you will find you are consciously and subconsciously taking in information in the form of visual and verbal clues and cues. This will help you feel your way into the interview, deciding on your approach. When interviewing corporate elites in the City of London, economic geographer Linda McDowell reported that she 'played dumb' with an older, charming and rather patriarchal interviewee. On the other hand, she acted 'sisterly' with another female informant of similar age (McDowell, 1998). Jennifer has also experienced how research outcomes can be influenced by the respondent's perception of the interviewee's knowledge in her work on advanced manufacturing. When faced with un-charming and overtly misogynistic older male interviewees, she sought ways to turn their attitude to her advantage. In some cases she pretended to have limited knowledge and asked the interviewees to explain complex tasks and processes to her. This revealed insights into precisely what they understood these to be and their significance, thereby uncovering different approaches in thought and some inaccuracies.

Where to interview

Where you interview can make a difference to your research design and the kind of data you collect. An individual who meets you in their office will present themself differently in the conversation and will emphasise different things compared to being interviewed in their home. Historian Valerie Yow (2015: 154) tells us:

> Once a student of mine, recording in ethnic communities in Providence, Rhode Island, interviewed the proprietor of an Irish bar inside the bar he owned. The narrator declared several times that it is a myth that Irish men drink a lot, but in the background were the tinkle of glasses and the gurgle of liquids. His testimony would have been more convincing if the recording had been done in a different setting.

You may not have control over where you interview (or it may be a specific factor in your research design, see the **mobile interviewing** methods below), but where you interview will impact on your research. For example, interviews with companies are typically held in offices – which enables observation of the organisation – or in coffee shops. It can be useful to hold interviews outside organisations, as individuals may be less reticent to speak openly if they do not fear being overheard. In general, more neutral settings can result in a more relaxed atmosphere and may make it easier to ask difficult or probing questions. Conversely, if the issues are very sensitive it may be wise to conduct the interview in a private rather than public place. Remember too that some public places can be noisy so this may make recording an interview difficult.

When thinking about where to interview we encourage you to think beyond offices and cafés. Other locations might be appropriate for your research. A team of geographers led by Sarah Marie Hall and Laura Pottinger conducted research on the personal and political potential of cookery classes in low-income communities in Manchester. They did so by using cook-along and food-for-thought methods, using observations and interviews with participants while they were participating in cookery classes (Hall et al., 2020). Wherever you conduct the interview, choose a place in which both you and the interviewee are comfortable and bear in mind that you will be likely recording the interview so quieter places may be more suitable. If you are unable to find a safe place to conduct your interviews then you are in danger of causing harm to research participants and you should not be doing the research.

Interview structure

Interviews range from structured conversations in which the wording and sequence of questions is decided in advance and consistently applied through to unstructured exchanges that explore themes flexibly and openly. When you are designing your interviews, and deciding how structured they should be, you need to think about what suits your topic and field location.

More and less structured interviews each have strengths and weaknesses. A highly structured interview, on the one hand, can begin to resemble a questionnaire and with this come some downsides. The more constrained nature of the structured interview means there is less opportunity for discovery as the questions are led by the interviewer. On the other hand, the more structured an interview is, the easier it is to make direct comparison between interviews. More structured interviews can be quicker to complete as the number of specific, targeted questions can result in shorter interviewee responses. Structured interviews are suited to short interactions in busy fieldwork locations – for example, asking individuals about their consumer spending habits in a shopping centre or collecting data on travel patterns by interviewing commuters in a train station. Business researcher Amiruddin Ahamat (2019) used structured interviews combined with observation to understand entrepreneurial opportunities among biotechnology entrepreneurs in Malaysia, due in part to the busy schedules of the individuals involved in the study as structured interviews can be quicker to complete.

In contrast, unstructured interviews allow interviewees to guide the interviews, with the interviewer providing prompts. Neither the question nor answer categories are predetermined, relying instead on social interaction between the researcher and interviewee. This makes each interview unique and reduces direct comparison between interviews. They can be lengthy and are good for in-depth and/or sensitive issues. Unstructured interview research is illustrated by political scientist Rebecca Alder-Nissen's (2016) work on public perceptions of EU integration, and sociologist Monica Sassatelli's (2007) work on the ways in which artists engaged with a 'European City of Culture' project. In each case, the open-ended subject matter invited correspondingly open research methods, in which the researchers retained scope to feel their way, picking up on interesting topics that emerged in the course of their conversations. We should not mistake the lack of structure for a lack of preparation, or for a casual approach to research. On the contrary, their interviews testify to the craft of interviewing, the skill and practice required. However, unstructured interviews also have disadvantages. These interviews can veer off topic, particularly where the researcher is less experienced. They can take time, which the interviewee may not be prepared to give. They also demand particular conditions, such as quiet and safe locations, which may not be available in the field where you are researching.

Alternative Forms of Interviewing

This section focuses on alternative ways of interviewing in different field environments. The settings in which you conduct interviews – including a range of physical and virtual, static and mobile locations – will shape the data you are able to collect. This is true not only of geographical settings as people say different things in workplaces and cafés, for example, but also of cultural settings. The ways in which people speak and respond to interview questions varies from place to place, culture to culture, and in ways that we can sometimes barely begin to understand. For example, psychologists Isa Gustafsson Jertfelt, Alice Blanchin and Sihong Li (2016) generalise that Chinese interviewees tend to search for the correct answer to the interviewer's question and are keen to move on to the next question quickly. They also suggest that Chinese interviewees talk in more general terms, using broad examples rather than describing concrete experiences from their own lives (Gustafsson Jertfelt et al., 2016).

In Jennifer's research on temporary staffing agencies in Japan she found her corporate interviewees to be extremely well prepared (Coe et al., 2012). The senior executives she interviewed attended interviews with folders full of corporate documents and data they were willing to share. However, interviewees found it much harder to answer questions about topics that were less fact-based, such as changes in corporate strategy. This contrasted greatly with Jennifer's interviews in Australia for the same research project (Coe et al., 2009). In this field context, the senior executives were quite happy to talk expansively about 'big issues' like their growth strategies, but much less willing to share factual data. This reflects different national business cultures around what information is able to be shared through interviewing and the executives' ideas around what data is valuable and what is not.

Walking interviewing

Some of the above examples of interviews have involved interviewee and interviewer sat opposite each other in dialogue. But interviewing need not be static. There is little to stop you interviewing research participants while moving – in fact, we positively encourage it, if you are able. Researchers have been increasingly using mobile interviewing to capture respondents' observations and thoughts while in particular environments. For example, interviewing women as they walk through their local urban environments to discuss how they perceive and respond to risks to their personal safety. Similarly, projects looking at people's mobilities interview participants as they go about their daily commute rather than when they are at home or at work. This will yield different data as a result of interviewing people during the act of *doing* rather than recalling the act later.

Walking interviewing involves walking with participants and talking along the way. They can be highly structured tours in specific, predetermined locations designed to elicit responses or they can involve wandering through places chatting to participants (Evans and Jones, 2011). Walking interviews can reveal responses connected to the surrounding environment and participants may feel less guarded, producing more genuine responses to questions. Researcher Olivia Mason used walking interviews alongside ethnography to examine the politics of identity and territory through the narration and analysis of everyday accounts of walking in Jordan (Mason, 2021). Geographers Mark Holton and Mark Riley used walking interviews with undergraduate students in Manchester to better understand their use of the different spaces in the city. Their work highlights the multifarious ways in which being in, and moving through, places influence the research encounter and encourages participants to reflect on places in the moment and to move away from superficial or rehearsed narratives of the place. This gives 'an understanding of the more everyday, mundane and less easily storied spaces which might be overlooked within a more conventional sedentary interview' (Holton and Riley, 2014: 65). Think also about how this approach might be applied to inside spaces such as shopping centres, factories or hospitals.

There are some practical issues to consider. Is it safe? Will you carry your interview schedule with you or try to memorise it? If outdoors, bad weather may make the conversation difficult (unless of course your topic is related to poor weather conditions). How will you record the interview? Note taking may be tricky and a Dictaphone/mobile phone may not capture all the interview due to background noise or interference. How do you complete any required paperwork (participant information sheet and consent form, for example)? These are not insurmountable barriers but may require some advance planning. Note also that, like all methods, walking interviewing does exclude some researchers and some individuals may not wish to be seen to be interviewed. Some adaptation may be needed for particular groups of people. Geographer Saskia Warren uses walking interviews with Muslim women in UK cities to question how different Muslim women experience urban space and the impact of anti-Muslim acts on walking practices. She implores us to take seriously the stasis caused by physical and perceptual barriers to mobility, such as the threat of violence (Warren, 2021).

Self-interviewing

Interviewing may not involve other people at all. Self-interviews have predominantly been used in studies where the content is sensitive or highly personal – for example, in medicine. However, COVID-19 has significantly increased awareness and use of interviewing techniques that avoid close physical interaction and opened up a range of previously less considered options for social science data collection. Self-interviews allow us to express our own thoughts and observations, working within the structure and questions we apply to interviews with others. Geographer Lyndsey Stoodley (2020) provides an example of self-interviewing as a means of investigating her experiences as a surfer. Self-interviewing with the aid of a video camera, attached to her surfboard, she captures the nuances of movement and motion as they are happening, and in the physical environment she wishes to understand. The important point here is that imagination was shown in terms of the technical set-up – which is determined by the offshore field location – and in the strong desire to take the research to the place where the act of surfing takes place. Similar to walking interviewing, the self-interview can provide access to practices and contexts that we may at first think of as inaccessible to research.

Self-interviewing can also be useful for more mundane subjects and settings, not just action-packed situations like surfing or mountaineering. An example of this is provided by Richard's research with undergraduate students, in a study of the loneliness they experienced during the COVID-19 pandemic, when they were confined to student residences and unable to access the social opportunities and settings that normally enrich the student experience. Because loneliness is difficult to talk about – given that it is stigmatised and sensitive – conventional interviews on the subject can be awkward, including silences and nervous laughter. To explore this subject in depth then, and with an honesty that is usually reserved for private diaries and close friends, the students agreed to turn their interview questions inward, asking themselves the questions they had originally intended for others. Doing so, they learned that self-interviews can be productive, revealing experiences and truths that conventional interviews may miss. The students also learned that self-interviews are challenging, involving as much practical preparation and ethical consideration as any other interview (Phillips et al., 2022).

Self-interviews, like other interviews, benefit from piloting, so it can be helpful to test your interview schedule before interviewing yourself. You can do this either by interviewing others or, more appropriately, asking them to use it to interview themselves, finally providing you with feedback on what worked well and what questions could be improved. Extending this method further, if you are working in groups in the field you may want to individually self-interview using the same questions and then compare the answers. This could help you track your thoughts and experiences during fieldwork in a different, maybe more systematic and reflective way, than using a research diary.

Try this

Interview yourself about an activity. This could be anything you regularly do: shopping, rock climbing or crocheting, for example. First, write down five questions to ask yourself. You can either speak out loud and audio/video record your answers or make notes as you go along, trying to be as specific as possible in recording your precise words. Later, listen or read through your interview and consider how effective your questions were and how self-interviewing can elicit different responses to interviewing others.

Online Interviewing

Interviewing can take place online. This is an established method of interviewing that has had a huge upsurge in popularity due to the restrictions on face-to-face contact that accompanied the COVID-19 pandemic. The assumption that face-to-face interviewing is the 'gold standard' in terms of validity and rigour (McCoyd and Kerson, 2006) has been challenged. Now the online interview can be regarded as a viable option rather than as an alternative or secondary choice when face-to-face interviews cannot be achieved (Deakin and Wakefield, 2014).

Online interviewing has several practical advantages. The world is almost your oyster in terms of who you can interview, it is quicker to arrange and conduct as you remove travel time for you and the interviewee and it is potentially safer as you are not entering an unfamiliar physical space to do your research. However, you are limited to interviewing people who have a stable internet connection; there are some dangers online you should be aware of (your online safety and issues around verifying who you are talking to) (for further discussion see Chapter 10, Digital Fieldwork).

Online interviewing means that you lack the subtle nuances of being in physical proximity to your interviewer and their/your environment, but this is often outweighed by the practical time savings of conducting the interview online, and where sensitive subjects are being discussed interviewees may appreciate the relative distance, feeling more secure when the conversation is mediated by technology. In some cases an interview simply would not happen without being held online. Online interviewing can involve using online video calls, or can be more distanced – for example, by using email interviews. Digital researcher Elizabeth Dean and her team used online tools to conduct cognitive interviews – where respondents describe their thoughts as they are answering questions – using video conferencing and via a virtual world (known as Second Life). In the virtual world interviews were conducted between two personal avatars, one representing the interviewer and one the participant, simulating a face-to-face interaction in real time using voice chat with their real voices (Dean et al., 2013).

Email interviews can be used in fieldwork in instances where the respondent may prefer more time to consider their responses. Social work researchers Judith McCoyd and Toba Kerson offered a choice of interview type, including email interviews, to research the experiences of women who had undergone a traumatic medical procedure. They found that email interviews were preferred by participants for two reasons. First, those interviewees for whom English was not their first language (the interviews were conducted in English). One stated 'I prefer to continue the interview via email since it gives time to think and write' (Connie, quoted in McCoyd and Kerson, 2006: 398). Second, it gave space for the women to respond in their own time and gave them a greater feeling of control. The researchers found that email interviews provided extensive, longitudinal communication (the email interviews tended to be longer, typically three to eight pages longer than in-person interviews and six to twelve pages longer than telephone interviews); they provided written text responses (no need for transcription); there was less social pressure on respondents. They concluded that when researching an emotive topic, the email interviews increased the well-being and dignity of the respondents. When we are in the field we should pause to think about the type of interview we should conduct, based not on convenience for us as researchers, but on consideration of the most appropriate form for our interviewees.

━━━━ Postcard 7.1 ━━━━

Conducting qualitative interviews with people who have life-limiting illness, by Geraldine Foley

I conduct qualitative research with people who have life-limiting illness to identify and explain their perspective on different aspects of healthcare. I have used predominantly qualitative interviews as a method for data collection to capture their perspective. Knowing how and why people who live with an eventually fatal condition have certain preferences for and expectations of care, including end-of-life care, is very relevant because it allows researchers like me and healthcare professionals in the field to know whether the criteria we use to judge care outcomes are consonant with the actual concerns facing people who live with life-limiting illness.

There is some consensus that conducting qualitative interviews with people who have life-limiting illness is invariably more challenging than conducting qualitative interviews with other groups – given the physical and/or high level of emotional or psychological distress encountered by them. Hence, I need to be fully sensitive to participants' abilities to engage in an interview. For example, in a study focused on patient preferences for healthcare services in motor neurone disease (a rapidly progressive and terminal condition), I did not exclude potential participants simply because they had difficulty communicating or would tire quickly in the interview. Rather, I adjusted procedures to compensate for participants' varying abilities to communicate and facilitated participants to be in control of how much time and effort it was possible for them to expend in the interview.

COVID-19 has required qualitative researchers to conduct online interviews with participants because of the social distancing measures imposed by the pandemic. Prior to COVID-19, I had not encountered the need to conduct online interviews in my research. Indeed, recording of interviews in palliative care research was in itself far from routine – given the sensitivities associated with life-limiting illness. Since the onset of the pandemic, qualitative interviews with research participants have been conducted remotely through a variety of online platforms (e.g., Zoom, Microsoft Teams) in multiple fields. However, at the time of writing this postcard (July 2022), it is not yet known the degree to which researchers have conducted online interviews during COVID-19 with people who have life-limiting illness.

As a qualitative researcher, I now ask – what are key benefits and/or limitations for conducting online interviews with people who have life-limiting illness, particularly in situations when it is no longer necessary to conduct remote interviews? An obvious advantage is convenience for participants themselves when it is not possible to accommodate me as a researcher in the same physical environs where formal and informal caregiving takes place. From my experience of interviewing research participants at the end of their life, creating a safe place to discuss sensitive topics has required participants to be in or at least feel in control of all proceedings. Face-to-face interviews which are not in-person could help some participants exert more control in relation to their privacy.

However, it is also possible that online interviews with people who have life-limiting illness are more challenging to conduct than traditional in-person interviews. An obvious limitation of online interviews is that they limit participation along the lines of the 'digital divide' – for example, in the case of disadvantaged or older people, but who otherwise would meet criteria for participating in my research. Online platforms may also lessen my ability to observe key incidents and behaviours that arise in the qualitative interview, important observations which are needed to contextualise what participants communicate to me in the interview. Rapport building between me the interviewer and interviewee is fundamentally a co-constructive process and online interviewing could lessen my capacity to respond effectively to participants' distress and remain fully sensitive to what participants share with me in their interview. The dissemination of qualitative research conducted during COVID-19 with people who have life-limiting illness should help pinpoint how best to proceed with online interviews, even in the absence of COVID-19 restrictions.

Narrative Interviewing

> We can think about the narrative interview as an origami. Initially, the origami is in the paper as potential: that is, the paper can or cannot become an origami. After the figure has been created, the paper can become a flat sheet again, which – despite the wrinkles – can be moulded into a new figure. Like an origami, untold and forgotten memories exist as potentials of one's constructions of the past. (Gemignani, 2014: 132)

Narrative interviewing is a means of collecting people's own stories about their experiences of particular issues, allowing them to express their experiences and views through telling stories or narratives. At the heart of narrative interviewing is the 'basic idea . . . to reconstruct social events from the perspective of informants as directly as possible' (Jovchelovitch and Bauer, 2000: 59). Without a set agenda (often lacking any interview prompts), the interviewee controls the content of the interview and determines the pace of the conversation. This avoids it becoming like a media interview, potentially making the interview a closer representation of the interviewees' lives. However, the interviews are typically not generalisable and tend to be conducted in comparatively small numbers. The approach has been used in medical studies as a means of collecting people's own stories about their experiences of health and illness to help researchers to better understand people's experiences and behaviours (Anderson and Kirkpatrick, 2016).

Narrative interviewing is intimately related to fieldwork as it enables researchers to build up pictures of individuals' stories and to aggregate interviews to build a rich picture of the social and informational world in which the participants live (Bates, 2004). Information researcher Jessica Bates uses narrative interviewing in her work on understanding the everyday informational needs of individuals in Northern Ireland. This method allows her to take a person-centred approach to human information behaviour. International business scholar Anne-Marie Søderberg used narrative interviews to study a quadruple Nordic business merger that led to the formation of the firm Nordea. Her team used the interview to collect individual stories about critical events and actions in relation to merger negotiations and the subsequent change processes. She states that the method gave 'voice to multiplicity of organizational actors, representing different nationalities, business areas, staff functions, professions and hierarchical positions' (Søderberg, 2006: 403).

Episodic interviewing is a particular narrative interview technique or genre that elicits descriptions of particular episodes or features in the interviewee's daily life. It was developed by psychologist Uwe Flick during a study on the social representation of technological change in everyday life in 1996. He suggests that an episodic interview be designed to 'combine invitations to recount concrete events ... and be open enough to allow the interviewee to select the episodes or situation he or she wants to recount' (Flick, 2000: 77). Catrinel Craciun and Uwe Flick (2014) use episodic interviewing to study perceptions of ageing in precarious and financially secure middle-aged Germans. They asked eleven questions on people's perceptions of ageing, representations of positive ageing and resources for growing old in a healthy way, such as 'Can you give me an example to illustrate what you associate with ageing?' or 'What would positive ageing mean to you?'

Oral History Interviewing

Related to narrative interviewing, oral history tells us less about *events* and more about their *meaning* (Portelli, 1991). Recollections of the past are related through the interviews between the historian-researcher (as this method terms the interviewer) and an interviewee with firsthand experience of the period under research. The aural nature of oral sources is important and interview transcripts are analysed not only for the words and phrases used, but *how* they are used as we look to understand the feelings and deeper meanings that may lie behind the words. Traditionally used by historians, oral history interviews can be used to research a wide range of topics. Historian Daniel James uses this method to understand the problem of modern memory for working-class communities faced with deindustrialisation and the destruction of sites for personal and collective memory in Argentina (James, 2000). Sociologist turned politician Belinda Bozzoli, with her colleague Mmantho Nkotsoe, used oral history interviews to study 22 black South African women migrants from one small town in the Western Transvaal and the complexities of the formation of the modern state of South Africa (Bozzoli with Nkotsoe, 1991). Richard Ward, a researcher of ageing and dementia, and colleagues used interviewing as part of the 'Hair and Care' project, which explored questions of appearance and the meanings it holds with people with dementia (Ward et al., 2014). The researchers used 'appearance biographies', a method which allows for a range of topics to be considered about appearance through the life course of interviewees, allowing for reminiscence and life story work.

Design historian Alison Slater (2020: 44) reminds us that 'oral history is one of the first research methods we learn, even if we do not think of it in this way. We grow up hearing stories from those around us. Oral histories shape our family histories and individual ideas about who we are.' She uses oral history interviewing to study dress history, using the oral testimonies collected with women who lived in the North West of England during the Second World War to learn what their clothing memories say about their lives at that time.

Often oral history interviewing is conducted with just one interviewee, primarily to ensure rapport is established and trust built with the researcher. However, some circumstances may require more than one person to be present. Medical anthropologist Linda Bennett and social worker Katharine McAvity (1994) discussed their research methods for a psychosocial research project on alcoholism and family heritage. They argued that there are advantages to interviewing couples together when marital negotiation of family identity is the general aim of research. This is the easiest way to detect lack of consensus on an issue as the spouses provoke each other to expand on information and to clarify differences. Other researchers, however, have found that information comes out that can create or exacerbate problems (Yow, 2015). You will have to make a judgement call about the circumstances under which you may interview more than one person at the same time.

Try this

This exercise will help you to practise interviewing before you enter the field.

Interview someone you know about a shared interest; such as food or sport. First prepare by writing down five questions to ask them. Your questions should be worded to invite detail, but you will probably need to ask follow-up questions to probe for more information. Probing questions include phrases like 'why?', 'do you mean that …', 'give me an example of …' or 'tell me more about …'.

You must be both listening to the interviewee's responses to understand what they are trying to say and, at the same time, thinking about the next question and whether you have the level of depth and detail you need. Wengraf (2001) calls this 'double attention'. Listening is an important skill which most of us need to practise.

Postcard 7.2

Being present in an interview, by Jennifer Johns

My research on 3D printing and the impact of digital technologies on global value chains has involved interviewing industry representatives across the United Kingdom, United States and Germany. When compared to conducting interviews in other industry sectors I had to modify my interviewing in several ways to suit the engineers I was speaking with. First, it became essential to reframe my research questions not as questions, but rather as problems that needed to be solved. This was necessary in order to fully communicate what the aims of the research were to elicit consent to interview and to explain the purpose of the interview questions. Second, the ways in which interviewees conducted the interviews in physical space were different to interviews I had conducted in the past (which were typically conducted in an office sat either side of a desk, or in a coffee shop). As the interviewees were working in an exciting new technological space, they tended to start our meeting by enthusiastically showing me their workspaces and machinery. This could be 3D printers they had manufactured, or new post-processing technologies, or wind tunnels in which prototyped parts were tested. When I interviewed a Formula 1 racing team head designer I was immediately given a tour of the whole production facility, including the construction areas. This meant that my interview schedule had to adapt to follow the order of the physical spaces I was touring, jumping from design to production to strategy, the order varying with every interview and demanding a lot from my interviewing skills. The interviewees felt it was essential for me to see, and admire, their manufacturing facilities before we could sit down and tackle some of the broader, more strategic questions in the interview. For them, how else could I possibly understand what they were talking about?

Third, the importance of being shown and holding objects became very apparent. In every interview I conducted at least one part, or associated object, would be physically shown to me. There would be much pride in the handing over of this object as the interviewee explained how it had been printed. They would explain how it was superior to a conventionally manufactured part and what the exciting applications of the object were. I was expected to handle the object with care and to pay great attention to it. The object was symbolic of production, of generating a physical object that had an important use in the world. It represented the interviewees' engineering prowess, their innovation, their contribution to society. To not pay attention to it would have been seriously detrimental to the interview and my reputation within the sector. Indeed, when I see interviewees again at trade shows or other industry events, I often mention the particular object(s) they had shown me. The interviewees are pleased that I remember, generating further trust and goodwill for my ongoing research.

Through interviewing engineers working in the 3D printing space, I have a renewed appreciation for the importance of 'being there', of being physically present in a location to be able to hold, discuss and appreciate the production of an object. Holding all these objects throughout my research has enabled me to piece together the global value chains of 3D printing, forming a broader perspective based on these micro-interactions.

Figure 7.2   A 3D printed object. Photograph by Jonathan Rowley

Interviewing using artefacts/contemporary objects

As we saw in Postcard 7.2, in which Jennifer referred to interviews with manufacturers, artefacts such as physical objects, maps, drawing, photographs and videoclips can be used to yield contributions from interviewees that are difficult to achieve by verbal exchanges alone (Crilly et al., 2006). Your interviewees are recalling events that occurred in the past and/or reflecting on their thoughts on contemporary issues. Because these are challenging tasks – calling upon the participant (and the researcher as well) to use cognitive skills including remembering, paying attention, understanding questions, reflecting and communicating (Gemignani, 2014), they are likely to appreciate the prompts you offer. It helps to think about how you can use things around you to aid in this process – walking interviews can connect interviewees with particular places and prompt place-specific responses. Also think about other prompts you or the interviewee could use to provoke deeper or clearer recall or aid in communicating complex ideas. For example, showing an interviewee a book you are reading that is related to your topic, sharing an old photograph or holding your grandmother's knitting needles. The tactile act of holding, examining and engaging with the process of producing this object will likely produce more in-depth and open discussion by the interviewee.

The work of political scientist Kristina Saunders also illustrates the advantages of using stimuli in interviews. In an attempt to minimise the hierarchical research relationship between interviewee and interviewer, Saunders used concept cards when interviewing women in the UK about their reproductive decision-making. The cards were printed with words related to reproduction and the key themes from the literature – for example, choice, responsibility, contraception, motherhood. Blank cards were also included so participants could add what they felt was important (Saunders, 2021). Similarly, in their work in Australia, Susanne Bahn and Llandis Barratt-Pugh (2013) found that considerable worthwhile information was obtained from young male construction workers through the use of visual artefacts to encourage discussion and revelation of workplace safety values and scenarios. Historical artefacts can also be an excellent conversation opener or can be used to encourage interviewees to consider alternative viewpoints or to explain their own versions of past events.

When public health researcher Peter Rothe and his team tried to interview members of a First Nations community in Alberta, Canada, they quickly realised their methodology required adaptation as traditional (Anglo-centric) methods 'may not be optimal for researching non-mainstream cultures' (Rothe et al., 2009: 335). In order to research how the community experiences and deals with disproportionate levels of injuries arising from impaired driving, the team developed a new interview method using the community's 'Sharing Circle'. The interviews were held in a culturally relevant location where rituals can be held, with participants recruited by community leaders. Interviews were conducted with several individuals for between three and eight hours, with the interviewer as a participant in the Sharing Circle. A cultural artefact such as a feather or 'talking' stick was passed on to the next speaker as the research topic was discussed. We emphasise that interviewing in the field may require careful thought about the most appropriate type of interviewing, and flexibility and adaptation to suit the geographical context.

Reflections on Interviewing

Like all methods, the success of interviewing in yielding the data we need or expect is dependent on many factors. These include your preparation, your selection of interviewees and the access you have gained, your skills as an active listener and some luck thrown in. Throughout the interviewing process it is important to reflect on our use of this method to question whose voices are/should be heard. Geographer Linda McDowell (2009: 170) reminds us that:

> as interviewers, we cannot and should not evade the academic and political responsibility of speaking for/on behalf of others through interpretations of the world that start, if not end, with the personal interactions that take place in interviews and the ways in which we interpret these through the lens of our philosophical, theoretical and political frameworks.

It is important to recognise the limitations of interviews, in terms of their ability to provide the quality and quantity of data you may be looking for. Critics of interviewing as a method have flagged questions about the reliability of the data they generate – how can you know the interviewee is telling you the truth as they know it and how can you interpret their words if not – and how can you see through the 'performance' that interviews generally entail (Hammersley, 2008; Murphy et al., 1998: 120–123; Atkinson and Coffey, 2002; Potter and Hepburn, 2005)? It is important to be aware of the limitations of interviews – as of any method – in order to make informed decisions about how and when to use (or not to use) them, and how to interpret the results they generate. Sociologist Martyn Hammersley builds upon criticisms of interviews as a research method, drawing out tips for researchers who decide to go ahead and use this method in their research (Figure 7.3).

- **Don't assume:** Interviews don't automatically give us the low-down on what has happened in particular situations. Even when you assume people are being honest, you can't assume that what interviewees tell us about themselves is a direct representation of how they think and feel.
- **Question assumptions:** Recognise that both interviewee accounts and researcher interpretations of those accounts always depend on assumptions, some of which may turn out to be false. You therefore need to understand your assumptions, and those of others, and be prepared to challenge them.
- **Context matters:** Interview situations are peculiar. You need to remember that what is said in them is shaped in various ways by the nature of the situation.
- **Look deeper:** Don't treat what people have said in interviews as obvious in its meaning and its implications. Researchers tend to read interview material uncritically, especially where it doesn't conflict with what the researcher already believes to be true.

Figure 7.3 Learning points from radical critiques of interviewing
Source: Adapted from Hammersley (2008: 8–10).

Conclusion

At best, qualitative interviewing can provide us with rich insight into the views and experiences of others. Interviewing is a common and accessible research method for fieldwork but its use should always be the result of consideration and selection rather than as a default method. This chapter has offered some insights into the considerations around interviewing with an emphasis on the different variations on qualitative interviewing that are open to us in the field. Interviewing can be relatively straightforward to design and data collection can be enjoyable. Interacting with individuals in the field is very rewarding and can create lifelong memories – whether you are interviewing a female business owner while sipping Jasmine tea in the Shibuya district of Tokyo, or sitting in a simple café while a homeless person tells you about their life on the streets, or walking through the Peak District National Park in England chatting with ramblers. This method can generate rich data on the lived experiences of individuals. It is a popular research method but there are still many opportunities to extend how and where we interview.

There are some limitations to interviewing, however. It isn't always appropriate to interview, based on the research topic (it may be too sensitive, or people may be unwilling to be interviewed) or on the challenges of gaining access. We should make sure we consider the context of interviewing, be it virtual or physical, and find appropriate forms of interviewing to suit the field and our research topic. Don't jump straight to using interviews without deciding if the method is most appropriate and, if it is, who you will interview, the kinds of data it will generate and the impact it may have on your research participants.

Key terms

Artefacts – objects that can be used during interviews to prompt discussion. They can be postcards, images, videos or even blank pages that elicit more open dialogue.

Interviewing – an interactive form of data collection involving dialogue between the interviewer and interviewee. It can vary in the degree to which it is structured and the ways in which it is enacted.

Mobile interviewing – interviewing conducted on the move, in contrast to traditional interviewing methods which tend to be static.

Online interviewing – the use of internet technologies to conduct interviews rather than conducting them face-to-face.

Further Reading

Cassell, Catherine (2015) *Conducting Research Interviews for Business and Management Students*. Sage.
Although written for business and management students, this book has wider applicability across the social sciences. Focusing on research interviews only, the book takes the reader through conceptualising the interview, preparing the research interview, conducting the interview, examples of interviews, conclusions and next steps.

Newing, Helen, Eagle, Christine, Puri, Rajindra & Watson, C. Bill (2010) *Conducting Research in Conservation: Social Science Methods and Practice*. Taylor and Francis.
Chapter 6 on 'Qualitative interviews and focus groups' is a really useful and informative summary of the different types of interview, practical guidance on preparing for interviews, advice on conducting a good interview including neutral prompts and different sources of inaccuracy in what people say and how to deal with them.

Jacob, Stacey A. & Furgerson, S. Paige (2012) Protocols and conducting interviews: Tips for students new to the field of qualitative research. *The Qualitative Report*, 17(6): 1–10. Available from: https://files.eric.ed.gov/fulltext/EJ990034.pdf. Last accessed 27 April 2021.

This short article is packed full of useful practical guidance for students. It contains guidance on writing your interview schedule, techniques to use when conducting the interviews and general practical advice. A must-read for those new to interviewing, with some advanced guidance for those with some experience too.

Bryson, John R., Billing, Chloe, Hales, Chantal, Mulhall, Rachel & Ronayne, Megan (2022) Corporate interviewing and accessing elites in manufacturing companies: A framework to guide qualitative semi-structured interviews. In Bryson, J. R., Billing, C., Graves, W. & Yeung, G. (eds.), *A Research Agenda for Manufacturing Industries in the Global Economy*. Edward Elgar, pp. 193–210.

This book chapter provides insight into interviewing with a focus on accessing interviewees, expanding on the guidance provided in this chapter. While it draws upon interviews with corporate elites, much of the discussion is broadly applicable.

8
PARTICIPANT OBSERVATION AND PARTICIPATORY FIELDWORK

In this chapter you will learn

- what participant observation and participatory fieldwork involve;
- to appreciate the conceptual, ethical and practical challenges of participant observation and participatory research;
- how to record, write up and interpret your observational findings.

Introduction

In this chapter we meet an undergraduate who investigated recreational soft drugs by attending club nights and house parties. We hear from drama students who collected stories from users of a park in Pakistan, distilling these into a performance piece. We hear of researchers who conducted fieldwork by attending medical clinics, and others who did so by gambling in casinos. By getting involved, each of these students were able to conduct a form of social research, finding out things that some more detached methods might have missed. Their fieldwork used **participant observation** – the field method we explain in this chapter.

Participant observers – in contrast with their orthodox cousins: non-participant observers – get involved in the social world, making observations and collecting data as they go. As its name suggests, participant observation has two components: observing and participating. Geographer Eric Laurier, who has used this technique in a study of café culture, explains that participant observation involves investigating people or communities by being, living or working with them (Laurier, 2010). This is a form of ethnography: a more generic and eclectic set of research methods originating in anthropology, cultural studies and urban sociology. Ethnographers traditionally immerse themselves in the field: variously eating, working, playing and living with 'the investigated population' (Davies et al., 2014: 253). Researchers have adopted and adapted these methods selectively and creatively, according to new times, places and research imperatives.

Some participant observers get involved with other people, and with things they are already doing, whereas others tend to initiate events and relationships, building and sustaining community relationships and partnerships. Doing so, they tend to involve participants as partners in the research process, and as beneficiaries and stakeholders (Macaulay, 2017). A radical form of **participatory research** is known as participatory action research (Reason and Bradbury, 2005). Action researchers consider beneficiaries and impacts from the outset (Kindon et al., 2007; Cahill, 2007), framing their work 'as a collaborative process of research, education and action, explicitly oriented toward social transformation' (Kindon et al., 2007: 9). Exemplifying this approach, disability studies researchers Hazel McFarlane and Nancy Hansen (2007: 88) wanted to conduct 'emancipatory research' that would involve and empower women with disabilities. Introducing themselves 'as life-long disabled women' (McFarlane and Hansen, 2007: 91), they convened participatory research, inviting women with disabilities to explore their personal relationships. Ambitious as it is – seeking to build relationships and effecting changes in the lives of groups including people with disabilities (McFarlane and Hansen, 2007), migrant workers (Pratt, 2007) and indigenous peoples (Hume-Cook et al., 2007) – participatory action research is beyond the scope and timescale of most undergraduate student fieldwork. For this reason, we have decided to focus this chapter upon the methods and approaches that we think will be most useful to most students: participant observation in which the researcher gets involved but does not set out to effect radical change, or promise too much to participants.

To begin to get a feel for participant observation – what it is and what it offers – we invite you to try the following Try this exercise.

——— Try this ———

Imagine you are planning some research for a supermarket that is opening a branch in a new location. You want to understand more about how people there shop for food.

1. First, consider what questions you could ask people about this subject. What might they tell you? What might they not be able, or not want, to put into words?
2. Now, consider what else you could learn if you were to live with people there, shopping and eating with them. What insights might you gain from this participant observation?
3. What ethical issues might this research raise? What harm might it cause and is there anything you could do to reduce this risk?

Insights

Participant observation can be effective in exploring issues that people find difficult to put into words, which more direct methods such as interviews, questionnaires and focus groups can therefore miss or stifle. These issues include aspects of social life that people tend to show rather than tell. For example, if we follow feminist theorist Judith Butler (2011) in understanding gender as a performative construct – something we perform through repeated actions and presentations of the self – then it makes sense to observe rather than ask about gender. This is why cultural geographer Phil Crang (1994) explored gendered and sexualised service work and emotional labour through participant observation. Working as a waiter in a Mexican restaurant in Britain, he was able to make observations that he would likely have missed had he stuck to interviewing co-workers and customers. A second, related point is that participant observation can be used to address issues that some people see as sensitive, personal, even taboo – and therefore difficult to talk about. Mpoe Johannah Keikelame – a health researcher with a doctorate in psychology – investigated experiences of accessing health services through participant observation in the waiting rooms of an epilepsy clinic in Cape Town (Postcard 2.2). This came with challenges – from the ethical complexity of the project to the necessary investment of time and emotional energy – but it revealed things that people in the clinic might not have said if asked directly (see also Parr, 1998).

Learning by Doing

Like swimming or dancing, we can only really understand participant observation – how to do it and what it can teach us – by having a go: learning through practice, trial and error. To begin to explore participant observation, we turn to some activities that you are likely to experience in the field, whether or not you think of these as part of your fieldwork. First, eating is an important part of any field trip and one that you can turn from a mere necessity to a research opportunity. We explore human settings not only by looking at them, but also using our other senses, becoming conscious of their sounds, smells and tastes (as discussed in Chapters 9 and 12 on visual and multisensory fieldwork, respectively). Whether this means going out to local cafés and restaurants in search of 'authentic' experiences, eating in national and global chain restaurants, or buying food in shops and markets to cook in your hotel or hostel, eating and drinking can tell you a lot about a place and the people who live there. Food and the ways in which people acquire, prepare and consume it speak to a wide range of social, cultural, religious, economic and geographical issues, all of which make food an illuminating subject for social research. An interest in food is something that fieldworkers share with tourists and travellers. But while a typical – possibly stereotypical – tourist may be interested in 'sampling other cultures through their food' (Bell and Valentine, 1997: 4), fieldwork involves thinking critically and analytically about the meanings, uses and experiences of food. This means interrogating notions of authenticity and adventurous eating, unsettling ideas of culinary exoticism in which 'we' eat 'their' food (Heldke, 2015; see also Wilk and Barbosa, 2012). It also means reaching beyond your own expectations and experiences to find out about how others engage with food. This is challenging. A good starting point is to read work by people with backgrounds different to your own including those who live in the areas where you are conducting your fieldwork. Examples of this include work on food and identity (Duruz and Khoo, 2014), 'culinary journeys' (Duruz, 2005: 51) and cross-cultural cuisine (Chi and Jackson, 2011).

Whereas eating is something you must do on a fieldtrip, going out to bars and clubs is something you might choose to do, particularly if yours is an urban field trip. This fieldwork 'tradition' can be ethically problematic as we have explained in previous chapters and its associations with alcohol and recreational drugs can be alienating to other students for personal, cultural and religious reasons (Rose, 1993). Still, however you spend them, your evenings and nights out are likely to provide some of your strongest impressions of the area in which you conduct your fieldwork. In cafés and bars, music venues and clubs, you can encounter strangers and overhear conversations and get a feel for the place you find yourself in. In this free time you can gain insights into broader issues – everything from cultures of consumption and the night-time economy, alcohol and recreational drug use, soundscapes and musical cultures to broad issues of identity, gender and sexuality (Malbon, 1999; Schofield and Rellensmann, 2015). Going out can be a form of participant observation.

Another thing you may find yourself doing in the course of your field trip – depending on your mobility and circumstances – is simply wandering around. Jane Jacobs, the author of a pioneering critique of modern city planning, illustrated how it is possible to learn from walking around and engaging with people and places. Enchanted by a neighbourhood she has come across in Boston, USA, Jacobs recalls the spontaneous desire to participate in some way.

> The general street atmosphere of buoyancy, friendliness and good health was so infectious that I began asking directions of people just for the fun of getting in on some talk. I had seen a lot of Boston in the past couple of days, most of it sorely distressing, and it struck me, with relief, as the healthiest place in the city. (Jacobs, 1962: 9)

Walking and chatting, Jacobs experimented with and practised a form of participant observation (though she did not call it that), gleaning insights that had been left out of official statistics and formal social scientific surveys that defined the area as a problem. Jacobs phoned a city planner and offered some unsolicited advice: 'You ought to be down here learning as much as you can from it' (Jacobs, 1962: 9). From her participant observation – mingling in the life of the street, noticing what people do and paying attention to their actions and routines – Jacobs drew broader conclusions about the 'intricacy of sidewalk use' and the 'complex order' of the city (Jacobs, 1962: 50). There are important lessons in Jacobs' participant observation: we can use this seemingly informal fieldwork method to generate data capable of informing both practice and theory.

Everyday actions like the ones we have mentioned here – eating, clubbing and wandering – illustrate just some of the opportunities for participant observation that you may find in the course of a field trip. On the surface they might seem 'easy' but to get the most from them and perhaps refine them into more sustained fieldwork, you will need to develop and practise skills.

If you have not tried participant observation before, we recommend you do so before your field trip begins. You can do this somewhere nearby and accessible such as a street, market or café or even in a student residence. Getting started is largely about gaining confidence and finding ways to interact that feel natural but are also insightful. You can begin, like Jacobs did in Boston, by trying to engage with people in ways that seem appropriate and comfortable, not forcing yourself on anyone but simply asking directions or the time. Then, whether or not this is part of your assigned or assessed fieldwork, we suggest you keep a diary of your participant observation when you are in the field. If you are somewhere unfamiliar, you may find yourself noticing more than you would at home. As geographers Jaquelin Burgess and Peter Jackson (1992: 153) explain, 'Your perceptions may be more acute than an insider's less focussed curiosity, dulled by routine observation and habitual experience.' Particularly during the first few days when everything feels new, experiences in the field can spark questions and interests, some of which you may distil and develop over time.

We go on in this chapter, building upon participant observation in which you may fit in with what other people are already doing, to participatory fieldwork in which you more actively involve other people in your research. To illustrate this, and provide some inspiration, we turn to a postcard by Sobia Zaidi, an interdisciplinary performance artist, researcher and teacher based in Pakistan. Here, she describes participatory research in which she worked with students and users of a local park to collect and distil their stories and glean insights into local lives and personal histories (Postcard 8.1).

Postcard 8.1

Collecting and performing stories at a park in Lahore, by Sobia Zaidi

This is a postcard from Model Town Park in Lahore, Pakistan. It tells how a group of drama students explored this park as a setting for performance, but also as a subject for social research. At first, we were simply interested in an outdoor space in which to work. But when the park users took an interest in us, watching us while we rehearsed, we began to reciprocate, taking an interest in them.

After the pandemic hit and the campus closed, we decided to take our theatre classes outdoors. Parks seemed like friendly places where we could practise social distancing while working together. We chose Model Town Park, a large green space within the city, bounded by a jogging track, cooled and shaded by mature trees. There, you will find people reading, singing or having a picnic and young couples holding hands.

For the first class, we decided to gather at the centre of the park. We set out together, looking for a place that was quiet, calling out to check the acoustics. We chose a spot by two old trees where the sound seemed right, perhaps because of the canopy that worked like a dome. We familiarised

Continued

ourselves with the space by walking and stretching into it. We made a circle and played games to warm up. We noticed people gathering around the circle, curious young children with their more reserved mothers, and teenagers who formed an outer circle. One of the students – Haseeb – tried to tell them that it was a class and we were not performing, but they stayed and we decided to let them watch. With this impromptu audience, the students became less self-conscious and their performances improved as a result.

Gradually we became more interested in the park users. We wanted our work to be relevant to them. The students went out into the park, conducting informal interviews and gathering stories. Then we wove the stories together in the form of a script. We invited those who had shared their stories to watch our performances in the park and to provide feedback and suggestions. Here are some of the stories, which we gathered and explored:

- A recently married couple in their 40s told us about their love story. They waited for each other for 18 years to get married because their parents didn't agree. He was sent to Dubai. She resisted and broke two engagements her families had arranged. Their parents finally gave in and they got married.
- A cricket coach, who had trained many cricket stars, was never selected to play for the national team. He didn't understand why. Eventually he gave up playing cricket. But his passion for the sport remained and he decided to coach children in the park.

Through this work, the students learned to gather and tell other people's stories. They learned to be responsible with ethical questions surrounding representation. They also learned to pay attention to their informants, who actively engaged in the process of theatre making and storytelling.

But this was not the end of the story. The next step was to take these performance pieces from the settings in which they were created. Translating them to perform elsewhere, we also found that we had distilled some broader findings. Our site-specific participatory research, spontaneous as it was, had helped us to explore aspects of human life in contemporary Lahore, then to share our findings with others.

Ethics

It is best not to become too set on participant observation or make excessively detailed plans for how you might do this before considering about how it might affect others, including the people you are interested in. These are fundamentally ethical considerations (see Kara, 2018; Warwick-Booth et al., 2021).

The first ethical consideration – as we explain in more detail in Chapter 5 on fieldwork ethics – is to anticipate and avoid harm. Researching youth gangs in Nicaragua, anthropologist Dennis Rodgers decided to conduct participant observation. He soon learned about initiation rituals – requiring new members to prove their allegiance – involving violence against rivals. Rodgers highlights the particularly stark risks associated with conducting field research in violent contexts (Jones and Rodgers, 2019; Koonings et al., 2019). Investigating soft drug use by students in Sheffield, Max Johnson participated in club nights and house parties in which students were taking recreational soft drugs, some of which were illegal (Postcard 8.2). This project raised ethical questions, which Max worked through before conducting and writing up his research, and which we considered before deciding to publish it. Though he did not instigate or encourage this risk-taking behaviour, Max felt compelled to consider whether he was complicit and whether he bore any responsibility for what might happen. He demonstrated that his research would not only not cause harm – the ethical minimum for fieldwork, as we explain in Chapter 5 on ethics. More positively, Max also argued that his research could be beneficial to participants and their wider student communities if it could bring into the open an issue that had lurked in the shadows. These contrasting examples illustrate some of the ethical considerations that fieldworkers necessarily confront when they get involved in situations rather than observing from afar. The postcard also raises practical issues – about writing – which is why we have saved it for later in the chapter, where we provide tips on the practicalities of participant observation.

Participation can also be risky for the researcher. You may not be planning anything as dangerous to others and yourself as street gangs or recreational drug use, but you may still find yourself in a difficult situation. Some risks revolve around personal safety. Others are subjective and emotional. When investigating HIV/AIDS in South Africa, members of a team of community researchers formed close relationships with participants. They learned from these encounters but lacked the skills to cope with what they witnessed and were told. Though their findings had informed the development of a new online platform for survivors of sexual abuse, these researchers had become closer to participants than they were able to manage and some were left with trauma (Visser, 2012). Finally, it is worth noting that participatory fieldwork presents particular kinds of risk to the researcher because it typically involves working away from home where you may not have personal contacts for support.

Another ethical challenge specific to participant observation is how to present yourself to the people you will be participating with and observing. Unlike some other research methods such as interviewing, it is not always possible to explain the purposes of participant observation studies to everyone who is potentially involved. Imagine Jane Jacobs walking along the street in Boston and explaining herself to everyone she chats to or passes; it would not work. It may be possible to find alternatives, though, such as explaining your project to a community leader or trusted individual. Sometimes, where there is no practical way of conducting research openly or because doing so might make people self-conscious and behave unnaturally, researchers choose to act covertly. Sociologist Jun Li, whose study of gambling is discussed in Chapter 3, Curiosity and Research Design, originally planned covert participant observation, anticipating that gamblers would behave more naturally if they did not know they were being watched. But Li had second thoughts. She explains: 'I felt that my disguised interaction with these female gamblers had unintentionally infringed their right to privacy, and also subjected myself to psychological pressure and inner conflicts' (Li, 2008: 106). In consequence she shifted to overt participant observation, recording the gambling activities she observed and the spontaneous conversations she overheard in the field (rather than instigating or being involved in any of these conversations). Li's experience is instructive. Covert research can sometimes be justified, but it can be ethically problematic. Conducting your own participant observation, you will need to decide whether you will tell people what you are doing; whether to show them your notes and/or provide feedback; whether and how to anonymise the people and organisations you observe (Richardson, 2015); and whether you can justify these decisions (Warwick-Booth et al., 2021).

Some social researchers, seeking to do more than simply avoid harm, set out to benefit participants and their communities, adopting participatory action research methods in order to effect 'social change' (Kindon et al., 2007: i; Monk, 2007: xxiii; Mattingly, 2001). This hands the ownership of the project over to participants who can ideally decide where they want to take it and what they want from it (Heron and Reason, 2005: 144; Campbell and Pahl, 2018). Pam Richardson's postcard on digital storytelling illustrates a form of participatory research in which participants play an active part from the start, initiating the project by reaching out to the researcher (Postcard 11.2) (see also Nagar and Ali, 2003: 361). Richardson presents an inspiring model for research. She also illustrates the level of commitment and investment in building and sustaining the trusting relationships that participatory action research tends to require. Students, embarking upon relatively short spells of fieldwork, may not have the time or resources to build such relationships and partnerships. A good rule of thumb is to avoid making promises or plans that you may not be able to keep. Avoid rushing into a life or situation, trying to make a difference that you may not fully understand. As we explain in Chapter 5 on ethics, it is important to plan for and communicate the depth and duration of your commitment to participants so that when you do 'exit the field' you will not leave a trail of disappointment (see Postcard 5.3 by Sarah Marie Hall). The next section turns to practical questions: how to do participant observation, and then how to record and interpret your findings.

Doing Participant Observation

To learn how to do participant observation and participatory fieldwork, it helps to learn from others who have attempted something similar, paying attention to their methods, insights, ethics and findings, learning from their achievements and their failures too.

Geographer Robyn Longhurst attended a 'shared lunch' attended by migrants at the Waikato Migrant Resource Centre (WMRC) in Hamilton, Aotearoa New Zealand. She and co-researchers used participant observation to investigate 'the roles played by food in women's domestic lives and spaces' (Longhurst et al., 2008: 210–211). They participated by bringing food, eating with the others who were seated on a long table and joining in the conversation. They observed how others approached their food: what food they took; how they combined different dishes; how they divided their meal into courses; how they interacted with each other. Their observations were concerned less with what people said than with what they did – their actions and body language. They noticed how some people combined spicy dishes such as kimch'i (fermented vegetables, associated with Korea) and sweet dishes such as pavlova (a dessert, which some New Zealanders regard as their national dish) on the same plates. In their field diaries, these researchers observed a 'crinkling of the nose' and 'screwing up of the face' when someone tasted something they did not seem to like or expect (Longhurst et al., 2008: 211). They recorded their own experiences: their behaviour, emotions and sensations. They admitted their reluctance to eat dishes such as spicy sheep stomach, which took them outside their 'food comfort zone' (Longhurst et al., 2008: 211). Writing up these findings, Longhurst and her co-authors worked towards some broader conclusions about experiences of migration and for embodied research methodologies.

Whereas Longhurst, Ho and Johnston attended a lunch that was already planned, some other researchers more proactively initiate or co-produce participatory events, which form part of their research as well as assuming significance in the lives of participants. Pamela Richardson, a development and environment researcher based in the UK, worked with community members and organisations in Zimbabwe to co-produce participatory video (Figure 8.1). In Postcard 11.2 she explains how the project members used online communication platforms to connect and collaborate. Together they worked to make and use video as a tool for fundraising. Other examples of participatory fieldwork include drama workshops involving teenagers in City Heights, San Diego (Mattingly, 2001), migrant workers in Vancouver (Pratt, 2012; Pratt and Johnston, 2017) and women affected by austerity in the North East of England (Raynor, 2017). As a student, you may not be able to replicate the scale or access the resources behind some of the larger projects described here. Still, some form of participatory research may be feasible for you – think back to the postcard by Sobia Zaidi (Postcard 8.1).

Figure 8.1 Participants from Ruwa in Zimbabwe engage in remotely facilitated participatory video activities, as part of online video-making workshops led by Pamela Richardson (see Postcard 11.2)

Practicalities

Now it is time to consider the practicalities. We make some suggestions that will be helpful once you have decided that participant observation is right for you and have settled on a topic.

First identify and, if possible and appropriate, gain access to a setting. Some places, such as the streets described by Jane Jacobs, are easy to access. Others including semi-public spaces such as shopping malls and train stations and semi-private spaces such as community centres and churches may be policed by security staff and through CCTV cameras and may have written or unwritten rules of conduct, which may make it difficult, unethical or impossible for you to access. You may need permission, possibly from formal authorities, landowners or informal 'gatekeepers'. Gatekeepers are trusted and influential individuals who may be able to welcome you and introduce you to others and perhaps to give you tips on how to participate when you are there.

Sometimes, getting access to a setting can mean showing you fit in. To get into a venue, as Ben Malbon explained in his book about clubbing, you may need to dress in a particular way and interact appropriately with the host at the door. Gaining access can also mean writing polite letters of introduction and patiently waiting for invitations. Or, as with Phil Crang's research in a Mexican restaurant, it can mean applying for a job, being hired and trained, then working for a sustained period of time. It can help if you already have contacts in a place or community. If not you may need to cultivate connections, allowing for the time this can take and accepting the possibility of failure. One compromise is to select a location in which you are a stranger but not completely out of place (Kearns, 2005), then conduct some groundwork and identify people to reach out to in advance of the fieldwork period. Heather Castleden, Vanessa Sloan Morgan and Christopher Lamb (2012: 160), framing their participatory creative research with First Nations Peoples in Canada, put it this way: 'I spent the first year drinking tea'. If you don't have so much time to play with you may need to scale back your ambitions, doing what is realistic for you.

Second, decide how to present yourself. While the way you dress and present physically can determine whether you are admitted to a place or event, it can also influence your ability to participate and interact with people there. Staff in many customer-facing service industries – from airline cabin crew to shop assistants – are required to groom themselves in particular ways. And bodily presentation is not all about clothing. Hester Parr (1998), conducting participant observation in a mental health centre, decided to hold back on perfumed deodorant and shampoo when she sensed this grooming was setting her apart from others. There are, of course, limits to how far one can dress in order to blend into a situation. You may not be able to afford to dress for a fashion show in Milan or a corporate event in Tokyo. And you may decide that it would not be ethical or convincing if you were to adopt cross-cultural clothing or to dress as a member of another gender.

Third, decide on how and how much to participate. Participant observation takes many different forms and involves different degrees of participation. Are you a participant-as-observer who gets involved in a situation or alternatively an observer-as-participant who stands back to play a less active role? What suits you as a person? Which approach is most suited to your research question or problem? If you were researching mental health services and their users, would you try to blend in and participate as Hester Parr did or would you follow Robin Kearns' (2005: 202) example of 'inconspicuously observing events under the guise of reading a newspaper'? Another decision you may need to make is whether to work individually or with others. In a group you might feel safer but be more conspicuous. You need to make your own judgements about these questions, considering the places and events you are participating in and the ways in which others behave there. If you opt for a proactive form of participatory fieldwork, you will face further decisions about how to approach and recruit potential participants and how to set up workshops and other events (see Lykes, 2006; Phillips and Kara, 2021).

Writing up and Interpreting Findings

Writing – recording and interpreting field notes – is fundamental to participant observation. Putting what you see into words will not only generate data; it will help you see it better. This echoes the central place of writing within the ethnographic traditions defined by figures such as Clifford Geertz and Claude Levi-Strauss, who were not only excellent field researchers but also highly accomplished writers. Social researchers across a range of disciplines have taken their lead: for example in management studies (Gabriel and Connell, 2010), geography (Barnes and Duncan, 2013) and socio-legal studies (Fish, 1980). The fieldworker-writers we have encountered in this chapter – from Jane Jacobs through Robyn Longhurst – put down their pens while they joined in lunches, went clubbing and wandered the city streets. Still, their research revolved around the words they used to describe and interpret those experiences. So it is important to pay some attention to writing as an aspect of fieldwork.

To explore the role of writing in participant observation, let's look at how a research student called Ben Malbon wrote up his participant observation of clubbing. First, he made notes during and immediately after nights out, and later he fleshed these out in more detail. For example:

> 2 am – main dance floor, chaos: The music dominated the dance floor. Everyone was dancing – on the balcony, on the little stages that projected out onto the dance floor like catwalks (look at me, 'cos I'm looking at you!), in the bar, behind the bar, *on* the bar. I really enjoyed dancing. I felt myself slipping in and out of submission to the music. No sooner had I forgotten what I was doing, and my dancing had become almost automatic, than I was suddenly aware of myself again, conscious of moving my feet, looking at what my arms were doing. I looked at people dancing and noticed how overtly they were looking at everyone else. I don't just mean glancing either. I mean really *looking* at someone, as though that was completely normal. I could feel myself being scanned, but wasn't affronted or anything by this. We all seemed to want the music to take us over; to *become* us in some way. Okay, so we each stamped our individuality on it in our own way – a neat little step here, an arm movement there – but the clubbers were essentially doing the same thing as each other and in the same place and at the same time. (Malbon, 1999: xii, emphasis original)

What do you notice about Ben Malbon's writing? What did he achieve by writing in this way? What were the limitations of this way of writing? Is this something you could do yourself? Would you want to? When would it be appropriate to write in this way? When not?

Malbon's field diary is written in the first person. Given the mixed messages students receive about writing in the first person (Phillips and Kara, 2021), it is important to explain why this can be legitimate and insightful. The critical race scholar bell hooks illustrates first-person field writing at its best. Here is an example from *Belonging: A Culture of Place* (hooks, 2009: 106).

> Riding in the car, away from the town, riding in the country we were surrounded by fields and fields of tobacco. Growing up in Kentucky I learned the reverence for the tobacco plant that had been handed down from generation to generation. In those days tobacco was not demonized. Tobacco was a sacred plant, cherished and deemed precious by the old folks who knew its properties and its potentialities.
>
> I cannot recall any time in my childhood when tobacco did not have meaning and presence. Whether it came from watching Big Mama smoke her pipe, or emptying the coffee cans that were used to spit out chewing tobacco, or watching mama's mother Baba braid tobacco leaves for use to ward off bugs …
>
> The history of black folks and the history of tobacco like braided leaves were once deeply intertwined.

Here, hooks writes about Kentucky and develops broader theoretical points about place and belonging, race and class. Putting herself in the picture, she tells a story that is immediate, engaging and theoretically searching.

Try this

1. Next time you have a snack or a meal make notes on what, where and how you eat and drink. You may also want to make and label photographs of what you consume.
2. Writing in a different colour, go back and annotate your diary, underlining any details that seem important or interesting, though you may not yet know why.
3. Finally, in a third colour, go through your diary and identify any broader questions or themes that your observations seem to raise. These may range from observations about where the food or drink originates, for example, to the sensory experience of consuming it.
4. Write a few words to explain the significance of these details.

Another thing you may notice about Malbon's and hooks' writing is the inclusion of details, which bring the writing to life. Here is another example of a field journal in which specific details accumulate, building up a picture of human life. This is by a postal delivery worker whose blogs about his round in the northern English town of Huddersfield attracted a following and were reprinted in book-form. The following piece is headed 'Friday, 16 August 2019':

> It starts to rain heavily and a thick petrichor scent fugs up from the busily embellished gardens of the cluttered over-60s retirement village; an eerie 1970s time machine of moorland park homes. The ambient scent around here is more usually best described as a blend of damp Players No.6 infused Austin Maxi upholstery and stewing steak. The perms and the glasses are big around here and the dogs are small. There are owl themed knick-knacks on the windowsills and chintzy cane furniture in the conservatories. Bookshelves are stuffed with faded spines: Giles, Thelwell, Richard Adams, Willie Carson, Jimmy Greaves, a Haynes Car Manual for a Fiat Strada … Gravel paths are sewn with couch grass, dandelions and bent old poppy heads. (Boniface, 2019, source: www.themostdifficultthingever.com)

Details such as these, trivial though they may seem, bring a field notebook to life and convey a sense of place and time, which enhances field writing.

Here are some tips that will help you get started as you write up and begin to interpret your participant observation. First, choose a notebook (physical or digital) in which to make your field notes. In some settings it is normal and acceptable to tap into a device; in others the use of mobile phones and computers is discouraged or forbidden. Paper and pens are acceptable in most places, but will attract attention in some. You may want to make notes in private or quiet moments when doing so will not disrupt the flow of activities.

Now you are ready to start writing, start with a simple description. Describe the setting you have chosen for your fieldwork, the people there and the things they are doing. Your observations and notes are likely to revolve around a series of simple questions, which can help you to observe more carefully. These may include: 'What is happening? When is it happening? Where is it happening? Who is (and is not) engaging in what kinds of activities? How are people responding to what is happening?' (Davies et al., 2014: 276). Try to make your notes straightforward and detailed, describing what you see and what happens rather than what you think these things mean; there will be time for this kind of interpretation later. Your notes will often be in the first person, describing what *you* are seeing, doing and feeling. They may be in the present or past tense. These notes will also be wide-ranging because when you make them you will not be sure what is important or why; much of this will come into focus later on (Silvey, 2003).

The next step is to analyse your field notes. When we make initial observations and notes we do not always know what will become important; this usually emerges as we reflect on what we have observed and bring our projects into focus. The analysis of field notes often accelerates when we transcribe and edit them. You may wish to do this as soon as possible, not only because some of your notes may be cryptic, scribbled down in haste, but also because you may be able to add to and develop them while the field experience is still fresh in your mind.

Some researchers use qualitative data analysis software (Davies et al., 2014) or card indexing systems (Silvey, 2003) to analyse field notes but this may be overkill. It is probably enough to re-read your notes, annotating them with reflections and interpretations. It can be a good idea to use a different colour pen or font to distinguish initial observations from subsequent interpretations (Schensul et al., 1999).

The importance of writing – in field notes and their subsequent interpretation – is illustrated in Postcard 8.2, where Max Johnson explores recreational drug use by students.

Postcard 8.2

Students' recreational drug use, by Max Johnson

I already had first-hand knowledge of recreational drug use among students when I chose this for my dissertation topic. Drugs were a part of nights out with my friends. Nights *in* too – because a lot of student drug taking happens at home, in after-parties and gatherings. My dissertation prompted me to find out more about student drug use: how we do it, why and what it means, all from the perspective of students who actually take some drugs.

This project made me think a lot about how I write – and to learn to write in a particular way that I wasn't used to – because I wanted to convey a sense of what student drug culture is like without being formal, sanctimonious or judgemental. This meant using the sorts of words that my friends would use rather than stilted academic language. I wanted to use my descriptions to do something analytical, understanding more about why some students sometimes take drugs, the pleasures they get from this, and the ways in which they acknowledged and navigate risk.

The words I found – to evoke and explore these themes – came from the time I spent with friends and research participants who had granted me permission to join and observe them. We spent whole nights together: pre-drinks, club or house party and after-parties. I tried to be unobtrusive, but paid more attention than I might have otherwise done to what people were doing and saying. I took notes on my phone, using these as the basis for my research diary. The following extracts give a flavour of my written descriptions and interpretations of what took place. In the first, some people are using nitrous oxide – what we call nos:

> As the group crack their nos into the balloon, Becky exclaims 'We need to make the perfect set up'. When I ask what they mean, they explain they have found the perfect setting for the room to make the nos 'mental'. They move all of the sofas to the sides of the room, turn on their colourful lights which are an array of pink, green, blue and yellow lamps with fairy lights draping the wall, and put on some trippy visuals on the TV. They sit with their backs to the radiator, which is on quite high, yet also with the door open, put a song on and begin to slowly inhale the gas in and out, in silence, taking in what's around them.

While this first diary entry gives a sense of the environments in which students like to take drugs, the next entries draw out the themes that really interested me: the ways in which drugs involve measured risks, and lead to pleasures.

Everyone starts to split their ecstasy into bombs using micro-scales to weigh out their amounts. The three girls all put between 0.06-0.1g in each one and make around three each. When I enquired into the reasoning for this, Becky said 'I dunno, it's better to take it like this in case it's strong or bad shit you know … I just want to have a dance and love you all'. David, who is sat forward on the sofa, long curly hair drooping into his face, pours out a small pile of powdered cocaine onto the table. He splits it up with his bank card into four separate lines, one for each person, and rolls a £10 note into a sort of tube for snortings. The people sat around him all seem to get a buzz off their prepared lines, before all hoovering them up.

I like these diary extracts because they remind me of how it felt to be a student among friends trying drugs, some for the first time. I also hope they convey, for a reader who wasn't there, the pleasure and adventure we found, and the ways we mostly supported each other. The words I use to describe and make sense of these experiences helped me to describe and interpret something more resonant.

When you are writing up your fieldwork in the form of a report or paper, you will need to decide how to draw upon your field notes. Taking inspiration from the writers quoted in this chapter, you may wish to quote your field diary in inset paragraphs or text boxes. Doing so allows you to write in two voices: including field notes that may be immediate and vivid, written in the first person and present tense; and setting these field notes in the context of more polished and formal academic writing, with conventional citations and formal arguments. But there is no single formula for writing up participant observation and participatory fieldwork. We suggest you read widely and practise writing, to find what works for you and suits your project.

Conclusion

At best, participant observation offers distinctive perspectives on human life, illuminating subjects that may be difficult to put into words and impossible to observe from a distance. Participant observation is feasible for students. So long as you are realistic about what you can do with the time available, and so long as you navigate the ethical issues raised by particular projects, you will hopefully find participant observation insightful and enjoyable. And since this fieldwork revolves around evocative and interpretive writing, it can encourage you to develop and expand your writing skills, and produce strong written work.

The flip side of the challenges, presented by participant and participatory research, are concerned with the difficulty of getting it right. We have distinguished between participant observation and other participatory approaches including participatory action research, warning that the latter can sometimes be beyond the reach of students, more appropriate to sustained and funded research. Researchers experienced in participant and participatory research stress the time required to develop skills, negotiate access, form and manage relationships (Bennett, 2002: 148). So we encourage you to try participant observation in your fieldwork but to do so cautiously, understanding why this is difficult to conduct and write up and perhaps spreading your risks by backing up this work with complementary methods. Sensing that it was not appropriate to explicitly discuss certain issues at the shared lunch, Longhurst, Ho and Johnston (2008: 213) saved some of their questions for formal and private interviews afterwards. This is known as triangulation: using different approaches to explore the same issues and comparing findings. Whether participant observation and participatory research are your main fieldwork methods, or part of a wider project, they will provide insight and inspiration, conveying a sense of being there and learning through doing.

Key terms

Ethnography – derived from the terms *ethnos* (people) and *graphein* (writing) – involves writing about people. Ethnographers seek to 'provide rich, holistic insights into people's views and actions, as well as the nature of the location they inhabit' (Warwick-Booth et al., 2021: 199; after Reeves et al., 2008).

Participant observation is a form of ethnography that involves spending time – being, living and perhaps working, playing and eating – with people or communities in order to understand them (Laurier, 2010; Laurier, 2013). Whereas ethnographies tend to take months or years, participant observation can be carried out over relatively brief periods, which are feasible within student fieldwork.

Participatory research involves participants as partners rather than mere informants (Israel et al., 2010) and frames the research process around the needs and interests of those participants, as 'beneficiaries, users and stakeholders of the research' (Macaulay, 2017: 256). Participatory research is an approach rather than a specific method.

Further Reading

Bennett, Katy (2002) Participant observation. In Shurmer-Smith, Pam (ed.), *Doing Cultural Geography*. Sage, pp. 139–149.
This chapter includes a useful exercise in participant observation, which helps the beginner develop and practise skills.

Cohen, Jeffrey H. (2015) *Eating Soup Without a Spoon: Anthropological Theory and Method in the Real World*. University of Texas Press.
This ethnography is both readable and methodologically explicit. The author is transparent about the ups and downs of his fieldwork: what worked and what didn't, what he got right and what he didn't and why it all mattered.

Warwick-Booth, Louise, Bagnall, Anne-Marie and Coan, Susan (2021) *Creating Participatory Research: Principles, Practice and Reality*. Policy Press.
This accessible and informative book provides a practical approach to understanding and doing participatory research.

Reeves, Scott, Kuper, Ayelet and Hodges, Brian David (2008) Qualitative research methodologies: Ethnography. *British Medical Journal*, 337(7688): 512–514.
Originating in anthropology, ethnography is now widely adopted by researchers in other disciplines. This chapter explains ethnographic methods to researchers in fields where ethnography remains novel: health studies and medical research.

9
VISUAL FIELDWORK

In this chapter you will learn

- why, when and how to make visual observations including sketches, written descriptions and photographs;
- how to ensure that your visual encounters are ethical;
- how to observe other people's visual practices; their ways of seeing.

Introduction

Looking and seeing are central to fieldwork. When you go on a field trip, particularly one away from home, you probably won't need to be told to take a camera (or camera-enabled device) to look around you, take lots of photographs, then use these in your field reports and share them with friends and family. Digital fieldwork is equally visual, involving sustained screen time, looking at images and words and exploring primarily through your eyes. To get the most out of these experiences and to ensure that where possible this supports your work, it will help to think more deeply about how you structure, record and interpret visual observations of people and places.

This chapter introduces the practical, ethical and intellectual dimensions of visual observation and description. We discuss when and how to use cameras and explain how you can structure, record and interpret your visual observations. We also acknowledge the limitations of visual fieldwork, the reasons why some researchers are 'reluctant to use their eyes as well as their ears' or to trust what their eyes seem to be telling them (Silverman, 2020: 376). Finally, we encourage you to work with visual methods where doing so is insightful and ethical.

It will not be feasible to cover all possible visual methods or technologies, given their recent proliferation. Examples of those beyond the scope of this chapter are cameras mounted on kites (Pánek et al., 2018), drones (Munck Petersen, 2020), animals and human bodies (Edmonds, 2021) and simulated images and films (Thorndycraft et al., 2009). We leave some visual methods and technologies to other parts of the book including Chapter 8, Participant Observation and Participatory Fieldwork, Chapter 7, Interviewing in the Field, and Chapter 14, Understanding and Handling Your Data. Here we concentrate on exploring, explaining and exemplifying visual approaches to fieldwork.

Insights

According to cultural theorist Raymond Williams (1961: 23), 'we learn to see a thing by learning to describe it'. Imagine you are interested in how people buy and prepare food. You can take in a lot of information by watching them shopping and cooking, but you will deepen your understanding if you describe what you are seeing. You can do this verbally – to another person or into a voice recorder – or by making written notes. It can also help to sketch what you are seeing and perhaps to take photos and films. Describing what we see – through sketches, words, photographs and other visual means – we may see and understand it better.

Visual fieldwork responds to three key questions, the answers to which promise real and distinctive insights. First, how can we see the world better through our fieldwork? Visual fieldwork methods – including photography, drawing and verbal description – can be vehicles for noticing (Walker, 2019), for seeing more, seeing better and sometimes for seeing differently. Second, how can we record what we see? The literature on visual fieldwork presents many good ideas for describing and documenting the social world, while it also provides points of departure for students seeking to bring their own creative imaginations to fieldwork. Fieldwork is not just about what we see and our ways of seeing; it is also about other people and what and how they see. So, third, how can we observe and describe other people's ways of seeing, their visual encounters and the ways in which they look at their lives? Visual ethnographers bring these questions to a wide range of human settings and subjects, from the tourist photography investigated by sociologists Jonas Larsen and John Urry (e.g., Larsen, 2005; Urry and Larsen, 2011) to the home-making practices studied by geographer Divya Tolia-Kelly (2007).

These three questions have provided points of departure for some exciting developments in visual fieldwork, which is bypassing the limitations of the written and spoken word and reaching into experiences and lives that other methods can miss. Not surprisingly then, a growing number of social researchers are getting out cameras and sketch pads (Soukup, 2014; Kuschnir, 2011, 2016; Heath and Chapman, 2020). Doing so, some are reaching beyond the traditional boundaries of their social science and humanities disciplines. Sarah Pink, a pioneer of visual ethnography, challenged the distrust of visual observation and representation that she detected in anthropology and sociology (Pink, 2012, 2020; Martiniello, 2017; Becker, 1974; Collier and Collier, 1986). Following through on this critique, Pink showed how researchers can use cameras and other visual devices as research tools, and also study the ways in which the people and communities they study use these devices in their lives. Pink's work has been influential; visual methods and studies are increasingly accepted methods and subjects of social research (Banks, 2001; Ruby, 2000; El Guindi, 2004; Emmison and Smith, 2000; Grimshaw, 2001; Grimshaw and Ravetz, 2005; Halford and Knowles, 2005; Knowles and Sweetman, 2004; O'Neill, 2001; Pink, 2005; Pink et al., 2004; Pole, 2004). Moreover, visual fieldwork remains a vibrant field with plenty of space for new ideas and innovations, openings for students and fresh ideas.

Ethics

Visual encounters with others can be ethically and practically challenging – requiring care and attention – but they are rich with possibility. On the one hand, we don't always like being looked at; most of us are sensitive to how people look at us, particularly if they have a camera or a notebook in their hands. On the other hand, we sometimes welcome attention and are happy to be acknowledged and recognised. This raises some questions for those conducting fieldwork: how to make visual contact with others; how to interact sensitively and appropriately with them; whether and how to look; how to seek their permission before looking too closely; how they are able to give this permission; and what to do with any visual data you collect.

First, the pitfalls. This is about taking care in how we look at others, and not intruding on their privacy and dignity. Rosemarie Garland-Thomson is a professor of English Literature and Disability Studies in the United States. She is also disabled and knows what it means to be looked at by strangers, even stared at (Garland-Thomson, 2017). She observes that 'curious looking' can be unkind and intrusive (Garland-Thomson, 2009: 3). Other people who stand out from the crowd recognise this point. Muslim women in Western countries have to contend with the prying eyes and furtive looks of those who wonder about their headscarves and religious garments (Johnson, 2017). The intrusion can be particularly damaging where cameras are involved – risking a kind of voyeurism (Sontag, 1973).

But visual fieldwork is also rich with possibilities for acting ethically. This means finding ways to be sensitive, careful about how we look and what we do with the visual records we collect. Some people actively want and seek out visual attention on their own terms. The lesson for fieldwork? Pick up on cues and invitations from potential research participants, allowing them to lead where they show signs of wanting to do so. More generally, approach the ethics of visual fieldwork proactively, considering opportunities as well as risks. Consider how you look at others and how this might affect them. Ask whether you might learn to look better, more insightfully and ethically, or perhaps not at all.

These considerations of pitfalls and possibilities translate to rules of thumb for ethical photographic and visual fieldwork: dos and don'ts. These are starting points to be considered rather than followed blindly – we must all come to our conclusions about what is acceptable and desirable, and justify our ethical choices to ethics committees, ourselves and participants.

- Do use your camera as a catalyst for connecting with other people. You might do this by asking permission to take a photograph, whether of a person or a thing. Visual sociologist Elizabeth Chaplin, who often takes pictures of people in the course of her work, finds that most people gladly grant permission and many ask her about her research, striking up informative conversations (Chaplin, 2004: 45).
- Do not point a camera at anyone at close range unless you can demonstrate that they have agreed to this.
- Do offer to share or send your pictures to those who appear in them.

- Do not share or publish photographs in which people are recognisable, except where they have granted written permission for you to do this.
- Do take note of how people respond to the pictures you take or the act of taking them. These pictures and practices can be vehicles for striking up informative conversations, which can be freer and less contrived than formal interviews.
- Do not photograph children or those who are vulnerable. Permission to take and use photographs can only be granted by adults who are able to understand and make decisions about being photographed.
- Do try to develop and reflect upon the skills you acquire while working with cameras, people and places. Make notes on what you are doing, what you are doing well and what you would like to do better.

Notice that some of these rules of thumb for photographic fieldwork come with caveats and exceptions. If you want to take a photograph in a crowded place or a setting in which people are on the go and at a distance, it may not be practical to ask everyone's permission. You may also want your pictures to retain a natural feel, which might be lost if people knew they were being photographed. In such circumstances you may have to make practical decisions about the kind of permission that is possible and desirable, not only before you take a photograph, but before you do anything with it. Other forms of visual encounter are even harder to negotiate. Ways of seeing and looking at other people usually require non-verbal negotiations and judgement, as do other non-photographic enquiries. Should you ask before drawing someone? Lynne Chapman, who sketches people in public places, says that she 'never, ever' asks permission (see Heath and Chapman, 2020). If you do that, she explains, 'you're stuck drawing a portrait' and may feel obliged to achieve a likeness and flatter the subject. Drawing people need not be voyeuristic – one-sided and extractive; on the contrary, it can be a catalyst for reciprocal encounters. It is not unusual for subjects – when they realise they are being sketched – to come over for a look and a chat.

It is not always ethical to produce a camera and point it at people, even if they have agreed to this. Doing so may not even be legal or permitted. Minors cannot grant permission, nor can adults with vulnerabilities that impair their understanding of the consequences of permission. Cameras are not allowed in some places – courts of law; factory floors where sensitive equipment and practices may be visible; schools and other settings where children are present; airports and other places where security is at risk; swimming pools and changing rooms where bodies are visible – and so on. In any case, pointing-and-shooting is not always the most insightful way of collecting visual data. Cameras can get in the way of seeing and come between researchers and participants. Other forms of visual observation and description may be more sensitive and appropriate in some situations. Will Haynes, a geographer investigating the seeing and unseeing of homeless migrants who sleep rough and spend their days in and around Rome's Termini station, sensed that it would have been wrong to use his camera in his fieldwork and turned instead to sketching (Haynes, 2021). Will's field sketches, featured in Postcard 5.2 in Chapter 5, Ethical Fieldwork, do not identify individuals in any recognisable way, but they are rich with insights into the lives of homeless people.

Doing Visual Fieldwork: Recording Findings

Visual fieldwork takes many different forms. We begin this section on the practicalities of visual fieldwork by turning to a medium that prompts sustained attention and close looking: sketching.

Sketching and drawing

Amanda Crawley Jackson, a specialist in cultural and heritage studies who has been researching post-traumatic landscapes on the fringes of post-industrial Sheffield, has a bulging field notebook. Over a period of years, Crawley Jackson has studied the landscape closely, observing and recording traces of streets that have been cleared and demolished. She has also built up relationships with nearby residents, getting to know their names and families, their pets and possessions, their ways of life. Her notebook is crammed with notes, maps and sketches she has made and collected on site and in other settings including libraries and online. A photographer once worked here, taking a series of portraits of the local area, including the material landscape and also the people and their homes. But Amanda says she feels that photography is not right for her. Sketching, she finds, is less intrusive and it helps her to look more closely, and from vantage points she might not be able to reach in person. With coloured pencils, Amanda sketches streets and rivers, caravans and cars, works of art and scraps of rubbish. She doesn't draw people, not just because portraits are so difficult, but also because drawings of things can be equally effective in capturing and telling stories. She adds to sketches with notes, maps and artefacts she has gathered in archives and collected on site: fragments of fabric and wallpaper, for example. Selections from her field notebooks are shown in Figure 9.1a–b.

In the past, weather-beaten field notebooks like Amanda's were less unusual in the field. Researchers carried paper, pens and notebooks around with them. In some disciplines, sketching and draughtsmanship skills were actively encouraged, taught and learned. The preface to a textbook on landscape interpretation, published in 1960, advised students that 'there is no better way of becoming seized of the characteristic features of any landscape than by sitting down and making a drawing of it', adding that this may be a step towards 'understanding' what one sees (Linton, 1960: vii). Students of art and design have been encouraged to do the same. This is why you may have noticed students sitting in front of paintings and sculptures in galleries and museums, making detailed sketches when they could simply have taken a photograph and moved on.

But how can a social researcher, without experience or training in the visual arts, set about drawing? How should we overcome our initial embarrassment or shyness about trying something we may not have attempted since childhood? How should we use the results? Lynne Chapman, who is both a social researcher and a member of the online 'urban sketchers' movement, offers some tips that can help first-time sketchers get started and then get better, whether as a hobby or for purposes of research (Urban Sketchers, 2022; Campanario, 2012). Sketches posted on this website tend to be accomplished and as such may be a little intimidating to those of us who may not feel very artistic. But artistic merit is not the point of observational

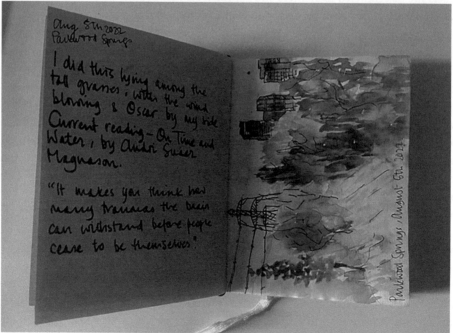

Figures 9.1a–b Amanda Crawley Jackson's field notebook

sketching, and less artistically accomplished sketches can be productive as catalysts for observation and encounter in the field. The following 'Try This' exercise, building on ideas by Sue Heath and Lynne Chapman (2020), provides practical tips for getting started – making your first observational sketches.

Try this

Go to a place where you will be free to stay for a while. This may be a park bench, the foyer of an office, a library, a shopping centre, a café, a hospital waiting room … Find an object that interests you and seems significant. This should be quite small, such as a chair or ashtray, a piece of rubbish on the ground or an item on sale.

Draw the outline of this object. This is called 'contour-line drawing' and involves a continuous line, describing the shape of your object. Draw while you are looking at the object rather than at the paper and draw without stopping, without taking your pencil off the paper. You have just one minute to do this, so time yourself and stop when the minute is up.

Next, think about what your drawing says or reveals. Write a caption or short description about this object and what it means or suggests to you (don't simply label it). Sue Heath and Lynne Chapman suggest wrapping the text around the drawing and using the words as part of your visual design, your drawing.

As you sketch, you may find you attract some interest and that some people may come up to you and ask what you are doing. This can lead to some interesting encounters and observations, which can feed into your fieldwork. Some questions, worth considering and reflecting upon in your research diary, are: Did anyone seem to notice you drawing? Did they speak to you and, if so, what did you say to each other? How might this experience compare to one of taking a photograph? How might the images compare?

Following these tips – summarised in the 'Try This' exercise – Richard tried some observational sketching with a group of students in Sheffield (Postcard 9.1).

Postcard 9.1

Observational sketches in Sheffield, by Richard Phillips

I spent a day sketching with students in Neepsend, an industrial area in Sheffield. We based ourselves in the 'Steel Yard', a stylish development with a cluster of shops and cafés, named after Sheffield's most famous industry, which has declined but not disappeared. From there, we wandered around nearby streets and along the bank of the River Don, past factories that looked derelict but turned out not to be. Amanda Crawley Jackson, whose work in the area is introduced above, accompanied us, pointing out some features and encouraging us to explore for ourselves. There, we heard the sounds of industry – machines banging and radios playing – dodged the heavy traffic and petted a local residents' dog that came rushing up to us.

Continued

Figure 9.2 Richard and a group of students sketching objects. Photograph by Ben Giles

Having gained a feel for the area and returned to the Steel Yard, we all started out with a minute sketch, using the method explained in the 'Try This' exercise above. Each of us chose something that seemed significant and spent no more than a minute drawing its outline. Olivia drew an umbrella, while Izzy traced the outline of a factory, and I sketched a glass of the rather expensive elderflower cordial I'd bought so that we could occupy this table.

The speed of this activity helped us get over our inhibitions about drawing. Some of us had not drawn for a while and felt shy about doing so. Without time to worry about this, we soon found we were enjoying ourselves and also seeing differently: noticing things around us (see Kuschnir, 2016). Olivia focused on a folded-up umbrella. She said it spoke of the moment – a cool afternoon in April, where there was neither sun nor rain to fend off – and the place where the scattering of customers left tables empty and umbrellas unused, where the gentrification that some people hoped for had yet to gather pace.

We ventured into a derelict street, cleared for redevelopment that had yet to happen and attempted some more sustained drawings (Figure 9.3). Once again, we found that sketching was prompting us to look for longer, notice details and explore these through our pencils. Dan was struck by a children's toy, discarded among broken tiles (presumably from houses that had been demolished) and condom wrappers (more recent additions to this place, which belied the impression that this place was simply abandoned) (Figure 9.4). Other students sketched plants like rhubarb that may once have grown in a domestic garden alongside weeds and trees, opportunists here.

By now we were making more sustained observations and gaining some confidence, if not in our artistic abilities then in the observational powers, which we were honing as we drew. Some students found this harder, others easier. Joe, who said he had never learned to love all the writing his degree demanded of him, found he enjoyed sketching and felt it freed him up and sparked something unexpected and fluent in him. George, who was more practised in drawing, produced some accomplished images (Figure 9.5), reflecting that these helped him to imagine people and animals whose faint traces he senses and spotted on his visit to this seemingly empty quarter.

VISUAL FIELDWORK | 141

Figure 9.3 Katie sketching in the site of an abandoned city street. Photograph by Ben Giles

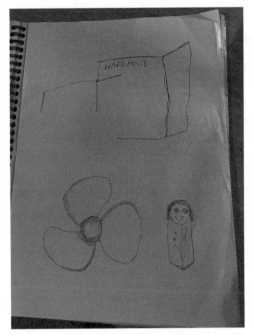

Figure 9.4 Field sketches by Dan: a fan blade, a building, a children's toy

Figure 9.5 Sketch by George: imagined streetscape with dog

Photographic surveys and diaries

Camera-enabled mobile devices have sped up and simplified field photography, such that taking pictures is now the first thing many people do when they begin fieldwork. We have set out some reasons to think twice before snapping (taking photos quickly) – including ethical risks – and we will go on to suggest some of the advantages of considered, slow field photography in which one holds back, conducts groundwork and builds relationships before getting one's camera out. But there is a place for snapping – particularly in an easy-to-use form such as a mobile phone – as a form of exploratory note-taking.

David Adjaye, the Ghanaian-British architect, has used digital photography as a kind of electronic sketchbook as part of his extensive survey of African cities. Feeling free to point and snap 'without the need to dwell on it for a long time', Adjaye collects images and reflects on them later. 'For me it's a sketch diary of the urban environment,' as an initial response to an environment or circumstance:

> When I land in a place I jump in a local taxi and spend the whole day criss-crossing the entire city. I work out the scale of the city and its key criteria. It isn't about me trying to find buildings I like or find interesting ... because of the digital camera I shoot what there is, what I see. (Adjaye, quoted by Jacobs, 2010)

In this relatively brief project, Adjaye visited 46 cities and took a huge number of pictures – 36,000 in total – of which he exhibited around 3,000 at London's Design Museum and online (in an exhibition entitled *Urban Africa: A Photographic Survey*, 2010) (Figure 9.6). Juxtaposing so many visual impressions, he explored 'the sense of place and how it varied from one city to another', identifying 'common threads and areas of difference'. The sheer number of photographs depicted diversity and afforded contrast and comparison that selective and studied photography might not have revealed.

Whether one takes pictures in quick succession like Adjaye did when he was criss-crossing Africa or slowly and selectively, the camera can help you to see more and see better – for example, seeing things we usually miss because they are so familiar. Elizabeth Chaplin, a sociologist who keeps a photo diary, explains that 'the camera helps you to see actively, to pinpoint the taken for granted' (Chaplin, 2004: 47). Whereas most people take pictures of the remarkable and interesting, she aims to do the opposite: to document the routine and the everyday. Chaplin reflects that keeping a photographic diary 'makes you look more closely' at the world around you (Chaplin, 2004: 43).

Photographic studies

In contrast with Adjaye's photographic sketches and extensive observations, we can also approach photography slowly and intensively, using the camera within engaged and sustained social fieldwork. Rather than the first thing you do in the field, taking a photograph may be the final stage, documenting or 'fixing' your findings (Trowell, 2019: 200).

Figure 9.6 *Urban Africa: A Photographic Survey*, by David Adjaye, exhibited at the Design Museum, London, 2010. Photograph by Richard Phillips

'Ex-Offenders' is a series of portraits of convicted criminals. South African photographer David Goldblatt invited ex-offenders to join him at the scene of their crime, where he would photograph and interview them, exploring how they had come to their crimes and contextualising those events. One such portrait – *Kapou Maaneveld where he robbed a man on Darling Street, Cape Town in 1987* (2010) – depicts a person who had been imprisoned for stealing a wallet in that location. Kapou Maaneveld is shown wearing a Carnival costume, a present from a friend whose brother he protected in prison (Higgins, 2014: 259–260).

As an eminent photographer, widely respected in South African communities, David Goldblatt was able to mobilise relationships of trust, also to access resources and exhibition spaces beyond the reach of most students. Still, it is possible to learn from the methods he employed including his investment in relationships with the individuals and communities he eventually photographed. In a similar vein but on a smaller scale, some students in London worked with an artist to investigate their communities. Their fieldwork included taking photographs and films and seeking out visual documents in picture archives and the local library. This culminated in *The School Looks Around*, an exhibition at the Whitechapel Gallery. Lead artist Amy Feneck explained that photography involved students 'looking at their local area differently, taking pictures of signs, symbols, also re-developments and changes that were happening in the area' (Feneck and Plender, 2010). An example of their work, shown in Figure 9.7, captures conflicting experiences of change. At the time, artists and city workers were buying up properties and spending money in fashionable shops, bars and restaurants, while others were excluded and left in poverty. This photograph also speaks of the disconnection between residents – between people of different social classes (rich investors and poorer long-term residents) and different generations (adult property owners and presumably younger authors

Figure 9.7 Photographic fieldwork. *Source*: Phillips (2017: 10)

of graffiti, for example). This project, comprising a sustained but low-budget local survey and culminating in an exhibition, is a realistic example for students to follow and adapt.

Photo-elicitation

Through visual fieldwork we can open windows on the social world, reflecting upon and perfecting our ways of seeing. But this need not be all about us as researchers and what we see. Photography can also be used to explore how other people see their worlds and encounters.

Photo-elicitation, also known as auto-photography and self-directed photography, with variants such as participatory film-making, puts cameras into the hands of research participants in a bid to see their lives through their own eyes (Harper, 2002). Photo-elicitation techniques have been used in a variety of social research projects to explore the life-worlds of homeless people and street children, for example. Geographers Sarah Johnsen, Jon May and Paul Cloke (2008) investigated experiences of homeless people, while Lorraine Young and Hazel Barrett (2001) used this technique to explore the life-worlds of street children in the African city of Kampala. Meanwhile, health researchers Alan Radley and Diane Taylor (2003a, b) used photo-elicitation to explore hospital stays from the perspectives of patients, while psychologist Brinton Lykes (2006) worked with photography in participatory action research in Guatemala. Each of these examples illustrate the possibilities of researching difficult-to-reach individuals and communities, who may not be responsive to more direct forms of enquiry such as interviews.

Photo-elicitation can engage research participants, challenging and inverting the unequal power relations between researcher and participant by allowing the latter to negotiate the research agenda in various ways: from choosing what to photograph to explaining its significance. Research participants often say they enjoy the projects in which they are involved and are pleased to receive copies of the pictures. Johnsen et al. (2008) observed that the homeless people involved in their auto-photography project appreciated the photographs in a time of their life that was passing largely unrecorded.

In its simplest form, photo-elicitation involves loaning cameras to research participants, providing some instructions on how to use them and what they should photograph, and then collecting in the images as a form of data (Ziller, 1990). There are a number of stages to this including: selecting and recruiting participants; setting and explaining guidelines for the use of cameras; collecting and interpreting photographs. To select potential participants, you may wish to conduct screening interviews. Then, you will need to provide a camera and give simple instructions on what to photograph and how. Sociologist Sue Heath and educationist Elizabeth Cleaver (2004: 70) gave the following instructions in their study of the spaces of shared rental housing:

> We would like you to make a visual record of what to you are the significant and meaningful aspects of living in a shared house and a shared household. Your photos may be related to any or none of the topics we have previously discussed with you. It's your camera and your record.

You may wish to follow up with interviews in which you use the pictures as interview probes, and perhaps with other activities such as asking participants to suggest captions (Johnsen et al., 2008: 197) or tell stories, sparked by the images (Phillips and Kara, 2021).

Photo-elicitation was pioneered in the 1990s, in the heyday of the disposable (chemical) camera when it became technically and economically viable to distribute cameras to research participants. This technique has evolved with the evolution of photography, assuming new forms with digital photography and camera-enabled devices, which are more expensive than their disposable predecessors but also more ubiquitous, such that research participants are more likely to have access to photographic equipment. Rather than distributing disposable or otherwise-affordable cameras, researchers have moved towards the use of crowd-sourced photography as vehicles for photo-elicitation (Bonacchi et al., 2014; Sessions et al., 2016).

Photo-elicitation overlaps with several other visual methods, including participatory methods in which researchers and participants work together, co-producing images and interpretations. Gabrielle Bendiner-Viani (2013: 712) invited people to take her on 'tours' of their everyday places, which she later photographed herself, before using the photographs as prompts for storytelling. Canadian researchers Ashlee Cunsolo Willox, Sherilee Harper and Victoria Edge used visual prompts in a similar way, but invited participants to bring in their own photographs and artwork (Kara, 2020; Harper et al., 2012). Other researchers have elicited more sustained visual works in the form of participatory film-making. Examples of this work include an action research project in Aotearoa New Zealand, in which participants explored their relationships within and with a local area by making a film together (Hume-Cook et al., 2007), and another project in which young British Muslims made an animated film together, as a vehicle for exploring and expressing their attitudes towards sexual relationships (Phillips et al., 2020). Until recently, participatory film-making has been too costly, technically challenging, time consuming and logistically complicated for some student fieldwork. But technological advances in film recording and editing have changed this, particularly for students with access to smartphones and laptops. Pamela Richardson's postcard about collaborative fieldwork in Zimbabwe illustrates some of the possibilities of participatory film-making in the field (Postcard 11.2). This postcard can be read alongside Richardson's other published work, which provides practical tips for students wishing to get started in this visual fieldwork (Richardson, 2022; Richardson-Ngwenya et al., 2019; see also Mitchell et al., 2016).

Found images and visual ethnography

To go a step beyond photo-elicitation – asking participants to take photographs – it is possible to collect and interpret images that people are already taking. Researchers have found photographs in the field: in peoples' photo albums and in their homes, in the images they post online and other public places, in archives and photographic collections, and in published form such as postcards and prints (Kürti, 2004). We can search for images, for example, in picture libraries, though we can also find them by chance. Researching a book about riots that took place in Liverpool in 1981, Richard went to the city archives in search of evidence. But his co-investigator Diane Frost heard rumours that a driving instructor had a shoebox full of photographs he had taken the morning after the riots. With the help of others, Richard and Diane eventually traced the box of photographs and obtained permission to publish them (Frost and Phillips, 2011).

Other researchers focus less on the images themselves than on the visual cultures surrounding them, such as the ways in which people are already using cameras and other visual devices and what they do with the images they have taken. Today, as visual ethnographer Sarah Pink (2020, 2012, 2005) observes, photography is pervasive: in consumer culture (Bourdieu and Whiteside, 1990), family photography (Chalfen, 1987), tourist photography (Crawshaw and Urry, 1997; Edensor, 2008; Urry, 1990), and in everyday life (Trowell, 2019). Visual ethnographers explore the ways in which cameras are embedded in people's lives, mediating and shaping their ways of seeing and self-understandings (Lury, 2013). Mohan Li and colleagues in the field of management studies investigated the ways in which Chinese tourists use cameras, and thereby investigated their ways of seeing through the lens (Li et al., 2019).

Seeing self-reflexively and differently

Though seeing can seem very natural – something we are already doing – we tend to see the same things in the same ways wherever we go. When we take photographs we tend to work within conventional but unconscious norms and genres, which shape our subject matter and approach. Like chemical photographers who worked (and in some cases still work) with different kinds of film, filters and lenses and made choices about shutter speeds and apertures, contemporary digital photographers have many decisions to make, all of which shape their product. Even with the simplest point-and-shoot camera-enabled devices, we make decisions about composition, contrast and colour, depth of field and focus, that extend through the editing and manipulation of images. Without realising it we 'work within genres and conform to expectations of what a good photograph is' (Rose, 2022: 4), which we have absorbed through the pictures we have seen and the things we have heard other people say about photographs they consider good or bad. We may have had feedback, whether from parents or siblings commenting on our family snaps or from friends liking or ignoring our posts on social media, such as the pictures we take when travelling or eating out. Without quite knowing or remembering why, we increasingly and repeatedly take the same kinds of photographs, which make sense within our visual cultures, ways of seeing that are sufficiently common that we barely notice them. As a result, our visual experiences tend to be blinkered, derivative and repetitive.

But we can train ourselves to notice. Paying attention to fieldwork practices such as note-taking and sketching, we can learn to see taken-for-granted aspects of everyday life afresh. Drawing, we can focus upon things and happenings that we might otherwise have overlooked: things 'too mundane, too ordinary, to merit our attention, yet which, when looked at in new ways, can often speak volumes about the nature of the social world around us'

(Heath and Chapman, 2020: 105). It can also help to try exercises in taking pictures differently. One thing we can do is to consciously set and follow rules for how to take and frame photographs, which can help us to break out of unconscious habits. The following 'Try This' exercise provides one example of how we can break out of – and become reflexive about – habitual ways of taking photographs. This exercise is adapted from research into the 'tourist gaze' (Urry, 1990), which has shown that tourists tend to see the places they visit in particular ways, filtering and framing perceptions according to the expectations and conventions of tourism. This 'counter-tourism' exercise is designed to disrupt the tourist gaze, to help us break out of perceptual habits and learn to see the world afresh (Antony and Henry, 2005: 101).

Try this

Take three photographs in a public place in the town or village where you live. After you have taken each picture, turn around and take a second picture of whatever you see. Do not stop to compose the secondary images. You may even try doing it with your eyes closed: spinning around and snapping.

Now, compare each pair of photographs. What are the differences between the first and second photographs in each pair? Pay attention to what you have included, how you have composed the picture and how you have framed it. What does each photograph in the pair reveal and what does it conceal?

While counter-tourism can prompt us to look in the opposite direction – turning away from things that normally claim our attention – it can also lead us to subjects that we have previously dismissed as unimportant. Rather than turning around in a literal sense, then, we may do so metaphorically, attending to seemingly odd and unimportant subjects. The French historian and philosopher Michel Foucault argued that this deep curiosity – fundamental to searching fieldwork – begins with an intellectually healthy 'lack of respect for the traditional hierarchies of what is important and fundamental' (Foucault, 1988: 328). Looking in unexpected directions and pointing our cameras away from usual suspects, we may also turn to different spatial scales. Rosa, a student attempting to apply the principles of counter-tourism during fieldwork in New York (Phillips, 2015), set out to look differently at a city that is closely associated with a particular set of visual clichés and conventions (Balshaw and Kennedy, 2000). Marketed as the *Big* Apple, New York is of course famous for all things large. Seeking to see the city afresh, Rosa decided to focus on the very small and the close-up – for example, the detail of a door (Figure 9.8) (Phillips, 2015).

Along similar lines, researchers have devised additional rules for taking photographs with the intention of disrupting and bypassing habitual ways of seeing, which can conceal as much as they reveal. Investigating gentrification, sociologist Charles Suchar (2004: 162) devised a formal sampling frame to direct the camera at ordinary rather than interesting subjects. His strategy 'was to systematically photograph' and build up a representative 'photographic

Figure 9.8 Small things: detail of door, photograph by Rosa, a student who conducted fieldwork in New York. This close-up, cropped photograph is decontextualised and abstracted, its subject de-familiarised. *Source*: Phillips (2015).

inventory' capable of 'discerning comparable patterns of use, function and transformation' (Suchar, 2004: 151). This method has the advantage of imposing discipline upon photographic fieldwork and revealing broader patterns that the human eye – drawn to the interesting and exceptional and socialised and steeped in a particular visual culture – might otherwise miss. It also aids in recording, observing and reflecting upon chronological changes in environments and can be applied over different periods of time. This could be charting change over years (and even decades if secondary photographic sources are available), weeks or days (in order to observe changes in how spaces are used and by whom, for example).

Interpreting Findings

Images do not speak for themselves. In his influential book (and TV series), *Ways of Seeing*, John Berger explained that 'photographs are not, as is often assumed, a mechanical record' of their subject, but are shaped by the photographer's way of seeing.

> Every time we look at a photograph, we are aware, however slightly, of the photographer selecting that sight from an infinity of other possible sights. This is true even in the most casual family snapshot. The photographer's way of seeing is reflected in his [*sic*] choice of subject … (Berger, 1972: 10)

The challenge, then, is to know how to read or interpret a photograph or other image.

Whether or not you have taken photographs, invited participants to take them or acquired them by some other means, the next challenge is to interpret (Van Leeuwen and Jewitt, 2001). The same is true of sketches and visual descriptions you have made and visual documents and evidence you have collected in the field – everything from postcards you may have bought in a street market to confectionery wrappers picked up in the street.

Feminist visual researcher Gillian Rose proposes some questions that can help here. Some of these focus on the production of the image (including when, where, by whom and why it was produced) and its audiences (who consumed, stored and circulated the image). Other questions are concerned with the image itself, and these are most likely to be relevant to you if, on your field trip, you have either taken or asked others to take photographs, or have collected visual material yourself and now want to interpret these images (Rose, 2022: 189). She starts with a deceptively complex question: 'What is being shown?' This question is central to the analysis of visual data, which many researchers frame as a form of content analysis, and address through qualitative analysis of visual discourse and quantitative analysis of the contents of images.

Rose goes on to pose a series of increasingly challenging questions, which frame a 'critical visual methodology', in which the researcher is reflexive about their 'own way of looking at images' (Rose, 2022: 16) and alert to 'the social conditions and effects of visual objects' (Rose, 2022: 15). Rose (2022: 189–190) challenges us to ask:

- what are the components of the image?
- how are they arranged?
- where is the viewer's eye drawn to in the image, and why?
- what do the different components of an image signify?
- what is the vantage point of the image?
- how has its technology affected the text?
- to what extent does the image draw on the characteristics of its genre?
- what do the different components of an image signify?
- what knowledges are being deployed?
- whose knowledges are excluded from this representation?

These questions apply to all sorts of visual data: photographs, of course, but also sketches and visual descriptions. We can adapt these questions to different datasets, ranging from detailed exploration of individual images to content analysis of larger datasets. Thus, for example, Rose uses these questions to guide her through detailed readings of selected images, whereas Dodman (2003) uses them to frame a content analysis of upwards of 800 photographs, generated in a photo-elicitation study on environmental knowledge involving Jamaican school children.

Visual data analysis is complicated by the fluidity of its objects. Photographs are not made in a single moment. Whether chemical or digital, they are made and remade through a series of processes: these include developing and printing chemical film, and the storage and editing of digital images. Photographs are also transformed and reproduced through their reproduction, storage, processing, management, distribution and consumption (Mitchell, 2003). The editing and manipulation of these images is also part of the ongoing process of handling and interpreting visual data, and indeed fabricating this data. William Mitchell, a professor of architecture and media in the United States, warns that digital editing can lead down a 'disturbingly slippery slope' since there is no point at which 'a trivially retouched image becomes a fictional construction rather than a documentary record' (Mitchell, 2003: 290). Accepting that photographs are actively made rather than passively taken and that they always more-than-mirror their subjects, you can feel free to manipulate and edit images that you have taken or, more precisely, produced. Rather than a linear three-stage process of taking or collecting photographs, then interpreting them, then disseminating findings, the process of making and interpreting these and other visual images is continuous.

You do not need to do all the interpretive work yourself. You can talk to other people about the images they are making and may be posting or sharing, and your images too. Cameras and photographs can also be conversation-starters. The photographer Diane Arbus (1923–1971), who is best remembered for her portraits of people on the margins of twentieth-century American society – such as crossdressers, nudists and people with disabilities – said she regarded photography as a catalyst for conversations and curiosity that would otherwise have been impossible to express (Blyn, 2013). As she put it, 'the camera is a kind of licence' (Diane Arbus, quoted by Doon Arbus and Martin Israel, 1972: 1). Social researchers have made similar observations, regarding the camera as a 'can-opener' that can help to establish rapport with informants and provide a licence for observing and engaging with them (e.g., Collier and Collier, 1986). When she arrived in the Mid-Western American town of Waucoma – where she was planning ethnographic research – anthropologist Dona Schartz (1992) began by taking photographs of buildings and landscapes. Taking pictures without intruding into anyone's privacy, she was able to introduce herself to local residents, chatting to some and answering questions posed by others. Camera in hand, she did the groundwork for closer engagement and enquiry (see Pink, 2020). You can also use photographs as prompts for interviews and research activities. You might ask participants to provide captions, for example, or to discuss the content and significance of these images (e.g., Johnsen et al., 2008: 197).

Conclusion

'Observe the world around you as if you've never seen it before' (Smith, 2008: 1, 83). At best, visual research can fulfil this promise, reaching beyond everyday ways of seeing and beyond other research methods (Pink, 2020). It can help us to open our own eyes – noticing more, seeing more and better, and sometimes differently – and it can help us to see how others see their social worlds.

That said, visual methods have limitations. The act of looking can set fieldworkers apart from the people and places they encounter in the field, reducing the latter to a distant and 'ghostly absence' (Crang, 2003: 499). As Susan Sontag (1973) warned, looking at people can be voyeuristic and extractive. Mechanising visual surveillance, newer visual technologies such as CCTV and drones are only exacerbating this risk.

Exploring the possibilities of visual research, while facing up to these risks, it is important to use visual field methods to engage with people rather than simply standing back and looking at them. We may start by talking, building relationships before making any visual record, or using our cameras or sketch pads to start conversations. And we can learn to look in ways that launch constructive and insightful encounters with others. And, when others look at us, we can take this as an opportunity to interact with them.

Key terms

Photo-elicitation, and variations known as auto-photography and self-directed photography, puts cameras into the hands of research participants in a bid to see their lives through their own eyes, and to enter worlds that are otherwise off-limits to the researcher (Harper, 2002).

Vision is 'what the human eye is physiologically capable of seeing' (Rose, 2022: 6).

Visuality refers to the ways in which vision is constructed: 'how we see, how we are able, allowed or made to see, and how we see this seeing and the unseeing therein' (Foster, 1988: ix). Throughout the modern period, the Western world is said to have become increasingly and exceptionally visual or ocular (Jay, 1993).

Further Reading

Causey, Andrew (2017) *Drawn to See: Drawing as an Ethnographic Method*. University of Toronto Press.
This book is helpful for those who are new to sketching, or feel we are not very good at it but would like to improve, for the purposes of our research and fieldwork.

Pink, Sarah (2020) *Doing Visual Ethnography*, 2nd ed. Sage.
Sarah Pink is the author of a series of books about visual methods for social research, which argue the case for visual research and fieldwork and suggest how this might be done.

Rose, Gillian (2022) *Visual Methodologies: An Introduction to Researching with Visual Materials*, 5th ed. Sage.
This book provides a wide-ranging, conceptually rich and practically useful discussion of visual sources and methods. It is particularly strong on the interpretation of secondary visual texts such as photographs and films.

10
DIGITAL FIELDWORK

In this chapter you will learn

- what digital fieldwork is and how you can use it in your research;
- where digital fieldwork can take place;
- what digital tools and data sources are available to you;
- how digital fieldwork can be combined with other types of fieldwork and under what circumstances;
- how to be aware of ethical challenges around digital fieldwork.

Introduction

> Our desk-field is ... a window onto a whole universe of human sociality and cultural creativity that happens somewhere in between material infrastructures, international treaties and corporate policies that make up the World Wide Web. (Góralska, 2020: 50)

Anthropologist Magdelena Góralska (2020) refers to her 'desk-field' in a play on the terms 'desk research' and the 'field'. Until relatively recently the two were considered separate, but the rise of **digital technologies** facilitating digital fieldwork has enabled us to conduct our fieldwork from our desks, mediated by the internet, and through using new digital technologies. You are probably familiar with some of these digital technologies – such as mobile phones, digital television and radio, desktop computers, laptops and tablets that can be used to access digital environments connected to the internet. You may also have experience of **immersive technologies** like **virtual reality** (VR), **augmented reality** (AR) and mixed reality (MR). There is a multitude of resources, communities, virtual worlds and experiences open to us as researchers – the possibilities are exciting and emerging as digital technologies innovate.

On first consideration, the process of conducting digital fieldwork may seem easy and straightforward given that many students have personal familiarity with digital spaces. However, there are several considerations around using digital fieldwork in our research. Where do you start? What types of data are you looking for? Given the (often substantial but not always complete) amount of data available, how do you systematically collect your data and organise it?

Given the expansive virtual environments we can research, how do we impose boundaries on our fieldwork? What potential dangers and ethical concerns do you face and how do you mitigate against these? This chapter will discuss how, when and why you can use digital fieldwork and what you stand to gain from using digital methods.

Insights

Since the introduction of digital technologies within society, digital fieldwork has been gradually used in research. Physical fieldwork has continued to dominate, due in part to habit, the design of courses involving fieldwork and some hesitancy around exactly how and why the digital can contribute to fieldwork. We have witnessed greater use of digital technologies during the physical data collection phase of research – for example, using video material, digital voice recording and use of satellite technology to move around and within field sites. Yet, until recently, the efforts of researchers across the social sciences to develop digital fieldwork techniques have received arguably less attention than they should have. This is especially surprising when we think of the depth and scope of the impact that digital technologies have on many aspects of economic and social life.

The global COVID-19 pandemic starting in early 2020 shook things up for researchers. Suddenly students and academics were prevented from travelling and conducting face-to-face fieldwork and scrambled to find alternatives. In consequence, much progress has been made across the social sciences by researchers working on digital fieldwork and associated digital methods. Digital technologies have vastly increased the ability of the average individual to capture, obtain and share information. For example, online discussion groups and virtual worlds have presented compelling new settings of social activity (Burrell, 2009) and virtual reality creates new artificial (or hybrid) environments. It is now much more typical for researchers to consider digital fieldwork as part (or all) of their fieldwork. It can be the sole approach to fieldwork – that is, staying entirely in the digital realm – or it can be combined with physical fieldwork.

Where Can Digital Fieldwork Take Place?

Digital fieldwork involves the collection of data from the digital environment. Broadly speaking we can divide digital fieldwork into two types. First, the use of digital tools and methods in researching any topic. Second, the specific research of digital media, either with the media themselves as the object of enquiry or using digital media to source data. 'A researcher might examine messages from new media whenever s/he desires to study human communication by examining the textual residue of human interaction' (Webb, 2017: 1).

In this chapter we focus on the former, examining the digital tools and environments we can use in our fieldwork.

In today's data-rich society, finding sources of information and/or accessing people relevant to a particular topic can appear to be relatively easy. In reality, the plethora of potential data sources can be overwhelming, making it challenging to identify the most fruitful and appropriate environments to study. This is particularly true of digital fieldwork where it can seem hard to identify discrete and bounded environments to research. The range of different environments range from the rich visual data (such as panoptical views provided by satellite data and street images), audio-visual representations of place (such as online videos) through to synthetic digital environments (such as video games and virtual reality). How we access these digital environments as field sites and the ways in which we can use these as tools in our research varies according to our research topic and our research objectives. Some of us may use digital environments to support physical data collection. Others may conduct all their fieldwork in digital environments.

Many 'traditional' fieldwork methods can take place virtually, with researchers using their computers and other devices to connect to places, digital archives, communities and individuals. For example, for several years Jennifer and Richard took students to Vancouver, Canada, on a field trip. One of the topics was how the large Asian-Canadian community in Vancouver has changed over time. We took students to the Japanese gardens, visited the historical Chinatown and modern shopping malls where many contemporary Canadians of Asian heritage shop and socialise. Since then, many more resources have been made available online, including digital museum resources documenting the history of Japanese Canadians (see https://open.library.ubc.ca/collections/jphotos). Access to those resources would have greatly enriched our teaching and the student learning experience. In the following sections we will highlight the importance of seeing the digital not as a separate field site, but as another dimension that we either dip our toes into, or completely immerse ourselves in.

Digital fieldwork can occur in one or all stages of research. First, the initial encounter with digital environments in fieldwork tends to be in the planning stages of research. This can be in the process of getting a feel for places or settings we are due to visit (in person or virtually) and/or exploration to identify a field site. Second, digital field sites can then become the sole field location/setting or can be used in support of physical fieldwork. Third, we can use digital environments to share our results (with research participants or as part of assignments) and as a dissemination tool. The degree to which we engage with digital fieldwork over these three stages can be determined by our familiarity and existing digital skills, but it also offers an opportunity to develop those skills. There are a number of digital tools we can use, detailed in Table 10.1.

Table 10.1 Digital tools and their fieldwork applications

Tool	Features	Fieldwork applications
Google Earth	Worldwide satellite imagery, aerial photography and GIS data on a 3D globe	• Explore your physical field site and surrounding areas • Use other resources for higher street-level resolution
Google Street View	Interactive panoramas of many streets in the world based on photographs taken on the ground	• Finer level of exploration of field sites is possible • Take in the images, architecture, traffic, people, retail, climate
360° Cities	Collated resource of stock 360° images and videos	• Review the curated sets which are collated according to different topics • Get a feel for the physical field locations you may be visiting – what do others think is important to upload to represent these places? • Upload your own field images to share
Google Arts and Culture	A series of images and 360° videos collated by different topics and themes	• Investigate themes and topics related to your research • Play with the music and sound functions in relation to your topic and field location
YouTube 360°	Watch VR180 and 360° videos	• Experience a more immersive experience of places • You can upload your own 360° as part of your research process – if you have technical knowledge and equipment
Roundme	Create 360° virtual tours on desktop and mobile	• Access virtual tours made by others • Create your own virtual tours for presentations • Create your own virtual tours to share with research participants (your findings)
StoryMaps	ArcGis StoryMaps enables you to create immersive stories using interactive maps, multimedia content and explanatory text	• Embed interactive maps in your work to provide richer context and/or explanatory power
Actionbound	Allows you to create digital scavenger hunts called 'bounds'	• Set up scavenger hunts for research participants to facilitate their exploration of different places and topics • Can replicate physical walking interviews in a virtual environment

Continued

Table 10.1 Digital tools and their fieldwork applications (Continued)

Tool	Features	Fieldwork applications
Thinglink	Editorial programme that allows you to add hotspots to images, videos, 360°/VR and 3D models and combine them into an engaging scenario	• Create a powerful tool to engage with research participants, either to introduce the research or to use as a research tool • The tool will collect feedback and track engagement so it could be a useful dissemination medium
Wonda VR	Immersive storytelling tool, an alternative to Thinglink but it includes presentations and 360° live events	• As above, but also to: • Create live stories while you are in the field

Source: Adapted from www.sheffield.ac.uk/staff/elevate/guidance/teaching-practice/fieldwork-alternatives

Try this

Imagine you will be visiting either Kyzylorda, Kazakhstan or Manhattan, United States, and want to find out more about their Korean heritage communities.

Access some or one of the digital tools listed in Table 10.1 and see what you can find out about these communities and the places where they live. Explore at different scales, from bird's eye view to street level in the neighbourhoods. What do you observe? Make a list of what you have learned. What has it been difficult to find?

How does this prepare you for your fieldwork? In what ways can you use digital resources like these?

Online Qualitative Methods and New Media

You can use online qualitative methods to collect data. There are several advantages to using these methods as explained by Lynne Webb and Yan Wang (2013), with some reflections added.

1 There is no initial investment in equipment as we may already own the tools we need, so researchers can harvest datasets. Remember though that students working with datasets will need some data management skills. We may have the physical infrastructure (e.g., a computer), but we also need the right research know-how.
2 As the data pre-exists in the public domain many issues around data collection and storage regulations are avoided (see though discussion on the ethics of using secondary data in the Secondary Sources chapter).
3 Data collection becomes almost instantaneous as researchers can collect data as quickly as they can download text. While downloading the data may be quick, working with large volumes of data is challenging and time consuming, and not all datasets are complete.
4 Recently downloaded text is contemporary and immediate, allowing timely research of important and relevant topics.

There are several types of online resources that you can access. First, there are open data sources provided by governments and other organisations. The US government launched Data.gov (www.data.gov) in 2009 to increase data transparency and in 2015 the UK's data portal (www.data.gov.uk) reported more than 22,000 published datasets (Corti & Fielding, 2016). There are other sources of public or open-source data – for example, 'smart city' initiatives involve the collection and sharing of a plethora of different real-time data feeds on climate, traffic, trade etc. Second, there are commercial datasets where data is collected and collated by private companies. These typically have to be paid for, with costs often being high. You may want to check your university or college's access to some commercial datasets. Third, archives of digital social research. As significant resources are invested in quality assessing and documenting data collections, these archives contain good-quality data that is high in integrity and increasingly accept a more diverse range of digital data from historical databases to qualitative interviews (Corti & Fielding, 2016).

In an example of the use of social media as a data source, communications studies scholar Catherine Knight Steele researches the history of black feminist techno-culture in the United States and its ability to decentre white supremacy and patriarchy in conversations about the future of technology (Steele, 2021). Her research uses letters, news articles and essays of black feminist writers of the past and a digital archive of blog posts, tweets and Instagram stories of some of the most well-known black feminist writers of our time. The research involves a conversation between methods that does not typically take place – she uses historical and archival analysis and empirical internet studies together. Here Steele is using publicly available digital resources to draw together an important narrative about an under-represented group of writers.

Digital Spaces: The Example of Video Games

In this section we will discuss a specific form of digital space – that of video games. Video games are a digital environment that is rich in potential for social science researchers. Digital games are – to differing degrees – complex constructions of visuals, sound, architecture world-building, narrative, rules and game mechanics (Heidbrink et al., 2014). They can be researched in terms of their landscapes or topographies (the worlds created in the games) the modes of play (the 'game play') and the communities they create. Religious studies scholar Simone Heidbrink and her co-authors (Heidbrink et al., 2014) conducted a case study on *Smite*, a multiplayer online battle arena game published by Hi-Rez in 2014. They did so to examine the religious content in the game. They immersed themselves in the *Smite* gameworld and they identified three levels of engagement with games when researching: first, studying the design, rules and mechanics of the game – which can be achieved by talking to the developers of the game; second, observing others play, reading their reports and reviews and hoping that their knowledge is representative and their play competent; third, by playing the game themselves. They cite Aarseth (2003: 3) who states that 'while all three methods are valid, the third way is clearly the best, especially if combined or reinforced by the other two'.

These researchers are advocating for a degree of immersion and engagement in the gameworld but also caution us to consider the large investments of time that are required to gain knowledge, skill or even 'reputation' (Taylor, 2006). It could be argued that the same is true of other forms of research into digital communities – the amount of time spent by the researcher in that environment is likely to impact on the data they collect as a more established community presence is probably going to lead to better access and understanding of the digital environment. Heidbrink et al. (2014) offer suggestions about how to structure and record game playing for research (clearly just playing is not enough). They recommend taking notes during (if possible) and after playing, and taking screenshots, video and audio recordings and storing them systematically.

Through this example of gameworlds, we can see that it is possible to conduct fieldwork entirely digitally, and to see how it can be perceived as entering a different field site. Interestingly, some recent research on video games highlights the interaction between gameworlds and physical environments. Anthropologist and folklore scholar Nathan Young studied *Pokémon GO* – a mobile app-based, augmented-reality game that requires physical travel to virtually capture and evolve hundreds of digital 'pocket monsters' or Pokémon, a shortened form applied to the wider Japanese franchise of games, media and merchandise (Young, 2020). *Pokémon GO* is a game that relies on networking and geographical/spatial exploration, with the gameplaying bringing people together into both physical and virtual spaces. His research therefore took place online, in the *Pokémon GO* gameworld *and* in physical field sites where he observed and participated in the physical encounters that players engaged in in seeking pocket monsters. For Young, the research was really important in highlighting how handheld digital technology mediates relationships.

This discussion of video games as digital field sites highlights the potential for research to be an experience in which the researcher participates – and in some cases is required to be an experienced participant in order to gain the 'reputation' required to gain access to research subjects. Next, we will discuss **digital ethnography** and examples of research where digital and physical spaces are combined before exploring the emerging fully immersive digital environments for research.

Digital Ethnographies

There are many topics you would associate with traditional physical field methods that you can research using digital methods. In this section we will discuss some examples of recent work that is based primarily on digital fieldwork, some supported with physical fieldwork, others without. Each uses a range of different digital spaces to collect data on particular communities, using digital fieldwork to access particular groups of people that would arguably be harder to reach using 'conventional' in-person methods – the digital spaces provide more accessible entry points to these groupings. This type of research can be described as 'digital ethnography' – a method used to study societies and cultures in the digital space.

This includes using different types of interviews, focus groups and observation to collect data within digital spaces.

Digital methods can provide rich data on the everyday and 'lived experiences' of groups and individuals. Social and cultural geographer Catherine Oliver researched masculinity and veganism, using seven in-depth semi-structured interviews and discourse analysis of the Instagram accounts of male vegans who are full-time paid influencer-activists based in the UK, US and Australia (Oliver, 2021). Her methodology provides us with insight into how to conduct such an analysis. Catherine Oliver analysed posts within a set time period (2015–2020), collecting and recording posts that show men's representations of themselves online, with captions about masculinity, protein, meat and/or their past. She analysed ten posts in-depth for each influencer based on their hashtags and caption content, coding according to themes of: (mock) meat, animals, activism, past, compassion and protein. These codes allowed her to analyse the role of the influencers and the ways in which masculinity was expressed by the male vegan influencers. Instagram proved to be a valuable resource in which individuals are expressing themselves in public in particular ways. The methodological task of finding men prepared to openly discuss masculinity and veganism would have been much more difficult without digital resources. In addition, Oliver was able to research across three distant countries using this methodology.

Digital Field Environments: Combining Digital and Physical Spaces

One of the advantages of digital fieldwork is the ability to mix and match, combining with physical fieldwork based on the needs of the research topic. Geographer Di Wu (2022) used a multi-method approach, combining interviewing, participant observation and digital fieldwork to investigate the revival of the Jingdezhen ceramics industry cluster in China. As the study focused on understanding the role of individuals in the revival, Wu examined the use of digital spaces, following research participants on WeChat and using the digital space to find and recruit participants. She interacted with the ceramics community frequently in virtual space, regularly 'hanging out' online (Jeffrey et al., 2021) and took notes on participants' posts or discussion. The data Wu collected included written texts, still and moving images, field notes and screenshots. Wu reflected on her use of digital fieldwork, concluding that it helped her to build trust and credibility with her participants.

> Some of my informants told me that they often saw my posts on WeChat about my time researching in Jingdezhen (conducting interviews, participating in various local events, or meeting other local actors for meals or coffee). They also told me that they noticed my comments and likes on their friends' posts and my presence in some online discussion groups. They revealed that because of this visibility, they came to not only trust my role as a researcher studying the local industry, but also felt closer to me, as if I was an insider and part of their community. (Wu, 2022: 92)

Sometimes we can be presented with challenges in physical field spaces that can be addressed with digital methods. In her work on the use of digital technologies by the urban youth of Ghana, information scholar Jenna Burrell integrated several field sites into her research (Burrell, 2012). Her physical fieldwork in Ghana began with participant observation in internet cafés in Accra. But her observations were not what she expected – instead of observing a vibrant community with interaction between the young people, she observed irregular attendance by individuals and little communication between people in the café. Burrell realised that she needed to expand her field locations.

> The cafés were focal points of circulation and intersection from which I was able to expand outward, tracing the contours of the social phenomenon of Internet use. This was accomplished by both following the movement of Internet users through the city and by intercepting the flow of media through the Internet as it arrived in the Internet café. (Burrell, 2009: 196)

Burrell conceived of her field site as a network composed of fixed and moving points including spaces, people and objects. This allowed her to jump between her physical and digital field sites in a way that suited her research and answered her research questions. Her physical field locations were starting points that allowed her to access the activities of her research participants on and via the internet.

Our field research can surprise us and require us to develop our methodologies. The example of Burrell's research shows the need to change our research at the start of the research process. Later changes might also be needed and the use of digital tools can facilitate these adaptations. For example, management scholars Onajomo Akemu and Samer Abdelnour spent several years researching a Dutch start-up firm (Akemu & Abdelnour, 2018), researching the management of the company. They began by using participant observation of the company executives, through gaining access to board and senior management team meetings. However, the company grew at a fast rate and soon went through many office expansions and reconfigurations. Soon the firm was spread over multiple office locations and observation became a practical challenge. During their research up to this point, Onajomo and Samer had observed the importance of online meetings in company operations. They decided to adapt their methodology and began conducting observations of team members in online meetings as part of their research, claiming that otherwise they would have found their overview of the company's growth and strategy to be partial. These researchers therefore supplemented their physical fieldwork with the use of digital tools to allow their research to continue in light of changes in the geographical footprint of the case study company they were investigating.

Onajomo and Samer's research methodology reminds us that the people, organisations and communities we are researching are likely themselves using digital tools and environments, necessitating us to also engage in the digital. Burrell's example illustrates how we can move away from thinking of fieldwork as occurring within a particular, bounded location and that it may be essential to our research to consider not only a particular place, but also different ways in which people, information, things and practices move within and through these spaces. Remember too that the act of defining our field sites is a necessary methodological (and sometimes conceptual) process but it is both an act of exclusion and inclusion (as discussed in the ethics section of this chapter). These examples illustrate how we can use everyday digital technologies as field tools and field locations. The next section introduces the more advanced technologies of virtual, augmented and mixed reality and metaverse digital environments. We end this section with a postcard – by Korean geographer Minsung Kim – that illustrates how digital technologies can be used alongside more established fieldwork methods.

━━━ Postcard 10.1 ━━━

Renewing fieldwork traditions using digital techniques, by Minsung Kim

Digital devices and capabilities are opening up new and exciting possibilities for fieldwork. Sometimes digital fieldwork is entirely new; in other cases it builds upon existing traditions and techniques. We can learn from fieldwork traditions and from methods that have been tried and tested, but we need to renew and reinvent these traditions, especially when we are translating them from one place to another, and when we are working with new technologies. This postcard describes fieldwork in twenty-first-century South Korea, which takes inspiration from methods that originated in mid-twentieth-century Paris, while taking advantage of twenty-first-century technologies for recording and exploring sights and sounds in the field.

I set out to explore Yeongdo – an island south of Busan, the second largest city in South Korea – through a technique that originated in Europe in the 1950s: the psychogeographic walk or drift. Psychogeographers walk without a specific purpose. Walking provides an opportunity for embodied spatial understanding through interactions between the body and the environment.

I found myself in a village called Kangkangee, a place known for its industrial heritage in heavy industry. The word Kangkangee is onomatopoeic, evoking the hammering sounds of ship construction and repair work. Indeed, one of the first things that struck me there was the sound, loud and abrasive, which echoed around me. Wondering about the source of all this noise, I found the Tanaka Shipyard, and learned that this was Korea's first modern shipyard, still in operation. Walking behind the Tanaka Shipyard, I came across artworks inspired by the sounds and sights of industry: including a sculpture of a hammer and a mural depicting an industrial worker, a kangkangee woman (Figure 10.1).

Noticing these sounds and sights, I found myself repeatedly reaching for my phone, taking photos and recording sounds. This, I reflected, was something the original Situationists would not have done. Sound recording equipment and photography were both very different, much more cumbersome in 1950s Paris than in South Korea today. This got me thinking about the continuity and also the changes in fieldwork practices. We inherit traditions, and take inspiration from those who have gone before us, but we can also renew and reinvent these methods and ideas.

In particular, my psychogeographical practice introduces diverse digital tools and strategies. I took pictures, made short videos and recorded sounds. Now that I was using more of the tools available to me, I decided to play around with VR tools, PowerPoint and Illustrator programs, and with apps that might be helpful. I even found a smartphone application that would enable me to renew the exercise

Figure 10.1 Mural of an industrial worker, a kangkangee woman, Tanaka Shipyard, South Korea. Photograph by Minsung Kim

that early Situationists attempted when they attempted to navigate one city with a map of another: this app promised to help me get lost! In this way, I renewed a fieldwork tradition from another time and place to explore an area associated with Korea's industrial heritage, and I did so by working with the possibilities afforded by contemporary South Korea's advanced technology infrastructure.

Immersive Digital Fieldwork

In addition to the everyday digital environments, we can engage with, newer digital technologies such as augmented, virtual and mixed realities which are offering more immersive spaces. These use tools such as headsets, cameras, smart glasses, optical sensors, gloves and other bodywear to create digital, multisensory environments. Virtual reality (VR) is fully enclosed in a completely digital world that effectively deceives the human mind to believe it is located in a reconstructed reality. Augmented reality (AR) creates a digital information overlay on top of the real world, with the digital enhancing the real. Mixed reality (MR) allows interactions and manipulation of the physical and virtual worlds. Each type of reality provides different opportunities for research, creating potential field locations with varying degrees of interactivity. It is easy to see how AR and MR technologies can enhance physical fieldwork, enabling students to interact with places digitally while also being physically present. We can envisage more fieldwork of infuture in which digital technologies overlay the vision and hearing of students in physical field locations with topic-specific data and visuals. Imagine visiting Rome and having your experience augmented with overlays of the historic streets and buildings, sounds of the past and data informing you of what occurred over 2,000 years ago in the streets in which you are standing. Or visiting the New York stock exchange with your headset overlaying your vision with graphics showing the digital trade, the flows of capital in and out of the stock exchange. These imaginings are possible now, and we should see an increase in the number of students using these technologies in fieldwork.

Moving on from AR and MR, where the physical is integrated into the digital, the most immersive technology is virtual reality. Virtual reality is already being used as a research platform in many fields (Hubbard & Aguinis, 2023). These include psychology (Brummelman et al., 2022), linguistics (Peeters, 2020), medicine (Mahtab & Egorova, 2022), tourism and hospitality studies (Beck et al., 2019), marketing (Javornik et al., 2021) and others. Related to virtual reality is the 'metaverse' – the next generation of the internet and Web, where immersive, interconnected, shared and persistent 3D virtual spaces coexist (Caulfield, 2021). It utilises VR headsets, blockchain technology and avatars (a user-created digital representation that symbolises the user's presence in the metaverse) within a new integration of the physical and virtual worlds. The metaverse complements the real world in various ways with tasks (e.g., exploring remote areas, psychological treatment and training individuals for dangerous assignments like disaster recovery) that are difficult to do in reality (Dwivedi et al., 2022). While the possibilities for the enhancement of our experiences and interactions are seemingly endless, there are challenges around ethics, data security, regulation and reports of antisocial and undesirable behaviour in the metaverse (Jamison & Glavish, 2022).

The metaverse itself is the study of increasing academic attention, but its potential to provide locations in which to conduct fieldwork is not yet fully explored. Hubbard and Aguinis (2023) suggest that VR and the metaverse are a useful addition to the methodological toolkit for researchers and it is particularly valuable for examining phenomena that are poorly understood. This is because it can mimic real-world phenomena in a standardised and controlled environment. Using VR in the metaverse can create digital environments in which participants can be inserted to see how they actually behave in different situations, rather than collecting data on how participants report they might behave (Aguinis & Bradley, 2014). Examples could be conducting experiments to see how phenomena or situations change with adjustments made to the gender, ethnicity or age of the participants by modifying their avatars.

The immersive nature of these technologies means that the experience for the researcher can be intense and data capture can be challenging, although online interactions can be saved as digital records. As part of his 'netnography' method, Kozinets (2022: 107) recommends using an 'immersion notebook' – the digital equivalent of a physical field diary – that captures electronically mediated research experiences with the purpose of recording them. Different digital data collection methods could include in-depth interviews, saved online interactions between the researcher and other social actors or other interpersonal data collection methods such as digital diaries.

There are still relatively few studies upon which to draw insight on fieldwork using immersive digital methods. The primary use of immersive technologies in research is still in the hard sciences (particularly engineering and medicine). Within social research, studies are still limited by the cost and availability of the equipment and it is therefore not routinely available to students for fieldwork. We are likely on the tipping point of these technologies becoming more widely used in fieldwork and we can appreciate how and why we might use these technologies. The implications are exciting and challenging. Could immersive technologies render the international field trip obsolete? Could these technologies help reduce the ecological impact of fieldwork? Would research methodologies have to be adapted to these environments? Some of the ethical issues are already known and will be discussed in the ethical section below, following discussion of the use of immersive technologies in marketing (Postcard 10.2).

Postcard 10.2

Using immersive technologies to explore digital fields, by Ana Javornick

I have been working with immersive technologies for over a decade, using them to answer research questions across marketing, consumer behaviour and human–computer interaction. Immersive technologies come with their own challenges when it comes to conducting fieldwork, but also many opportunities.

In one of my recent projects, I studied the motivations that drive people to use augmented-reality (AR) filters on social media to understand why so many social media users choose to filter their selfies and stories that they post and share. The study was completely virtual, taking place in different digital fields: I conducted interviews with participants on Zoom and, as part of the interview, the interviewees were asked to show me on their phones what AR filters they used. In that sense I was able to enter their personal AR spaces. They were excited to explain which filters they preferred, why in some cases they are avoiding the beautifying filters and how they are using this virtual overlay to signal to their community what causes they support. It is so important to capture these interactions and uses as closely as possible. In this case, many details related to the use of the filters and associated motivations were uncovered only because the participants were directly showing me specific details. Observing the actual interactions thus adds an important value, which can remain hidden if people are only describing the experience without actually being in the virtual spaces.

Another project relates to the metaverse. My student observed how people in Roblox (a famous virtual environment) play games in a virtual space developed by the luxury brand Gucci. In order to be able to interview the participants, she first had to spend time in the field – Roblox – to develop

Continued

relationships with the members of the online community. Over time she gained their trust. Many were rather reluctant to participate in the research at first, because they typically adopt a very different identity when on Roblox and wish to protect their anonymity in this virtual space. My student had to find ways to reassure them that no one would be able to identify them if they participated in an interview. Eventually, we got many different insights, such as how multisensory aesthetics draw participants to explore such worlds and the social aspects including having fun (and sometimes competing) with other players.

Using immersive technologies for research is fun. For me, it has been an exciting journey in which I have had the opportunity to conduct numerous studies that showed how immersive technologies are changing the way people consume products and services and how they interact both with each other and with physical surroundings. When approached as fieldwork locations, these new realities are often sensorially very rich, so it is crucial for the researcher to carefully choose such environments that both they and participants feel comfortable in, are able to navigate quite intuitively and do not feel overwhelmed. It is also important to consider how much participants should be familiar with certain technologies, as completely new experiences might elicit a lot of excitement in the first instance, but that can fade away after continuous use.

Challenges of Digital Fieldwork

Digital fieldwork, although filled with exciting possibilities, also brings challenges. These include:

- delimiting the digital space/environment. Think carefully about what your digital field site is. Where does it begin and end? Why is it important for you to decide this? The almost limitless range of digital contexts and communities means that it might be difficult for you to contain your research within the parameters you have been set. This may be particularly challenging where the physical and virtual are blurring, and in expansive metaverse settings;
- when do you enter and exit the digital field? When we can access our field sites from our desks and/or mobile phones it can be harder to identify when the research process begins and ends and this is exacerbated when we engage with virtual environments, particularly immersive ones;
- which methods are most appropriate and do 'conventional' (non-digital) methods require adaptation? Often it is possible to collect and analyse your data in ways that are very similar to those you would use in physical spaces – the main difference being your method of communication is facilitated differently;
- recording your data may be more challenging as the combination of video and audio recordings, screenshots and messages may be a little overwhelming. A systematic way of recording this data will be needed (see also Chapter 14, Understanding and Handling Your Data).

Remember that some people and places are less well represented online than others. How do we reach communities that are under-served, under-resourced and under-represented? We need to be aware of who we are including and, crucially, who we might be excluding through our engagement in digital environments. This is particularly challenging for digital fieldwork as we are not always fully aware of exactly who we are engaging with, or the extent to which different voices can be heard in the spaces we inhabit online.

There are some physical spaces – most notably due to national regulations or lack of digital infrastructure – where internet use and access is restricted in particular ways, and not every subject is covered exhaustively online. Some online spaces are commercially owned, their data hidden behind paywalls and regulatory restrictions. The provision of internet infrastructure is still far from universal in global terms, rendering the world an uneven research landscape. As not all digital fieldwork takes place from a desktop at home or work, this has implications for students in terms of how and where you can conduct this kind of fieldwork.

How can we minimise exclusion – and conversely maximise inclusion and coverage – in our research? You should be aware of potential causes of exclusion and try to design your research to include multiple voices. This may require adoption of multi-method approaches such as combining digital and physical fieldwork, or conducting digital fieldwork across different platforms. We also need to step away from our own familiar engagement with digital environments to think more critically about where, how and why we are engaging with particular individuals and communities.

Ethics

Having outlined some of the challenges of digital fieldwork, we will now discuss the ethical considerations we should make. Psychologist Lynne Roberts encourages us to go beyond 'procedural ethics' to examine 'ethics in practice' (Roberts, 2015: 315). She identifies important areas that need to be considered when researching online communities.

- *Public/private space:* being able to identify whether spaces are public and private and, by association, what the expectations are of those individuals in those spaces. For example, individuals in a private space would typically have an expectation of privacy. Some researchers contend that even sites that require registration can be viewed as public spaces (e.g., Schotanus-Dijkstra et al., 2014). In immersive multisensory environments, such as the metaverse, unwanted and privacy-invasive content may be felt as more intrusive and is likely to have a greater negative impact on the users or victims (Dwivedi et al., 2022).
- *Authorship versus human research participants:* how can we conceive of the online data produced by individuals? There is some debate over whether the data should be conceptualised as human subject research and require ethical approval, or merely as secondary textual analysis. Are the producers of the data authors with associated copyright ownership? This raises questions about how the data is attributed and how material is quoted (offline

identity or pseudonym and/or specific naming of online communities). Social geographer Nadia von Benzon researched home education blogs (von Benzon, 2019) and reflected on the use and ownership of these blogs. She advocates for the use of online, publicly available data as this avoids putting a vulnerable person at risk of harm and demonstrates 'the utmost respect for the writer of the blog as "author"'(von Benzon, 2019: 186).

- *Anonymity and pseudonymity:* how to gain consent and protect individual identities. The use of pseudonyms, screen names, avatars etc. obscures our knowledge of who we are really talking to, often making gaining consent more difficult. To get around this you can use publicly available data (for example, on Instagram or Twitter) where consent is not required (although it is polite to obtain via a simple request and explanation of what you will be using the images/data for). Or you can negotiate access carefully over time and build up deeper knowledge of individuals to find out their real identities. If this occurs you then need to pay attention to how you will then protect those identities. Roberts (2015) encourages us to be sensitive to the preferences of research participants and actively discuss the preferred attributions of quotes. Do online pseudonyms or avatars require protection? It may be possible for others to link a pseudonym to an offline identity. Quotations should be anonymised and paraphrased and checked using search engines to make sure they are not traceable.

Gaining consent in digital fieldwork is an area that we will now discuss further. Informed consent is the term used to describe the processes researchers use to make sure research participants are informed about the study and the recording of those individuals' consent to participate. This involves the exchange of information – which is often much harder to do online where there are fewer opportunities for conversational explanations of formal documents (Salmons, 2021). Do users of online spaces care about consent to be researched? Computing researchers James Hudson and Amy Bruckman conducted research to test the attitudes of chatroom users to researchers' presence (Hudson and Bruckman, 2004). The researchers sent three types of messages to users in chatrooms: (1) a message only to inform the chatroom users of their presence as researchers; (2) a message with a provision for people to opt out of the research; and (3) a message with provision for people to opt into the research. The researcher was ejected from the chatroom within five minutes 63 per cent of the time (across all three message types), indicating that many online users do not deem research without consent to be acceptable. This sends us a clear message that consent is important and regardless of the digital space we are entering we should assume that we need to gain the consent of the community we are engaging with.

How do we gain informed consent when researching in digital environments? We must remember that consent processes can be less straightforward for online research. There are fewer opportunities for conversational explanations of formal documents. Education policy scholar J. Kessa Roberts and her team used virtual qualitative methods to study student homelessness in Huston, Texas, United States (2021). One of the key ethical considerations in their study they had to grapple with was how to obtain consent virtually. While obtaining consent via email is a typical way of replacing in-person consent, this team decided against this method as it does not allow for two-way conversation necessary to explain the research and for participants to ask questions in real time. Asking participants to return a written consent form prior to data collection can place burdens on participants and can require a printer and scanner/smartphone (Carter et al., 2021). Roberts and her team decided to use the Qualtrics survey platform as participants could electronically sign the form from multiple devices without specialised software. Participants either used their phones to sign at the start of the interview or used the device upon which they were conducting the interview. Public health scholar Stacy Carter and her team also emphasised the need to ensure that participants' digital literacy did not create barriers to participation, encouraging researchers to be flexible so methods suit participants' comfort and capabilities.

Just as the method of gaining informed consent is important, it is vital that we adapt the ways in which we explain our research in online environments. Table 10.2 highlights the key areas in which we should modify our consent information to acknowledge the specificities of online research.

Table 10.2 Key questions in online consent information

Conducting the study	Where can a potential participant learn about the researcher and verify that the study is legitimate? • Include links to credible information on the researcher(s) where possible – i.e., institutional webpages or blogs • Include information on the supervisor of the study if the researcher is a student
Recording interactions	How will interactions with the researcher be recorded, saved or archived online? • Note whether you will download original files of recordings, interview chat records or posts, and ensure they are safe from hacking or public release
Participant review or correction of information	Can participants review transcripts or recordings? • Make sure that participants have the digital skills to access the materials in the ways you have chosen to make them accessible • Be clear on procedures for participants to communicate any corrections
Participation	What does participation mean in terms of duration, time commitment and types of interactions? • If the interactions are part of a group, explain how the participants' individual identities will be protected • Explain what types of technologies will be used for communications with the researcher
Protecting confidentiality and anonymity	How to ensure confidentiality and anonymity of data collected online? Is personal information contained in metadata?

Source: Adapted from Salmons (2017: Table 1).

If you find it challenging to think through all the ethical aspects of conducting online research, don't despair as you are not alone. Scholars like Christine Hine (2015) and Nadia von Benzon (2019) have reflected on the incapacity of institutionalised ethics procedures to adequately contend with online research spaces. Where does that leave you? Our advice would be to pause, think and reflect. Take on board the advice given to you here, and from other sources, and while you are doing online research acknowledge the fundamental aim to do no harm. Nadia von Benzon (2019: 187) reminds us that what is key is the:

> necessity to ground our work in a personal ethics of care (Capurro and Pingel, 2002) that seeks to do no harm and to improve the lived experiences of those in positions of less power. The ways in which we might do this are, of course, as many and varied as the potential researchers and participants themselves.

Conclusion

At best, using digital fieldwork can open up new ways of accessing research environments and exciting means of interacting with participants. We can become immersed in digital spaces and draw out rich and plentiful data for our fieldwork. This chapter has highlighted the different ways in which we can conduct digital fieldwork, combining Big Data's bird's-eye view using resources like Google Earth with participant observation, in-depth interviews and textual analysis to provide thick descriptions and deep localised knowledge of social processes (Wang and Liu, 2021).

There are some challenges to, and limitations of, using digital fieldwork. A significant one can be how to shift your thinking as a digital user/consumer to that of a digital researcher. This involves consideration of digital spaces as research sites/environments, thinking about the kinds of data we can collect, how we collect the data, what ethical considerations we have to make and how to store and analyse the data. It is not as simple as delving into a digital space and coming out the other side with a completed research project. This chapter has provided some insight into how students can think about digital fieldwork and encourages you to consider how and why you can use digital methods in your research.

Key terms

Digital ethnography – using ethnographic methods to research digital cultures and societies online without the necessity to travel. Can also be referred to as 'virtual ethnography', 'netnography' or 'cyber-ethnography'.

Digital fieldwork – the collection of data from the digital environment.

Digital technologies – technologies such as mobile phones, digital television and radio, desktop computers, laptops, tablets and video recorders that can be used to access digital environments that are often connected to the internet. It also includes more advanced immersive technologies.
Immersive technologies – these technologies provide new ways of being immersed in, or enabling interaction with, simulated objects and environments, bringing together users' sight, sound and even touch. The technologies range from 360-degree photography and video to **augmented reality** (AR – a digital experience in which the real world remains central but enhanced with virtual details) and **virtual reality** (VR – a fully enclosed synthetic experience in a fully digital environment with no sense of the real world).

Further Reading

Salmons, Janet, E. (2021) *Doing Qualitative Research Online*, 2nd ed. Sage.
This book covers the general methodological discussions around researching online, taking the reader through designing online studies, conducting studies ethically and the collection and analysis of online data. It sits in complement to this chapter and is a valuable source if you want to explore the methodologies of online data collection in more detail.

Webb, Lynne (2017) Online research methods, qualitative. In Matthes, Jörg, Davis, Christine S. & Potter, Robert F. (eds.), *The International Encyclopaedia of Communication Research Methods*. Wiley-Blackwell.
A short and accessible chapter contribution to an encyclopaedia. It focuses on the kinds of data we can use from new media sources and covers some of the methods of qualitative analysis that can be used.

Lupton, Deborah & Watson, Ash (2021) Towards more-than-human digital data studies: Developing research-creation methods. *Qualitative Research*, 21(4): 463–480.
A challenging but fascinating insight into the new interdisciplinary field of critical data studies. Helen Lupton and Ash Watson suggest a 'more-than-human' approach to digital methodologies that elicit the affective and multisensory contexts of people's feelings, practices and imaginaries concerning their digital data. A suggested reading for those students who are keen to push the contemporary boundaries of digital fieldwork.

Hine, Christine (ed.) (2005) *Virtual Methods: Issues in Social Research on the Internet*. Berg.
This text offers detailed exploration of the problems and opportunities surrounding internet-based research. It uses case studies combined with methodological discussion to highlight the problems researchers face in conducting virtual research and offers solutions.

11
SOCIAL MEDIA FOR FIELDWORK

In this chapter you will learn

- about the different forms of social media that you can use for fieldwork;
- how to use social media for fieldwork data collection;
- to think about the different communities and individuals you can reach through social media;
- to explore the various ways you can use social media as an active researcher engaging with the field and disseminating your findings.

Introduction

Where does fieldwork begin and end? Social media is blurring the separation between being 'in' or 'out' of the field, creating exciting and challenging opportunities for us to engage with research in new ways. It forces us to reconsider how our traditional research methods fit in digital contexts. What does it mean to conduct ethnography or interviews using social media? This chapter will discuss different forms of social media and discuss how they may be used during fieldwork, often necessitating a fresh approach to be taken to the research methods chosen, adapting them from physically situated context to digitally mediated social contexts. This has implications for how to plan research, the timings of engagement with the social media field and how social media can be used to recruit research participants. This chapter will discuss how social media can be used as a powerful way to transcend the physical and virtual in fieldwork, how to plan for this and overcome the challenges it presents in data collection, analysis and dissemination. You may find it helpful to read this chapter alongside Chapter 10, Digital Fieldwork.

Insights

While many of us are familiar with several forms of social media and may well engage with them on a daily basis, it is worth pausing here to establish exactly what types of social media we are referring to and how they relate to fieldwork. Kaplan and Haenlein (2010: 61) define social media as 'a group of Internet-based applications that build on the ideological and technological foundations of Web 2.0, and that allow the creation and exchange of User Generated Content'. The user process is open as users do not need technical expertise to easily produce and publish content on the internet (Gretzel, 2017). However, some argue that definitions of social media can only be dynamic and context specific:

> Our understanding of social media is temporally, spatially, and technologically sensitive – informed but not restricted by the definitions, practices, and materialities of a single time period or locale. How we have defined social media in societies has changed, and will continue to change. (Papacharissi, 2015: 1)

The emergence of social media technologies has been embraced by a growing number of users who post text messages, pictures and videos online, creating rich environments for study. As discussed in Chapter 10, Digital Fieldwork, we can consider the spaces created by social media as potential field sites, opening up exciting opportunities for engagement with social media users and the collection of multimedia data. In her review of social media research, educational technologist Chareen Snelson (2016) notes that social media technologies have attracted substantial attention among many types of users, including researchers. Following review of all the social science research conducted using social media before 2016, she informs us that the most commonly used research approaches involve collecting data from people through interview, focus group and survey methodologies. Content analysis was the second most commonly used approach where researchers use social networking sites and other social media content as a data source.

There are disciplinary differences in the degree to which social media has been embraced by researchers, with psychology paying particular attention to the psychological traits of Facebook (Meta) users (see Błachnio et al., 2013; Caers et al., 2013; Nadkarni & Hofmann, 2012) and education examining the use of social media spaces by students and teachers (see Hew, 2011; Manca & Ranieri, 2013). Other disciplines contain examples of ground-breaking research using social media, some of which is referenced in this chapter, but there is still ongoing debate around how and why social media can be utilised for social science research and the degree to which traditional methods need to be adapted for application to social media contexts. For example, archaeologist Lisa Wescott Wilkins @LisaWWilkins used social media her desire for her discipline to better engage with its key audiences and stakeholders. She laments that archaeology has still not resolved to accept modern technologies and possibilities in research, fieldwork or welcoming innovation, viewing social media as superfluous to the 'real world', despite the significance of social media in recent events like the Arab Spring (see Figure 11.1).

In the following sections, we distinguish nine forms of social media, varying in the degree of interaction between users and in the types of information exchanged (see Table 11.1). Social media can be used in fieldwork in a number of different ways, ranging from using social media

SOCIAL MEDIA FOR FIELDWORK | 175

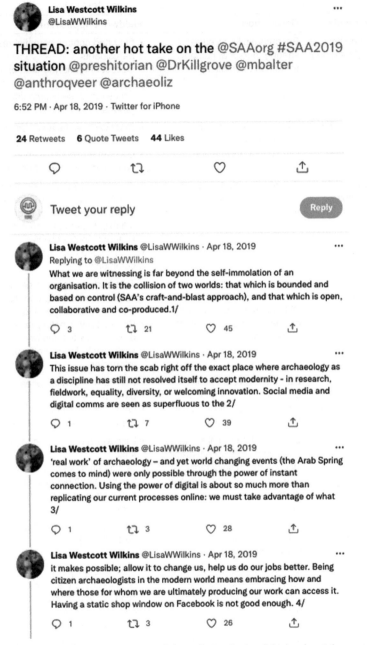

Figure 11.1 Lisa Wescott Wilkins uses social media to start a debate about the purpose of archaeology as a discipline

Table 11.1 Forms of social media and fieldwork, in order of greatest utility

Form of social media	Description	Fieldwork applications
Social networking sites, e.g., Facebook (Meta), (X), LinkedIn	Encourages knowledge sharing, personal human-to-human interaction	• Find and contact potential research participants • Collect and analyse data on different communities (may require gaining access to closed communities and groups)
Image and video sharing sites, e.g., Pinterest, Youtube, Vimeo	Users create, curate and share unique images that can spark conversation	• Discover images and videos related to your topic • Gain an audio-visual impression of your field before you begin fieldwork
Community blogs, e.g., Medium, Tumblr, Blogger	Space for users to express their thoughts and connect with readers	• Access to a range of opinions and insights on a topic (with the usual caveats about lack of peer review and reliability), not to be confused with academic publications • Identify and connect with different communities
Discussion sites, e.g., Reddit, Quora	A more anonymous forum than social networking sites. Different sub-communities discuss a wide range of often niche topics	• Find and engage with people interested in your research topic to discover what they are discussing (and how) • Conduct participatory research on the discussion sites and/or use to recruit participants for online focus groups/interviews
Online games communities, e.g., Second Life, Animal Crossing. Monster Hunter	Gamers form communities and social connections with other gamers. Interaction is focused on the game	• Source of potential research participants • Games form 'other worlds' that themselves can be a site of study
Social news, e.g., Digg, Reddit	Users post news links and other items to external articles. Users vote on said items, making those with highest votes most prominently displayed	• Discover news articles related to your topic • Textual analysis of the news articles • Insight into different user communities and their ranking of particular viewpoints
Bookmarking sites, e.g., Mix.com, Discuvver, Flipboard	Users can save and organise links to any number of online resources and websites	• Access resource generated by users on particular topics
Sharing economy networks, e.g., Airbnb, Kickstarter	Brings together people who have something to share together with people who need it	• A participatory approach may be required here that may be beyond the scope of your fieldwork due to financial resources required • Observation of social economy possible
Social review sites, e.g., Yelp, Tripadvisor, Foursquare	Reviews from community members for all kinds of locations and experiences First-person points of view	• Research your field in advance, explore topics that are being discussed by communities in that space • Review and analyse attitudes to products, services and/or activities

to explore field locations to gain formal and tacit knowledge in advance of entering the field, through to full immersion in social media to collect data, engage with communities and to disseminate findings. Social media can support your fieldwork, or it can be the whole focus of your fieldwork. There are many options for you to explore. For example, you could use social media to help you recruit participants. We discuss these options then focus on specific social media qualitative research methodologies. It then outlines ways to use social media to disseminate project findings and engage with fieldwork communities in meaningful ways.

Ethics

The relative youth of social media as a medium means that less attention has typically been paid to ethical issues of research using social media. As a result, it is important to pause to think about any ethical issues that may be specific to social media in relation to your fieldwork. If required, your university or college will advise you about ethics approval so this section concentrates on understanding how we might view the humans behind the post or avatar, and how we can use social media in fieldwork in ways that are sensitive to the people who have created it.

Most social media platforms require users to set their own privacy setting. This is an important indication to us about how they view their interaction with the world and we can respond accordingly with our research practices. Don't collect or disseminate information that you have accessed in environments that are not public unless you have express permission to do so from all individuals concerned. For example, if you join a private online community to conduct research be upfront and honest. Inform the community why you are there and what you will do with the data. Give all individuals the opportunity to opt out. Because the data we collect using social media is mediated through a computer or mobile screen it can feel distanced from the people behind it. This does not give us licence to think or behave unethically. In some instances, the individuals we are researching on social media can seem very real to us as they provide a wealth of rich and personal information using blogs, videos, photos. Remember too that this data should be treated sensitively. If in doubt, ask permission.

Another ethical consideration to make is regarding the anonymity of social media. Individuals are likely to not be using their offline identities. We discuss the ethical implications of this in Chapter 5, Ethical Fieldwork, and Chapter 10, Digital Fieldwork, and pay greater attention to consent across digital environments in general. Table 11.2 explores ethical issues in social media in more detail.

A common theme running throughout all chapters in this book regards the ethics of fieldwork and the avoidance of harm to those individuals with whom we interact during our research and ourselves. This applies to digital platforms, for example Facebook. In her research in Indonesia, Isabelle Côté notes that Facebook is the most widely used social media application in Indonesia with over 129 million users, nearly 62.5 per cent of the population (Statista Research Department, 2022). As her postcard (Postcard 11.1) outlines, this presented opportunities and challenges for her research.

Table 11.2 Ethical considerations for social media research

1. Sound application and conduct of social research methods

- Social media techniques/data should be the most appropriate method to use to answer the research questions and not used on any other basis
- Methods should be used professionally and appropriately
- As social media methods often make use of existing, publicly available data, the burden on respondents can be reduced. However, researchers should consider the implications of using existing data on ensuring data is robust and valid
- Where appropriate, researchers should make details of their project publicly available, including the research purpose and the data being used

2. Participation based on informed consent

- The terms and conditions which users agree to when signing up to a social media platform may cover the use of their data for research. While this can provide a legal gateway, researchers should consider whether specific research projects reasonably meet user expectations of the collection, analysis and use of their data
- If individual informed consent is sought, researchers should consider appropriate ways to contact users
- Users can post data to social media platforms and subsequently delete it. If that data has been retrieved by a researcher before deletion, it is not clear whether the user's initial consent for their data to be used remains intact. Depending on the sensitivity of the data and analysis researchers should agree up front how to manage this issue

3. Enable participation

- Certain groups are more likely to use social media than others and significant differences can exist between social media platforms. Researchers should consider whether any groups are being inappropriately excluded given the nature of the research questions. Actions to enable participation where possible (e.g., collecting data through a number of different platforms)

4. Avoidance of personal and social harm

- Researchers must consider privacy settings to understand whether data is public or private. Any research involving private consent should only be conducted with explicit informed consent from the user
- The collection of unnecessary personal data should be minimised. This could include limiting the amount of information collected or stripping out personal or irrelevant data after collection

5. Non-disclosure of identity

- There can be no guarantee of full anonymity within social media research. Aggregated findings may provide anonymity but any raw data will not be anonymous even if stripped of the author field as the content could be searched for online. In addition, removing the author field may be problematic with some social media platforms – you should check the terms of use of the platforms you are drawing from.
- It may be possible to 'mask' content by altering the content so that the meaning is maintained but it is not traceable back to the source but it is unlikely this will guarantee anonymity. There is a trade-off here between accurately quoting what was said and by whom, for academic scrutiny
- If researchers wish to use verbatim content, they should consider contacting social media users to ask them if they would be happy for their content to be cited. Make sure to build in time to address this in your fieldwork.

Source: Adapted from GSR (2016: 16–18).

---------- **Postcard 11.1** ----------

Do no harm? Social media and the ethics of fieldwork, by Isabelle Côté

As I went out to discover the neighbourhood where I was staying in Indonesia, the chants of 'You, Facebook? You, Facebook?' welcomed me nearly everywhere. This was not surprising given how widespread use of the platform is there. In themselves, those impromptu social media friendship requests posed little problems as most people simply wanted to befriend someone from abroad or practise their English. As a researcher, they also yielded important benefits. Social media helped me recruit participants (and even research assistants!) and provided me with unequalled access to a huge pool of information that would have otherwise remained outside my reach as a non-local (i.e., non-insider). It also allowed me to gain – and maintain – participants' trust long after I left the proverbial 'field'.

But as I quickly came to realise, whether or not to engage with my participants on social media sites raised important – though still largely unaddressed – ethical issues that ran the risks of compromising my ability to uphold the 'do no harm' principle guiding all academic research.

For instance, some participants in my study sent me a Facebook request after I interviewed them. While it is not new for ethnographic researchers to maintain a connection with their participants after their study is completed, the fact that such interactions are now taking place on a visible public platform could potentially jeopardise participants' confidentiality and anonymity. Such risks are particularly high for vulnerable populations, like the members of local ethnic minority groups I interviewed.

What if psychological or legal harm is inflicted to a participant due to what they write on my 'wall'? What if a potentially controversial – and anonymised – statement included in my research is traced back to an individual due to our interactions on social media? Is it the researcher's responsibility to remind participants of the risks these virtual post-study interactions may bring on them, even if it is the participants who chose to post such comments or to seek the researcher's 'friendship' in the first place?

While this has fortunately not affected me and my research participants (yet), these dilemmas are no longer mere ethical conjunctures. Under Indonesia's 2008 ITE Law, an individual who allegedly posts defamatory statements on the internet can be imprisoned and/or fined. Shortly after completing my fieldwork in Indonesia, an Indonesian civil servant who had denied the existence of God on his Facebook page – that is, a violation of Indonesia law according to Pancasila, the founding principle of the country – was sentenced to two-and-a-half years in prison and fined the equivalent of then US$10,600. But this was not a unique case as dozens of individuals have been prosecuted.

Researchers who intend to use social media in their fieldwork need to be informed about and reflect on the risks such a decision entails, keeping their specific region and population of studies in mind. Whether or not to engage with participants on social networking sites and whether or not limits to privacy and confidentiality exist on social media are questions that need to be better addressed by researchers in the ethics review process. And yet, despite raising important ethical challenges to social scientists, social media's sky-rocketing growth and the methodological potential mentioned above makes it a 'beast' well worth taming.

Using Social Media in the Field

The characteristics of social media that make it conducive to social science research include its potential as a participant recruitment platform, its reach into particular demographics and the access it provides to data on behaviours, attitudes and perceptions (McCay-Peet and Quan-Haase, 2017). Social phenomena such as involvement in social movements, charitable giving and political participation and consumption can be examined through an analysis of social media data. For example, sociologist Tressie McMillan Cottom used Facebook to research the experiences of black female scholars doing online PhDs as part of her work on black cyberfeminism. In her research she found that her target population didn't tend to have open social media profiles so she had to negotiate access to closed Facebook groups which had been pre-screened 'the group moderator [of one group], Janice, said that she used Facebook profile pictures to screen potential new members' (McMillan Cottom, 2017: 220). We will address the issue of public and private social media profiles later in the chapter. The general point remains – social media platforms can be a way for students to navigate identities that are more complex than single analytical frames like race, class, gender and sexuality can fully capture.

— Try this —

Think of a research topic that interests you. It could be based on a course you've taken, from a book you've read or a conversation you've had. Identify three or four keywords. Use the keywords to search for content on a social media platform of your choice. What kinds of results does it generate after a five-minute search? Depending on the platform you are using the results could be social media posts, links to news articles, reshared data and facts, photographs and videos, press releases and many more. How much of the content is relevant? The art of using social media in research is to learn how to categorise, validate and prioritise different types of data so you don't get lost in it all.

When using social media in fieldwork students should remember that it can help us to identify and research different social contexts. Social context refers to the social, political, economic, work and personal phenomena or characteristics that underlie users' social networks within social media sites, including the size and nature of these local and global networks (e.g., a small, close-knit peer group; a large, diffuse network of social activists) (McCay-Peet and Quan-Haase, 2017). There is an issue of scale – social media can expand our research horizons. It also creates some challenges for us around how to find, access and engage with different research contexts. When thinking about fieldwork, there are three key aspects to consider – access and recruitment, placing social media research and how to combine social media with traditional methods.

Accessing Research Communities Using Social Media

As suggested above, a compelling characteristic of social media research is its ability to make finding and accessing different communities comparatively easy. This does, however, vary according to the types of community that we are seeking to gain access to. When seeking to explore the challenges faced by foreign direct investors in the South African banking sector, management researcher Efrider Maramwidze-Merrison struggled to get access organisational elites, due in part to their use of subordinate staff to screen contacts and Maramwidze-Merrison's lack of deep enough personal network connections to the sector. In response, she developed an 'online social and professional media window access strategy' (Maramwidze-Merrison, 2016). Maramwidze-Merrison used social network tools such as LinkedIn and Facebook to identify and initiate a professional relationship and to facilitate direct communication in approaching research participants. It was more successful than her earlier efforts to contact individuals via their office phone numbers or emails.

Maramwidze-Merrison's example shows that social media can be used in the initial stages of fieldwork to identify research participants and gain access and can be particularly helpful where geographical distance prohibits personal network connections. Many of us use social media platforms in this way, but it is important to acknowledge this use and to note it in our methodologies. In their research on politicians in Australia, Canada, South Africa, the United Kingdom and the United States, Alex Marland and Anna Lennox Esselment (2019) suggest that researchers should tailor their approach when placing interview requests to elected officials and make careful use of email, websites, social media and online reputation management. Finding gatekeepers willing to make contacts and referrals was essential to their research. They argue that researchers are not making full use of social media resources, recommending that we start the research process by broadcasting our research plans using our own social media to start making connections. This is a reminder that engagement with social media is two-way – you can both use social media to find participants *and* to 'advertise' your fieldwork.

These social media-informed ways of accessing research participants can occur when entering the field and while in the field. In addition to approaching organisational elites, we can also consider social media as an important tool in reaching permanently or temporarily displaced communities. Anthropologist Julia Gerster used social media to conduct ethnographic research in North East Japan after the March 2011 earthquake, tsunami and nuclear disaster. She used Facebook as a tool to build rapport and enact reciprocity in her research and claims that this gave her research informants agency at a time when they were particularly vulnerable (Gerster, 2018). Similarly, Noomi Weinryb, Nils Gustafsson and Cecilia Gullberg analysed Facebook groups to understand the use of money – how it was communicated and accounted for – in emotional and rationalised ways by refugees on the island of Lesbos. Access to these groups provided data and the basis for their focus group interview questions (Weinryb et al., 2021).

You can use social media to contact communities that may be hard to reach because they are scattered across the globe or less visible. One of the key appeals of social media is its large user numbers (often in the millions or even billions), but a key consideration for the researcher is how to find the particular populations needed for research – considerable reduction in those numbers will be needed for typical qualitative fieldwork research. Think then about how to access the specific individuals relevant to your research and don't overlook sources such as online video games. Telehealth researchers Saira Haque and Jodi Swicegood used Second Life – a virtual world where individuals represent themselves through avatars – to recruit research participants with chronic conditions to support the design and implementation of targeted health interventions. At the time of their research, in 2013, Second Life had over 29 million registered users and some communities had arisen organically to support users of these conditions, many of whom are housebound due to their conditions. The researchers were able to gain access to a more diverse pool of research respondents than traditional methods offer (Haque & Swicegood, 2013).

You may want to pause and reflect on your own engagement with social media. Think about the platforms you use (if you do) and the different types of people you are connecting with. If a researcher were to view your social media presence, what do you think it might say about you and your life? If you don't have a social media presence, why not? You might want to think about what the implications of this are for your own research – it helps us to acknowledge that not everyone accesses social media and those that do use it in very different ways. We will be likely to view social media, and our own activities using it, differently when we start to consider it a research tool.

Placing Social Media Research

The digital world should not be considered as separate from the non-digital (as we explain in Chapter 10, Digital Fieldwork). On the contrary, social media can 'amplify social phenomena' that exist in other spheres (McCay-Peet and Quan-Haase, 2017: 11). In fieldwork, this challenges students to negotiate the digital and, often physical, environments in which research is being conducted. Hjorth and Hinton (2019) note that the recognition that online experiences were grounded in real-world settings led to what they term an 'ethnographic shift' in internet studies. They cite Daniel Miller and Don Slater's (2000) study of the use of internet by Trinidadians, which considered the ways in which their internet intersects with other (offline) cultural activities. Miller and Slater stressed that the internet is 'embedded' within specific places, 'which it also transforms' (Miller and Slater, 2000: 21; see also Hu et al., 2013; Hochman et al., 2014). Thus, the seemingly infinite and placeless digital realm is actually far from unrooted in place, and social media is no different. Cultural studies researcher Nadav Hochman (2016) argues that, far from placeless and abstract, social media tends towards hyperlocality, revolving around tightly focused geographic niches and communities (Metzgar et al., 2011).

While social media can be a vehicle for fieldwork, it can also be a topic for research. Exemplifying the latter, Nadav Hochman investigated a social media campaign, linked to an art installation by the British artist Banksy in New York. Banksy installed works at different locations in the city and online. With his tacit encouragement, information about each location spread online. Banksy's own posts – on Instagram – were amplified by those of followers, who posted with a special hashtag: #banksyny. In many cases, the only way to detect the location of the physical works was to search for their earlier representations online, posted via the #banksyny hashtag (Hochman, 2016: 370).

As you conduct your fieldwork, we encourage you to identify forms of social media that suit the geographical scale of your enquiries. You can find meaningful signals in the noise of social media streams, either through your own search and analysis, or through the use of digital tools. For example, there are tools that can automatically extract and summarise hyperlocal information about events, topics, people and places from social media posts (Hu et al., 2013). There are also narrowly bounded place-specific social media platforms, such as the Nextdoor social network for users living in houses in contiguous neighbourhoods and the Tripadvisor website for travellers and consumers of services. Not only situated in particular spaces – from the local to the global – these platforms also construct representations of these spaces. Sociologist Trevor Jamerson, investigating travel and social media, concluded that both the content and the form of the Tripadvisor platform reproduces contemporary discourses about racial difference (Jamerson, 2017). He notes that the reviews posted on Tripadvisor constitute a contemporary version of a much older narrative form – the traveller's tale – which is heavily implicated in the ways Western construction of social, cultural, gendered, racial and ethnic types of 'otherness' are formed (Said, 1978).

> TripAdvisor is the world's largest travel-related social media site. It exemplifies what Henry Jenkins (2006) calls a 'convergence culture' where different types of media – in this case, the traveller's tale and digital social media – converge to create a new type of media culture. (Jamerson, 2017: 120)

Students should therefore be aware that while social media platforms are comparatively new, the activities that are mediated through them are often replicating older and more entrenched perspectives. For this reason it can be effective to combine data collected using social media with other methodologies. Social media research is narrow and exclusively digital but may also be integrated with other methods, both physical and digital. Some examples of mixed-methods fieldwork, conducted by established researchers, can guide and inspire us to attempt similarly hybrid fieldwork ourselves. Justine Gangneux combines the use of Facebook activity logs and search history as digital probes during interviews. She notes that there is a long tradition of using digital and non-digital artefacts – such as photographs, videos, graphics, maps and diaries – as probes in qualitative research to elicit discussion and encourage participants to reflect on their lives and past experiences (Gangneux, 2019: 1252). Meanwhile, marketing researchers Jan Brace-Govan and Vlad Demsar combined interviews and digital ethnography to examine the phenomenon of video game trade-in, where gamers exchange products. Their research included interviews with participants selected through online forums and gaming communities (Brace-Govan & Demsar, 2014), but also included immersive participant observation in online gaming.

Challenges of Social Media Research

The use of social media in research can be exciting and feels contemporary. We hope that this chapter inspires you to engage with social media and integrate it into your fieldwork. However, as with all research methods, there are some perils and downsides to be aware of. First, we should question the reliability of factual data presented in social media, just as we do with all non-academic sources that are not peer reviewed. This is part of your existing academic skillset, so utilise it to question the origin of facts and check them out. For example, track back the sources of factual statements where possible to reveal their origins and make a judgement call about their reliability. Remember also that much social media data, certainly qualitative data, is highly personalised and opinion-based, so not 'reliable', but this doesn't matter if you are seeking lived experiences in your fieldwork research.

Second, students need to be mindful of some of the perils of using social media to reach fieldwork participants. Nursing scholar Margaret Salinas used social media to recruit participants for a survey on the experiences of older adults in the United States who live alone. She used Amazon Mechanical Turk, Facebook groups and email distribution lists to recruit older adults. Of 738 recorded participants, 117 responses were retained in the final sample (Salinas, 2023). Salinas identified many fraudulent survey takers and reflected on the use of social media in recruitment. A strong protocol for identifying non-credible responses using the IP address (to make sure multiple attempts haven't been made), longitude and latitude (to make sure the respondent is from the target location/country), completion time (too fast is suspicious) and nonsensical or conflicting answers (may indicate that a 'bot' has answered the survey) helped her identify fraudulent participants (Bell et al., 2020). Salinas concluded that, while using social media can initially seem like a great way to access large numbers of people, she was more successful when she used a snowball approach involving individuals and organisations sending the link to other people they knew who met the survey criteria. This resulted in only one survey being discarded for incomplete data and no surveys were flagged as suspicious. This was supported by the work of Chambers et al. (2020) who found snowball recruitment to be more successful than social media. For them, Facebook advertisement generated thousands of clicks, but zero participants (Chambers et al., 2020).

Students should be aware that while social media can help you reach people, you should also take time to think about what that means for your fieldwork and the methods you use. A balanced approach may be needed in which you use social media to expand your available pool of potential research participants or, better yet, use it to recruit a known group of human research participants. This means you will have greater certainty about who is engaging with your fieldwork and why.

Third, be aware of the 'fake news' that spreads rapidly through social media. Vosoughi et al. (2018) compared the differential diffusion of over 126,000 verified true and false stories through social media. They found that false stories spread much faster, further and more broadly than true new stories did. The appropriation of others' voices (ranging from debates on social media about the 'stealing' of posts, through to more serious replication and modification of work by people other than the original authors), is another concern, as well as the tendency for social media networks to connect like-minded individuals. Social media networks can be made up of 'people like us'; when we follow others' networks we will see a replication in opinions and viewpoints.

Social media can often acutely reflect social divisions, be they around responses to a global pandemic or political changes like Brexit (the withdrawal of the United Kingdom from the European Union in 2020) or war. For many social media users, 'engagement' can feel like speaking into an echo chamber, getting back the same opinions. It is important to acknowledge this when we act as researchers using social media. Public policy and data science researcher Chris Bail reminds us that academic research on political polarisation often fails to acknowledge the extent to which social media can reflect and distort people's attitudes (Bail, 2021). Media anthropologist Sahana Udupa conducted research on the digital practices of right-wing Hindu nationalist volunteers in India. She combined interviews and observations with content analysis of online texts to show the online assembling of facts, figures and treatises as an ideological exercise by net-savvy 'non-expert' volunteers. For Shana, this practice of 'online archiving' constitutes a distinct politics of history-making which she views as religion's interface with cyberspace and one of the varied ways in which online users participate in religious politics. 'Online archiving for religious politics offers a sobering, and even troubling, picture of the digital commons, and unsettles some of the universalist claims underlying much celebrated user-generated content' (Udupa, 2016: 212). Be wary. Social media is not a neutral platform.

Using Social Media as a Research Dissemination Tool

We live in an age where the sharing of research findings and ideas is no longer confined to people with access to academic libraries or scientific journals. Social media have permitted knowledge and ideas to be shared with unprecedented speed and magnitude (Dijkstra et al., 2018). This is relevant to students wishing to get their fieldwork findings 'out there'. There is an increasing literature on how academics can use social media to disseminate their findings, increase and improve their professional networks and link to other research institutes and universities, and some research on how social media can improve communication between teaching staff and students. However, there is less specific guidance on how students can use social media. This section will outline some of the ways students can use social media when in the field.

Before you enter the field explore the social media platforms most relevant to your topic and field location. Begin to form a mental map of how that place is represented on different social media platforms and who the key people and organisations are. Start following those people on social media, request notifications for updates to relevant blogs. Think about how social media can help you with the planning of your research (discussed in Chapter 3, Curiosity and Research Design). How can it support your identification or approach of potential research participants or communities? Pause to think about how to communicate your research in lay terms. Write a one-page summary of your research plans that is stripped of academic terminology and concepts (it is harder than you might think to do this, it feels like undoing years of education, but it is an important skill to learn how to communicate your ideas to a wider audience). In this summary explain what you will be doing and why. What is the context? Why is the research important now and in this place? What problems are you solving? What questions are you answering? Include details on what you will ask of research participants and include your contact details. You now have a short, accessible summary that you can distribute to potential research participants. The next step is to crystallise this one step further to produce a short, three- or four-sentence summary to publicise your research on your own social media networks. If you want to keep your work and private identities separate, create a work-focused social media profile.

During the research process the ways in which you use social media may vary according to the research methods you have chosen. If you are researching an aspect of social media itself you may well be very active during the research stage, using social media to connect to research participants, to observe, to engage with them. If you are relying on offline methods, take heed of the advice in the sections above about using social media to reach particular communities in research. It is likely social media will inform your data collection process.

Remember that the research process is not completely linear. As soon as you begin to collect data you can start to disseminate initial findings back to your research communities. This is more engaged and responsive. It can accelerate your research as awareness of the project increases and some of the fruits of your labours become apparent. These findings should be in lay terms, easily accessible and short. Summarise some of the things that strike you as important and get short statements out there, using social media, blogs etc. Don't cite academic literature, feel liberated to write snappy, relevant pieces that will spark wider interest. Manage your expectations as to the engagement you will get with this initial dissemination and don't feel disheartened if your summaries get fewer likes or shares than the photos of your puppy you posted the week previously. It is all part of a process, and this is the start of the research dissemination journey. You aren't speaking into a void and are likely to receive comments on your work that can help shape the direction of your fieldwork in real time. The immediacy of social media becomes a great asset, particularly when we are conducting time-pressured fieldwork.

After you have completed your fieldwork you can use social media as a way to fill any gaps in data collection. You may be able to do some online interviews or conduct more analysis of an online community once you have left the field. Be aware that once you have started a social media presence and established a social media network with key individuals, organisations and your research participants, it can be hard to identify when we 'leave' the field. Our digital footprint remains and we also have an obligation to try to feed back our full findings to those who gave us their time in the research project. Think about the ways in which you want to distribute the findings and how you will respond to comments (and possibly criticisms). A couple of longer blog posts may be appropriate, rather than a copy of your academic work which may be dry and less accessible to the community or individuals you studied. Explain what you have done and summarise your findings. Discuss the implications for them and/or society in general. You may also wish to talk about what you hope might come of the research. Find out if your academic institution has a social media channel(s) and use them to help publicise your research. Regardless of your stage in academia, it is highly likely that your research will generate relevant and interesting research that has meaning for wider society.

The following postcard – by Pamela Richardson – illustrates the potential to use social media as a vehicle for fieldwork. It describes a remotely facilitated (online) digital storytelling and participatory video making, which used the communication platform WhatsApp to work together.

Postcard 11.2

Digital storytelling: Building feminist solidarities through a women's WhatsApp story circle, by Pamela Richardson

In 2021, the leaders of a capacity-building programme in Zimbabwe – 'Women Are Medicine' – reached out to me. Their programme involves bringing women together from different communities to train in leadership, facilitation and project management skills, then supporting them to establish 'women's circles' in their own communities. This project was interrupted by the COVID-19 pandemic, which prevented participants and facilitators from meeting in person. This called for other ways of working together.

This project involving women in rural southern Africa faced particular challenges. Women in Zimbabwe are less likely than their male counterparts to travel the distances required to access stable internet connection. This is partly a reflection of caregiving responsibilities, which make it harder for women to travel to find a signal. Given these practical constraints, the women involved in the project needed to work with an accessible communication platform. We opted for WhatsApp, which has relatively low data usage and connectivity requirements and can be used for asynchronous communication. As it is already widely used by participants, it was the most appropriate option for hosting the online workshop series.

At the programme leaders' invitation, I recruited a team of other women (two Zimbabwean and one British) to support me to co-facilitate what we called a 'digital story circle'. Aware of the postcolonial dynamics of such an arrangement, the Zimbabwean co-facilitators ensured that English-language messages were translated and that participants were supported to tell their stories in their own languages and in their own way, to each other. The participants received free data bundles. Over a

Continued

period of two to three months, 23 workshop participants created audio and video stories, sharing experiences from their different communities. Each week, we hosted a live, half-day workshop on WhatsApp. We started with structured discussions around our various hopes and then co-created group rules. Each session, a strong emphasis was put on paying attention to how we listen (especially in our context of connection across distance and time).

Over the weeks, we covered topics of storytelling, camera handling, shot types, storyboards, ethics and video editing. The common story prompt that everyone was asked to respond to was: 'tell a story about a positive change you have personally observed or experienced in your community, as a result of women coming together'. Participants recorded voice-notes and listened to each other's stories, watched each other's video clips and gave each other feedback, using the WhatsApp 'groups' function. Texts, emojis, voice-notes and video clips flowed and multiplied.

It must be said that initially I had been REALLY sceptical about using WhatsApp to host a 'participatory' learning circle. Personally, I often multitask with WhatsApp, respond late and in 'text-speak'; I was worried that perhaps we would ALL behave (rather rudely!) like this and only give half our attention to the learning group. However, I was surprised by the level of group engagement and interaction, and the genuine sense of connection that I experienced. Sharing personal stories, we learned about each other's life experience, reaching beyond our most immediate objectives. Working together and finding new ways to listen to each other, we developed empathy and solidarity, found friendship and joy, and developed and shared practical and technical skills.

Participatory, digital storytelling and video methods, involving accessible communication platforms such as WhatsApp, are increasingly feasible for students conducting fieldwork on a low budget and over relatively short periods of time.

Conclusion

Academic researchers are beginning to catch up with the rapid rise in the use and scope of social media, developing new methodologies like digital ethnography and adapting traditional methodological approaches to allow social media to be used as a research tool. At best, social media can enable fieldwork to be more immersive, allowing the research new insights into a wide range of topics. It can also be an important supporting tool in the suite of research environments open to the researcher. It offers you an exciting opportunity to use social media in new ways, to push the boundaries of existing practice to gain the answers to your research questions.

There are some challenges and limitations of social media in research, requiring us to pause and think more deeply about what we are researching, how and why. Social media is not likely to be a useful tool if we are researching marginalised communities with reduced or no access to the internet, for example. Nor is it always the best way to tackle personally sensitive topics. We also need to think about where the research is taking place – that is, how we identify/delimit the 'field', the ethical implications of conducting research on social media and how we can best use social media to engage with the community/individuals/organisations we are researching.

Key terms

Digital ethnography – an adaptation of ethnography for the online world that allows us to study social media that is also termed 'netnography'. Specific practices include locating communities and topics and analysing digitally contextualised data.

Social media – a group of internet-based applications that enable the sharing of user-generated content. The term covers social networking, review, image and video sharing sites, community blogs, discussion sites and sharing economy networks.

Further Reading

Hill, Craig A., Dean, Elizabeth & Murphy, Joe (eds.) *Social Media, Sociality and Survey Research*. Wiley & Sons.
This book is organised around social media interactions that are either broadcast, conversational or community-based – a conceptual framework that may be of interest to the more advanced student. While it is focused on the use of surveys, it contains some useful contemporary chapters for students – on social media and virtual interviewing, diaries and recruitment, for example.

Hjorth, Larissa & Hinton, Sam (2019) *Understanding Social Media*, 2nd ed. Sage.
An interesting book that explores the diversity of complex social media practices, cultures and industries that have emerged over recent years. It is worth reading if you are thinking of researching social media as a topic, but also contains some interesting examples of research methodologies using social media, including work on location-based mobile gaming, emojis, selfies and surveillance practices.

Sloan, Luke & Quan-Hasse, Anabel (eds.) (2017) *The Sage Handbook of Social Media Research Methods*. Sage.
An accessible book that covers some foundational issues for those new to social media research, as well as extending into more complex forms of research. It covers the conceptualisation and design of social media research, how to collect and store social media data, quantitative and qualitative approaches to social media research. Later chapters cover research and analytical tools and examine a range of different social media platforms.

12
MULTISENSORY AND EMBODIED FIELDWORK

In this chapter you will learn

- why it is important – and sometimes creative and original – to use all of your senses in fieldwork;
- how and why it is important to pay attention to other people's sensory experiences;
- how to collect, represent and interpret multisensory data in the field;
- how a wide range of fieldwork is (already) embodied and why this matters.

Introduction

This chapter does two things. First, it shows us how all the senses and the ways in which they interact can be useful in fieldwork: in collecting, representing and interpreting data. This applies to both physical and virtual fieldwork; although we don't physically enter a digital site, we can't do virtual fieldwork without our bodies (Ellingson, 2017). We provide practical suggestions to help students get started at and better in **multisensory fieldwork**. Second, this chapter also encourages and guides you to become more conscious of the ways in which you are already using your body in the fieldwork you do. You can benefit from being more conscious of this – more reflexive about it.

Though multisensory and **embodied fieldwork** practice involves more conscious use of your own body in fieldwork, this is not all about you. This approach can also help you to understand more about other people and how they experience events, encounters, relationships and predicaments in their lives. In this way, multisensory and embodied fieldwork can be a form of creative, innovative and original social research.

Insights

Multisensory fieldwork promises two kinds of insight. First, by using all of your senses you stand to develop fuller pictures of human experience (Crang, 2003; Zardini, 2005; Rodaway, 1994; Cowan and Steward, 2007; Degen, 2008). Sensory fieldwork enables you to see more of the social world, which people can't or won't put into words. Visual sources and methods are an important first step, countering 'disembodied' social science research methods (Thanem and Knights, 2019; see also Leigh and Brown, 2021). But the visual is the most detached of all the senses, tending to separate and distance the observer from the observed, the thing or people they are investigating, and missing crucial messages. Seeing a street but not hearing or smelling it, we miss much of the human experience of that place, the smells of bodies or engines, food or refuse; the sounds of traffic and vendors; the feel of the surfaces and textures that make life harder or easier for a person with a wheelchair or skateboard.

Our senses work together. We lean in to smell a flower we have seen; we taste more of a berry we can smell. Sensing the world, being immersed in it, we come to see it better, but are also provoked to ask further questions about it. Educational philosopher Mark Zuss explains that 'questions arise from the filaments of our senses' (Zuss, 2012: 122). For this to happen, we need to listen to our bodies and become attuned to the particular sounds, smells, tastes and textures of the world around us, the people and things we encounter (Phillips, 2015). We need to learn – or remember – to use our senses in particular ways. A doctor must learn to read an x-ray chart that remains inscrutable to the patient; a connoisseur or sommelier must work equally hard before they can detect and articulate the qualities of a wine that most others can only say is 'nice'. Equally, in our first attempt to hear and then name or describe a sound or smell, many of us may struggle, though practice will help as will learning from those who have developed and practised fieldwork involving these senses.

A second insight revolves around understanding how much of what we have already been doing in the field involves the body as an instrument – in other words, this research is 'embodied'. If, as the phenomenologist Maurice Merleau-Ponty (2013, first published in 1945) argued, we understand the world through our bodies (Thanem and Knights, 2019: 28), then it is better that we should become conscious of this and that we should understand the implications. Sometimes we try to ignore the messages our bodies are sending. Reflecting on her first day conducting research for a new topic, mental health researcher Hester Parr (2001) recounts a feeling that many fieldworkers will recognise but also remember trying to suppress: her 'stomach churned'. After a similar experience – feeling nervous before a first interview – management studies professor Torkild Thanem reflected that if we listen to our bodies we can learn from them. Students who have participated in field trips that force them to walk further or faster than they are comfortable doing, or to be out of range of a suitable toilet, have another appreciation of how fieldwork is embodied. Struggling to walk or desperate for the toilet, they may feel embarrassment and pressured to fit into fieldwork that is stacked against them (Rose, 1993; Rose, 2020). We develop these points in Chapter 4, Working Together (also covering travelling), particularly in the section on disability.

Other fieldwork is embodied in more mundane ways – accepting a coffee while conducting an interview, for example. Sometimes the physicality of fieldwork is pleasurable, even exhilarating, as in the adrenaline-fuelled urban exploration and parkour described by cultural geographer Bradley Garrett (2013; see also Bennett, 2013). Through the limitations of our stomachs and nerves, our limbs and bladders, and sometimes through more comfortable or exciting bodily sensations, we can understand more of how 'people live, work and interact with their bodies within the social world' (Thanem and Knights, 2019: i). Though much of the fieldwork we discuss in this chapter is overtly embodied, focusing upon the senses, some other fieldwork is more subtly so. Interviews and focus groups, even those that take place over the phone or online, rely upon embodied communication skills such as tone of voice, eye contact, body language and so on. We illustrate this point in Postcard 7.2, where Jennifer explains the value of conducting (some) interviews face-to-face and bringing objects for interviewees to see and hold, as stimuli for conversation. Where they take place in person, these exchanges typically involve embodied acts such as sitting down, drinking tea and eating together, none of which are incidental to the exchange.

Doing Multisensory Fieldwork

In this section we outline what it might mean for you to do multisensory fieldwork. Different senses demand varied research methods, though there are also similarities which would make it repetitive to run through each of the senses in turn. We have chosen to illustrate multisensory methods through hearing and touch and to save some other senses for later in the chapter. Recurring themes are techniques for noticing – paying attention to particular sensory experiences – and documenting sensory experiences.

Sounds and noises: hearing and listening

Sociologist Les Back challenges social researchers to learn to listen as seriously as we have become accustomed to looking (Back, 2003; Bull and Back, 2003; Sullivan and Gill, 1975). In social research, listening begins with registering what is said: with the words and other sounds that people make when we speak, whisper, sing and shout, when we express ourselves and communicate with others. In addition to picking up on more subtle expressions such as awkward silences and ambiguous laughter, listening to people involves more than one's ears and brain. Whether it takes place online, over the phone or face-to-face, listening is an embodied practice that involves means of communication that we can learn and improve upon. These include eye contact, body language and silent attentiveness: 'listening well' and being seen to listen well (Sennett, 2012: 6). In *You're Not Listening* (2020), American journalist Kate Murphy illustrates how people are learning to listen better: couples attending counselling sessions to explore and improve their communication; businesses commissioning training sessions; communities running workshops to bring increasingly divided neighbours back together; individuals turning to self-help books or simply resolving to make an effort.

Listening better is partly a matter of technique – such as paying attention to others and showing that we are doing so – which we can learn, practise and improve. But listening also depends upon something more fundamental and less straightforward – curiosity. When we are curious about people and their lives, we have a chance of hearing what they are saying, including things we might not have expected, which might sound strange and even counter-intuitive (Ware, 2006; McAvoy, 2014). We can also learn to be more curious – more genuinely interested in people and what they are saying – as we explained in Chapter 3, Curiosity and Research Design.

Listening can take many different forms. We listen to others in conversations and focus groups; we overhear their conversations, shouts, laughter and other utterances. We can also find ourselves listening to crowds of people or human settings, to places with human and non-human sounds and noises. But how to listen? How to get started? The following 'Try This' exercise, adapting a sound mapping exercise suggested by Keri Smith (2008: 57; see also Butler 2006), will help you get started.

Try this

1. Find a place where you are free to spend some time, and where it is possible and ethical to make some observations. Focus on the sounds in that place, and document them in your own words. Spend fifteen minutes doing this.
2. Make a sound recording in the same place, using the simplest device you can lay your hands on, such as a sound recording app on a mobile phone, or a voice recorder such as a Dictaphone.
3. Reflect on what you have described and on the recording you have made. How have you described sounds and noises? How have you documented the ways in which they unfold over time? How have you positioned them in geographical space? What challenges has this presented? What do you notice about the sound recording? How does it differ from the sounds you heard? How might you improve it?
4. What has this exercise helped you to notice for the first time?

Taking the first part of this exercise first – documenting sounds by labelling them or transcribing them – is challenging. Attempting this in everyday life, we often fall back on identifying the source of a particular noise, such as the hammer or the engine, the baby or the bird, though it is best if we can find words for the sound itself. Doing so is largely a matter of practice, of finding and perfecting a vocabulary for particular sounds and noises, though we can also learn from others who have done this, perfecting acoustic vocabularies and notation systems. Take bird sounds. If you heard a bird when you were carrying out the 'Try This' exercise, you might have used words like tweeting and chirping to describe it. Or you might have compared the particular bird song or call to another familiar sound. Trying to capture the call of a bird he encountered while attempting this exercise, Richard compared the Common Magpie to a football rattle. This kind of comparison would be most helpful to someone who knows what a football rattle is and how it sounds – loud, abrasive, persistent, wooden, energetic, irritated and irritating – but it would be lost on others who may not share the same cultural references. To go one step further, describing without presuming any background knowledge, you may want to describe a sound directly and precisely, in terms of what it is rather than what it is like. Illustrating how this can be done, a popular bird guide describes the Common Magpie's 'voice':

> Most calls hoarse and unmusical. Perhaps best known is the alarm against cat or owl, long drawn-out, fast, very hoarse staccato series, 'tsche-tsche-tsche-tsche …' Other calls include hard, hoarse and whining sounds; disyllabic, clicking 'cha-ka!', 'chia-cha' etc. in conversation. Song more rarely heard, a quiet, harsh twittering 'subsong'. (Svensson, 2009: 360)

Some other bird guides are much more evocative, and convey a sense of the possibilities that can arise as we pay attention to and describe sounds. The Grey-Headed Bushshrike – a bird found in southern Africa – is more often heard than seen because it spends much of its time in dense vegetation. 'Its presence is usually given away by the male's mournful, drawn-out, rather ghostly 'whoooooo' whistle, which explains its Afrikaans name (literally "ghost bird")' – Spookvoel (Tarboton and Ryan, 2016: 172). These descriptions – variously technical and evocative – illustrate how we can expand sonic vocabularies. This applies not only to birds, but also to the sounds and noises of other animals, machines, vehicles, instruments and more – the sounds of life.

Transcribing the spoken word – whether from an interview recording or a conversation in real time – can be equally challenging and equally insightful. This includes but reaches beyond the actual words that are spoken to include other utterances: laughter, specific types of laughter, other audible expressions, silences and pauses; and noting the tone, pitch and volume of spoken words, and their form, such as whispering, shouting and imitating. Here is one example from an interview in which one student asked another about their educational experiences during the COVID-19 pandemic, and enquired about face-to-face teaching. The bare transcript quoted the interviewee as saying that face-to-face teaching 'may as well have not happened'; but the student who conducted the interview described the exchange in more detail, attending to everything they had heard. As they put it, the interviewee 'laughed and made a rasping noise' and stated that face-to-face teaching 'may as well have not happened' (Phillips et al., 2022: section 4).

The 'Try This' exercise also involved a sound recording, starting with a simple device such as a mobile phone or Dictaphone. When you listen to your recording, you will see that this exercise is not as simple as it may have seemed. If you worked outside or in a public place – anywhere but a quiet room – the volume and variety of sounds and noises in the recording might surprise you. (And even quiet rooms have their noises: scraping chairs, passing vehicles, the hum of an air conditioner or projector, the sounds of a laptop or device, clicking pens, clothes brushing against surfaces, people breathing.) Likely, you only described a few of these sounds in your written description. Whether or not you did so deliberately, you would have been selecting from the cacophony of sounds around you, filtering and focusing these sounds to make sense of your environment.

Within the sonic environment, we can distinguish three broad dimensions: ambient sounds, noise(s) and specific sounds. Your simple sound recording, as we have said, is likely to have picked up a range of noises. If you have ever tried to record an interview in a public place or outside, you may have found the same thing, and struggled to pick out the interviewee's words above the hubbub of ambient sounds: vehicle engines; footsteps; spoken words; coughs and sneezes; sounds of eating and footsteps on the ground; perhaps some background music or a nearby television; calling and singing birds and barking dogs; the sounds of wind and rain; machinery and industry: computers, telephones, kettles, ovens; and more (Bull and Back, 2003; Lashua et al., 2014; Murphy, 2012). You may have also picked up some of your own sounds: your clothes rustling; your breathing; your footsteps and, perhaps, your voice if you spoke to someone. As we see in Chapter 8, Participant Observation and Participatory Fieldwork, you are always part of the picture.

Ambient sounds can coalesce into increasingly amorphous noise (Fisher, 1973), which is hard to record, harder still to describe. Though our brains may be efficient at filtering out noise as we focus upon listening to specific sounds – the person speaking to us or whispering a secret to someone else, or the announcement we need to hear – we stand to learn from noise if we tune into it. Listening, we may begin to detect an acoustic backdrop to social life that is 'discordant, disorderly and irregular' (Butler, 2006; Hetherington, 2013) or alternatively harmonious and rhythmic. Noise also varies in intensity – it can be loud, but is sometimes quiet – and in its temporality and spatiality: how long and how far it reaches. This general noise can be difficult to describe; its volume and frequency can be measured and often are, not least by disturbed and litigious neighbours, environmental planning officers and inspectors. A range of devices are available for measuring noise levels and frequencies, some of which are affordable and easy to use.

If you are interested in specific sounds you may need more focused and advanced recording skills. Here it is possible to learn from sound artists and technicians who record human and environmental sounds – such as fences flapping in the wind, customers ordering coffee, rain falling on roofs, machines in operation – and embed these found sounds in their compositions. Environmental sound artist Kate Carr explains that her 'music blurs the boundaries between instruments and field recordings, underlining the intersections and overlaps between nature and culture' (https://katecarr.bandcamp.com/). Other sound artists explore the sounds of machines and vehicles, bringing these into their musical compositions and soundscapes (Russolo, 1986, originally published in 1913). You may be able to record sounds on your phone, though you may get better results if you use a microphone and/or recording device, which you may be able to borrow from your university or college. These devices range from general purpose microphones to more specialist gadgets, capable of picking up more specific sounds from electromagnetic impulses to very high or low frequencies such as the sounds emitted by bats. Whether or not you are actually recording, it can be helpful to attach these microphones to your recording devices and wear headphones. Doing so will enable you to experience sounds that may not be audible or clear to your naked ears.

Once you have improved the quality of your noise and sound recordings – if necessary – you will need to decide what to do with them. One possibility is to edit them, creating sound recordings as outputs of your fieldwork. Selecting, describing, recording, editing and mixing sounds, media sociologist Brett Laschua – whose sound research in the Canadian city of Edmonton is described in Postcard 12.1 – worked with students to create rather than just collect soundscapes: 'sonic collages'. He also edited initial recordings to remove distractions and amplify particular sounds. This editing stage may sound like cheating or distorting the truth; but it is part of the process of making and handling data. We legitimately focus on particular sounds when we listen.

When we describe sounds in words, and when we make and edit sound recordings, we bring our own ears and selves – our positionalities – to the soundscapes we create. Not everyone hears the same sounds in the same ways. Teenagers pick up frequencies such as the high-pitched sounds emitted by bats that adults do not. Many older people struggle to hear lower frequencies, particularly if they are in places with hard surfaces where sounds echo. Different individuals also have different hearing abilities, of course, and some are hearing impaired. We also respond differently to the sounds and noises we hear. Traffic noise or bird sounds may be unpleasant and disturbing to one person, taken for granted by another and reassuring or comforting to a third (Law, 2013). These differences are personal but also cultural and social since some groups of people are more accustomed to some sounds and noises, more tolerant of them and more acoustically literate, understanding them better. This tells us that, though measurement and recording devices have a place in fieldwork involving noise and sound and though we can get a long way by listening and describing, we cannot investigate the social soundscape without also involving other people: finding out about what they hear and how they understand it. This is just one of the ways in which soundscapes open windows on the social world.

While we can think of sound descriptions and recordings as research outputs in their own right, we can also see them as data, awaiting interpretation, which we can use to explore the social world. Brett Laschua's soundwalk (Postcard 12.1) illustrates how it is possible to reach beyond description and venture interpretations of this social world. Listening to Edmonton by day and night, Laschua illuminates the parallel lives of older and younger people, mainstream and minoritised communities, illustrating how soundscapes can throw light on the social worlds that produce them.

Touching and Feeling: Haptic Fieldwork

Fieldwork involving touch – haptic fieldwork – is more often advocated than actually done, largely because it is difficult. Cultural geographer Mike Crang once observed that, though they are 'often derided for being somehow soft and touchy-feely', qualitative research methods have in practice 'been rather limited in touching and feeling' (Crang, 2003: 494). But things are changing. Advances in this field provide examples and points of departure for those who wish to try it. Anne Volvey (2012) set out an agenda for haptic research methods and illustrated some of the forms it might take, in researching the material world that we experience through touch and also the human contacts, which are fundamental to relationships and social life. Three haptic fieldwork methods, which we introduce here, involve noticing rules and norms regarding touch; noticing and describing what and whom you touch; noticing and describing the people and things that touch you.

First, touch is governed by rules and norms about who can or cannot, should or should not, must or must not touch what and whom. Richard was once told off for touching an interviewee's crystal; the interviewee said it would drain the object's energy. And Jennifer was reprimanded for feeling a sculptural vase, printed in 3D, which was made of a material that was toxic (having not yet been made safe through heat treatment). Touching other people is equally risky. One form of haptic fieldwork involves noticing these rules, which are variously explicit and implicit, actively policed and informally upheld.

The simplest haptic fieldwork involves noticing and recording rules of touch and ways in which people respond to these rules. These rules are spelled out in some settings. 'Do not touch' signs are common in museums and art galleries, food counters and market stalls. Touch came into focus, perhaps as never before, in the course of the COVID-19 pandemic. Believing that the virus spread through contact with infected people and things, many people became aware of 'high-touch surfaces' and of how we use our hands. All this was reinforced by notices and announcements, reminding us to be careful of what and how we touch (Figure 12.1).

Figure 12.1 Notices posted in Derbyshire, England, in Summer 2020, the height of the COVID-19 pandemic, warning pedestrians of the risks of high-touch surfaces and of proximity to other people. Photograph by Richard Phillips

Where rules about touch are not so explicit and are coded in behavioural norms and unwritten forms, other fieldwork methods may be required. You might use the methods we introduced in Chapter 8, Participant Observation and Participatory Fieldwork, to explore haptic practices such as social greetings and business interactions involving touch. You might also consult rulebooks – whether these be legal statutes or perhaps the rulebooks for particular sports – which specify the forms of contact that are permitted between particular body parts and sporting equipment such as balls and nets. Many players and fans learn these rules – or some version of them – through word of mouth. The same applies to the rules of touch that govern everyday life. To investigate these unwritten rules, it may be necessary to conduct some form of participant observation.

Here, it helps to read work by researchers whose participant observation involved touch. Sociologist Loïc Wacquant (2004) provides a sustained example of haptic fieldwork – and an important example of embodied social research more generally – in the form of participatory research in a boxing club. Through the gym on the South Side of Chicago, Wacquant investigated everyday lives of young black men. Using his body as an instrument for research, he experienced physical contact with other boxers, throwing and taking punches, and with the gym and the objects in it including the punch bags and towels (see Thanem and Knights, 2019: 9). Boxing is not all about touching and being touched; it is largely about avoiding the latter, though it necessarily revolves around the possibility of this physical contact. Wacquant's research diary reflected this, recording a 'straight smack in the face' through unforgiving competition gloves (Wacquant, 2004; Wacquant, 2005; see also Thanem and Knights, 2019: 26).

Other projects, providing points of departure and inspiration for haptic fieldwork, explore embodied mobility in the form of cycling and climbing. In *Cyclogeography* (2015), cycle courier Jon Day evokes a city he experiences through touch and in physically demanding work that revolves around a close relationship between body and space. Through the tyres, he feels the texture of the streets, the smooth surfaces, cobbles, potholes and kerbs. Through the greater and lesser effort he puts into cycling his sometimes heavily laden bike, this cyclist apprehends the topography of the city. Cycling through vehicle exhaust and drizzle, sometimes in the warmth of the sun, retained and reflected by masonry, Day also touches the urban atmosphere and feels its temperature and humidity, sometimes its rain and wind. Referencing psychogeography – through the pun in his title: *Cyclogeography* – Day claims to explore the city against its grain. Working as a courier and therefore constrained and directed by the schedules and logistics of the courier industry, he is also moving with the demands of the urban economy.

Another tribe of haptic fieldworkers, climbers feel through their hands and feet, which make more intimate contact with surfaces, textures and micro-topographies (Foster, 2007; Chiu, 2009; Holmes and Hall, 2020). This kind of fieldwork is feasible for some students, as we see from the example of fieldwork, conducted by a student called Henry during a field trip in New York. Henry wanted to explore New York through his body, and most directly his hands and feet: by climbing over its surfaces. As an experienced climber he had already developed the skills needed both to climb and to describe how he climbs and what he finds. Such mindful, active touch arguably brings experience of the material world to life as a 'textured part of an overall body experience' (Degen, 2008: 42). Having learned to climb on small but challenging rock surfaces in the Peak District in Northern England where he grew up, Henry was drawn to the schist boulders of Central Park. He explains:

> By going climbing in New York, I was able to personally experience the tactile city, not having to rely on descriptions from others, but instead being able to compare these to my own sensory findings. Other climbers have suggested that this activity allows them to detach themselves from the sensory overload ordinarily experienced in cities such as New York. (Henry, quoted by Phillips, 2015: 622)

The specific form of climbing practised here – bouldering – allows close intimate contact between body and rock: an 'increased awareness of the sense of touch' (Foster, 2007: 1), which can be entirely absorbing, akin to a form of mindfulness in the concentration it demands, both upon one's own body as it climbs, and also upon the surfaces being climbed.

> I was on a boulder problem next to a children's play area, so there were many aural and visual distractions happening around me; however, as soon as I started climbing I was concentrating so hard on my sense of touch, assessing whether I could maintain my grip on the holds and completing each move on the problem, that I completely zoned out to all of the noise and movement happening around me, effectively switching my brain off to any distractions. (Henry, quoted by Phillips, 2015: 622–623)

But the other climbers were more than mere distractions. Henry 'noticed that many children were trying to scramble up the rock next to [him]'. Interpreting their curiosity and their attempts to mimic his actions, Henry speculated that the children were also following his lead as they explored and evaluated the environment by touching it (Rodaway, 1994: 51). In this way, his haptic fieldwork was relational, no longer just about the person doing the fieldwork.

While these examples – of boxing, cycling and climbing and less active practices such as sitting and sipping a hot drink – all illustrate forms of touch that the researcher has chosen, other aspects of the haptic are involuntary and may be less comfortable, and these are concerned with being touched. This fieldwork involves noticing the people and things that touch you and the ways in which they do this, which may involve asking and/or gaining your permission to be touched. This touch takes many different forms. Offering a hand, hug or social kiss, one person can apply pressure without actually compelling the other person to touch. Other forms of physical contact, apparently incidental, include rubbing up against others on a train or a dance floor. In some cases people touch more deliberately and assertively. 'When I was pregnant,' a friend recalled, 'people behaved as if they had the right to touch me.' Parents with small children and owners of dogs often say the same, that strangers reach in and touch their child or pet, often without asking first. Touch takes many different forms then: people bumping into and brushing up against each other, touching sensually and clinically, gently and violently, consensually and invasively (Rodaway, 1994). And touch means many different things – affection, sexual desire, compassion, support, curiosity and so on – though the toucher and touchee may not share the same understandings of a particular encounter. Haptic fieldwork, noticing and documenting these active and passive, consensual and unwelcome forms of touch, offers to open windows on social life including relationships structured by gender, sexuality and intergenerational difference.

Try this

1. Choose two of the following forms of movement (or others if you can think of them) if you are able: walking, running, cycling, driving, climbing, skateboarding or scootering and so on. Travel for ten minutes using one of these forms of travel, and then return to your starting point using another. For example, walk to the next bus stop then get the bus back.
2. Document your movements and the ways in which you perceive or interact with the surfaces you are travelling over and the people and things you encounter as you go, including everything you feel or notice. You may be describing things you are already conscious of, such as how to move along on a skateboard or bicycle if you find these challenging. Or you may need to develop an awareness of things you do routinely and without thinking, such as walking (if that is easy for you to do) or riding a bike (if you are a confident cyclist).
3. This exercise introduces the idea that in order to understand embodiment it is not enough to sit and think about it; we need to observe and describe bodily actions, movements, gestures and appearances: our own, and those of others.

Recording and Describing

To record and convey a taste, smell or tangible feeling, we still rely largely on written and spoken words (Pullen, 2018). Finding the right words, we can document and communicate a sensory experience; we can also sharpen that experience by training our senses. 'We learn to see a thing' better 'by learning to describe it' better (Williams, 1961: 23). There is no simple formula for description – for finding the right words – but it is helpful to start by reading others who have described well. Here are two examples to learn from and enjoy. First, Kevin Boniface, a postal worker and writer, describes his round in Huddersfield, a town in northern England. His blog illustrates the power of words as means of registering and documenting multisensory experiences: streets walked down (in order to deliver letters and parcels), seen and smelled. Smells are prominent in his blog (www.themostdifficultthingever.com: Friday, 16 August 2019).

> It starts to rain heavily and a thick petrichor scent fugs up from the busily embellished gardens of the cluttered over-60s retirement village; an eerie 1970s time machine of

moorland park homes. The ambient scent around here is more usually best described as a blend of damp Players No. 6 infused Austin Maxi upholstery and stewing steak.

For a second and more sustained example of sensory fieldwork in which words matter, we now turn to Brett Lashua, a specialist in media and education, who describes the soundwalks he conducted in the Canadian city of Edmonton (Postcard 12.1). Lashua describes a city that is sometimes noisy, sometimes eerily and tellingly quiet. The silences are an important part of the picture he paints through words.

──────── **Postcard 12.1** ────────

Edmonton soundwalks, by Brett Lashua

When I taught music production at an alternative high school in Edmonton, we created soundscapes by first going on soundwalks. Soundwalks are journeys around the city centre with a portable recorder, paying attention to and 'collecting' sounds along the way. We'd traipse through urban passageways – like many Canadian cities, Edmonton has labyrinthine walkways (underground pedways, above-ground skyways) so pedestrians may navigate the city without ever stepping into the bitter cold outside – capturing everything that passed by our microphones. Back at school, we'd edit and mix these 'found sounds' into sonic collages (soundscape compositions), sometimes adding in students' spoken-word poetry or rap lyrics (for mixing, free digital sound editing apps and software are available).

Removed from taken-for-granted contexts and with sounds oddly juxtaposed, soundscapes called my attention to the 'other' city that young people inhabited. For example, one student recorded train station announcements and wrote rap lyrics that name-checked the stations; he stopped before University station because he 'would never go there'. Like many North American cities, Edmonton emptied of office workers after 6pm and was largely deserted by adults. Come night time the city took on a different pace, hum and rhythm. A 24-hour coffee shop populated with suited civil servants during the day overflowed at night with teenagers in hip-hop clothing. The bus shelters near the City Centre Mall – sites of arriving, departing and simply meeting up – swam with young people at night. Shops were closed, food courts shuttered, but young people lingered, noisily, in passageways and in-between spaces: there are few acceptable places or times for teenagers to be in the city. Later there were those who didn't want to go home or didn't have homes to go to. Some were students I worked with at the alternative school. Labelled 'youth at-risk', most had failed or were expelled from 'regular' high schools; poverty, addictions, gangs, violence (as perpetrators and victims), homelessness and lack of social support caused other difficulties. Most were First Nations (Aboriginal-Canadians) and racism and discrimination compounded the challenges of their lives. They often spoke of treatment as second-class citizens, daily abuse and verbal taunts of 'fucking Indians'.

I began to hear these social relations in the city soundscape. One young woman spoke of how different the underground pedways sounded during daytime, when full of voices, versus the quiet of night. During the day she felt out of place, as if young, First Nations people did not belong in the city of white, middle-class professionals. Similarly, familiar busy night time spaces were deserted during the day, such as the gritty alleyways leading to 'after-hours' clubs where she would dance from 11pm until 7am. During our soundwalking tours she told me I was learning to see (and hear) things 'from a street kid's perspective'. That is, I learned that when struggling, impoverished, homeless, trying to stay high or simply stay alive, there were different movements and places to know – where to go, where and when to sleep or to stay awake, where to keep warm, where to find comfort and joy in spite of all other difficulties.

My Edmonton soundwalks alerted me to the persistence of what the author China Miéville (2009) called 'the city and the city', where citizens of one municipality are unable to see inhabitants of the other, although – bizarrely – the cities share the same space. Edmonton comprises at least two cities, used differently at different times by inhabitants who do not interact. One is a city of power, privilege, affluence; one is a city of poverty, discrimination and disadvantage. Walking through one city, I had been unaware of the other, until these young people taught me to listen to it.

Documenting Smells

Smellscape research, an area of fieldwork that has leapt forward in recent years, shows how it is possible to learn to describe sensory experiences, not only verbally but also through visual and other means. Victoria Henshaw, working in urban studies and planning, published a landmark text – *Urban Smellscapes: Understanding and Designing City Smell Environments* (2013) – which advanced methods for researching smellscapes and ways in which planners and designers can work with smell to shape and improve living environments. Taking this project forward by applying her skills in art and design, Kate McLean has devised innovative vocabularies, cartographies, charts and other means of describing and recording smells (Henshaw et al., 2017). Her work is illustrated in Postcard 12.2 and on her website: www.sensorymaps.com. Other researchers have tried techniques ranging from recording diaries of smell walks (Bouchard, 2021; Riach and Warren, 2015) to preserving smell samples in airtight jars, distilling smells in scratch-and-sniff cards (Lockard, 2013), developing 'olfactometers' (gadgets for detecting and measuring odours) (Henshaw, 2013) and using smells as pedagogical devices and stimuli (Allen, 2022). This body of smellscape research is instructive in two ways: when we are training and sharpening our sense of smell; and when we are recording and describing what we smell.

Getting started in smellscape research, it helps to distinguish between the smells that come to you and those you seek out. McLean distinguishes between smell catching (noticing the ambient smells, which one tends to experience passively and which are differentiated between background and episodic or localised smells) and smell hunting (smells that one must actively seek out, perhaps by sniffing a herb, crushed between one's fingers). McLean invites participants on the smell walks she leads to name a series of smells in each of these categories. They are then asked to assess each smell (on a seven-point scale) in terms of its intensity, duration and appeal, to state whether it was expected or not (in a particular setting) and to add further comments and thoughts.

These methods challenge us to do more than label smells by their source (such as coffee, or diesel). They encourage us to evoke the smell itself, through descriptions that are lateral rather than literal. Marshalling her skills as an artist, McLean works with colour and shade to suggest experiences of smell, and she encourages participants on smell walks to do the same

(McLean, 2018). Thus, for example, a smell is identified as 'chocolate powder' and colour-coded 'pale beige'; another is described as 'old books, attics, smoky damp' and colour-coded 'sage green' (McLean, 2017). Though an individual smell researcher might devise their own terms and colours, smellscape research involving multiple participants benefits from shared verbal vocabulary and colour codes (McLean, 2017). These principles underpin more scientific smellscape research. Systematic means of identifying odours and/or describing experiences of smell include an 'odour descriptor wheel' (Fisher et al., 2018; Henshaw, 2013: 17), a visual chart originating in water and environmental management practice, which helps users to distinguish between and label odours.

Postcard 12.2

Smells of a hospital, by Kate McLean

In the early days of the COVID-19 pandemic, a network of healthcare researchers – known as Sensing Spaces of Healthcare – asked me to produce an olfactory map of a hospital. They approached me because they had heard about my previous work exploring and visualising urban smellscapes.

Like so much other fieldwork, smellscape research was constrained during the pandemic, when most people had lost their freedom of movement. Hospitals were locked down in a way that prevented me from working as I normally would: walking around with a group, recording smell instances. I turned instead to friends and acquaintances, asking them to share smell-related hospital memories.

The dataset we created was personal, alluding to some major surgeries and recoveries while focusing on smells and concomitant emotions such as 'soap in a bowl of hot water used to find a vein for chemo' and 'first cup of tea after general anaesthetic (cosy and warm)'. I ensured that every respondent was included in the final smellmap, which identified and grouped the smells associated with hospital environments such as waiting rooms, wards and canteens. Some of the participant smellnotes comprised unlikely 'combination smells' such as 'rubber, disinfectant, mince and an acrid smell that cut through from the dressings cupboards'.

My process for visualising smells involves a series of interrelated stages. First, I allocated colours and shapes to particular smells. I selected colours based on previous smell mapping projects. The synthetic smells are purple in hue whereas disinfectant and astringent smells are blue and green in hue. Food smells are yellow and brown. I use lighter and less saturated shades for the weaker smells and combination smells make use of two colours linked with a gradient. The smell shapes emulate the physical sensation of smelling, the 'sweaty/sticky/stale odour of a waiting room' is circular, incessant and self-contained as a doughnut shape and the 'nail varnish remover' is long and sharp. I placed these colours and shapes on plans and maps, locating the smells and showing how they overlap and where they extend. In their visual language, typography and layout, these plans reference NHS (the UK's National Health Service) brand guidelines. These maps speak to a broader conceptual question, which I was interested in exploring, and concerned the ways in which smells might mingle. The smellmap we created (Figure 12.2) shows smells in relation to the layout of corridors, showing how smells emanate from particular rooms and seep into common areas, mingling and moving in the airflow and along the corridors. This smellmap brings a new dimension to the representation of a hospital – shifting the focus from practical room-locating to the experiential depiction of connective space.

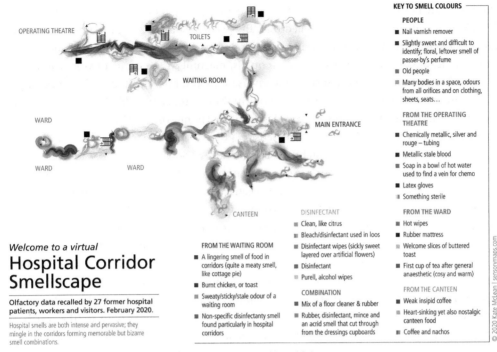

Figure 12.2 Hospital corridor smellscape. *Source*: Kate McLean

Fieldwork is more than simply work conducted in situ. It derives from knowing the field, anticipating the field and honouring the data in ways that communicate to virtual, potential and previous visitors to the space. Working with participants to record olfactory data often includes reference to associated memories. In this case the memories are poignant and personal with the potential to elicit empathic responses. The smellscape may need to be redefined from simply being a perceived phenomenon to a combination of both external sources and internal smell memories in acknowledgement of the powerful emotive olfactory memories that contribute to imagining hospital environments.

Interpreting Findings

The interpretation of sensory experience is a continuous process, extending from the moment in which you recognise and name an experience and continuing long after, when you go on to ask what these newly revealed sensory experiences say about the social world. Here are some starting points, concerning the significance of sensory observations.

First, the soundscapes, smellscapes and other sensory worlds that researchers are bringing into view tell us a lot about the social worlds that produce them. Les Back argues that sounds and noises are both a backdrop to human life and an expression of that life (Back, 2003: 272–273). Walter Benjamin (1985: 53) argued that 'the peculiar sounds of transit are the signature tunes of modern cities'. Clattering trains, vibrations of combustion engines, announcements, street traffic, buskers, wind, construction, footfalls, machinery, the drone of voices and snippets of conversations and more sustained conversations and interviews too; all of these speak of human lives, experiences, relationships and rhythms (Atkinson, 2007; Barns, 2013; Lefebvre, 2013; Raimbault and Dubois, 2005; Schafer, 1977; Thompson, 2002).

Second, sounds, smells, sights and other sensory phenomena have social and political significance so there is a politics to researching them (Smith, 1994, 2000). Who has to live or work in noisy places where it is difficult to sleep or concentrate? Who can retreat to a quiet place when they choose? Who gets a view of the ocean? Who is surrounded by unpleasant smells and by the toxins that emit them? Prompted by questions like these, William (Bill) Bunge, an activist and community researcher who lived in Toronto and Detroit in the early 1970s, led community fieldwork projects involving volunteers. With Bunge's direction, the community researchers pioneered a politicised form of multisensory fieldwork. They recorded smells – naming and locating them – that reflected the quality of life and culture of their neighbourhood (in the smells of cooking) but also the hazards and pollution endured there, the smells belched out by factories, too close to schools and housing. Attending both to 'the smells of ripe grapes, tomatoes and peppers' that 'fill the air' at particular times of the day and the year, and also to the stench of 'roasting oil from the near-by Planter's peanuts factory', Bordessa and Bunge (1975: 15–16) identified environmental hazards while presenting a very humane picture of the neighbourhood. In both senses, they politicised multisensory fieldwork, mobilising this as a form of activism.

Third, though multisensory fieldwork opens windows on the social world – on noisy workplaces, smelly neighbourhoods and apartments with beautiful views – it also speaks of the social world closest in: the body of the researcher and the **embodiment** of sensory experience. What is possible for one field worker is not possible for another. Fieldwork in some disciplines – including geography and anthropology – has traditionally depended upon a certain kind of physicality, an ability to walk a certain distance or manage without a toilet for an extended period of time. These are unrealistic expectations as we saw in Chapter 4, Working Together, because bodies vary and change over time, as we grow and age and as our health and fitness fluctuate and eventually decline (Rose, 2020). It is not that some bodies are complete and in their prime whereas others are impaired or deteriorated. Rather, all bodies and sensory experiences are socially conditioned, made rather than born, in their infinite variety. We experience the world through the bodies that we have learned to inhabit: boys learning to stride around confidently and occupy as much space as possible, girls to walk, run and sit more modestly and defensively (Young, 1990; see also Bourdieu, 1990; Thanem and Knights, 2019; Haynes, 2012). And while bodies are gendered, they are also socialised in other ways, freed, constrained and trained in specific ways, which affect our sensory experiences.

Conclusion

Human bodies can be sophisticated instruments for fieldwork. Researchers are learning to use more of our senses, to use them better and to record and interpret what they tell us. Multisensory fieldwork can be akin to the state of enchantment described by Jane Bennett (2001: 5) in which 'you notice new colours, discern details previously ignored, hear extraordinary sounds, as familiar landscapes of sense sharpen and intensify'. That said, multisensory research is not necessarily enchanting in a pleasurable sense. The sensory worlds inhabited by pickers scavenging a living in a waste dump (where there are overpowering smells), by workers in a deep mine (with its uncanny darkness, artificial lighting and cold damp air) or by patients in a hospital (where disinfectants mask and interact with other odours) are important to an appreciation of those settings but are not necessarily pleasurable.

Multisensory fieldwork also comes with risk. Because it can be fun and many people find it novel, sensory fieldwork can be gimmicky and shallow. Numerous manuals, guidebooks and self-help books recycle the same sensory exercises and activities. Though many of these books are lively and inspiring, serving their purposes, these can be derivative and repetitive. This presents you with a challenging question: how do you take inspiration from multisensory fieldwork manuals and published work without simply repeating their methods and findings? How, in other words, do you remain as creative and innovative as those who invented these exercises?

Happily, there are many examples of multisensory fieldwork that remain creative and innovative, productive and original. In smellscape research, for example, we have seen continued methodological advances through the application of art and design principles to the detection and description of particular odours, and we have also seen applications that bring new meaning and significance to this work, including in the theory and practice of urban design and planning. Moreover, as an emerging field with plenty of space for creativity and innovation, multisensory fieldwork presents students with many points of departure for ideas and original experiments. We encourage you to take up this challenge.

Key terms

Embodied fieldwork can involve the body as an instrument of field research, an 'active subject' in the production of knowledge, and/or as 'an object of knowledge and a topic of research' (Thanem and Knights, 2019: 43).

Embodiment is a theoretical term that recognises the social construction and socialisation of human bodies, leading to divergence between different bodily experiences and competences in different times and places (see Cresswell, 1999: 176; see also Grosz, 2020).

Multisensory fieldwork brings more than one of the researcher's senses to field research, typically reaching beyond the most commonly used sense – seeing – to include the other senses and the interactions between these senses.

Further Reading

Ellingson, Laura L. (2017) *Embodiment in Qualitative Research*. Routledge.
This book explores why and how researchers use their bodies as tools for fieldwork. Embodied researchers pay attention to sensations, feelings, emotions and experiences, using each of these to collect and interpret field data.

Henshaw, Victoria (2013) *Urban Smellscapes: Understanding and Designing City Smell Environments*. Routledge.
Victoria Henshaw, an urban design expert, gives practical tips to those interested in experiencing and describing the urban smellscape. She argues that smell environments can be designed and planned.

Pink, Sarah (2015) *Doing Sensory Ethnography*. Sage.
Anthropologist Sarah Pink is a leading authority on visual ethnography. In this book she turns her attention to a wider set of sensory ethnographic practices.

Thanem, Torkild and Knights, David (2019) *Embodied Research Methods*. Sage.
Drawing upon their own experiences, the authors explain how researchers can use their bodies as tools for fieldwork, for making observations and collecting data. The book really comes alive through the authors' searching and good-humoured reflections on their own embodied research and gendered embodiment.

13
EXPLORING WITH SECONDARY SOURCES

In this chapter you will learn

- what secondary sources are and how you can use them in your fieldwork;
- the different types of secondary sources you might seek out in the field;
- how to use and analyse secondary sources critically and ethically;
- how secondary research may be combined with other methods in your fieldwork.

Introduction

While visiting Liverpool's International Slavery Museum a few years ago – Jennifer writes – a particular object fascinated me and my collaborator, business historian Andrew Smith. It was a nineteenth-century sugar bowl made by Wedgwood decorated with the words 'The Produce of Free Labour'. This object inspired us to dig a little deeper to find out more about 'free labour sugar' and how that could help us understand ethical consumption and modern slavery today. We used secondary sources and archives to research this category of sugar, searching historical texts, parliamentary or governmental papers, British Library newspapers, *The Times* and *Economist* archives and the Slavery and Anti-Slavery Archive (for more detail see Smith and Johns, 2019). We discovered that James Cropper, a Quaker merchant in Liverpool, was significant in creating this anti-slavery sugar so we visited the Liverpool Maritime Museum to access the remaining documents from his company. Our research conclusions included evidence that consumers do not necessarily become more ethical over time and that there is always a danger that ethical products (like today's Fairtrade) can be removed from the market (see Johns, 2019).

When we see ourselves entering the field, we typically imagine being present in exciting, colourful and/or inspirational settings. Chapter 6, Decolonising Fieldwork, has reminded us to be cautious of seeing some places as exotic, and open to the possibility of conducting our fieldwork in ordinary places closer to home. We have illustrated how fascinating research can be sparked by a trip to a local museum, for example. However, not many of us imagine that some, or all, of our time in the field could be spent in museums, libraries or archives that we might think of as quiet and dusty. This type of data collection involves different skills, a more detective-like mindset. It involves the identification, collection and interpretation of what we call secondary data.

Secondary data is the information and material that other people have collected or produced (Tight, 2019). **Secondary research** involves accessing and interpreting data that already exist: written documents such as newspapers, websites, articles and books, numerical records such as census data and voting records, and artefacts such as photographs and household belongings. Secondary sources encompass a variety of media including on paper, online, on film and microfilm, and three-dimensional. There is certainly space for all of us to consider how to use such sources in our fieldwork.

Secondary sources and research methods are distinguished from primary sources and methods, which involve direct observation and the collection of new data. Primary research involves observing or recording phenomena or events and generating entirely new data, whereas secondary research involves accessing and interpreting data that already exist. As we have seen throughout this book, primary research is central to fieldwork. That said, secondary sources and methods have important parts to play too, and you can do original fieldwork with 'old' data (Hakim, 1982: 12).

Even if you are required to collect primary data, or if you decide this is what you want to do, it is likely you could benefit from incorporating secondary sources into your fieldwork. Fieldworkers engage secondary sources at every stage of research projects: beginning with preparation and framing prior to data collection, through time in the field, when we may come across secondary sources in situ, and seek them out in libraries, archives and other repositories. Secondary sources can be handled in a multitude of different ways. They may be physically collated, or they may be recorded, transcribed, copied or described.

In this chapter we will talk through some of the secondary sources and methods you may use in your fieldwork, and discuss how you can combine these with other sources and methods. We recognise that you are likely to already possess skills in finding and analysing some secondary sources – particularly journal articles and academic books (Denyer and Tranfield, 2009; Tight, 2019) – so here we focus on other kinds of secondary sources and methods of data collection and analysis that you are less likely to have tried. You will find these sources and methods can enhance your other fieldwork and open new windows on the social world.

Insights

Though it might superficially resemble 'armchair' scholarship – seeming passive and an easy option – secondary research can be as productive and dynamic as any other form of fieldwork (Jacobsson, 2016). To understand this point it is important to see where secondary research can fit into your work, and to develop a deeper sense of what secondary data and sources comprise. This means asking what you can learn or gain from secondary sources, and how you can use them in your fieldwork. Here, we identify four possibilities.

First, secondary research can be helpful when you are planning fieldwork. You can use it to inform your research design and establish the context for primary research you may conduct. Here, secondary research plays a supporting role within fieldwork. It may be that you want to establish some background data and/or gain some insight into your chosen topic. Secondary sources may give you an idea of the size and scope of the phenomenon or problem you are investigating. For example, if you were researching garment factories in Dhaka, Bangladesh, you could access official data to see how many factories are in the city to determine your sample size. Doing so would give you background information on the efforts of the government to improve working conditions since the Rana Plaza disaster of 2013. By conducting secondary research before visiting a field site, you may be able to identify potential organisations, locations or individuals to investigate when you arrive, and you may find their contact details, enabling you to make arrangements in advance so that you make the most of your time in the field.

You can also use secondary research to design the primary research you conduct in the field. You will get much more out of interviews – and show more respect for interviewees' time – if you prepare in advance by finding out what interviewees and/or organisations have already said or published about your topic – for example, on their websites or in public statements. You will also find that background research will help you to design specific research questions, which generate genuinely new data. Public policy researcher Simon Parker used documentary research to prepare for observations and interviews in his research on the attitudes of participants attending strategic boards in public services. Parker was interested in the values within – sometimes between the lines of – policy documents (Parker, 2015). Because these values were more often implied than stated explicitly, he had to use good detective skills to read and understand the documents. Doing so, he was then able to devise a list of interview questions that discussed and probed his findings from the documentary research.

Second, it can be helpful to conduct secondary research while you are in the field, particularly if this involves spending time in a place where you may find resources such as local libraries and community archives, which can only be accessed in person, and which may be interesting in themselves, perhaps as settings in which people gather and in which events take place. This secondary research may be part of your fieldwork, but not necessarily the primary focus. This is an example of mixed methods research, in which different methods are brought together. This enables you to triangulate findings – cross-checking the data generated by different methods. It can be helpful to triangulate qualitative observations you make yourself with quantitative data you gather through secondary research, or interview findings against **documentary sources** on the same subject. For example, education sociologist Shinichi Aizawa investigated changes in school education in post-war Japan through a mixed methods approach, combining interviews with the collection and analysis of Japanese government papers: annual government reports known as White Papers. He found these documents 'as dry as dust' (Aizawa & Watanabe, 2020: 256), but the combination of primary and secondary fieldwork methods was effective in understanding how policy-makers recognise social issues, laws and social institutions. Furthermore, mixed methodologies provide a safety net so that if one method fails – if interviewees cancel, for example, or you are unable to access an ethnographic site, or an archive is closed – you are still able to complete your project, without unnecessary stress, and to explore more dimensions of an issue than a single approach might reveal.

Another inspiring example of mixed methods – primary and secondary – research comes from the work of sociologist Daniel Mato, who used field and documentary research to examine the transnational networks of indigenous peoples' organisations in Latin America. He combined interviews with documentary research, examining the documentation produced by local, community groups and global organisations such as non-governmental organisations (NGOs). Doing so, Mato found that the global stakeholders had notable advantages in terms of their transnational experience and privileged access to archives, libraries and other documentary sources (Mato, 2000). We see here how Mato draws on the documentary evidence but also reflects on the unequal power relations inherent within access to the documents themselves by different stakeholders. We pick up these points later in the chapter, explaining what it means to conduct secondary research critically and ethically, which includes asking challenging questions about who does and does not have access to secondary sources.

Third, you may wish to conduct fieldwork that is primarily informed by secondary sources and methods. This is a legitimate form of fieldwork, not only in historical studies where this is the default method, but also in other social science and humanities disciplines.

Fourth, and finally, you may want to conduct secondary research towards the end of your project while writing up. This can be particularly helpful where you identify loose ends or gaps, but are not on site to collect primary data. It can also be helpful where primary research uncovers leads – such as mentions of events and organisations – that you can find out more about through secondary sources.

Having outlined different ways in which secondary sources may be useful in your fieldwork, we now turn to a more sustained illustration, which shows how this may work in practice. This example of secondary research within fieldwork takes the form of a postcard by Maayan Niezna, who researches modern slavery and human rights.

Postcard 13.1

Beyond judgments: Using case files and court archives for empirical research, by Maayan Niezna

It is a cold December day and I'm sitting on the floor outside the registry in the Supreme Court building in Jerusalem, Israel, surrounded by boxes full of documents. It is a lot better than it might sound for two reasons. First, one of the administrative workers took pity on me and brought me tea and biscuits, having seen that I'd been at the registry a while. Second, I am diving into court archives and discovering some wonderful treasures.

My research asked what the policies and practices are that result in trafficking for labour exploitation, focusing on non-citizen workers in Israel. This discussion relied on analysis of various sources. I looked at regulations, parliamentary discussions and policy documents, and conducted qualitative expert interviews to consider concrete developments in the responses to trafficking for labour exploitation in Israel over the past two decades. Most of my material came from court archives, where I read not just judgments, but everything that was in the file: submissions of the parties, protocols and interim orders. Many submissions included annexes and support evidence, such as correspondence, statistics, newspaper articles and references to other proceedings. I relied on these too. This sort of work is not typical in legal research. When lawyers want to know what the law is, they read a judgment. The judgment is likely to include a summary of the parties' arguments as presented in the court, so one could get a sense of the position of different actors in addition to the court itself. For some questions this is enough. But accessing the case file allows one to answer additional, or different, questions: Why were certain decisions made? How did implementation look in practice? What happened outside the court during and after the proceedings? Can a change in the position of the different parties be identified? While judgments inform the study of 'law in books', case files can help researchers learn more about law in action. They can also help the study of courts as actors, as settings for different interactions, or as social institutions.

Most of the cases I focused on were constitutional and administrative proceedings, where a ministry, or the government, was a party to the proceedings. While in many such cases the courts may aim to simply interpret and apply the law as it is, in some cases, the position of the court as an institution, or the position of individual judges, could be identified. This is especially true as in my research I considered highly politicised questions: migration policy and migration control measures, labour market regulation and criminal law enforcement. Thus, in some cases a clear distinction could be identified between judges that tend to adopt a liberal, or even neo-liberal, approach to contracts of employment, and judges emphasising the power gaps between workers and employers, and structural vulnerabilities of the former. Some judges are more trusting of law-makers and law enforcement, while others are more sceptical – a distinction that will often reflect in 'activist' or 'conservative' approach to how much the court should intervene in, for example, a visa regime. The use of case files allows us to distinguish between 'what the law is' and 'what the court does'. Case files can include, for example, arguments made by the parties that were not reflected in the judgment itself. When such a situation could be identified, it raises interesting questions for the researcher – why was this point not mentioned? Is it because it is so irrelevant the court simply ignored it? Or maybe it is the other way around – could it be that the argument would be hard to reconcile with the court's analysis? Case files are a rich source of data, but they should be approached with great care and following careful planning. Getting access to files can be a lengthy process, and copying, reading and coding the material will also take time. I had to be strategic and have clear reasons for reading each case.

In my socio-legal approach I sought to consider the law in its broader context, looking at legal proceedings beyond judgments. I therefore gathered evidence as to what happened outside the court during the legal procedures and after a judgment has been issued, and assessed how such decisions were implemented and how state agencies and other policy actors reacted in practice. The method of process tracing, often used by historians and political scientists, informed how I approached the causes and impact of legal and political developments, though my analysis included significant doctrinal elements and critical legal analysis. This way, the judgment is an important part – but only one part – of the consideration of legal developments and the law as it is in a specific context.

Documentary and Secondary Sources

Secondary sources include a range of pre-existing data, documents and artefacts, which other people have produced (McCulloch and Richardson, 2000). The terms 'secondary sources' and 'documentary sources' are closely related – but not quite synonymous – because not all secondary sources are documentary. Documents are 'content or objects which include written, graphical or pictorial matter, or a combination of these types of content, in order to transmit or store information or meaning' (Grant, 2018: 11). This definition encompasses a wide range of materials, both those in hard and digital copies and formal and informal documents. Documents of one kind or another are hugely important in most people's lives, even though social researchers do not always recognise this. Ethnographic and other primary research can be enriched through the collection and interpretation of documentary sources: everything from newspaper articles to advertisements, policy documents, government reports, blogs, schedules, letters, posters, pamphlets, brochures, campaign materials, cartoons, films and more (Weller and da Silva, 2011; Baltruschat, 2000; Bounegru and Forceville, 2011). The following 'Try This' activity will help you to begin to appreciate the range of documents in contemporary life.

Try this

List all the documents you have created and/or accessed today. Write them down and, while you do, think about who wrote or made them and what their purpose was. Put these into categories.

You will notice your list contains a variety of physical and online documents, some of which are not permanent. What reflections can you make about your list? How many of those documents will be around in a month's time? What would a historian 100 years in the future make of your day if they collected and analysed your day's documents?

When trying this exercise one day around noon – Jennifer writes – I reviewed my morning and found there were three categories of documents with a mixture of physical and virtual. I reflected on what I found: 'One category included my academic documents – physical books, online books, journal articles and teaching materials. Another category was administrative, including a word-processed plan for an academic workshop and many email exchanges. The final category contained personal documents. It covered domestic tasks like a permission slip for a school trip, a label for a dress to be returned to the retailer and a shopping list (just a short one noting milk, flowers, a birthday card and potatoes). I realised how high the volume of documents is that I interact with daily and noticed how many were still physical despite efforts to go paperless.' Secondary research involves collecting and analysing secondary data like these.

What forms of secondary data are likely to be useful in your fieldwork? To answer this question, we shall now introduce five overlapping secondary data sources: (1) official records kept by governments and other authorities; (2) records kept by organisations such as businesses and community groups; (3) personal documents such as diaries, letters, biographies; (4) previously published research findings; and (5) material artefacts. These examples are illustrative rather than exhaustive, given the enormous variety that secondary sources can take.

First, official records including official statistics and government papers, variously intended for internal use and external communications. Many national governments provide access to data on a wide range of topics, typically using online resources and offering links to other data providers and archives. Examples include the UK Data Service (ukdataservice.ac.uk), Research Data Australia, the National Opinion Research Center and Social Science Data Archive (United States) and the Israel Social Sciences Data Center. Archives are not the preserve of countries in the Global North. There are extensive archives to be found including the Indian Council of Social Science Research, the South African Data Archive and the National Archives of Malaysia. Each country will offer access to a range of different databases. In the UK these include national surveys such as the Family Expenditure Survey (carried out since 1957) and the Labour Force Survey (since 1973). There are cross-national surveys too, including the European Quality of Life Survey (since 2003), which you can access data via international data providers such as Eurostat, the Organisation for Economic Cooperation and Development (OECD) and the United Nations (Tight, 2019). When seeking out these official records, a good place to start can be your own institution's library website and search facilities. It is always a good idea to speak to your university librarian, who may be able to guide you through the full range of the databases you can access covering data on international disasters, financial inclusion, assassinations, corruption and mortality rates among others.

Some researchers seek out official records before they enter the field; others chance upon them when their fieldwork has already begun. Political scientist Robert Vitalis (2006: 5–6) began his research on multinational firms in construction and infrastructure development in Cairo. This research took him all over the world, starting with declassified State Department records in Washington (United States) that covered embassy telegrams, dispatches and memoranda of conversations. When he reached Egypt his research took an unexpected turn. He found himself doing fewer interviews and spending more time in libraries, the Egyptian National Archive and even visiting National Library collections in Kew and Oxford (United Kingdom). Vitalis's research became more historical, examining investment conflicts between 1920 and 1950, which he realised were essential to understanding the contemporary political economy of investment in Egypt. This experience shows us how our time in the field can take our research in new directions, requiring us to think about our methodological choices and being open to different forms of data collection.

A second example of secondary data source, which is important to fieldwork, is records kept by organisations such as businesses and community groups. In some cases, records relate to the organisation's activities. For example, the multinational manufacturing firm Unilever has an extensive online archive of its business activities, which includes its annual reports and accounts (as far back as 1929). Community archives are also valuable sources for secondary research, both historical and contemporary. Conducting fieldwork on feminist youth work in the Northwest of England, for example, political scientist Niamh Moore came across an archive on this subject, created by a collective of academics and non-academics called Feminist Webs. This includes over 50 years' worth of oral histories and documentary records (Moore et al., 2016). The archive, and the secondary data contained within it, provided powerful insights, complementing other methods and sources. Drawing upon the work of historian Helen Verran, Moore et al. (2016) point to the empirical possibilities and intellectual challenges of secondary data collection and interpretation, in 'the everyday messing about with murky, obdurate stuff, and in the conversations and other texts – official and unofficial' (Verran, 1998: 252).

Third, personal documents such as diaries, letters and memoirs open windows on the everyday lives of individuals and happenings within organisations, and as such they are powerful research tools. The diary has been defined as the regular, personal record of an individual life, kept in real time (Alasazewski, 2006), though it is not just individuals who keep diaries: families, communities and organisations do too. There are three main types of diary – private, political and official. Private diaries are those written by individuals for their own purposes, to record their daily lives. Political diaries are often diarising a political career where the author wishes to document their activities, thoughts and opinions as a historical record. Official diaries are kept as a requirement of one's position in an institution – for example, as a ship's captain (McCulloch, 2004) – and these may be kept by the named office holder or by a colleague or assistant. As with all personal accounts, diaries have strengths and weaknesses that result from research participants in that they are 'partial and reflect the interests and perspectives of their authors' (Hammersley and Atkinson, 1995: 165). That said, diaries have specific uses in 'picking up' the minutiae of experiences and events in a way that other forms of solicited information, questionnaires and interviews do not (Morrison, 2012). For these reasons, diaries can be valuable sources for research. Examples of social research employing diaries range from Fay Bound Alberti's historical study of loneliness (Alberti, 2019) to George Adamson's employment of private diaries as sources on climate change (Adamson, 2015). These private diaries constitute a unique set of materials within climate change research because they provide information both on past climate variability and on the ways that people live within, and interact with, climate. Diaries can also be a way of reaching participants that might respond differently to observation or interview – for example, children. Burgess and Morrison (1998) used diaries with primary school children to study their eating and food choices. International relations researcher Roger MacGinty (2021) uses war memoirs and personal diaries (specifically from the First and Second World Wars) to inform the study of contemporary peace and conflict. He argues that a growing number of studies in his field are recognising the everyday, the individual and the small group as appropriate levels of analysis. MacGinty (2021) identifies five factors that recommend personal diaries and related personal documents such as memoirs as sources for research:

1   They have a first-hand immediacy as the authors were present and/or participating in the event described.
2   They often contain individual or subaltern voices that frequently go unheard.

3 Memoirs and diaries may be in a vernacular and have textual richness, without an affected tone. They weren't written to be presented in a book.
4 The sources are not prompted by academic enquiry (such as with interview questions) so they do not take the form of answers to questions. This can take the research in new directions.
5 They offer personal, intimate and sociological details that may be difficult to access through other sources.

Like diaries, letters may be personal documents, opening windows on individual lives, or they may be produced by and for organisations (Grant, 2018). These documents can reveal personal and private attitudes, aspirations and ambitions (McCulloch, 2004). In their analysis of the attitudes and practices of Soviet citizens in the 1930s, historians Lewis Siegelbaum and Andrei Sokolov accessed declassified archives using letters written by individuals sent to newspapers as well as party and state leaders and institutions. They were surprised by the sheer volume of letters received. For example, in the month of July 1935 *Krest'ianskaia Gazeta* (the *Peasant's Newspaper*) received over 26,000 letters (Siegelbaum and Sokolov, 2000). In a contemporary example, scientist Doreén Pick and management scientist Stephan Zielke studied letters from German utility companies, in which they found that companies sought to hide price increases from customers (Pick and Zielke, 2015).

Fourth, secondary sources also include findings that other researchers have generated or assembled and either shared online or placed in repositories and data banks, which other researchers are able to access, or published. These secondary sources take a huge variety of forms, from academic papers to biographies aimed at academic, specific or general audiences. Examples of the latter include business historian Alusine Jalloh's (2002) biographies of entrepreneurs in the post-independence era. These prove powerful sources to understand African business history, providing rich contextual information about the lived experiences of the authors. Another example of published biographical and autobiographical material – which we are treating as a form of secondary data – is provided in Postcard 13.2.

Postcard 13.2

Working with African political autobiographies, by Anaïs Angelo

When I first arrived in Kenya in 2011, I knew, from my academic readings, that the autobiographical genre was booming: most prominent male politicians were publishing autobiographies or commissioned their biography. In a large bookshop in Nairobi, I could find the latest autobiographies published. I was recommended to ask the bookseller for his personal advice: I later learned that some biographies were printed in limited number and that to get one, one had to be informed on the specific delivery date. I bought everything I could bring back in my luggage and, more importantly, everything I knew I would never be able to buy on the internet.

Continued

For someone working on African history and elite politics, and more particularly on the transition from colonialism to postcolonialism, these autobiographies are a useful addition to state archives. They restore the unbalance of documentary sources largely produced by colonial authorities and which, very often, silenced African voices. They also offer a unique insight into an elite world, which consists in informal social networks and discussions that are unlikely to be set down in writing.

These autobiographies constitute, nonetheless, a political performance. The publication of a book provides the author with a specific social status: that of the writer, scholar and historian. It is also used by the author to deliver his own version of past events, to settle his scores with those who were once opponents or enemies. When reading the autobiography and using it as a source, I was not only interested in what was said, but more specifically how it was said (with insistence, derision, pride, or violence?) as much as I looked for what was not said: which events, actors, well-known rumours were left out? Crossing these biographical narratives with other historical sources (written and oral), my aim was to discover why an author had decided to depict his life in a particular way.

It did not immediately occur to me that most of these political autobiographies were written by powerful men and spoke almost exclusively of male actors. It is only when I embarked on a project dealing with African women's political history that I realised that very few Kenyan women have published an autobiography. This dearth of female autobiographies reflects the profound marginalising of Kenyan women in politics (an observation that applies to many other African countries). Clearly, the autobiographical genre is the reserved field of powerful politicians and patriarchal politics. Why? And can this trend be challenged?

I came to encounter Kenyan women who had had a rich political career though not in state institutions. I conducted interviews, but as I asked them about their political activities, discussion about their biographies came naturally. One of them confided to me that she would like to write her autobiography, but has not yet been able to. This enterprise demands extensive resources: material and financial (access to a recorder, a computer, perhaps even to funding to support the research and publication process) as well as social resources (access to someone to assist with the transcription and research, access to the publishing world). For veteran (female) politicians, this may not be an easy thing.

The production of African political autobiographies is profoundly political and profoundly gendered. In these conditions, the publication of the historical testimonies of African female leaders is a work in progress, but one that could teach us a lot. When I read available female autobiographies, I search for the way their public and private lives overlapped, the way they fought for their ideas to be heard, the way they want to be remembered. And whenever I have an autobiography in my hands, or conduct a biographical interview, I am more aware of the power relationship playing in, asking myself who is giving them the power not only to speak, but to be heard and/or read?

A fifth example of secondary data, which may be important and useful in your fieldwork, consists of material artefacts: things. These include things stored in museums and archives, and objects you may find in your own or other people's houses, or on the street, or for sale in markets and shops. When Richard was in Paris with a group of students, exploring connections between communities in France and Algeria, he came across some old postcards, for sale in a market stall. The images and inscriptions on these cards, which had been sent from settlers in Algeria to friends and relatives in metropolitan France, offer glimpses of everyday life within a colony, prior to its anti-colonial uprising and eventual independence (Figure 13.1a–b).

Figure 13.1a–b Postcards sent from Algeria to France. *Source*: Richard Phillips.

For another example of tangible secondary sources, recall that we began this chapter with an artefact – a sugar bowl, displayed in a museum – which both prompted and formed the subject of a research project. The following 'Try This' exercise introduces another kind of material artefact, and another example of where and how you may collect and interpret secondary data. This exercise is inspired by Croatian journalist and writer Slavenka Drakulić's work on feminism, communism and post-communism, articulating the everyday experiences of women. In her 1993 book, *How We Survived Communism and Even Laughed,* she describes how she catalogued the contents of her grandmother's cupboard. What would we discover if we did the same with our own kitchen cupboard?

Try this

This exercise explores the variety of archives, secondary sources and artefacts we are surrounded by, including everyday items. Open a drawer, cupboard or fridge. It can belong to someone else if you have permission. Make a list of the contents. You can also make a drawing or take a photograph. Review the contents and answer these questions:

1 What do the items tell you about their owner?
2 What do they tell you about the socio-economic context in which they exist?
3 If they represent a moment in history, what moment, and what does it tell us?

Jennifer tried this exercise, exploring the kitchen cupboard shown in Figure 13.2. Here, she explains what she learned, working through the three questions in the exercise to explore what the photograph reveals. The cupboard documents a moment in history. In this way, it is just like Slavenka's grandmother's cupboard. What can we surmise? It is a well-stocked cupboard – the family is not struggling to feed itself. Reaching to the back of the cupboard can reveal older

Figure 13.2 A kitchen cupboard. Photograph by Jennifer Johns

items with surprisingly low prices; the items and price tags tell us something about a moment in economic history, a period of high inflation. There are some unusual ingredients including banana blossoms, Thai fish sauce and caper berries, perhaps the family has wide ranging tastes and likes to cook. There are non-alcoholic drinks, reflecting a recent trend in the United Kingdom to drink less alcohol. All this is contained within the ubiquitous IKEA kitchen cupboard. What do you see when you look inside your own cupboard? Or a friend or relative's cupboard?

Getting Started: Finding and Accessing Secondary Sources

Secondary data is all around us if we know where to look and are open to what we find, whether deliberately or by chance. An obvious place to start are the repositories where published and unpublished materials are stored and made available to the public or authorised users.

Archives can house a wide range of physical and digital materials: the wide range of secondary sources we have seen in this chapter including written texts, photographs, sound recordings, postcards, medical records, printed materials and material artefacts. An archive is 'a repository of some kind' that may be housed in 'a building, cardboard-box, photograph album, internet website' or other physical or virtual setting (Moore et al., 2016: 1). More fundamentally, the archive can be understood as a 'discourse of interconnected ideas such as community heritage and shared memory' (Moore et al., 2016: 1). There are many different types of archives based on the information they hold and the interests of those organisations who have established and funded them. These range from national archives to corporate archives, and include the archives of religious and community organisations, all of which tend to hold a mixture of historical and more contemporary materials. Every archive tells the story of its owners' interests and priorities. For example, when she was researching the manufacturing history of Japan, social and cultural historian Katja Schmidtpott asked curators of a large consumer products manufacturer's archive about how they decide which materials to preserve. They answered frankly, explaining that they keep only materials that testified to the successful development of new products, and dispose of materials on accidents or failures (Schmidtpott & Schölz, 2020). Remember then that in all archives a decision has been made about what to retain and what not to include. Motivations driving these choices vary based on the type of archive and the purposes for which is has been established.

Archives and libraries, once rather intimidating places for first-time researchers, have become much more accessible as many have digitised and scanned their holdings, making it possible to search and access materials online. Programmes have been launched specifically to find, catalogue, digitise and preserve the world's archives. The Endangered Archives Programme (https://eap.bl.uk/about-programme) has a searchable online archive (https://eap.bl.uk/search). It contains archives as varied as the ecclesiastical and notarial archives in Colombia and Brazil (Landers et al., 2015), Iranian National Radio recordings of Persian classical poetry and music (Lewisohn, 2015), archives of a Cameroonian photographic studio (Zeitlyn, 2015), preservation of *Lepcha* (a Tibeto-Burman language) manuscripts (Plaisier, 2015) and early Roma organisation, church and newspaper records (Mariushakova & Popov, 2015). Digitisation is helping archives to preserve materials that might otherwise be lost, as numerous holdings have been over the years due to fires, floods, wars and simple wear-and-tear. A devastating fire in 2018 prompted archivists at Brazil's *Museu Nacional* (National Museum) to redouble their digitisation project (Roth, 2018). Since then, the museum curators have been collecting digital copies of documents from past researchers to try to rebuild some of the collection.

Once you have identified an archive that might be useful to you, how can you get started? We have already suggested you start with an online search. First, identify archives that might be useful to you. Next, look at their websites for an overview of their holdings and, if you are lucky, access to catalogues and actual holdings. Figure 13.3 provides a practical guide to using archives.

Finding

- Conduct some background secondary research using online sources before you enter the field.
- Read academic sources on your topic AND on your field location to see what archives researchers have used before.
- Talk to a historian/expert about the relevant archival collection you are interested in. Even better, if they work in the place (and time) that you are interested in. Find out:
    - where they are located
    - get a sense of what you will find there
    - will someone be onsite that will be able to help you? Is there an archivist who can help you?
    - are there any printed guides that can help you in advance of your trip?

Preparing

- In addition to finding the archives you wish to visit, you can prepare and practise your archival techniques in advance of entering the field.
- Few social science courses teach archival research techniques so if you are nervous and/or feel at a loss when you enter an archive you are not alone. Good preparation can help a great deal.
- Plan to spend more time at the archive than you think you need. Always best to over-estimate. That way you allow yourself time to explore the archive and are open to unexpected findings.
- Prepare yourself for entering the archive. You will be overwhelmed by the bewildering array of collections, much of which is mundane and tedious.
- Your most accessible archive is that of your own university or institution. They will likely have a guide to citing the records held there, and you can learn how collections are filed and what aids exist to make it easier to access the records.

Mapping

- Take a few days to learn the protocols around the organisation of the archive. You'll need to work out, and note, preferably in a field diary:
    - how the collection is organised, what is included and excluded
    - what are the bulk of the contents focused on?
    - does the archive permit you to take digital photographs? If so, how are you going to take photos? How will you store and organise them?
- Scope the collection first. If there are four boxes or fewer, skim the contents of all. If there are five or more, skim the first, last and middle boxes. Skim means to quickly scan all the contents to get a sense of what is in each box and noting high points.
- Develop a system of precise and consistent record keeping to be able to demonstrate transparency and verifiability.

Reflecting

- Be aware of the limitations of archival resources and the need for you to interrogate records rather than read them naively. Jordanova (2000) is an excellent source to kickstart reflection.
- Think about whether your archival research is complete, or if you need to return to the archive, or visit a new archive.

Figure 13.3 A practical guide to archival research
Source: Adapted from Stanley (2016) and Vitalis (2006).

Though most archives have websites, not all have online catalogues or digitised holdings. This means you may need to arrange to visit in person when you are conducting your fieldwork. It is important that you check opening hours and access rules. Not all archives are open to the public and even those that are may require you to apply for a reader's pass, which may only be available to some people and on certain conditions. Access to some archives is highly restricted – for example, corporate archives that are maintained for employees and in-house researchers, and archives that hold materials that are restricted for reasons of confidentiality and privacy. When Katja Schmidtpott (Schmidtpott & Schölz, 2020) was researching the economic history of Japanese businesses, she noted that companies create their own rules for their own archives – determining who can access them and when. If you check these details in advance of your fieldwork, you won't be disappointed or waste precious time when you are in the field.

Even if the archives you intend to access are partially or wholly digitised, you can learn a lot from visiting them in person. Some students, participating in a field trip we were leading in Vancouver, were interested in Chinese-Canadian communities and spaces. Their projects took them to areas of the city where members of this large community tend to live, work, shop and socialise, but some students also visited libraries and archives. There, they were able to glean additional information including press cuttings in Vancouver Public Library (Figure 13.4), and also to see displays and leaf through books and magazines, all providing additional insights into this community and their experiences, past and present. Though some of the material would have been available online, this was not the case for all of it, and the assemblage of these sources added to their value, as did the students' observations of how local people were using and interacting with these collections. Though digital archives create a wealth of resources, the 'digital search offers release from place-based research' (Putnam, 2016: 379). Historian Lara Putman calls on us to take context seriously, to acknowledge that via digitalisation we

Figure 13.4 Resources on Chinese-Canadian community history, accessed at Vancouver Public Library. Photograph by Richard Phillips

are removing contextual browsing and intimacy with archives. Cultural geographer Hayden Lorimer acknowledges that we need to balance the demand of archive-oriented travel itineraries and the financial costs incurred, which can be punitive, but that the intellectual and social rewards that come from being 'present' are very often greater still.

> It is impossible to generalise about what might be lost, missed, overlooked or simply put beyond reach if the scope of archival study is limited to those documents available online. Though there will never be verifiable evidence to support the claim, the likelihood of making that serendipitous (and all-important) archival discovery would seem to be greatly reduced for the remote researcher. There is, for sure, a case to be made for the creative responsibilities of being present, spending time in situ. (Lorimer, 2010: 256)

Another geographer – Timur Hammond (2020) – conducts research using archives in Istanbul. He clearly remembers, and cherishes, his memories of first working with the archive in Istanbul. Working remotely now takes him back, imaginatively, to the place in which he first encountered the documents. Through his previous physical presence, he feels he is better able to imagine and understand how the documents were produced, circulated and used. Visiting archives in person, you have a chance to gain a sense of their context, as Hammond illustrates. You may also be able to speak to an archivist, who may know their collection intimately and be able to guide you through it in ways that search engines might not; search engines only work if you know the keywords to enter, of course.

Practical, Critical and Ethical Challenges

Although as researchers we are familiar with reading and analysing documents, much of our expertise lies in understanding academic journals and books, and easily accessed internet sources like news and blogs. While you may not feel experienced or confident in deeper and more systematic engagement with secondary sources, you have a lot to gain and learn if you give it a try. If you've received training in researching using secondary sources, you are lucky and should try to make the most of it, you have a head start on many others. This chapter has aimed to guide you through some of the places you can find secondary sources and to think about how you will engage with them. In this final section we draw out three key challenges of working with secondary sources: practical, critical and ethical.

First, secondary research presents practical challenges. These include dealing with the volume of materials you are likely to encounter as soon as you start to scratch the surface of archives, documents and other sources. This can feel overwhelming, so pause, breathe and think about how to systematically work through the sources. There is something wonderful, almost meditative, about working with documents, images, objects etc., particularly when we are in the field and can use all our senses while we inhabit archives, museums and other spaces. A key challenge when using secondary methods in fieldwork is in finding a balance and acknowledging what we as individuals (and potentially members of a team) want to get out of our time in the field. The lure of intense engagement with others through interviews, or participant observation, or the appeal of walking through different landscapes, often leaves less consideration of how we can use the secondary sources we may come across, or actively seek, in the field. We challenge you to make time for secondary research in fieldwork, to experience fieldwork in a way that has a different rhythm and reflective experience than other research methods with more human engagement.

Secondary fieldwork also presents critical challenges. When we start looking for, collecting and analysing secondary data we need to think critically about them. Rather than taking documents at face value, for example, we need to assess their 'quality' (Scott, 1990). We provide guidance on doing this in Table 13.1. We encourage you to ask the questions, posed in Table 13.1, of every documentary source you plan to use. You may not be able to answer all questions positively, but you should be able to see how and why some documents may have less authenticity, credibility, representativeness or meaning than others.

Thinking critically about secondary sources, you will need to consider who the author of the document is and what their intended audience is. For example, there is a vast difference between a persuasive pamphlet written by a local government encouraging us to recycle and a company's annual report written to reassure stakeholders. Both are crafted in particular ways to elicit specific ideas and actions from the reader. When we are in the field, we need to be particularly sensitive to these questions as we may not be as familiar in new contexts with subtleties around authorship.

You will also need to consider who and what is represented within an archive or library, and who is not. For example, if you are working with published biographies, you will soon notice

Table 13.1 Criteria to assess documentary sources

Criteria	Questions
Authenticity	• Is it the original document or a high-quality copy? Is the document fully readable? • Is the full text available? • Is it clear who the author was? • Has the document been translated? If so, by whom?
Credibility	• Does the author report sincerely on their experience? • Does the author describe an accurate narrative?
Representativeness	• Does the document offer a representative sample of the whole population? Does it need to? • Is the document available to researchers?
Meaning	• Can you understand the language used and decipher the handwriting (if not typed)? • Can you combine the document with an understanding of the context to be able to interpret its meaning?

Source: Adapted from Scott, 1990: 19–35.

how these accounts tend to focus on the life stories of 'great men' such as male politicians, scientists, sporting figures and religious leaders. This point came through strongly in Anaïs Angelo's postcard on African political biographies. Since few people still accept the 'great man theory' of history – which claims that history is made by individuals (mostly men) – it is important to ask whose biographies have not been written or published, and to think about how you might access them. Doing so might mean turning from published biographies to other published works (Magedera, 2014; Smith, 2012; Wengraf et al., 2012) and then to less obvious sources, in which the lives of less privileged people may be recorded or otherwise leave a trace.

Within archives and secondary data, exclusion and inclusion affect entire groups. We have already noted that archives are set up and maintained by those with the resources and expertise to do so – with nation states, international bodies and powerful corporations strongly represented – and the flip side of this is that people with less money and power are less able to establish and maintain such resources. For example, London's Black Cultural Archives (https://blackculturalarchives.org), which was established in 1981 to preserve and share the histories of African and Caribbean people in Britain, has been poorly and unreliably funded (Weale, 2018). It now struggles to survive on a patchwork of funding including public donations. The precarious position of archives such as this challenges us to ask: which secondary sources are not saved, preserved or available to view?

If you are lucky enough to be granted access to an archive or library, you might also consider who else is and is not present in the room, whether it be physical or virtual. Who does and doesn't have access to these secondary sources? Daniel Mato, the sociologist we encountered earlier in the chapter, found that access to archives, libraries and other documentary sources on his research subject was highly unequal. He found that global stakeholders – highly educated individuals with cultural capital, financial resources and affiliations to universities and businesses – had more access to significant archives on the subject of indigenous peoples (Mato, 2000). Drawing on the documentary evidence, while also reflecting on the unequal power relations inherent within access to the documents, Mato provides an example that we would do well to follow in our own secondary research.

Last, but not least, it is important to consider the ethics of secondary research. As we have explained in Chapter 5, Ethical Fieldwork, you will be bound by your university or organisation's ethical approval procedure though we have encouraged you to go beyond this ethical minimum. The use of secondary and documentary materials does not always prompt intensive ethical scrutiny by institutional ethical reviewers. But this does not mean that there are no ethical issues to consider and research using secondary sources will likely require some ethical clearance. As secondary sources may have been collected by someone else, or the data may not have been collected specifically for research reasons, we need to be reassured that we are re-analysing data that have been collected ethically and that participants have consented to others viewing and analysing their responses (Barker and Allred, 2012). There may be potential for participants to be upset or harmed, especially if the public (re)release of information causes distress to individuals or communities and groups. It is your responsibility as researchers to ensure privacy and anonymity, where it can reasonably be expected.

Conclusion

At best secondary research can be the foundation of our fieldwork research, generating rich, insightful and potentially evocative findings. We can spend time in spaces imbued with a deep sense of history, accessing evidence from the distant or recent history to inform our understandings of either a different time period, or of our contemporary world. Through documentary research we can gain really valuable research and transferable skills, testing our organisational skills and challenging us to reflect on how secondary sources are created, who stores them and who has access to them.

The challenges of secondary research lie in stepping beyond our initial instinct to use such materials in a limited way. Often, we use documents to provide context to other research methods, particularly when in the field. We encourage you to reflect on two things. First, how can we think creatively to make space for secondary research in the field? It can greatly complement our use of other methods, or even be the sole method we adopt. Second, while many secondary sources are available digitally, how can we find time in our fieldwork schedule for this type of research? How do you feel about the arguments put forward about the importance of viewing secondary sources in their context, to see and feel the materials in situ? In many respects, the future of archives lie in the hands of us as researchers and the ways in which we interact with them.

Key terms

Archives are repositories or collections of published and unpublished sources such as letters, minutes of meetings, reports, maps, sound recordings and digital files. They may be publicly or privately owned and can have a specific focus such as a particular region or a special theme.

Documentary sources – a record, typically but not always written, that is published or unpublished and can be extracted and used in research. The term includes personal documents such as diaries, notes, letters, memoirs, photographs, records kept by companies and organisations, and public documents.

Secondary data is the information and material that other people have collected or produced (Tight, 2019). Secondary sources include written documents such as newspapers, websites, articles and books, numerical records such as census data and voting records, and artefacts such as photographs and postcards.

Secondary research involves accessing and interpreting secondary data. Secondary research methods are distinguished from primary, the latter generating entirely new data.

Further Reading

Grant, Aimee (2018) *Doing Excellent Social Research with Documents: Practical Examples and Guidance for Qualitative Researchers*. Routledge.
This text explains how we can use written content and images in research to understand society. It is an accessible book, rich with examples. The 'how' of documentary research is supported with discussion of the 'why', providing the reader with a grounding in the theoretical and ethical context of research with documents.

Moore, Niamh, Salter, Andrea, Stanley, Liz & Tamboukou, Maria (2016) *The Archive Project: Archival Research in the Social Sciences*. Routledge.
An accessible how-to guide to archival research in social sciences. It tells the reader about how to use and analyse different kinds of archived data, how to devise methodologies to address the practicalities of conducting research using archives and the theories behind archival research.

Plummer, Ken (2001) *Documents of Life 2: An Invitation to a Critical Humanism*, 2nd ed. Sage.
This was originally published in 1983 and became a classic text. It champions the use of life stories and other personal documents in research. This 2001 edition is revised and expanded to include contemporary topics and documents.

Tight, Malcom (2019) *Documentary Research in the Social Sciences*. Sage.
This book aims to empower researchers to use documentary research methods to answer contemporary research problems. It outlines different types of documentary sources, research design, data collection and sharing research findings. It covers quantitative, qualitative and mixed methods and provides many case studies.

14
UNDERSTANDING AND HANDLING YOUR DATA

In this chapter you will learn

- to start exploring your data while you are still in the field;
- how to anticipate and avoid potential problems with managing your data;
- why it is important to go beyond data collection while you are still in the field;
- how and when data analysis can be conducted in the field.

Introduction

Fieldwork can produce a varied – but potentially confusing – array of data. Data need to be collated, recorded, organised (and possibly shared) during the research process. Some of this will occur while you are in the field, rather than waiting until you get home. This chapter will outline some of the important groundwork that begins before your fieldwork starts in terms of anticipating different forms of data and planning how you will handle them. It offers practical guidance on how you can record data (physically and digitally) and the tools that you can use to support this. New digital technologies have opened-up exciting possibilities for the research process to be accelerated in the field. These enable some field-based data analysis, boosting reflexivity and the ability to make modifications to data collection in response to initial findings.

Insights

Even before you begin your fieldwork proper, you will start to collect information and resources in a variety of different forms. Managing the accumulation of academic literature to support your fieldwork may be straightforward for you as you will already have experience of researching and writing using academic sources. What you may be less familiar with is how to identify, organise, analyse and write up the vast array of different types of data and documents you are likely to collect before, during and after your fieldwork period. The preceding chapters have talked through different methods and approaches, each resulting in different types of data being collected. For example, interviewing can generate some combination of written notes, audio files, video files (particularly if you interview online) and photographs. You may then transcribe your audio files, creating transcripts for analysis. Transcripts are another form of data (the oral data has become written text).

If you combine methods you will need to handle several different types of data simultaneously. Imagine you have conducted some participant observation, conducted some interviews and spent time in an archive looking at secondary sources. This will generate respectively: field notes, sketches and photographs; oral voice recordings (or possibly video); interview transcripts; written notes on secondary sources; and copies or photos of the sources. It is a range of different types of data, resulting from a fairly standard combination of methods. Be aware of just how quickly you will build up a substantial amount of data and supporting documents during your fieldwork.

In the past, research data was primarily in paper form. Changes in the makeup of research and data from analogue to digital have made collecting, processing and analysing data easier than ever (Ray, 2014). However, the improvements offered by digital research bring new challenges in terms of how to collect, store, process and analyse data (Eaker, 2016). An early decision to make before you enter the field is whether to fully digitise your data. This has advantages. If you scan/photograph documents, upload audio and video files and type up field notes, there are possibilities to use technology to both keep your data secure and to help manage and analyse that data. But digital technologies do not render physical records – particularly field notes and sketch books – obsolete. On the contrary, many fieldworkers find it helps to combine physical and digital data, although doing so requires a little thought and planning. This is further complicated if you are working in teams and need to handle data in collaborative ways.

Managing Different Types of Data

Throughout this book we have outlined a range of ways in which you might collect your data, and a variety of types of data (see Table 14.1). The potentially high volume of data presents new challenges: How do you collect, store and organise these forms of data and cross-reference them? One solution is to collate and store data by medium, with digital and perhaps physical folders for audio files (interview recordings, oral archives), video files (online interviews, observations), text (email interviews, research diary, interview transcripts, blog posts, secondary documents) and photos (field images, secondary images). (Many methodological textbooks refer to these different forms of data as 'text' though this should not be taken too literally, since these data 'text' files include more than words). In some cases, you may find that one piece of fieldwork generates data across different categories, prompting you to decide how best to store, cross-reference and link these files. For example, an interview may generate an audio recording, stored in the form of an audio file, which you transcribe by hand or through using transcription software, creating a word-based text file. You are likely to want to keep more than one of these files until your research is complete, or for as long as your ethical clearance allows, and this forces you to make decisions about where and how to store your data, which to keep for reference (perhaps the voice recording) and which to work with in your analysis (more likely the transcript in this example).

Table 14.1 Fieldwork data types, storage and processing

Data form	Data collection and storage	Data processing
Audio files from interviews, recording soundscapes, audio field notes	*Format:* Digital (mp3) *Collected* using a Dictaphone, mobile device or laptop and *stored* in a secure digital space	Mp3 needs to be converted into a transcript if it contains interview data or field notes. This is typically a word processing document. Transcripts can then be collated and can be analysed by hand or using CAQDAS software.
Photographs taken by the researcher of field sites, participants (with permission), participant observation, web/social media images	*Format:* digital (jpeg) *Collected* using a camera, or directly on mobile device or laptop and transferred to be *stored* in a secure digital space	Images need to be collated and ordered systematically. They should be labelled ready for analysis by hand or using CAQDAS software. Note the particular need to timestamp web/social media images, particularly where the data is dynamic.
Secondary photographs, documents, artefacts	*Format:* physical *Collected* in the field by hand and *stored* in a dry environment. Can be digitised to ensure back-up copies	Can be analysed in physical form or digitised and analysed using CAQDAS software.
Videos taken by the researcher	*Format:* Digital (mp4) *Collected* using a Dictaphone, mobile device or laptop and *stored* in a secure digital space	Files can be analysed by hand or using CAQDAS software. Mp3 files can be extracted from the video file to generate transcripts (see audio files). Note that large storage capacity will be needed.
Documents including publications, newspapers, pamphlets, maps etc.	*Format:* physical or digital *Collected* in the field and/or online. *Store* physically or in a secure digital space. You can digitise the physical documents (pre- or post-annotation)	Collate and order the documents in preparation for analysis. Documents can be analysed by hand or using CAQDAS software (if digitised).
Field notes	*Format:* typically physical but increasingly digital (typed straight into mobile device) *Collected* during the fieldwork process on a frequent basis *Stored* in a book or digitally	Collate and order your fieldnotes. This may be chronological or by theme/topic. Notes can be analysed by hand or using CAQDAS software (if digitised).
Supporting documents for data collection	Consent forms should be stored as per your institution's ethics guidance	n/a

---

Try this

Record a five-minute conversation on your phone or other recording device. It can be a conversation you have with someone (with their consent, advise them you are practising your research skills), an interview from the television or internet or even just five minutes of content on any topic. Transfer this file from your recording device to your computer. Now start to type up the content of the recording. Think about how you do this. Do you record *everything* (pauses and hesitations, interruptions, laughter) or just the words? How do you label the participants and separate the text? What format do you save the file in to make working with it easier later? The decisions you make will impact on the data you generate through this exercise. You may notice how long it takes to transcribe even a short excerpt of text.

Data management is receiving increased attention in this era of 'big data', not least due to the risks associated with the loss of data or failing to keep data secure. In 1998 Pixar employees nearly lost the files storing *Toy Story 2* (Harrison, 2022). The UK's Home Office lost data on over 80,000 prisoners when one employee transferred all that data from a secure server onto a USB stick, and then lost the USB stick (Satter, 2008). The Bank of America 'misplaced' a backup tape that contained over a million government employees' personal information and still hasn't located it (Lemos, 2005). In 2011 Flickr accidentally wiped an account, losing five years and 4,000 photos owned by a customer (TechCrunch, 2011). These well-publicised examples are the tip of the iceberg when we consider the amount of data that is lost, mishandled or stolen each year and they underline the need to organise and store data securely, for practical and ethical reasons.

The larger the research project, the greater the complexity of the data that needs to be managed, but even fieldwork projects conducted by students demand some form of data management. You will need to store data in ways that make it possible to find specific data again and to organise it so you are able to analyse it. And, as the examples of data breaches above show, you will need to store your data safely so that only those with permission are able to gain access. This is fundamental to the confidentiality and privacy assurances that you are likely to make to your research participants, as part of the ethics of your fieldwork. This is particularly challenging when you are working in a team and need to share access to data and keep 'live' files open and changeable. The explosion in the amount of available data and electronic means of storage challenge the day-to-day organisational practices of many students. Ward et al. (2011) found that many researchers do not take a systematic approach, instead organising their data in an *ad hoc* fashion. Instead, they simply do what seems easiest at the time. This poses difficulties with retrieval and reuse of data. Therefore, it is important to consider three fundamental questions of data management right from the start:

1   *volume* – how much data are you expecting to collect? What forms will it take? Will you digitise physical artefacts and sources (typically by taking photos)? If you are working in a group how will you divide this data collection up and then share it?

2. *recording* – which methods will you use to record your data? A physical field notebook can be a practical way to record thoughts and observations, particularly if your field location is remote and/or your activities are particularly mobile or exposed to the elements. Try to have backup methods of recording too. If you are interviewing, for example, don't reply solely on your recording device, take some notes as well in case your recording fails. If you are working in a group, make sure more than one person is recording your data as you collect it.
3. *storage* – how and where will you store data while you are in the field? How will you back up your data? What systems will you use to make sure you transfer data from mobile to fixed storage (such as transferring photographs taken on a mobile phone to cloud storage)? In the field we need accessible storage, but we also need to be systematic and prompt in storing and backing up this data. If you are working in a group, decide before you enter the field how you will access and share data.

Postcard 14.1

Critical judgements and qualitative data: Building and managing a corporate database in a research team, by Jennifer Johns, John R. Bryson and Vida Vanchan

While investigating sustainability in garment supply chains – a topic typically researched using interviews – our research team noticed that many eco-friendly activewear companies published a lot of information about their firms and their corporate social responsibility activities and credentials. This information was typically very detailed, including data on their factories (number of employees, gender breakdown, working conditions etc.), suppliers, logistics arrangements, materials (fabrics, accessories, packaging). We began to wonder why we needed to interview the firms as we would be given the same information as contained in their documentation – and likely annoy the interviewee in the process. Why take an hour of their time to ask them questions that are answered in documents open to the public?

So, we changed our methodology and decided to focus on the secondary materials, using a variety of sources to triangulate the information. We used several reputable eco-ranking publications and websites. These organisations investigate the claims of sustainable companies and publish rankings detailing where the companies are doing well and where they may be lacking. We were therefore trying to overcome the 'greenwashing' phenomenon in which companies claim to be more sustainable than they are. We use these rankings, company documents including corporate social responsibility statements and reports and company interviews and write-ups in the press. This allowed us to construct a dataset of 80 firms (40 from the United States, 40 from Europe). To make sure our ranking was robust we each *independently* researched each firm and met to discuss whether the firm was sustainable enough to be included. Many firms were rejected based on there being too little evidence to support their claims or where their activities were not as sustainable as they claimed. An example of this is the use of bamboo as a sustainable material, which is not always the case as bamboo agriculture is associated with deforestation, limiting of ecosystems through

Continued

monoculture and the use of chemicals. As we were making subjective decisions we had to develop, as a team, a set of inclusion and exclusion criteria for the firms. We had to collectively agree on what we understood sustainable practices to be. This meant a lot of meetings to discuss the firms, comparing notes and finally forming a list of 80 firms.

The next step was to collate and analyse all the available data on the firms, storing them in a shared online space. We grouped firms into three categories based on the nature of their sustainability practices, which once again involved us independently analysing the firms and discussing our findings to come up with shared decisions on their categorisation. This was time-consuming but we needed to make sure that our database was replicable and robust. When we submit papers to journals for review we will be able to include the dataset, much as students can include datasets in their assessed work. It is therefore really important that we pay sufficient time and attention to creating, managing and working with qualitative datasets. The next stage of our research may take us from our digital fieldwork to visiting the factories where the activewear garments are made, using our secondary data findings to inform our observations. If we do interview company owners it will be in more meaningful, engaging and probing ways.

Capturing and Recording Data: Technologies

In the early 1980s researchers started to use what they then termed 'microcomputers' in the field. The reduction in the size and cost of computing power made it possible for researchers to bring technology out of the university and into the field. In his ethnographic research in Southern Peru in 1983–1984, anthropologist David Guillet used a microcomputer in the field for the first time. He noted three important consequences that are still relevant for us today (Guillet, 1985). First, it allowed him to begin preliminary analysis of questionnaires and participant observation notes while still in the field. Second, as preliminary analysis can take place in the field rather than after completing fieldwork, research design can be much more quickly adjusted for unexpected field conditions. Third, he found that he had to devote much of his research time (in this case around a third) to working on the computer, recording, collating his data and conducting preliminary analysis. Though several decades have passed since the introduction of computing technologies into fieldwork, and though these technologies have changed almost out of recognition, some of Guillet's observations remain pertinent today. Computers can still be powerful tools for fieldwork, but they can also be time-consuming and distracting. In other words, you may not want to spend too much of your time in the field staring into a screen, and it may help to think strategically about this and budget the time and energy you devote to screen time in the field.

You now have many technologies that can support you in the field to make data management easier and enrich the research process. You may want to use mobile devices (any device that can record, transfer or provide information to the user in any location) (Masrom and Ismail, 2010), GPS tools, data management software, multimedia editing software, transcription software and many others. Mobile devices are useful in the field as they allow the transfer of information over wireless and Bluetooth connections, capturing and storing multimedia data along with a variety of analytical applications (Welsh et al., 2015). Remember though that your field location may not allow for the kinds of digital connections you are used to at home or on campus and you need to plan accordingly.

Data Analysis in the Field

The use of technologies in the field can speed up – and enhance the two-way relationship between – data collection and analysis. Instead of viewing research as a linear process, think instead of stages of the process that overlap and inform each other. Thus, you can understand that preliminary data analysis can be embedded within the data collection process. Figure 14.1 shows how we can embed feedback loops in our research process, using our data collection experiences to reinform our research design and using initial data analysis to modify our data analysis. You can make sure you plan time to examine your data for gaps and areas of improvement. When you pause to review your data you should reflect on two areas. First, the quality and security of your data to assess the effectiveness of your methodology and, second, your initial findings.

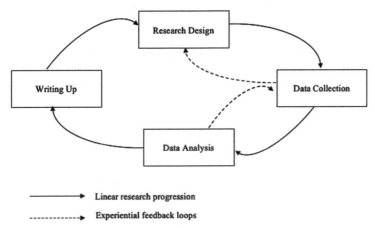

Figure 14.1 Feedback loops during fieldwork

Data Quality and Security

Once you have started data collection you can reflect on how it is going so far and assess the quality of that data. By doing this part way through your fieldwork, instead of at the end, you may have the opportunity to modify your methodology to enhance the data quality. Herrera and Kapur (2007) suggest that data quality can be measured by considering three elements:

1 *validity* – the relationship between the theoretical concepts and collected information, i.e., how well it answers your research questions;
2 *coverage* – how complete your data is, how far it avoids gaps;
3 *accuracy* – how 'correct' your data is, how far it avoids any errors – although for qualitative research this can be subjective and open to debate, as below.

When a laptop computer containing highly sensitive information was stolen from her home, law researcher Judith Aldridge and her team began to pay more attention to data security issues – an issue they suggest is rarely discussed by academic researchers (Aldridge et al., 2010). They highlight the 'principle of proliferation', reminding us of the increasing volume of data during the research process and the crucial importance of keeping track of all these forms – *and* making sure they are secure. Digitally held data is potentially stored in numerous locations during research, may be used by multiple individuals in a research team/group, may be stored on multiple devices and in numerous versions as analysis takes place (Aldridge et al., 2010). The theft, loss, confiscation or interception of digital data can be both physical (e.g., the theft of a laptop) and digital (e.g., unauthorised server access) (van Baalen, 2018). Aldridge and her team have developed guidelines on how to keep research data secure, summarised in Figure 14.2.

---

1 Agree a policy for managing and securing your data – which may be included in your ethics approval but you may go beyond this.
2 Use passwords to protect access to files, computers and devices.
3 Use encryption software to create 'encrypted space' on computers and storage media.
4 Ensure all team members are following the same guidelines on storing and deleting data.
5 Make pack-ups of data only to portable media that have been encrypted and store/carry these separately.
6 When making fieldnotes, if the data is potentially sensitive make sure to destroy all data that is not encrypted (paper notes, voice recordings) and transfer to more permanent encrypted storage away from the field setting.
7 Try to do as much on screen as you can to avoid generating paper copies.
8 When sharing data documents across a team use on encrypted documents.
9 Consider using tracker software so that lost or stolen computing equipment can be traced and tracked down.
10 Early anonymisation of interview transcripts and fieldwork notes is always the ideal.
11 Store data centrally, i.e., cloud locations, to reduce the production of multiple copies of data.

Figure 14.2 Guidelines on data security. *Source*: Adapted from Aldridge et al., 2010.

Remember that the guidelines provided in Figure 14.2 need to be considered in relation to your research and your field context. Cloud services may be useful in research (van Baalen, 2018); you should only use these services if you are sure they are properly encrypted or safe from hackers. Your university or college will have its own policy on cloud data storage, which you will have to follow, and which is likely to exclude certain commercial storage providers. Significantly, cloud companies can be forced to give up user data under certain legislation. So, we need to weigh up the benefits and risks for our research projects on a case-by-case basis.

Postcard 14.2

Managing sensitive interviews in Kuala Lumpur, by Kautsar Ramli

On a very hot day in July 2018, I made my way to one of the most important interviews of my PhD. I was conducting my fieldwork in my home country Malaysia, examining policies to support entrepreneurs. This included some controversial policies such as affirmative action. I travelled to Kuala Lumpur by car to interview an ex-minister who is still quite prominent in Malaysia and I felt nervous. We had arranged to meet at a not-so-popular hotel lounge, which was selected because it was quiet. I'd been introduced to the minister through a family member who also accompanied me for the interview – my family member had a good relationship with him which had helped me gain access and was reassuring for me on the day. As we entered the hotel lobby and met the ex-minister I was very intimidated. I was just a PhD researcher and he was there with his armed, uniformed bodyguards with walkie-talkies. We sat down and I was invited to order whatever I wanted. I chose some *cucur udang* (Malaysian prawn fritters) and an orange juice.

The ex-minister didn't seem to be concerned about what happened with the interview data. This wasn't my first interview with policy-makers and ex-politicians. The longer I had spent in the field the more I was trusted by the political community – they knew that I hadn't shared any confidential information and was handling the data I had been trusted with in the correct way. Had even the smallest detail been 'leaked' by me my research project would have been over, no-one would have agreed to talk to me, least of all this ex-minister. I'd informed the ex-minister that I would safely record and store the interview in a secure location but forgot to tell him it would be destroyed after five years. But I don't think that would have made any difference to him – he either trusted me with the information or he didn't.

After the interview I was confident about handling this sensitive data. I knew how to store it. But I was quite worried about the very secretive and sensitive information he had shared. It is easy to worry about losing data and to want to have multiple copies of audio files and transcripts, but I definitely couldn't do that in this case. Imagine if I'd lost a memory stick with the interview stored on it! Now when I look back, I was really pleased to have access to the ex-minister and was grateful that he was so open with me. As it turned out though, I wasn't able to use everything he talked about in the interview when I wrote up my research. Some quotes would have been too easily identifiable as being made by him. My analysis therefore involved quite a lot of time retracting really juicy quotes that I just could not use in my PhD. This interview really sticks in my mind when I think back to my fieldwork – getting through a high-pressure interview with armed bodyguards and then dealing with the pressures of handling the data securely.

No data set is 'perfect' and it is extremely likely that there will be some limitations in the data you have collected. Just make sure you reflect on this and are upfront about how and where your data could be improved. For example, are all your project objectives being met? Do you need to consider an additional method? With regard to your data coverage, are any types of respondent or any stakeholder or community voices absent? Do you need to consider the gender/age/race distribution of your participants and adjust accordingly? Finally, do you need to refine your methodology or expand your range of secondary data collection?

Do reflect on your data, looking for the positives and the negatives. It can result in some interesting observations. For example, political studies scholar Lee Ann Fujii (2010) encourages us to engage constructively with 'bad data'. She draws on her work with victims of violence in Rwanda to show how even accounts with historical inaccuracies yield insights. Fujii found much of her data to be 'flawed' as interviews contained rumours, errors, denials and silences. Rather than dismiss this data, she engaged with the 'flawed' accounts as a counterpoint to dominant, elite narratives about the experiences of individuals during war and violence. By acknowledging where inaccuracies existed, Lee Ann Fujii was able to adapt her interview questions to sensitively explore the individuals' recollections and better understand their individual responses to the horrors they had experienced.

Identifying Initial Findings

Regardless of the types of data you are generating in the field, finding the time and space to pause and reflect creates possibilities to develop the links between your empirical findings and the conceptual, academic ideas supporting your research.

The initial analysis process can begin in many places, but typically start with a review of your field notes – which we encourage you to keep throughout your research. In many ways, field notes are the first stage of analysis as the notes themselves are to a certain extent an analytical act (Evers, 2011). Field notes grow through gradual accretion as each day's writing is added to the next. These notes are typically not pre-determined or pre-specified and are therefore not collections of data in the same way that audio recordings can be, for example. When you write your notes you are making choices about what to write down, it is intuitive and they reflect your changing sense of what might possibly be made interesting or important (Emerson et al., 1995). When you review your jottings and process them into full notes you are also selecting, prioritising and discarding thoughts and observations and reflecting on the processes observed. This is preliminary analysis – you are seeking to develop a rough sense of the processes or phenomena you are studying and developing initial ideas to explain those processes or phenomena.

Reading through your notebook – while you are still in the field – can help you to see how your ideas, thoughts and experiences are evolving and how they might continue to develop. Your field notes tell you what you notice and find interesting. Reading them can help you to define and refine your research questions, then to become more analytical as you progress. Here are two tips from researchers with experience of using field notebooks, which can help you to get started.

1. Read and re-read your notes, the significance of which may not be immediately clear. If your notes are extensive it can help to index them in some way, noting recurring themes and patterns. Rachel Silvey, a researcher based in Toronto who conducts fieldwork among migrant workers, has used a 'simple, alphabetical indexing system at the back of the field notebook' and found this saved 'hours of research time' (Silvey, 2003: 99). If your notes are electronic, you might find other ways of indexing your notes and seeking out recurrent themes.
2. Reflect on the significance of your observations both for your research questions and in relation to wider debates you have read about in the academic literature. Ask yourself: 'Has your experience changed your perception of the research problem and the issues associated with it?' (Dummer et al., 2008: 477). The wider theoretical significance of what you have observed may only become apparent to you once you have had time to read your notes in the context of academic literature, perhaps after you have returned from the field.

As we saw in Chapters 9 and 12 on visual and multisensory methods, not all field notes take the form of words; we also take photographs and films, and record our field experiences in other ways including through sound recordings. It is not unusual, at the end of the day, to sit around looking at these notes and share them with others, whether in person or online. But how to handle these data? How to get the most out of it, not simply flicking through these images and other texts, adding a few captions and attracting a few likes before forgetting them? Here, we can learn something from Arianne Reis, who took many photographs in the course of her research on conflicts between hunters and recreational 'trampers' in New Zealand, arrived at three distinct ways of using these images. She used some of these images to illustrate her memories of the field. A second set, she used to explore other people's experiences. Others she edited, combining images and words, and embedded these in her text. Using photographs in these different ways, Reis explored 'layers of meanings and emotions' (Reis, 2011: 15). The lesson – for students conducting fieldwork – is to read and re-read all your field notes – verbal, visual and others too – while you are in the field, and while you still have time to respond to and build upon preliminary findings, as you shape your project and research questions.

When you reflect on your field notes – accompanied sometimes by sketches and photographs – you can begin to see writing as a form of fieldwork in its own right. As such, writing involves more than simply documenting findings and conclusions that you may have already reached – 'writing up'. This is particularly true of fieldwork traditions in which written notes and reports occupy centre stage – notably ethnography – but writing is important in a wide range of fieldwork. Rather, writing can be a way of making and interpreting observations, and doing so in real time, in the field rather than at some later date and in some other place.

Digital Analysis on the Go

Some other ways you can conduct initial analysis of your data, while still in the field, involve the use of digital technologies. If you have been processing your data while in the field, you may well have been analysing the data, possibly without realising it. For example, if you have been transcribing (either manually or using transcription software) your interviews, you have been reviewing your data and started to think about key themes. Taking time to look over the interviews you have done so far can allow you to make adjustments to your interview schedule to emphasise emerging themes and possibly to remove some lines of enquiry in favour of deepening your questions around themes you now feel to be more important based on initial analysis.

Earlier in this chapter we have encouraged you to think about how you will systematically record and collate your data. One technological tool at your disposal is **computer-aided qualitative data analysis software** (CAQDAS) (e.g., Nvivo, Atlas.ti, qcoder, Aquad, Quirkos, datagrav). Enter different types of data into CAQDAS software and find appropriate ways to organise them. It is possible to integrate all relevant data methods in one place to create a growing database already during the process of data collection (Friese, 2006). Field notes can be typed directly into a CAQDAS package, photos can be assigned, organised into groups according to specific criteria, such as dates and names. You can then start to immediately add comments and descriptions to photos and other files, beginning your interpretive and analytical processes. Interviews can be recorded on a laptop and immediately archived into the growing database inside the CAQDAS package (Friese, 2006).

While some students find CAQDAS software programmes useful, be aware that it can take a little time to familiarise yourself with whichever software you have access to (there are free versions and your institution will likely have a licence for at least one type). This requires preparation before entering the field so you can get to grips with how the software can help you record and analyse your data, and acknowledgement that even the process of uploading all the data can be time-consuming. If you are conducting fieldwork in a group, licensed versions of the software typically allow multi-user access and simultaneous work and editing. CAQDAS enables you to start analysing your data more easily in the field as you can immediately start to collate, order and interpret your data. The software can allow you to track your project progress as it contains an event log that is date- and time-stamped, and all textual documentation can later be exported as text files as well as summary information about the project as a whole.

Remember though that use of these software tools is not mandatory. It is possible to collect and organise your data using non-specialist word and data processing software, and you can use physical and cloud-based data storage. Regardless of which technologies you use to support your fieldwork, the key point to note is that you can review and start to analyse your data while still conducting fieldwork. You can also start to make connections between different types of data and between your empirical observations and your academic ideas before leaving the field.

What To Do Next?

- Adapt your methodology if you identify gaps in your existing research plan, i.e., new stakeholders to include, boosting representation of particularly significant groups.
- Re-evaluate your project research questions – if this is within the scope of your fieldwork task – based on having a greater understanding of the processes or phenomenon you are researching. Perhaps you want to emphasise a specific aspect or theme of your research or narrow your focus to allow greater analytical depth.
- Review the types of information you are collecting and whether it matches what you initially expected. Many methodological decisions are made based on these pre-field expectations, so once you are in the field you may want to alter our research plan to better reflect what you are actually hearing, seeing, reading and being told.
- Modify your data collection tools. You may adapt your interview schedule in light of initial analysis of the interviews you have conducted so far. You may revisit some of your archival data, looking with fresh eyes, seeking out a particular focus you didn't have when you first looked at the documentation/artefacts.
- Take the time to check that your data management processes are working effectively. Are your files logically titled? Are you able to find what you need easily? Are you able to make connections between data/sources? If not, come up with a new or adapted system.
- Make sure you keep a record of your initial analysis and the changes you make to your research process. It is an important record of how you conducted your research and demonstrates your reflexivity.
- Armed with some initial observations, think about how you can feed these into the research process and engagement with research participants. As noted in the social media chapter, it can be rewarding to feedback initial findings while you are in the field as part of your research, and as a way to give back to those who have participated in your research.

Postcard 14.3

Analysing images and texts in 'sustainable' supply chain research, by Lucy McCarthy and Anne Touboulic

We conduct research that uses secondary data in the form of images and texts to understand how 'sustainability' in supply chains is represented and constructed. We adopt an approach called multimodal discourse analysis. Discourse is the way we think, know and communicate about things. Discourse can take the form/mode of text, visuals and audio, and analysing these multiple forms makes it multimodal (i.e., more than one mode). It shapes our views and experiences around certain issues. Discourse is extremely powerful and we are all embedded in multiple and often competing discourses, some of which are dominant (i.e., the frame of reference used/imposed by the majority/

Continued

most powerful) and some of which are dissonant (i.e., traditionally less powerful, unheard or marginalised). It is often possible to identify the dominant voices and the marginalised ones; this is what we find the most interesting part of discourse analysis.

As part of our work on sustainable supply chains, we saw a trend of researchers becoming interested in corporate social responsibility (CSR) reporting and we found ourselves reading them too (and their reported 'facts') with increasing discomfort. We were finding the language and images used around suppliers – especially those from the Global South – particularly problematic. The suppliers were represented as passive and ignorant subjects in need of help and education from the large corporations. Our first attempt to conduct multimodal discourse analysis therefore was to analyse a series of CSR reports published by large companies across different sectors (pharmaceuticals, cosmetics, food, fashion and banking) to show how they were talking about their suppliers. It helped us expose power dynamics we were aware of in a different light.

So how did we do this? We combined an analysis of text and images. In the text, we searched for terminology used to describe suppliers (e.g., smallholder, strategic, local etc.) as well as the verbs and adjectives most often associated to the term supplier (e.g., follow rigorous standards; comply; communicate). In the images, we wanted to understand how suppliers were visually represented in CSR/sustainability reports and the symbolism behind these representations. We searched and analysed images of suppliers and focused on the frequencies of their appearances, on their roles and the locations and outfits they were portrayed in. Here is a representative sample of the images we analysed.

We found that the text and images in the CSR reports revealed underlying dynamics of legitimation, identity construction and responsibility on environmental and social issues. Suppliers were predominantly represented in a neo-colonial way, and relatedly the Western corporations were constructed as knowing best. Overall, this created a discourse around the need to educate the suppliers and bring them up to speed with sustainability.

This type of work also allowed us to consider what might be missing from the discourse on 'sustainability' and supply chains. Thinking about all the actors in a supply chain, we questioned whose voices and perspectives were included and whose were absent. Where were the suppliers' voices in these reports? As researchers we feel that we have a role in highlighting who is being excluded from the discourse and the implications that this has for practice. For instance, the discourse on educating suppliers and the associated neo-colonial representations serves the Western corporate interests under the umbrella of 'sustainable development'. Ultimately, it devalues local knowledge and work and highlights the importance of fieldwork to give voice to all stakeholders in the supply chain, particularly those who are poorly represented in many discourses.

Conclusion

Data management is an important part of the research process. It can be particularly challenging to record, collate and analyse our data when in the field. The development of technologies such as mobile devices and research software can offer us opportunities to conduct research differently, in ways that enhance our data collection and our reflexivity and adaptability while conducting fieldwork. It is easy to become overwhelmed by how much data we collect in the field, so having awareness of this and developing a plan to manage that data is really important. This chapter has highlighted some of the technologies you can use to support your data management.

A key point in this chapter is that you should devote time in your research schedule to manage your data and to pause to review and reflect on your data collection thus far. Preliminary analysis is possible – and desirable – in the field and can have some positive outcomes on your research including adaptation of your methodology to enhance data collection and increase data quality and through the development of initial findings than can be communicated to research participants.

Key terms

Computer-aided qualitative data analysis software (CAQDAS) – software designed to support qualitative research that can be used in the field.
Data – research data is the recorded, original factual material you have created or collated to conduct your research project that form the bases of your reasoning or discussion. Data is necessary to validate your research findings and can be digital or non-digital.
Data management – the practice of collecting, storing and using data securely and effectively.

Further Reading

France, Derek, Whalley, W. Brian, Mauchline, Alice, Powell, Victoria, Welsh, Katherine, Lerczak, Alex, Park, Julian & Bednarz, Robert S. (2015) *Enhancing Fieldwork Learning Using Mobile Technologies*. Springer.
A guide to using different technologies in the field. It introduces technologies that are appropriate to use during fieldwork and discusses their capabilities. The book focuses on the use of tablets and there are also chapters on using video and social media in the field.

Silver, Christina & Lewins, Ann (2014) *Using Software in Qualitative Research: A Step-by-Step Guide*, 2nd ed. Sage.
This book demystifies the use of software in qualitative research, explaining how and why researchers use software and working through some of the consequences (positive and negative) of its use. It uses case study examples and explains the specific analytical functions the software offers.

15
TAKEAWAYS: FOR WORK AND LIFE

In this concluding chapter you will learn

- to see and name the skills and experience you gain through your fieldwork;
- how to use these skills as you seek and find employment;
- to recognise personal qualities that you can cultivate through your fieldwork and take away in life.

Introduction

Your fieldwork is likely to come with demands and pressures such as the need to cooperate with others and complete assignments on time, but it is important to stand back, to reflect upon the bigger picture, asking where your fieldwork has taken you and where it may take you yet. What, in other words, can you take away from the field? This question challenges you to think beyond specific academic learning outcomes and short-term objectives.

This final chapter identifies some key 'takeaways' of fieldwork, with a view to supporting students who are looking forward to graduating and entering the world of work, but also contemplating life beyond university. This means different things for different people, of course. For some, the question will be practical, a matter of building a strong CV/resumé and presenting well in interviews. Others wonder what they can do about bigger questions, wanting to make a difference to environmental and social challenges at the global and local scales. Others, not sure quite what they want to do or achieve, start out with personal reflections about the kind of person they have become, the qualities they want to cultivate in themselves. But in reality most students – most people – are concerned with all of these things: finding work; shaping your world; and developing as a person.

For Work: Skills and Employability

You can use your fieldwork experience to enhance your employability. Employability encompasses achievements, skills, understandings and personal attributes that can help individuals gain employment and achieve success in their occupations (Yorke, 2006; see also

Pegg et al., 2012). This is not simply a matter of individual advancement in the workplace; your employability can also benefit others including your community, society and the economy (Yorke, 2006). The European Union's Bologna Process, designed to create a coherent European Higher Education Area, calls upon higher education institutions to enhance the 'employability' of graduates (Schaeper, 2009). Similar developments are taking place in other parts of the world, where governments and universities are calling upon universities to prepare students for work and employment. Universities from Australia to Canada to Sri Lanka are increasingly working to ensure that graduates are experienced and confident in transferable soft skills such as problem solving and teamwork that students can develop in the field (Jackson and Chapman, 2012; Finch et al., 2013).

It can help to mention your fieldwork experience when you are composing a CV/resumé or completing a job application and when you are presenting yourself in an interview. This means mapping your own experiences onto the employability attributes and skills that employers will be looking for – shown in Table 15.1. You can do this by keeping track of all aspects of your fieldwork, noting the different skills and experiences you took from them. This table distinguishes three broad sets of skills: subject-specific and technical skills (knowing things, and knowing how to do things); 'soft' skills (these revolve around interpersonal skills and problem solving); and practical experience (including decision-making and adapting to new tasks and circumstances). It is helpful, when you reflect on the skills you acquire, to use some of the language you see in this table. This can help you communicate with and where necessary sell yourself to an employer. For example, if you experienced a conflict with another student in the context of group work, you could describe what happened and what you learned (with the focus on the latter). You might reflect on how this initially unhappy experience prompted you to develop 'interpersonal skills' and gain experience in 'conflict resolution' – skills that will be useful in the workplace. Here it will help to refer back to Chapter 4, Working Together, where we discussed the challenges, risks and opportunities that arise in group fieldwork. For example, we suggested ways of navigating conflicts, working effectively in teams and making sure that everyone is included and involved.

For Life: Personal Qualities and Values

Fieldwork can be a time in which to define (or redefine) yourself, not only as a student but as a human being. Though some of the attributes you develop will interest employers, they can also have a higher purpose, concerned with the kind of person you would like to be and become. In this final section we identify four hallmarks of fieldwork, which have run through this book and are concerned with: finding out; seeing differently; acting differently; and making a difference. Some of these may appeal to you more than others, depending on your personality, priorities and values. These hallmarks of fieldwork show how fieldwork offers – more than academic success and professional advancement – opportunities for personal discovery and social engagement.

Table 15.1 Fieldwork skills and employability attributes. These skills are relevant to employability but also to other forms of academic and personal development

Employability attributes	Fieldwork skills that can make you more employable
Subject-specific and technical skills	Reinforcement and application of academic learning through field experience and observations, including research. Applying abstract (often theoretical) ideas to the real world and using critical thinking to use empirical data to challenge concepts and theories; developing the skills to question the validity of different data sources. Subject-specific skills vary across disciplines, some subjects focusing more on qualitative, some on quantitative data collection and handling, for example. Deep learning. This includes the acquisition of higher-order skills such as analysing, interpreting and evaluating information rather than simply amassing, reproducing and describing it (Hill and Woodland, 2002).
'Soft' skills	Learning about working practices (your own, and of others). Gaining self-confidence through independent work, sometimes in challenging circumstances. Communication and interpersonal skills in relationships with other students and research participants: demonstrating leadership, conflict resolution, empathy (listening to others' opinions), building relationships. Research skills like negotiating access to people or data, learning to relate to research subjects, networking, conducting research ethically. Learning to communicate with different audiences of academics, stakeholders and participants to disseminate your findings. Problem solving including organisation and planning (anticipating problems), working under pressure to solve problems, collaborative problem solving.
Experience	Strategic decision-making, taking ownership of particular tasks, responding to feedback (from peers and/or staff), changing approach after feedback, working in a new environment, understanding different cultures, using technology to find information and disseminate research.

Finding out – the first hallmark of fieldwork – begins with wondering, expressing curiosity and asking questions. The desire to see, know or learn something – curiosity – is a starting point for enquiry, whether in the library, the laboratory, the lecture theatre or the field. This is why some academic researchers celebrate curiosity as a catalyst for scientific and cultural advances (Phillips, 2010). It is why lecturers and teachers include curiosity in defined learning outcomes (Phillips and Johns, 2012). In this book we have argued a similar point – that curiosity can motivate you to learn and make enquiries in the field. Accordingly we have encouraged and guided you to be or become curious. We add a postscript here: curiosity is more than a means to an end. There is something 'free-ranging' (Lee, 2007: 109), open-ended, unpredictable, profound and anarchic about curiosity – a vitality – that you can take away from the field and into your life.

Fieldwork means finding out for yourself rather than taking someone else's word for it. Finding out often involves direct observation, not relying too heavily or trustingly on other books or academic papers, important though they are in context. Equally fieldwork means finding out in your own way. This is why, for all the suggestions and advice we have offered in this book, we have not written a manual or told you precisely what to do or how. We have deliberately left you with problems to solve, decisions to make, so that you learn from other people and traditions but don't just copy them. This leaves space for your creativity, imagination and independence. It simultaneously informs you about but also frees you from tradition and precedent, inviting you to adapt and innovate, making your own mark. An important takeaway of fieldwork is independence.

Second, fieldwork means seeing differently. Fieldwork can bring heightened emotional and sensory experiences, which political theorist and philosopher Jane Bennett identifies with enchantment. This means 'having one's nerves or circulation or concentration powers turned up or recharged – a shot in the arm, a fleeting return to childlike excitement about life' (Bennett, 2001: 5). 'You notice new colours, discern details previously ignored, hear extraordinary sounds, as familiar landscapes of sense sharpen and intensify' (Bennett, 2001: 5). It is possible to be enchanted anywhere and at any time but for many people this is particularly feasible in the course of fieldwork, away from the routines and absorptions of everyday life. Intense sensory and emotional experiences are more than by-products of fieldwork; they are 'inseparable parts of fieldwork learning' (Lai, 2000: 167). There are two lessons in this for us all. The first is to embrace the possibilities of 'affective-focused fieldwork' – a term coined by Kwok Chan Lai, an education researcher based in Hong Kong – in the fieldwork process. The second is to try to hold on to this way of being, carrying the vitality and intensity of fieldwork into life.

One of the catalysts for heightened experience in the field is risk. Fieldwork is not always comfortable; it can take us out of our comfort zones, dropping us into risky situations and exposing us to uncertainty. In the field we find ourselves attempting things that might not work, might be time-consuming and fruitless and where there is a danger of looking silly, amateurish or frivolous. Taking risks can be exciting and it can pay off, taking us to unexpected places and leading to unpredicted discoveries. This willingness to take certain controlled and considered risks – rather than always playing safe – is another thing we can take away from the field.

Seeing differently is closely related to the third in this series of takeaways – acting differently. One practical way in which we can escape habits of perception and action is through play. Management studies professor Michael Schrage argued that we should take play seriously, and never relegate it to childhood. 'Serious play' is experimental; it involves 'the challenge and thrill of confronting uncertainties' through improvisation and innovation (Schrage, 1999: 2; Sutton-Smith, 1997). Serious play has potential in many spheres of life: from the workplace to the hospital, the theatre to the sports field, as well as the classroom, lab and field. We have included many examples of playful fieldwork in this book – inviting you to let a dog take you for a walk, for example, and try seemingly silly exercises and missions that can get you exploring with fresh eyes (Antony and Henry, 2005; Smith, 2008). We have also noticed how students can find themselves playing spontaneously in the field, finding their own ways of being playful. Here as elsewhere play can also be a source of pleasure, joy, diversion and delight, all of which matter in life, lived well and happily. Play can also play a serious part in our lives, a way of thinking laterally and acting experimentally, prompting us to do things differently, to see new possibilities for how we might solve problems and live our lives.

Cycles of problem finding and problem solving, which can shape hands-on enquiry (Sennett, 2008), challenge us to think on our feet. When off-the-peg methods and theories are not enough and when they need adapting to research questions and circumstances, it can be helpful to explore new and different ways of doing and thinking. Creativity can produce something new (Runco and Jaeger, 2012), challenge orthodox ways of seeing and thinking (Jones and Leavy, 2014: 1) and challenge the disciplinary and intellectual boundaries (Kara, 2020: 6) that can both enable and constrain our understanding of the world. Creativity is close to innovation, which involves the development and/or implementation of new methods (see Holmes and Hall, 2020). Creativity and innovation can improve fieldwork, leading to unexpected findings and experiences and thus to fresh perspectives and originality. Conversely, fieldwork provides opportunities for us to develop and build confidence in creativity. This is not for everyone; some people affirm that they are not creative and don't want to be; some find the idea of creativity scary; others argue that it is idealised and over-rated (Mould, 2018). Still, many students find their creative feet in the field and some find this liberating. For them – perhaps for you – creativity not only pays an immediate dividend in terms of the quality of the fieldwork; it also helps you develop a personal quality with intrinsic value of its own.

Fourth and finally, skills and qualities gained in the field can help us to make a difference in the world. This includes a difference in ourselves. Health experts have evidence that 'taking notice' can be good for mental health and well-being (Atkinson and Joyce, 2011; Phillips et al., 2015). Noticing is akin to mindfulness: attending to the world (including people, animals, things and places) around you and simultaneously to what you are feeling (Walker, 2019). And, as we have seen, fieldwork can be a way of developing personal and interpersonal skills and dispositions such as creativity, curiosity, care and empathy. But while your fieldwork can be good for you, it can also make a positive difference to others. When we conduct fieldwork ethically we take responsibility for our actions (Jazeel and McFarlane, 2007), anticipating and avoiding harm and actively seeking the benefits it may bring to other people and perhaps also to non-human counterparts including animals, things and places. There are different ways of taking responsibility, ranging from expressions of active citizenship and community engagement to more transgressive forms of social and environmental action and activism. While it is important to do fieldwork and other forms of research responsibly, it is possible to go further than this, to bring the insights and habits you have learned in the field into other areas of your life, particularly where you can make a difference to others. Through fieldwork – what you take away from it and what you do with it – you can make a difference in yourself and in the world.

GLOSSARY

Ableism is a form of discrimination which favours able-bodied people. In fieldwork, ableism can take the form of assumptions about students' bodily capabilities, ranging from how far they can walk to how long they can manage away from a toilet, with the effect that some students are excluded from some activities, even from entire trips.

Active learning means finding out for yourself, making your own decisions and about what to study and how. Active fieldwork involves learning and enquiry through first-hand experience and observation in and of the social world.

Archives are repositories or collections of published and unpublished sources such as letters, minutes of meetings, reports, maps, sound recordings and digital files. They may be publicly or privately owned and can have a specific focus such as a particular region or a special theme.

Artefacts – objects that can be used during interviews to prompt discussion. They can be postcards, images, videos or even blank pages that elicit more open dialogue.

Colonialism begins with the appropriation of land, labour and resources, and often involves the establishment of settlements and governments in distant lands. Colonial empires have declined and have been succeeded by less overt and tangible configurations of power, but colonialism lives on, in a range of forms: including resilient forms of racism, colonial discourse, domination and subordination.

Computer-aided qualitative data analysis software (CAQDAS) – software designed to support qualitative research that can be used in the field.

Curiosity is the desire to know, see or learn something.

Data – research data is the recorded, original factual material you have created or collated to conduct your research project that form the bases of your reasoning or discussion. Data is necessary to validate your research findings and can be digital or non-digital.

Data management – the practice of collecting, storing and using data securely and effectively.

Decolonisation is one of a number of related terms – others including anti-colonialism and postcolonialism – that refer to activist and critical practices, concerned with dismantling and fighting contemporary colonialism in all its forms. Ngugi wa Thiong'o – the African scholar and writer – coined a term that helps to explain what it might mean to decolonise fieldwork and the wider curriculum: 'decolonising the mind' (wa Thiong'o, 1992).

Digital ethnography – using ethnographic methods to research digital cultures and societies online without the necessity to travel. Can also be referred to as 'virtual ethnography', 'netnography' or 'cyber-ethnography'.

Digital fieldwork – the collection of data from the digital environment.

Digital technologies – technologies such as mobile phones, digital television and radio, desktop computers, laptops, tablets and video recorders that can be used to access digital environments that are often connected to the internet. It also includes more advanced immersive technologies.

Documentary sources – a record, typically but not always written, that is published or unpublished and can be extracted and used in research. The term includes personal documents such as diaries, notes, letters, memoirs, photographs, records kept by companies and organisations, and public documents.

Embodied fieldwork can involve the body as an instrument of field research, an 'active subject' in the production of knowledge, and/or as 'an object of knowledge and a topic of research' (Thanem and Knights, 2019: 43).

Embodiment is a theoretical term that recognises the social construction and socialisation of human bodies, leading to divergence between different bodily experiences and competences in different times and places (see Cresswell, 1999: 176; see also Grosz, 2020).

Ethical review is the process that researchers are required to successfully complete before they are permitted to start fieldwork. Ethical review is administered by institutions – such as the college or university in which the researcher is studying or working – and also by funding bodies and regulators by organisations governing research within a disciplinary or national framework.

Ethics is a branch of philosophy, also known as moral philosophy, concerned with questions of right and wrong (Singer, 2016). Moral philosophers distinguish a series of ethical dimensions: the intrinsic virtues of individuals or acts, the values that lead them to behave that way, and the consequences of their actions. The latter – the ways in which research affects people – are particularly important considerations for those undertaking fieldwork for social research.

Ethnography – derived from the terms *ethnos* (people) and *graphein* (writing) – involves writing about people. Ethnographers seek to 'provide rich, holistic insights into people's views and actions, as well as the nature of the location they inhabit' (Warwick-Booth et al., 2021: 199; after Reeves et al., 2008).

The **field** is the site, place, time or context in which fieldwork takes place. The field may be real or virtual, material or representational, bounded or relational, singular or plural, far away or close to home.

A **field class** is a course component (known in some places as a module or unit) which includes fieldwork.

Fieldwork means finding out for yourself through contextual research. Fieldwork can involve one or more of a range of methods of data collection, analysis and communication.

Immersive technologies – these technologies provide new ways of being immersed in, or enabling interaction with, simulated objects and environments, bringing together users' sight, sound and even touch. The technologies range from 360-degree photography and video to **augmented reality** (AR – a digital experience in which the real world remains central but enhanced with virtual details) and **virtual reality** (VR – a fully enclosed synthetic experience in a fully digital environment with no sense of the real world).

Inclusion involves openness to, and respect for, forms of difference including gender, sexuality, religion, ethnicity, culture, heritage, race, bodily differences, neurodiversity and age. The pursuit of inclusion is often grouped together with that of equality and diversity within institutional equality, diversity and inclusion strategies, which are geared towards recognising differences and making alterations and reasonable adjustments. In educational settings, this means adjusting teaching and learning practices and the institutional settings in which they take place, ranging from classrooms to virtual learning environments to field sites (Ahmed, 2012).

Interviewing – an interactive form of data collection involving dialogue between the interviewer and interviewee. It can vary in the degree to which it is structured and the ways in which it is enacted.

Mobile interviewing – interviewing conducted on the move, in contrast to traditional interviewing methods which tend to be static.

Multisensory fieldwork brings more than one of the researcher's senses to field research, typically reaching beyond the most commonly used sense – seeing – to include the other senses and the interactions between these senses.

Neurodivergent refers to an individual or group of people who is/are not neurotypical (autistic, ADHD etc.). A **neurodiverse** group includes people who are variously neurodivergent and neurotypical.

Online interviewing – the use of internet technologies to conduct interviews rather than conducting them face-to-face.

Participant observation is a form of ethnography that involves spending time – being, living and perhaps working, playing and eating – with people or communities in order to understand them (Laurier, 2010; Laurier, 2013). Whereas ethnographies tend to take months or years, participant observation can be carried out over relatively brief periods, which are feasible within student fieldwork.

Participatory research involves participants as partners rather than mere informants (Israel et al., 2010) and frames the research process around the needs and interests of those participants, as 'beneficiaries, users and stakeholders of the research' (Macaulay, 2017: 256). Participatory research is an approach rather than a specific method.

Photo-elicitation, also known as auto-photography and self-directed photography, puts cameras into the hands of research participants in a bid to see their lives through their own eyes, and to enter worlds that are otherwise off-limits to the researcher (Harper, 2002).

Positionality refers to the circumstances in which knowledge is produced and shaped, and where we stand in relation to the people or topic we are investigating. By acknowledging our positionality, it is possible to be explicit about the origins, content and limits of what we know. Understanding our positionality, it is also possible to become more aware of our responsibilities to other people.

Reflexivity turns the focus inward upon the researcher, their positionality and practice. Being reflexive means being curious about how you are seen by others in the field, and about the power relations behind those perceptions and relationships. Being reflexive means reflecting critically upon your work and encounters in the field.

Research design is the strategy you develop to answer your research question or problem. It includes the data you collect, the methods you choose and the ways in which you analyse your data.

Secondary data is the information and material that other people have collected or produced (Tight, 2019). Secondary sources include written documents such as newspapers, websites, articles and books, numerical records such as census data and voting records, and artefacts such as photographs and postcards.

Secondary research involves accessing and interpreting secondary data. Secondary research methods are distinguished from primary, the latter generating entirely new data.

Teamwork skills are important for fieldwork and can be acquired through fieldwork. Teamwork skills take various forms, ranging from leadership (the role played by a project leader or chair) to supportive team membership (listening to others, cooperating with them, prioritising the needs of the group above personal concerns and so on). These skills can be valuable in future employment and also in life.

Vision is 'what the human eye is physiologically capable of seeing' (Rose, 2022: 6).

Visuality refers to the ways in which vision is constructed: 'how we see, how we are able, allowed or made to see, and how we see this seeing and the unseeing therein' (Foster, 1988: ix). Throughout the modern period, the Western world is said to have become increasingly and exceptionally visual or ocular (Jay, 1993).

BIBLIOGRAPHY

Aarseth, Espen J. (2003) Playing Research: Methodological approaches to game analysis. Papers from spilforskning.dk Conference, 28–29 August. Available from: https://pdfs.semanticscholar.org/527f/b6d570164582bf2ade79ba1899bfc7e7c039.pdf

Abbott, Dina (2006) Disrupting the 'whiteness' of fieldwork in geography. *Singapore Journal of Tropical Geography*, 27(3): 326–341.

Adams, Mike & Brown, Sally (eds.) (2006) *Towards Inclusive Learning in Higher Education: Developing Curricula for Disabled Students*. Routledge.

Adamson, George C. D. (2015) Private diaries as information sources in climate research. *WIREs Climate Change*, 6: 599–611. doi: 10.1002/wcc.365

Agbebiyi, Adeola (2013) Tiers of gatekeepers and ethical practice: Researching adolescent students and sexually explicit online material. *International Journal of Social Research Methodology*, 16(6): 535–540.

Aguinis, Herman & Bradley, Kyle J. (2014) Best-practice recommendations for designing and implementing experimental vignette methodology studies. *Organizational Research Methods*, 17(4): 351–371.

Ahamat, Amiruddin (2019) *Using Structured Interviews and Personal Observation to Study Entrepreneurial Opportunity: A Reflection*. Sage.

Ahmed, Sara (2012) *On Being Included: Racism and Diversity in Institutional Life*. Duke University Press.

Aizawa, Shinichi & Watanabe, Daisuke (2020) Accessing quantitative data for qualitative research: White Papers, official statistics and micro datasets. In Kottman, N. & Reiher, C. (eds.), *Studying Japan: Handbook of Research Designs, Fieldwork and Methods*. Nomos, pp. 256–260.

Akemu, Onajono & Abdelnour, Samer (2018) Confronting the digital: Doing ethnography in modern organizational settings. *Organizational Research Methods*, 23(2): 296–321.

Alasazewski, Andy (2006) *Using Diaries for Social Research*. Sage.

Alberti, Fay Bound (2019) *A Biography of Loneliness: The History of an Emotion*. Oxford University Press.

Alder-Nissen, Rebecca (2016) Towards a practice turn in EU studies: The everyday of European integration. *Journal of Common Market Studies*, 54(1): 87–103.

Aldridge, Judith, Medina, Juanjo & Ralphs, Robert (2010) The problem of proliferation: Guidelines for improving the security of qualitative data in a digital age. *Research Ethics*, 6(1): 3–9.

Ali, Nafhesa (2021) Reflexive storytelling: 'Muslim women laughing in the library'. In Phillips, Richard & Kara, Helen (eds.), *Creative Writing for Social Research*. Policy Press, pp. 99–107.

Allen, Louisa (2022) Smellwalks as sensuous pedagogy in sexuality education. *Sex Education*, May: 1–8.

Altheide, David (1980) Leaving the Newsroom. In Shaffir, W. B., Stebbins, R. A. and Turowetz, A. (eds.), *Fieldwork Experience: Qualitative Approaches to Social Research*. St Martin's Press, pp. 301–310.

Amit, V. (2000) *Constructing the Field*. Routledge.

Anderson, Claire & Kirkpatrick, Susan (2016) Narrative interviewing. *International Journal of Clinical Pharmacy*, 38: 631–635.

Ansell, N., Robson, E., Hajdu, F. & van Blerk, L. (2012) Learning from young people about their lives: Using participatory methods to research the impacts of AIDS in southern Africa. *Children's Geographies*, 10(2): 169–186.

Antony, Rachael & Henry, Joel (2005) *The Lonely Planet Guide to Experimental Travel*. Lonely Planet.

Arbus, Doon & Israel, Marvin (1972) *Diane Arbus*. Mullen.

Ardley, Barry & McIntosh, Eleanor (2019) Business strategy and business environment: The impact of virtual communities on value creation. *Strategic Change*, 28(5): 325–331.

Ardley, Barry & McIntosh, Eleanor (2021) Netnography, Facebook, and the adult fans of LEGO: Researching value creation processes in an online community. Sage Research Method Cases. Sage.

Asad, Talal (ed.) (1973) *Anthropology and the Colonial Encounter*. Ithaca Press.

Atkinson, Paul & Coffey, Amanda (2002) Revisiting the relationship between participant observation and interviewing. In Gubrium, Jaber F. & Holstein, James A. (eds.), *Handbook of Interview Research*. Sage, pp. 801–814.

Atkinson, Rowland (2007) Ecology of sound: The sonic order of urban space. *Urban Studies*, 44(10): 1905–1917.

Atkinson, Sarah & Joyce, Kerry E. (2011) The place and practices of well-being in local governance. *Environment and Planning C: Government and Policy*, 29(1): 133–148.

Back, Les (2003) Deep listening: Researching music and the cartographies of sound. In Blunt, A., Gruffudd, P., May, J., Ogborn, M. & Pinder, D. (eds.), *Cultural Geography in Practice*. Arnold, pp. 272–285.

Bahn, Susanne & Barratt-Pugh, Llandis (2013) Getting reticent young male participants to talk: Using artefact-mediated interviews to promote discursive interaction. *Qualitative Social Work*, 12(2): 186–199.

Bail, Chris (2021) *Breaking the Social Media Prism: How to Make Our Platforms Less Polarizing*. Princeton University Press.

Ball, P. (2012) *Curiosity: How Science Became Interested in Everything*. Random House.

Balshaw, Maria & Kennedy, Liam (2000) *Urban Space and Representation*. Pluto.

Baltruschat, Astrid (2000) The interpretation of films based on the documentary method. In Bohnsack, Ralf, Pfaff, Nicolle & Weller, Wivian (eds.), *Qualitative Analysis and Documentary Method in International Educational Research*. Barbara Budrich, pp. 311–342.

Banks, Glenn & Scheyvens, Regina (2014) Ethical issues. In Scheyvens, Regina (ed.), *Development Fieldwork: A Practical Guide*, 2nd ed. Sage, pp. 160–187.

Banks, Marcus (2001) *Visual Methods in Social Research*. Sage.

Barker, John & Alldred, Pam (2012) Documentary research and secondary data. In Bradford, Simon & Cullen, Fin (eds.), *Research and Research Methods for Youth Practitioners*. Routledge, pp. 140–161.

Barnes, Trevor J. & Duncan, James S. (2013) *Writing Worlds: Discourse, Text and Metaphor in the Representation of Landscape*, 2nd ed. Routledge.

Barns, Sarah (2013) Sounds different: Listening to the proliferating spaces of technological modernity in the city. *Space and Culture*, 17(1): 4–15.

Bates, Jessica A. (2004) Use of narrative interviewing in everyday information behavior research. *Library and Information Science Research*, 26: 15–28.
Beck, Julia, Rainoldi, Mattia & Egger, Roman (2019) Virtual reality in tourism: A state-of-the-art review. *Tourism Review*, 74(3): 586–612.
Becker, Howard S. (1974) Photography and sociology. *Studies in Visual Communication*, 1(1): 3–26.
Becker, Howard S. (1999) The Chicago School, so-called. *Qualitative Sociology*, 22(1): 3–12.
Bejarano, Carolina Alonso., López Juárez, Lucia, García, Mirian A. & Goldstein, Daniel M. (2019) Decolonizing ethnography: Undocumented immigrants and new directions in social science. *Anthropological Quarterly*, 93(1): 1613–1618.
Belbin, R. Meredith (1981) *Management Teams: Why They Succeed or Fail*. Heinemann.
Bell, Cynthia J., Spruit, Jessica L. & Kavanaugh, Karen L. (2020) Exposing the risks of social media recruitment in adolescents and young adults with cancer: #Beware. *Journal of Adolescent and Young Adult Oncology*, 9(5): 601–607. https://doi.org/10.1089/jaao.2020.0018
Bell, D. & Valentine, G. (eds.) (1997) *Consuming Geographies: We Are Where We Eat*. Routledge.
Bendiner-Viani, Gabrielle (2013) The big world in the small: Layered dynamics of meaning-making in the everyday. *Environment and Planning D: Society and Space*, 31(4): 708–726.
Benjamin, Walter (1985) *One Way Street and Other Writings*. Verso.
Bennett, Jane (2001) *The Enchantment of Modern Life: Attachments, Crossings and Ethics*. Princeton University Press.
Bennett, Katy (2002) Participant observation. In Shurmer-Smith, Pam (ed.), *Doing Cultural Geography*. Sage, pp. 139–149.
Bennett, Linda A. & McAvity, Katharine (1994) Family research: A case for interviewing couples. In Handel, Gerald (ed.), *The Psychosocial Interior of the Family*. Routledge, pp. 53–68.
Bennett, Luke (2013) Who goes there? Accounting for gender in the urge to explore abandoned military bunkers. *Gender, Place and Culture*, 20(5): 630–646.
Bennett, Luke & Crawley Jackson, Amanda (2017) Making common ground with strangers at Furnace Park. *Social and Cultural Geography*, 18(1): 92–108.
Berger, John (1972) *Ways of Seeing*. Penguin.
Bhakta, Amita, Dickinson, Jen, Moore, Kate, Mutinda, David, Mylam, Anna & Upton, Caroline (2015) Negotiating the responsibilities of collaborative undergraduate fieldcourses. *Area*, 47(3): 282–288.
Błachnio, Agata, Przepiórka, Aneta & Rudnicka, Patrycja (2013) Psychological determinants of using Facebook: A research review. *International Journal of Human–Computer Interaction*, 29: 775–787.
Blommaert, J. and Jie, D. (2020) *Ethnographic Fieldwork: A Beginner's Guide*. Multilingual Matters.
Blunt, Alison & Dowling, Robyn (2022) *Home*, 2nd ed. Routledge.
Blyn, Robin (2013) *The Freak-garde: Extraordinary Bodies and Revolutionary Art in America*. University of Minnesota Press.
Bonacchi, Chiara, Bevan, Andrew, Pett, Daniel, Keinan-Schoonbaert, Adi, Sparks, Rachel, Wexler, Jennifer & Wilkin, Neil (2014) Crowd-sourced archaeological research: The MicroPasts project. *Archaeology International*, 17: 61–68.
Boniface, K. (2019) Friday, 16 August 2019. Blog: www.themostdifficultthingever.com. Last accessed 6 September 2022.

Booth, K. I. (2015) What a difference place makes: Place gestalt and some methodological thoughts. *Qualitative Inquiry*, 21(1): 20–27.
Bordessa, Ronald & Bunge, William (1975) *The Canadian Alternative: Survival, Expeditions and Urban Change*. Department of Geography, Atkinson College.
Borland, John & James, Sue (1999) The learning experience of students with disabilities in higher education: A case study of a UK university. *Disability and Society*, 14(1): 85–101.
Bosch, Tanya (2022) Commentary: Decolonizing digital methods. *Communication Theory*, 32: 298–302.
Bouchard, Natalie (2021) Travelling on smell-time. In Bonnaud, X. & Fraigneau, V. (eds.), *Nouveau Territoires de l'Expérience Olfactive*. Infolio, pp. 91–111.
Bounegru, Liliana & Forceville, Charles (2011) Metaphors in editorial cartoons representing the global financial crisis. *Visual Communication*, 10(2): 209–229. doi: 10.1177/1470357211398446
Bourdieu, Pierre (1990) *The Logic of Practice*. Stanford University Press.
Bourdieu, P. & Whiteside, S. (1990) *Photography: A Middlebrow Art*. Stanford University Press.
Bozzoli, Belinda with Nkotsoe, Mmantho (1991) *Women of Phokeng: Consciousness, Life Strategy and Migrancy in South Africa, 1900–1983*. James Currey.
Brace-Govan, Jan & Demsar, Vlad (2014) Narrative inquiry, netnography and interviews: Triangulation in video gaming trade-in. Sage Research Method Cases. Sage.
Bradbeer, John, Healey, Mick & Kneale, Pauline (2004) Undergraduate geographers' understandings of geography, learning and teaching. *Journal of Geography in Higher Education*, 28(1): 17–34.
Bray, Lucy (2007) Developing an activity to aid informed assent when interviewing children and young people. *Journal of Research in Nursing*, 12(5): 447–457.
Brummelman, Eddie, Grapsas, Stathis & van der Kooij, Katinka (2022) Parental praise and children's exploration: A virtual reality experiment. *Scientific Reports*, 12: 1–11.
Brydon, Lynne (2006) Ethical practices in doing development research. In Potter, Rob B. & Desai, Vandana (eds.), *Doing Development Research*. Sage, pp. 25–33.
Bryman, Alan (2016) *Social Research Methods*. Oxford University Press.
Bryson, John R., Billing, Chloe, Hales, Chantal, Mulhall, Rachel & Ronayne, Megan (2022) Corporate interviewing and accessing elites in manufacturing companies: A framework to guide qualitative semi-structured interviews. In Bryson, J. R., Billing, C., Graves, W. & Yeung, G. (eds.), *A Research Agenda for Manufacturing Industries in the Global Economy*. Edward Elgar, pp. 193–210.
Bull, Michael & Back, Les (2003) *The Auditory Culture Reader*. Berg.
Burgess, Jaquelin & Jackson, Peter (1992) Streetwork: An encounter with place. *Journal of Geography in Higher Education*, 16(2): 151–157.
Burgess, Robert G. (1984) *In the Field*. Routledge.
Burgess, Robert G. & Morrison, Marlene (1998) Ethnographies of eating in an urban primary school. In Murcott, Anne (ed.), *The Nation's Diet: The Social Science of Food Choice*. Addison, Wesley, Longman, pp. 209–227.
Burrell, Jenna (2009) The field site as a network: A strategy for locating ethnographic research. *Field Methods*, 21(2): 181–199.
Burrell, Jenna (2012) *Invisible Users: Youth in the Internet Cafes of Urban Ghana*. MIT Press.

Burton, Susan K. (2015) Issues in cross-cultural interviewing: Japanese women in England. In Perks, Robert & Thomson, Alistair (eds.), *The Oral History Reader*, 3rd ed. Routledge, pp. 145–156.

Butler, Judith (2011) *Gender Trouble: Feminism and the Subversion of Identity*. Routledge.

Butler, Toby (2006) A walk of art: The potential of the sound walk as practice in cultural geography. *Social and Cultural Geography*, 7(6): 889–908.

Caers, Ralf, De Feyter, Tim, De Couck, Marijke, Stough, Talia, Vigna, Claudia & DuBois, Cind (2013) Facebook: A literature review. *New Media and Society*, 15: 982–1002.

Cahill, Caitlin (2007) Participatory data analysis. In Kingdon, S., Pain, R. & Kesby, M. (eds.), *Participatory Action Research Approaches and Methods*. Routledge, pp. 181–187.

Callaway, Ewen (2017) South Africa's San People issue ethics code to scientists. *Nature*, 543(7646): 475–476.

Calvey, David (2017) *Covert Research: The Art, Politics and Ethics of Undercover Fieldwork*. Sage.

Cameron, Harriet, Coleman, Bryan, Hervey, Tamara, Rahman, Sabrina & Rostant, Philip (2019) Equality law obligations in higher education: Reasonable adjustments under the Equality Act 2010 in assessment of students with unseen disabilities. *Legal Studies*, 39(2): 204–229.

Campanario, Gabriel (2012) *The Art of Urban Sketching: Drawing on Location around the World*. Quarry.

Campbell, Elizabeth & Pahl, Kate (eds.) (2018) *Re-imagining Contested Communities*. Policy Press.

Capurro, Rafael & Pingel, Christoph (2002) Ethical issues of online communication research. *Ethics and Information Technology*, 4: 189–194.

Carter, Stacy M., Shih, Patti, Williams, Jane, Degeling, Chris & Mooney-Somers, Julie (2021) Conducting qualitative research online: Challenges and solutions. *The Patient*, 14(6): 711–718.

Cassell, Catherine (2015) *Conducting Research Interviews for Business and Management Students*. Sage.

Castellano, Marlene Brant (2004) Ethics of Aboriginal research. *International Journal of Indigenous Health*, 1(1): 98–114.

Castleden, Heather, Morgan, Vanessa Sloan & Lamb, Christopher (2012) 'I spent the first year drinking tea': Exploring Canadian university researchers' perspectives on community-based participatory research involving Indigenous peoples. *The Canadian Geographer/Le Géographe canadien*, 56(2): 160–179.

Caulfield, Brian (2021) What is the metaverse? Available at: https://blogs.nvidia.com/blog/2021/08/10/what-is-the-metaverse/. Last accessed 1 February 2023.

Causey, Andrew (2017) *Drawn to See: Drawing as an Ethnographic Method*. University of Toronto Press.

Chabram, Angie (1990) Chicana/o studies as oppositional ethnography. *Cultural Studies*, 4(3): 228–247.

Chacko, Elizabeth (2004) Positionality and praxis: Fieldwork experiences in rural India. *Singapore Journal of Tropical Geography*, 25(1): 51–63.

Chalfen, Richard (1987) *Snapshot Versions of Life*. University of Wisconsin Press.

Chambers, Megan, Bliss, Katherine, & Rambur, Betty (2020) Recruiting research participants via traditional snowball vs Facebook advertisements and a website. *Western Journal of Nursing Research*, 42(10), 846–851. https://doi.org/10.1177/0193945920904445

Chaplin, Elizabeth (2004) My visual diary. In Knowles, Caroline & Sweetman, Paul (eds.), *Picturing the Social Landscape: Visual Methods and the Sociological Imagination*. Routledge, pp. 35–48.

Chapman, Lynne (2010) How to draw people: Sketching in public places. Available at: https://lynnechapman.blogspot.com/2010/06/sketching-people.html. Last accessed 6 September 2022.

Chi, Heng-Chang & Jackson, Peter (2011) Thai food in Taiwan: Tracing the contours of transnational taste. *New Formations*, 74: 65–81.

Chiarella, D. & Vurro, G. (2020) Fieldwork and disability: An overview for an inclusive experience. *Geological Magazine*, 157(11): 1933–1938.

Chilisa, Bagele (2019) *Indigenous Research Methodologies*. Sage.

Chiu, Chihsin (2009) Contestation and conformity street and park skateboarding in New York City public space. *Space and Culture*, 12(1): 25–42.

Chuan, G. K. & Poh, W. P. (2000) Status of fieldwork in the geography curriculum in South East Asia. In Gerber, R. & Chuan, G. K. (eds.), *Fieldwork in Geography: Reflections, Perspectives and Actions*. Kluwer Academic, pp. 99–117.

Clifford, J. (1997) *Routes: Travel and Translation in the Late Twentieth Century*. Harvard University Press.

Coe, Neil M., Johns, Jennifer L. & Ward, Kevin (2009) Slow growth: Fragmented markets and competitive margins in the Australian temporary staffing industry. *Journal of Economic Geography*, 9(1): 55–84.

Coe, Neil M., Johns, Jennifer L. & Ward, Kevin (2012) Limits to expansion: Transnational corporations and territorial embeddedness in the Japanese temporary staffing market. *Global Networks*, 12(1): 22–47.

Coe, Neil M. & Smyth, Fiona (2010) Students as tour guides: Innovation in fieldwork assessment. *Journal of Geography in Higher Education*, 34(1): 125–139.

Coffey, Amanda (1999) *The Ethnographic Self*. Sage.

Coffey, Amanda (2018) Sex in the field: Intimacy and intimidation. In Welland, T. & Pugsley, L. (eds.), *Ethical Dilemmas in Qualitative Research*. Routledge, pp. 57–74.

Cohen, Jeffrey H. (2015) *Eating Soup Without a Spoon: Anthropological Theory and Method in the Real World*. University of Texas Press.

Collier, John & Collier, Malcolm (1986) *Visual Anthropology: Photography as a Research Method*. Holt, Rinehart, and Winston.

Cook, I. (2005) Participant observation. In Flowerdew, R. & Martin, D. (eds.), *Methods in Human Geography*. Pearson, pp. 167–188.

Corti, Louise & Fielding, Nigel (2016) Opportunities from the digital revolution: Implications for researching, publishing, and consuming qualitative research. Sage Open. doi: 10.1177/2158244016678912

Cowan, Alexander and Steward, Jill (eds.) (2007) *The City and the Senses: Urban Culture Since 1500*. Ashgate.

Craciun, Catrinel & Flick, Uwe (2014) 'I will never be the granny with rosy cheeks': Perceptions of ageing in precarious and financially secure middle-aged Germans. *Journal of Aging Studies*, 29: 78–87.

Crane, Andrew (2017) Book review: Modern Slavery. *Organization Studies*, 40(1): 143–146.

Crang, Mike (2003) Qualitative methods: Touchy, feely, look-see? *Progress in Human Geography*, 27(4): 494–504.

Crang, Philip (1994) It's showtime: On the workplace geographies of display in a restaurant in southeast England. *Environment and Planning D: Society and Space*, 12(6): 675–704.

Crary, Jonathan (1992) *Techniques of the Observer: On Vision and Modernity in the Nineteenth Century*. MIT Press.

Crawshaw, Carol & Urry, John (1997) Tourism and the photographic eye. In Rojek, Chris & Urry, John (eds.), *Touring Cultures: Transformations of Travel and Theory*. Routledge, pp. 176–195.

Crenshaw, Kimberlé Williams (1989) Demarginalizing the intersection of race and sex: A black feminist critique of antidiscrimination doctrine, feminist theory and antiracist politics. *University of Chicago Legal Forum*, 1: 139–167.

Cresswell, Tim (1999) Embodiment, power and the politics of mobility: The case of female tramps and hobos. *Transactions of the Institute of British Geographers*, 24(2): 175–192.

Crilly, Nathan, Blackwell, Alan F. & Clarkson, P. John (2006) Graphic elicitation: Using research diagrams as interview stimuli. *Qualitative Research*, 6(3): 341–366.

Croskerry, Pat, Singhal, Geeta & Mamede, Silvia (2013) Cognitive debiasing 1: Origins of bias and theory of debiasing. *BMJ Quality and Safety*, 22(Suppl 2): ii58–ii64.

Cupples, Julie (2002) The field as a landscape of desire: Sex and sexuality in geographical fieldwork. *Area*, 34(4): 382–390.

Datta, Ayona (2008) Spatialising performance: Masculinities and femininities in a fragmented field. *Gender, Place and Culture*, 15(2): 191–207.

Davies, Andrew D. (2009) Ethnography, space and politics: Interrogating the process of protest in the Tibetan freedom movement. *Area*, 41(1): 19–25.

Davies, Anna, Hoggart, Keith & Lees, Loretta (2014) *Researching Human Geographies*, 2nd ed. Routledge.

Day, Jon (2015) *Cyclogeography: Journeys of a London Bicycle Courier*. Notting Hill Editions.

Deakin, Hannah & Wakefield, Kelly (2014) Skype interviewing: Reflections of two PhD researchers. *Qualitative Research*, 14(5): 603–616.

Dean, Elizabeth, Head, Brian & Swicegood, Jodie (2013) Virtual cognitive interviewing using skype and second life. In Hill, Craig A., Dean, Elizabeth & Murphy, Joe (eds.), *Social Media, Sociality and Survey Research*. John Wiley and Sons, pp. 107–132.

DeCarvalho, José Jorge and Flórez-Flórez, Juliana (2014) The meeting of knowledges: A project for the decolonisation of the university in Latin America. *Postcolonial Studies*, 17(2): 122–139.

Degen, Monica Montserrat (2008) *Sensing Cities: Regenerating Public life in Barcelona and Manchester*. Routledge.

Denyer, David & Tranfield, David (2009) Producing a systematic review. In Buchanan, David A. & Bryman, Alan (eds.), *The Sage Handbook of Organizational Research Methods*. Sage, pp. 671–689.

Desai, Vandana & Potter, Rob B. (eds.) (2006) *Doing Development Research*. Sage.

DfES (1999) *Skills Task Force Employer Skills Survey, 1999*. Department for Education and Skills, London.

Dijkstra, Suzan, Kok, Gautam, Ledford, Julie G., Sandalova, E. & Stevelink, Remi (2018) Possibilities and pitfalls of social media for translational medicine. *Frontiers in Translational Medicine*, 5: 345–351.

Do, Jaewoo & Yamagata, Lisa C. (2017) Designing and developing cell phone applications for qualitative research. *Qualitative Inquiry*, 23(10): 757–767.

Dodge, M. & Kitchin, R. (2006) Net: Geography fieldwork frequently asked questions. In Weiss, J., Nolan, J., Hunsinger, J. & Trifonas, P. (eds.), *The International Handbook of Virtual Learning Environments*. Springer, pp. 1175–1202.

Dodman, D. R. (2003) Shooting in the city: An autophotographic exploration of the urban environment in Kingston, Jamaica. *Area*, 35(3): 293–304.

Dowling, Robyn (2005) Power, subjectivity and ethics in qualitative research. In Hay, I. (ed.), *Qualitative Research Methods in Human Geography*. Oxford University Press, pp. 19–29.

Drakulić, Slavenka (1993) *How We Survived Communism and Even Laughed*. HarperCollins.

Driver, Felix (2000) Editorial: Field-work in geography. *Transactions of the Institute of British Geographers*, 25(3): 267–268.

Dummer, Trevor J. B., Cook, Ian G., Parker, Sara L., Barrett, Giles A. & Hull, Andrew P. (2008) Promoting and assessing 'deep learning' in geography fieldwork: An evaluation of reflective field diaries. *Journal of Geography in Higher Education*, 32(3): 459–479.

Dunbar-Ortiz, Roxanne (2014) *An Indigenous Peoples' History of the United States*, Vol. 3. Beacon Press.

Duruz, Jean (2005) Eating at the borders: Culinary journeys. *Environment and Planning D: Society and Space*, 23(1): 51–69.

Duruz, Jean & Khoo, G. C. (2014) *Eating Together: Food, Space, and Identity in Malaysia and Singapore*. Rowman & Littlefield.

Dutta, Urmitapa (2021) The politics and poetics of 'fieldnotes': Decolonizing ethnographic knowing. *Qualitative Inquiry*, 27(5): 598–607.

Dwivedi, Yogesh, K. et al. (2022) Metaverse beyond the hype: Multidisciplinary perspectives on emerging challenges, opportunities, and agenda for research, practice and policy. *International Journal of Information Management*, 66: 102542. https://doi.org/10.1016/j.ijinfomgt.2022.102542

Eaker, Chris (2016) What could possibly go wrong? The impact of poor data management. In Federer, Lisa (ed.), *The Medical Library Association's Guide to Data Management for Librarians*. Rowman & Littlefield, pp. 1–27.

Edensor, Tim (2008) *Tourists at the Taj: Performance and Meaning at a Symbolic Site*, 2nd ed. Routledge.

Edmonds, Rosalie (2021) Balancing research goals and community expectations: The affordances of body cameras and participant observation in the study of wildlife conservation. *Social Interaction: Video-Based Studies of Human Sociality*, 4(2). https://doi.org/10.7146/si.v4i2.127193

El Guindi, Fadwa (2004) *Visual Anthropology: Essential Theory and Method*. Altamira Press.

Ellingson, Laura L. (2017) *Embodiment in Qualitative Research*. Routledge.

Ellingson, Laura L. & Sotirin, P. (2020) *Making Data in Qualitative Research: Engagements, Ethics, and Entanglements*. Routledge.

Emerson, Robert M., Fretz, Rachel I. & Shaw, Linda L. (1995) *Writing Ethnographic Fieldnotes*. University of Chicago Press.

Emmison, Michael & Smith, Philip (2000) *Researching the Visual: Images, Objects, Contexts and Interactions in Social and Cultural Inquiry*. Sage.

England, Kim V. (1994) Getting personal: Reflexivity, positionality, and feminist research. *The Professional Geographer*, 46(1): 80–89.

Evans, Bethan, Bias, Stacy & Colls, Rachel (2021) The dys-appearing fat body: Bodily intensities and fatphobic sociomaterialities when flying while fat. *Annals of the American Association of Geographers*, 111(6): 1816–1832.

Evans, James & Jones, Phil (2011) The walking interview: Methodology, mobility and place. *Applied Geography*, 31: 849–858.

Evers, Jeanine, C. (2011) From the past into the future: How technological developments change our ways of data collection, transcription and analysis. *FQS Forum: Qualitative Social Research Sozial Forschung*, 12(1): 1–22.

Farrant, Finola (2014) Unconcealment: What happens when we tell stories. *Qualitative Inquiry*, 20(4): 461–470.

Feneck, Amy & Plender, Olivia (2010) *The School Looks Around*. Whitechapel Gallery, London. https://www.whitechapelgallery.org/exhibitions/artists-in-residence-the-school-looks-around/. Last accessed 6 September 2022.

Finch, David J., Hamilton, Leah, Baldwin, Riley & Zehner, Mark (2013) An exploratory study of factors affecting undergraduate employability. *Education + Training*, 55(7): 681–704.

Fish, Stanley (1980) *Is There a Text in this Class? The Authority of Interpretive Communities*. Harvard University Press.

Fisher, Gerald H. (1973) Current levels of noise in an urban environment. *Ergonomics*, 4(4): 211–218.

Fisher, Ruth M., Barczak, Radoslaw J., Hayes, James E. & Stuetz, Richard M. (2018) Framework for the use of odour wheels to manage odours throughout wastewater biosolids processing. *Science of the Total Environment*, 634: 214–223.

Flick, Uwe (2000) Episodic interviewing. In Bauer, M. W. & Gaskell, G. (eds.), *Qualitative Researching with Text, Image and Sound*. Sage, pp. 75–92.

Forsdick, Charles, Kinsley, Zoe & Walchester, Kathryn (eds.) (2019) *Keywords for Travel Writing Studies*. Anthem.

Foster, Hal (ed.) (1988) *Vision and Visuality: Discussions in Contemporary Culture*. Bay Press.

Foster, Roland J. (2007) 'It lets you use your feet more like you use your hands on the rock': A haptic geography of bouldering. Lincoln University: doctoral thesis.

Foucault, Michel (1988) The masked philosopher: Interview first published in *Le Monde*, April 6–7, 1980. In Kritzman, L. (ed.), *Politics, Philosophy, Culture: Interviews and Other Writings 1977–1984*, trans. A. Sheridan. Routledge, pp. 327–328.

France, Derek, Whalley, W. Brian, Mauchline, Alice, Powell, Victoria, Welsh, Katherine, Lerczak, Alex, Park, Julian & Bednarz, Robert S. (2015) *Enhancing Fieldwork Learning Using Mobile Technologies*. Springer.

Franco, Paolo & Yang, Ye (2021) Exiting fieldwork 'with Grace': Reflections on the unintended consequences of participant observation and researcher–participant relationships. *Qualitative Market Research: An International Journal*, 24(2): 358–374.

Frazier, Emily (2020) When fieldwork 'fails': Participatory visual methods and fieldwork encounters with resettled refugees. *Geographical Review*, 110(1–2): 133–144.

Freire, Paulo (2020) *Pedagogy of the Oppressed: Toward a Sociology of Education*. Routledge.

Friese, Susanne (2006) Software and fieldwork. In Hobbs, Dick & Wright, Richard (eds.), *The Sage Handbook of Fieldwork*. Sage, pp. 307–332.

Frost, Diane & Phillips, Richard (eds.) (2011) *Liverpool '81: Remembering the Riots*. Liverpool University Press.

Fujii, Lee Ann (2010) Shades of truth and lies: Interpreting testimonies of war and violence. *Journal of Peace Research*, 47(2): 231–241.

Fukuo, Wataru, Yoshiuchi, Kazuhiro, Ohashi, Ken, Togashi, Hitomi, Sekine, Rie, Kikuchi, Hiroe, Sakamoto, Noriyuki, Inada, S., Sato, F., Kadowaki, T. & Akabayashi, A. (2009) Development of a hand-held personal digital assistant-based food diary with food photographs for Japanese subjects. *Dietetic Journal of the American Association*, 109(7): 1232–1236.

Fuller, Ian, Edmondson, Sally, France, Derek, Higgitt, David & Ratinen, Ilkka (2006) International perspectives on the effectiveness of geography fieldwork for learning. *Journal of Geography in Higher Education*, 30(1): 89–101.

Fuller, Mary, Georgeson, Jan, Healey, Mich, Hurst, Alan, Kelly, Katie, Riddell, S., Roberts, H. & Weedon, E. (2009) *Improving Disabled Students' Learning: Experiences and Outcomes*. Routledge.

Fuller, Mary, Healey, Mick, Bradley, Andrew & Hall, Tim (2004) Barriers to learning: A systematic study of the experience of Disabled students in one university. *Studies in Higher Education*, 29(3): 303–318.

Gabb, Jacqui (2010) Home truths: Ethical issues in family research. *Qualitative Research*, 10(4): 461–478.

Gabriel, Yiannis and Connell, N. A. D. (2010) Co-creating stories: Collaborative experiments in storytelling. *Management Learning*, 41(5): 507–523.

Gangneux, Justine (2019) Rethinking social media for qualitative research: The use of Facebook Activity Logs and Search History in interview settings. *The Sociological Review*, 67(6): 1249–1264.

Garland-Thompson, Rosemarie (2009) *Staring: How We Look*. Oxford University Press.

Garland-Thomson, Rosemarie (2017) Becoming disabled. In Davis, Lennard J. (ed.), *Beginning with Disability*. Routledge, pp. 15–19.

Garrett, Bradley (2013) *Explore Everything: Place-Hacking the City*. Verso.

Gemignani, Marco (2014) Memory, remembering and oblivion in active narrative interviewing. *Qualitative Inquiry*, 20(2): 127–135.

Geography Collective (2010) *Mission:Explore*. Can of Worms Kids Press.

Geography Disability Network (2004) *Learning Support for Disabled Students: Undertaking Fieldwork and Related Activities*. Geography Disability Network.

Georges, R. A. & Jones, M. O. (1980) *People Studying People: The Human Element in Fieldwork*. University of California Press

Gerber, R. & Chuan, G. K. (eds.) (2000) *Fieldwork in Geography: Reflections, Perspectives and Actions*. Kluwer Academic.

Gerster, Julia (2018) The online–offline nexus: Social media and ethnographic fieldwork in post-3.11 North East Japan. *ASIEN*, 149: 14–32.

Giles, S., Jackson, C. & Stephen, N. (2020) Barriers to fieldwork in undergraduate geoscience degrees. *Nature Reviews Earth and Environment*, 1(2): 77–78.

Gillen, Jamie (2015) Rethinking whiteness and masculinity in geography: Drinking alcohol in the field in Vietnam. *Antipode*, 48(3): 584–602.

Glass, Michael R. (2015) International geography field courses: Practices and challenges. *Journal of Geography in Higher Education*, 39(4): 485–490.

Gold, J. R., Jenkins, A., Lee, R., Monk, J., Riley, J., Shepherd, I. & Unwin, D. (1991) *Teaching Geography in Higher Education: A Manual of Good Practice*. Blackwell.

Goldblatt, D. (2010) Ex-Offenders at the Scene of the Crime [exhibition]. Available at: https://blog.ormsdirect.co.za/exhibition-ex-offenders-by-david-goldblatt/. Last accessed 6 September 2022.

Gonzales, Roberto G. (2016) *Lives in Limbo: Undocumented and Coming of Age in America*. University of California Press.

Góralska, Magdalena (2020) Anthropology from home: Advice on digital ethnography for the pandemic times. *Anthropology in Action*, 27(1): 46–52.

gov.uk (2010) Equality Act. Available at: https://www.legislation.gov.uk/ukpga/2010/15/pdfs/ukpga_20100015_en.pdf. Last accessed 6 September 2022.

gov.uk (2022) Disability Rights: Education. Available at: https://www.gov.uk/rights-disabled-person/education-rights. Last accessed 6 September 2022.

Grady, J. (2004) Working with visible evidence: An invitation and some practical advice. In Knowles, Caroline & Sweetman, Paul (eds.), *Picturing the Social Landscape: Visual Methods and the Sociological Imagination*. Routledge, pp. 18–32.

Grant, Aimee (2018) *Doing Excellent Social Research with Documents: Practical Examples and Guidance for Qualitative Researchers*. Routledge.

Greene, Sarah, Ashley, Kate, Dunne, Emma, Edgar, Kirsty, Giles, Sam & Hanson, Emma (2020) Toilet stops in the field: An educational primer and recommended best practices for field-based teaching. Available at: https://doi:10.31219/osf.io/gnhj2. Last accessed 21 February 2022.

Gretzel, Ulrike (2017) Social media activism in tourism. *Journal of Hospitality and Tourism*, 15(2): 1–14.

Grierson, E. & Brearley, L. (2009) *Creative Arts Research: Narratives of Methodologies and Practices*. Sense.

Grimshaw, Anna (2001) *The Ethnographer's Eye*. Cambridge University Press.

Grimshaw, Anna & Ravetz, Amanda (2005) *Visualizing Anthropology: Experimenting with Image-Based Ethnography*. Intellect.

Grosz, Elizabeth (2020) *Volatile Bodies: Toward a Corporeal Feminism*. Routledge.

GSR (Government Social Research) (2016) Using social media for social research: An introduction. Social Media Research Group. Available from: https://assets.publishing.service.gov.uk/government/uploads/system/uploads/attachment_data/file/524750/GSR_Social_Media_Research_Guidance_-_Using_social_media_for_social_research.pdf. Last accessed 10 April 2021.

Guillet, David (1985) Microcomputers in fieldwork and the role of the anthropologist. *Human Organization*, 44(4): 369–371.

Gustafsson Jertfelt, Isa, Blanchin, Alice, & Li, Sihong (2016) Cultural perspective in open-ended interviews: The importance of being adaptable. *Culture and Psychology*, 22(3): 483–501.

Hackett, Abigail, Pool, Steve, Rowsell, Jennifer & Aghajan, Barsin (2015) Seen and unseen: Using video data in ethnographic fieldwork. *Qualitative Research Journal*, 15(4): 430–444.

Hakim, Catherine (1982) Secondary analysis and the relationship between official and academic social research. *Sociology*, 16(1): 12–28.

Halford, Susan & Knowles, Caroline (2005) More than words: Some reflections on working visually. *Sociological Research Online*, 10(1): 85–87.

Hall, S. M. (2009) Private life and work life: Difficulties and dilemmas when making and maintaining friendships with ethnographic participants. *Area*, 41(3): 263–272.

Hall, S. M. (2014) Ethics of ethnography with families: A geographical perspective. *Environment and Planning A: Economy and Space*, 46(9): 2175–2194.

Hall, Sarah M., Pottinger, Laura, Blake, Megan, Mills, Susanne, Reynolds, Christian & Wrieden, Wendy (2020) Food for thought? Material methods for exploring food and cooking. In Holmes, Helen & Hall, Sarah M. (eds.), *Mundane Methods: Innovative Ways to Research the Everyday*. Manchester University Press.

Hall, T. (2015) Reframing photographic research methods in human geography: A long-term reflection. *Journal of Geography in Higher Education*, 39(3): 328–342.

Hall, Tim & Healey, Mick (2005) Disabled students' experiences of fieldwork. *Area*, 37(4): 446–449.

Hall, Tim, Healey, Mick & Harrison, Margaret (2002) Fieldwork and Disabled students: Discourses of exclusion and inclusion. *Transactions of the Institute of British Geographers*, 27(2): 213–231.

Hammersley, Martyn (2008) *Questioning Qualitative Inquiry*. Sage.

Hammersley, Martin & Atkinson, Paul (1995) *Ethnography: Principles in Practice*, 2nd ed. Routledge.

Hammett, Dan, Jackson, Lucy & Vickers, Dan (2019) The ethics of (not) giving back. *Area*, 51(2): 380–386.

Hammett, Dan & Sporton, Deborah (2012) Paying for interviews? Negotiating ethics, power and expectation. *Area*, 44(4): 496–502.

Hammett, Dan, Twyman, C. & Graham, M. (2014) *Research and Fieldwork in Development*. Routledge.

Hammond, Timur (2020) Papering, arranging, and depositing: Learning from working with an Istanbul archive. *Area*, 52(1): 204–212.

Haque, Saria N. & Swicegood, Jodi (2013) Recruiting participants with chronic conditions in Second Life. In Hill, Craig A., Dean, Elizabeth & Murphy, Joe (eds.), *Social Media, Sociality and Survey Research*. Wiley & Sons, pp. 231–252.

Harper, Douglas (2002) Talking about pictures: A case for photo elicitation. *Visual Studies*, 17(1): 13–26.

Harper, S. L., Edge, V. L., Cunsolo Willox, A., & Rigolet Inuit Community Government. (2012) Using an EcoHealth approach to explore impacts of climate change on Inuit health. *EcoHealth*, 9, 89–101.

Harris, R. Cole (2001) Archival fieldwork. *Geographical Review*, 91(1–2): 328–335.

Harrison, Ellie (2022) Resurfaced tale details how Toy Story 2 was saved after being deleted – twice. *Independent*. Available from: www.independent.co.uk/arts-entertainment/films/news/lightyear-toy-story-2-deleted-b2017238.html. Last accessed 3 May 2022.

Harvey, Arlene & Russell-Mundine, Gabrielle (2019) Decolonising the curriculum: Using graduate qualities to embed indigenous knowledges at the academic cultural interface. *Teaching in Higher Education*, 24(6): 789–808.

Hatcher, William (2019) Teaching curiosity in public affairs programs. *Teaching Public Administration*, 37(3): 365–375.

Haynes, Kathryn (2012) Body beautiful? Gender, identity and the body in professional services firms. *Gender, Work and Organization*, 19(5): 489–507.

Haynes, William (2021) Counter-narratives of migrants on Termini TV. *The Sociological Review*, 3 August. Published online: https://doi.org/10.51428/tsr.meqx8905

Heath, Sue & Chapman, Lynne (2020) The art of the ordinary: Observational sketching as method. In Holmes, Helen & Hall, Sarah Marie (eds.), *Mundane Methods*. Manchester University Press, pp. 103–120.

Heath, Sue & Cleaver, Elizabeth (2004) Mapping the spatial in shared household life: A missed opportunity? In Knowles, Caroline & Sweetman, Paul (eds.), *Picturing the Social Landscape: Visual Methods and the Sociological Imagination*. Routledge, pp. 65–78.

Heidbrink, Simone, Knoll, Tobias & Wysocki, Jan (2014) Theorizing religion in digital games: Perspectives and approaches. In Heidbrink, Simone & Knoll, Tobias (eds.), *Religion in Digital Games: Multiperspective and Interdisciplinary Approaches*. Available from: http://journals.ub.uni-heidelberg.de/index.php/religions/article/view/12156. Last accessed 1 November 2021.

Heldke, Lisa (2015) *Exotic Appetites: Ruminations of a Food Adventurer*. Routledge.

Henshaw, Victoria (2013) *Urban Smellscapes: Understanding and Designing City Smell Environments*. Routledge.

Henshaw, Victoria, McLean, Kate, Medway, Dominic, Perkins, Chris & Warnaby, Gary (eds.) (2017) *Designing with Smell: Practices, Techniques and Challenges*. Routledge.

Heron, John & Reason, Peter (2005) The practice of co-operative inquiry: Research with rather than on people. In Reason, Peter and Bradbury, Hilary (eds.), *Handbook of Action Research*. Sage, pp. 144–154.

Herrera, Yoshiko M. & Kapur, Devesh (2007) Improving data quality: Actors, incentives, and capabilities. *Political Analysis*, 15: 365–386. doi:10.1093/pan/mpm007

Herrick, Clare (2010) Lost in the field: Ensuring student learning in the 'threatened' geography fieldtrip. *Area*, 42(1): 108–116.

Hetherington, Kevin (2013) Rhythm and noise: The city, memory and the archive. *The Sociological Review*, 61: 17–33.

Hew, Khe Foon (2011) Students' and teachers' use of Facebook. *Computers in Human Behavior*, 27: 662–676.

Higgins, Jackie (2014) *The World Atlas of Street Photography*. Yale University Press.

Hill, Craig A., Dean, Elizabeth & Murphy, Joe (eds.) (2013) *Social Media, Sociality and Survey Research*. Wiley & Sons.

Hill, Jenny & Woodland, Wendy (2002) An evaluation of foreign fieldwork in promoting deep learning: A preliminary investigation. *Assessment and Evaluation in Higher Education*, 27(6): 539–555.

Hine, Christine (ed.) (2005) *Virtual Methods: Issues in Social Research on the Internet*. Berg.

Hine, Christine (2015) *Ethnography for the Internet: Embedded, Embodied and Everyday*. Bloomsbury.

Hirvi, Laura & Snellman, Hanna (2012) *Where is the Field? The Experience of Migration Viewed through the Prism of Ethnographic Fieldwork*. Studia Fennica Ethnologica.

Hjorth, Larissa & Hinton, Sam (2019) *Understanding Social Media*, 2nd ed. Sage.

Hochman, Nadav (2016) From site-specificity to hyper-locality: Performances of place in social media. In Sloan, L. & Quan-Haase, A. (eds.), *The Sage Handbook of Social Media Research Methods*. Sage, pp. 367–385.

Hochman, Nadav, Manovich, Lev & Yazdani, Mehrdad (2014) On hyper-locality: Performances of place in social media. Association for the Advancement of Artificial Intelligence. Available from: http://manovich.net/content/04-projects/082-on-hyper-locality-performances-of-place-in-social-media/onhyperlocality.pdf. Last accessed 22 April 2021.

Holmes, Helen & Hall, Sarah Marie (eds.) (2020) *Mundane Methods: Innovative Ways to Research the Everyday*. Manchester University Press.

Holton, Mark & Riley, Mark (2014) Talking on the move: Place-based interviewing with undergraduate students. *Area*, 16(1): 59–65.

hooks, bell (2009) *Belonging: A Culture of Place*. Routledge.

Hope, M. (2009) The importance of direct experience: A philosophical defence of fieldwork in human geography. *Journal of Geography in Higher Education*, 33(2): 169–182.

Hu, Yuheng, Farnham, Shelly D. & Monroy-Hernandez, Andrés (2013) Whoo.ly: Facilitating information seeking for hyperlocal communities using social media. CHI Conference on Human Factors in Computing Systems: 3481–3490. https://doi.org/10.1145/2470654.2466478

Hubbard, Timothy D. & Aguinis, Herman (2023) Conducting phenomenon-driven research using virtual reality and the metaverse. *Academy of Management Perspectives*. https://doi.org/10.5465/amd.2023.0031

Hudson, James M. & Bruckman, Amy (2004) 'Go away': Participant objections to being studied and the ethics of chatroom research. *The Information Society*, 20(2): 127–139.

Hughes, Annie (2016) Exploring normative whiteness: Ensuring inclusive pedagogic practice in undergraduate fieldwork teaching and learning. *Journal of Geography in Higher Education*, 40(3): 1–18.

Hume-Cook, Geoff, Curtis, Thomas, Woods, Kirsty, Potaka, Joyce, Wagner, Tangaroa & Kindon, Sara (2007) Using participatory video in Aotearoa New Zealand. In Kindon, S., Pain, R. & Kesby, M. (eds.), *Participatory Action Research Approaches and Methods*. Routledge, pp. 160–169.

ILGA (2022) Maps: Sexual orientation laws. Available at: https://ilga.org/maps-sexual-orientation-laws. Last accessed 6 September 2022.

Inan, I. (2012) *The Philosophy of Curiosity*. Routledge.

Iser, Wolfgang (1997) The significance of fictionalizing. *Anthropoetics*, 3(2): 1–9.

Israel, Barbara A., Coombe, Chris M., Cheezum, Rebecca R., Schulz, Amy J., McGranaghan, Robert J., Lichtenstein, Richard, Reyes, Angela G., Clement, Jaye & Burris, Akosua (2010) Community-based participatory research: A capacity-building approach for policy advocacy aimed at eliminating health disparities. *American Journal of Public Health*, 100(11): 2094–2102.

Jackson, Denise & Chapman, Elaine (2012) Non-technical competencies in undergraduate business degree programs: Australian and UK perspectives. *Studies in Higher Education*, 37(5): 541–567.

Jacob, Stacey A. & Furgerson, S. Paige (2012) Protocols and conducting interviews: Tips for students new to the field of qualitative research. *The Qualitative Report*, 17(6): 1–10. Available from: https://files.eric.ed.gov/fulltext/EJ990034.pdf. Last accessed 27 April 2021.

Jacobs, Jane (1962) *The Death and Life of Great American Cities*. Jonathan Cape.

Jacobs, Sean (2010) David Adjaye's urban Africa. www.africasacountry.com/2010/09/david-adjayes-urban-africa. Last accessed 6 September 2022.

Jacobsson, Katarina (2016) Analysing documents through fieldwork. In Silverman, David (ed.), *Qualitative Research*, 4th ed. Sage, pp. 155–170.

Jacques, David & Salmon, Gilly (2007) *Learning in Groups: A Handbook for Face-to-face and Online Environments*, 4th ed. Routledge.

Jalloh, Alusine (2002) Reconstructing modern African business history. In Falola, Toyin (ed.), *Africanizing Knowledge*. Routledge, pp. 149–164.

Jamerson, Trevor (2017) Digital orientalism: TripAdvisor and online traveller's tales. In Daniels, Jessie, Gregory, Karen & McMillan Cottom, Tessie (eds.), *Digital Sociology*. Policy Press, pp. 119–136.

James, Daniel (2000) *Doña María's Story: Life History, Memory and Political Identity*. Duke University Press.

Jamison, Mark & Glavish, Matthew (2022) The dark side of the metaverse, Part 1. Available from: www.aei.org/technology-and-innovation/the-dark-side-of-the-metaverse-part-i/. Last accessed 24 April 2022.

Javornik, Ana, Marder, Ben, Pizzetti, Marta & Warlop, Luk (2021) Augmented self: The effects of virtual face augmentation on consumers' self-concept. *Journal of Business Research*, 13: 170–187.

Jay, Martin (1993) *Downcast Eyes: The Denigration of Vision in Twentieth-Century French Thought*. University of California Press.

Jazeel, Tariq & McFarlane, Colin (2007) Responsible learning: Cultures of knowledge production and the north–south divide. *Antipode*, 39(5): 781–789.

Jazeel, Tariq & McFarlane, Colin (2010) The limits of responsibility: A postcolonial politics of academic knowledge production. *Transactions of the Institute of British Geographers*, 35(1), 109–124.

Jeffrey, Heather L., Ashraf, Hamna & Paris, Cody M. (2021) Hanging out on Snapchat: Disrupting passive covert netnography in tourism research. *Tourism Geographies*, 23(1): 144–161. Available from: https://doi.org/10.1080/14616688.2019.1666159

John, Cédric Michaël & Khan, Saira Bano (2018) Mental health in the field. *Nature Geoscience*, 11: 618–620.

Johns, Jennifer (2019) What the 19th-century fad for anti-slavery sugar can teach us about ethical Christmas gifts. *The Conversation*. Available from: https://theconversation.com/what-the-19th-century-fad-for-anti-slavery-sugar-can-teach-us-about-ethical-christmas-gifts-128968

Johns, Jennifer & Hall, Sarah M. (2020) 'I have so little time […] I got shit I need to do': Critical perspectives on making and sharing in Manchester's FabLab. *Environment and Planning A: Economy and Space*, 52(7): 1232–1312.

Johnsen, Sarah, May, Jon & Cloke, Paul (2008) Imag(in)ing homeless places: Using auto-photography to (re)examine the geographies of homelessness. *Area*, 40(2): 194–207.

Johnson, Azeezat (2017) You're othered here and you're othered there: Centring the clothing practices of black Muslim women in Britain. University of Sheffield: PhD dissertation.

Johnson, M. (2020) In the name of pleasure: An ethnographic study of student drug consumption. University of Sheffield: BA dissertation.

Jones, Gareth A. & Rodgers, Dennis (2019) Ethnographies and/of violence. *Ethnography*, 20(3): 297–319.

Jones, Kip & Leavy, Patricia (2014) A conversation between Kip Jones and Patricia Leavy. *Qualitative Report*, 19(38): 1–7.

Jordanova, Ludmilla (2000) *History in Practice*. London: Arnold.

Joseph Mbembe, Achille (2016) Decolonizing the university: New directions. *Arts and Humanities in Higher Education*, 15(1): 29–45.

Jovchelovitch, Sandra & Bauer, Martin W. (2000) Narrative interviewing. In Bauer, Martin W. & Gaskell, George (eds.), *Qualitative Researching with Text, Image and Sound*. Sage, pp. 57–74.

Kaplan, Andreas & Haenlein, Michael (2010) Users of the world, unite! The challenges and opportunities of social media. *Business Horizons*, 53: 59–68.

Kapor, Vladimir (2019) Exotic. In Forsdick, Charles, Kinsley, Zoe & Walchester, Kathryn (eds.), *Keywords for Travel Writing Studies*. Anthem, pp. 87–89.

Kara, Helen (2018) *Research Ethics in the Real World: Euro-Western and Indigenous Perspectives*. Policy Press.

Kara, Helen (2020) *Creative Research Methods: A Practical Guide*, 2nd ed. Policy Press.

Kara, S. (2017) *Modern Slavery: A Global Perspective*. Columbia University Press.

Kaspar, Heidi & Landolt, Sara (2016) Flirting in the field: Shifting positionalities and power relations in innocuous sexualisations of research encounters. *Gender, Place and Culture*, 23(1): 107–119.

Katz, Cindi (1994) Playing the field: Questions of fieldwork in Geography. *Professional Geographer*, 46(1): 67–72.

Kaul, Vaibhav & Thornton, Thomas F. (2014) Resilience and adaptation to extremes in a changing Himalayan environment. *Regional Environmental Change*, 14(2): 683–698.

Keane, Moyra, Khupe, Constance & Seehawer, Maren (2017) Decolonising methodology: Who benefits from indigenous knowledge research? *Educational Research for Social Change*, 6(1): 12–24.

Kearns, Robin (2002) Back to the future/field: Doing fieldwork. *New Zealand Geographer*, 58(2): 75–76.

Kearns, Robin A. (2005) Knowing seeing? Undertaking observational research. In Hay, I. (ed.), *Qualitative Research Methods in Human Geography*. Oxford University Press, pp. 192–206.

Kedge, Stephen & Appleby, Ben (2009) Promoting a culture of curiosity within nursing practice. *British Journal of Nursing*, 18(10): 635–637.

Keikelame, Mpoe Johannah & Swartz, Leslie (2019) Decolonising research methodologies: Lessons from a qualitative research project, Cape Town, South Africa. *Global Health Action*, 12(1): 1561175.

Khupe, Constance & Keane, Moyra (2017) Towards an African education research methodology: Decolonising new knowledge. *Educational Research for Social Change*, 6(1): 25–37.

Kindon, Sara (2003) Participatory video in geographic research: A feminist practice of looking? *Area*, 35(2): 142–153.

Kindon, Sara, Pain, Rachel & Kesby, Mike (eds.) (2007) *Participatory Action Research Approaches and Methods*. Routledge.

Kingsbury, Cole G., Sibert, Elizabeth C., Killingback, Zachary & Atchison, Christopher L. (2020) 'Nothing about us without us': The perspectives of autistic geoscientists on inclusive instructional practices in geoscience education. *Journal of Geoscience Education*, 68(4): 302–310.

Knott, Eleanor (2019) Beyond the field: Ethics after fieldwork in politically dynamic contexts. *Perspectives on Politics*, 17(10): 140–153.

Knowles, Caroline & Sweetman, Paul (eds.) (2004) *Picturing the Social Landscape: Visual Methods and the Sociological Imagination*. Routledge.

Kominko, Maja (2015) *From Dust to Digital: 10 Years of the Endangered Archive Programme*. Open Books.

Koonings, Kees, Kruijt, Dirk & Rodgers, Dennis (eds.) (2019) *Ethnography as Risky Business: Field Research in Violent and Sensitive Contexts*. Rowman & Littlefield/Lexington.

Kozinets, Robert V. (2022) Immersive netnography: A novel method for service experience research in virtual reality, augmented reality and metaverse contexts. *Journal of Service Management*, 34(1): 100–125.

Krzywoszynska, Anna (2015) On being a foreign body in the field, or how reflexivity around translation can take us beyond language, *Area*, 47(3): 311–318.

Kumar, Neha (2016) Interviewing against the odds. In Kubitschko, Sebastian & Kaun, Anne (eds.), *Innovative Methods in Media and Communication Research*. Palgrave Macmillan, pp. 207–220.

Kürti, Laszlo (2004) Picture perfect: Community and commemoration in postcards. In Afonso, Ana Isabel, Kürti, Laszlo & Pink, Sarah (eds.), *Working Images: Visual Research and Representation in Ethnography*. Routledge, pp. 47–71.

Kuschnir, Karina (2011) Drawing the city: A proposal for an ethnographic study in Rio De Janeiro. *Vibrant: Virtual Brazilian Anthropology*, 8(2): 609–642.

Kuschnir, Karina (2016) Ethnographic drawing: Eleven benefits of using a sketchbook for fieldwork. *Visual Ethnography*, 5(1): 103–134.

Kwan, T. (2000) Fieldwork in geography teaching: The case in Hong Kong. In Gerber, R. & Chuan, G. K. (eds.), *Fieldwork in Geography: Reflections, Perspectives and Actions*. Kluwer Academic, pp. 119–130.

Lai, Kwok Chan (2000) Affective-focused geographical fieldwork. In Gerber, R. & Chuan, G. K. (eds.), *Fieldwork in Geography: Reflections, Perspectives and Actions*. Kluwer Academic, pp. 145–169.

Landers, Jane, Gómez, Pablo, Acuña, José P. & Cambell, Courtney J. (2015) Researching the history of slavery in Colombia and Brazil through ecclesiastical and notarial archives. In Kominko, Maja (ed.), *From Dust to Digital: 10 Years of the Endangered Archive Programme*. Open Books, pp. 259–330.

LaRocco, Annette Alfina., Shinn, Jamie E. & Madise, Kentse (2020) Reflections on positionalities in social science fieldwork in Northern Botswana: A call for decolonizing research. *Politics and Gender*, 16(3): 845–873.

Larsen, Jonas (2005) Families seen sightseeing: Performativity of tourist photography. *Space and Culture*, 8(4): 416–434.

Lashua, Brett, Spracklen, Karl & Long, Phil (2014) Introduction to the special issue: Music and tourism. *Tourist Studies*, 14(1): 3–9.

Laurier, Eric (2010) Participant observation. In Clifford, N., French, S. & Valentine, G. (eds.) *Key Methods in Geography*, 2nd ed. Sage, pp. 116–130.

Laurier, Eric (2013) Encounters at the counter: The relationship between regulars and staff. In Tolmie, Peter & Rouncefield, Mark (eds.), *Ethnomethodology at Play*. Ashgate, pp. 287–308.

Law, Lisa (2013) Urban senses. In Cloke, Paul, Crang, Philip & Goodwin, Mark (eds.), *Introducing Human Geographies*. Routledge, pp. 706–719.

Layton, E. & Blanco White, J. (1948) *The School Looks Around: A Book for Teachers About Local Surveys*. Longmans, Green & Co., with the Association for Education in Citizenship.

Le Grange, Lesley (2020) Decolonising the university curriculum: The what, why and how. In Lee, J. C. K. & Gough, N. (eds.), *Transnational Education and Curriculum Studies: International Perspectives*. Routledge, pp. 216–233.

Lee, Joanne (2007) Languages for learning to delight in art. In Beer, Gillian, Bowie, Malcolm & Perrey, Beate Julia (eds.), *In(ter) Discipline: New Languages for Criticism*. Legenda, pp. 107–113.

Lefebvre, Henri (2013) *Rhythmanalysis: Space, Time and Everyday Life*. Bloomsbury.

Leigh, Jennifer & Brown, Nicole (2021) *Embodied Inquiry: Research Methods*. Bloomsbury.

Lemos, Robert (2005) Bank of America loses a million customer records. CNET. Available from: www.cnet.com/news/privacy/bank-of-america-loses-a-million-customer-records/. Last accessed 2 May 2022.

Levin, Peter (2005) *Successful Teamwork! For Undergraduates and Taught Postgraduates Working on Group Projects*. Open University Press/McGraw Hill.

Lewisohn, Jane (2015) Conservation of the Iranian Golha radio programme and the heritage of Persian classical poetry and music. In Kominko, Maja (ed.), *From Dust to Digital: 10 Years of the Endangered Archive Programme*. Open Books, pp. 587–616.

Li, Jun (2008) Ethical challenges in participant observation: A reflection on ethnographic fieldwork. *The Qualitative Report*, 13(1): 100–115.

Li, Mohan, Sharpley, Richard & Gammon, Sean (2019) Towards an understanding of Chinese tourist photography: Evidence from the UK. *Current Issues in Tourism*, 22(5): 505–521.

Liamputtong, Pranee (2010) *Performing Qualitative Cross-Cultural Research*. Cambridge University Press.

Linton, David (1960) Foreword. In Hutchings, G. E. (ed.) *Landscape Drawing*. Methuen.

Livingstone, David N. (1992) *The Geographical Tradition: Episodes in the History of a Contested Enterprise*. Blackwell.

Livingstone, I., Matthews, H. and Castley, A. (1998) *Fieldwork and Dissertations in Geography*. Cheltenham: Geography Discipline Network.

Lockard, Brittany (2013) Sissel Tolaas, SmellScape KCK/KCMO. *Senses and Society*, 8(2): 245–250.

Lonergan, N. & Andersen, L. W. (1988) Field-based education: Some theoretical considerations. *Higher Education Research and Development*, 7(1): 63–77.

Longhurst, Robyn, Ho, Elsie & Johnston, Lynda (2008) Using the body as an instrument of research: Kimch'i and pavlova. *Area*, 40(2): 208–217.

Lorimer, Hayden (2010) Caught in the nick of time: Archives and fieldwork. In DeLyser, Dydia, Herbert, Steve, Aitken, Stuart, Crang, Mike & McDowell, Linda (eds.), *The Sage Handbook of Qualitative Geography*. Sage, pp. 248–273.

Lunn, Jenny (2014) *Fieldwork in the Global South: Ethical Challenges and Dilemmas*. Routledge.

Lupton, Deborah & Watson, Ash (2021) Towards more-than-human digital data studies: Developing research-creation methods. *Qualitative Research*, 21(4): 463–480.

Lury, Celia (2013) *Prosthetic Culture*. Routledge.
Lykes, M. Brinton (2006) Creative arts and photography in participatory action research in Guatemala. In Reason, P. & Bradbury, H. (eds.), *Handbook of Action Research*. Sage, pp. 269–278.
Macaulay, Ann C. (2017) Participatory research: What is the history? Has the purpose changed? *Family Practice*, 34(3): 256–258.
MacGinty, Roger (2021) Temporality and contextualisation in peace and conflict studies: The forgotten value of war memoirs and personal diaries. *Cooperation and Conflict*. https://doi.org/10.1177/00108367211027605
Maddrell, A. (2010) Academic geography as terra incognita: Lessons from the 'expedition debate' and another border to cross. *Transactions of the Institute of British Geographers*, 35(2): 149–153.
Magedera, Ian H. (2014) *Outsider Biographies*. Rodopi.
Mahtab, Edris A. F., & Egorova, Anastasia D. (2022) Current and future applications of virtual reality technology for cardiac interventions. *Nature Reviews Cardiology*, 19(12): 779–780.
Malbon, Ben (1999) *Clubbing: Dancing, Ecstasy and Vitality*. Routledge.
Manca, Stefania & Ranieri, Maria (2013) Is it a tool suitable for learning? A critical review of the literature on Facebook as a technology enhanced learning environment. *Journal of Computer Assisted Learning*, 29: 487–504.
Mannay, Dawn (2016) *Visual, Narrative and Creative Research Methods*. Routledge.
Maramwidze-Merrison, Efrider (2016) Innovative methodologies in qualitative research: Social media window for accessing organisational elites for interviews. *The Electronic Journal of Business Research Methods*, 14(2): 157–167.
Mare, Admire (2017) Tracing and archiving 'constructed' data on Facebook pages and groups: Reflections on fieldwork among young activists in Zimbabwe and South Africa. *Qualitative Research*, 17(6): 645–663.
Mariushakova, Elena & Popov, Vesselin (2015) The first Gypsy/Roma organisations, churches and newspapers. In Kominko, Maja (ed.), *From Dust to Digital: 10 Years of the Endangered Archive Programme*. Open Books, pp. 189–224.
Marland, Alex & Esselment, Anna L. (2019) Negotiating with gatekeepers to get interviews with politicians: Qualitative research recruitment in a digital media environment. *Qualitative Research*, 19(6): 685–702. https://doi.org/10.1177/1468794118803022
Marsden, B. (2000) A British historical perspective on fieldwork from the 1820s to the 1970s. In Gerber, R. & Chuan, G. K. (eds.), *Fieldwork in Geography: Reflections, Perspectives and Actions*. Kluwer Academic, pp. 15–36.
Martiniello, Marco (2017) Visual sociology approaches in migration, ethnic and racial studies. *Ethnic and Racial Studies*, 40(8): 1184–1190.
Maskall, John & Stokes, Alison (2009) *Designing Effective Fieldwork for the Environmental and Natural Sciences*. GEES Subject Centre Learning and Teaching Guide.
Mason, Jennifer (2002) *Qualitative Researching*, 2nd ed. Sage.
Mason, Olivia (2021) A political geography of walking in Jordan: Movement and politics. *Political Geography*, 88. https://doi.org/10.1016/j.polgeo.2021.102392
Masrom, Maslin & Ismail, Zuraini (2010) Benefits and barriers to the use of mobile learning in education: Review of literature. In Guy, Retta (ed.), *Mobile Learning: Pilot Projects and Initiatives*. Informing Science Press, pp. 9–26.

Massad, Joseph A. (2015) *Islam in Liberalism*. University of Chicago Press.
Massey, D. (1991) A global sense of place, *Marxism Today*, June: 24–29.
Massey, D. (2005) *For Space*. Sage.
Masson, Peter & Mata, Peter (1998) *Infelicities: Representations of the Exotic*. Johns Hopkins University Press.
Mathewson, K. (2001) Between 'in camp' and 'out of bounds': Notes on the history of fieldwork in American geography. *Geographical Review*, 91(1–2): 215–224.
Mato, Daniel (2000) Transnational networking and the social production of representations of identities by indigenous peoples' organisations of Latin America. *International Sociology*, 15(2): 343–360.
Mattingly, Doreen (2001) Place, teenagers and representations: Lessons from a community theatre project. *Social and Cultural Geography*, 2(4): 445–459.
Mawere, Munyaradzi (2015) 'Indigenous knowledge and public education in Sub-Saharan Africa'. *Africa Spectrum*, 50(2): 57–71.
Mawere, Munyaradzi & Mubaya, Tapuwa R. (2016) *African Philosophy and Thought Systems: A Search for a Culture and Philosophy of Belonging*. Langaa Rpcig.
Mazrui, Ali A. (2003) Towards re-Africanising African universities: Who killed intellectualism in the post-colonial era? *Alternatives: Turkish Journal of International Relations*, 2(3–4): 135–163.
McAvoy, P. (2014) Dementia communication using empathetic curiosity. *Nursing Times*, 110(24): 12–15.
McCay-Peet, Lori & Quan-Haase, Anabel (2017) What is social media and what questions can social media research help us answer? In Sloan, Luke & Quan-Haase, Anabel (eds.), *The Sage Handbook of Social Media Research Methods*. Sage, pp. 13–26.
McCoyd, Judith & Kerson, Toba (2006) Conducting intensive interviews using email: A serendipitous comparative opportunity. *Qualitative Social Work*, 5(3): 389–406.
McCulloch, Gary (2004) *Documentary Research: In Education, History and Social Sciences*. Routledge.
McCulloch, Gary & Richardson, William (2000) *Historical Research in Educational Settings*. Open University Press.
McDowell, Linda (1992) Doing gender: Feminism, feminists and research methods in human geography. *Transactions of the Institute of British Geographers*, 17(4): 399–416.
McDowell, Linda (1997) Women/gender/feminisms: Doing feminist geography. *Journal of Geography in Higher Education*, 21(3): 381–400.
McDowell, Linda (1998) Elites in the City of London: Some methodological considerations. *Environment and Planning A: Economy and Space*, 30: 2133–2146.
McDowell, Linda (2009) Interviewing: Fear and liking in the field. In DeLyser, Dydia, Herbert, Steve, Aitken, Stuart, Crang, Mike & McDowell, Linda (eds.), *The Sage Handbook of Qualitative Geography*. Sage, pp. 156–171.
McEwan, Cheryl (2006) Using images, films and photography. In Potter, Rob B. & Desai, Vandana (eds.), *Doing Development Research*. Sage, pp. 231–240.
McFarlane, Hazel & Hansen, Nancy E. (2007) Inclusive methodologies: Including Disabled People in participatory action research in Scotland and Canada. In Kingdon, S., Pain, R. & Kesby, M. (eds.), *Participatory Action Research Approaches and Methods*. Routledge, pp. 88–94.

McGregor, Deborah, Restoule, Jean-Paul & Johnston, Rochelle (eds.) (2018) *Indigenous Research: Theories, Practices and Relationships*. Canadian Scholars Press.

McLean, Kate (2017) Smellmap: Amsterdam: Olfactory art and smell visualization. *Leonardo*, 50(1): 92–93.

McLean, Kate (2018) Mapping the invisible and the ephemeral. In Kent, Alexander J. & Vujakovic, Peter (eds.), *The Routledge Handbook of Mapping and Cartography*. Routledge, pp. 500–515.

McMillan Cottom, Tressie (2017) Black cyberfeminism: Ways forward for intersectionality and digital sociology. In Daniels, Jessie, Gregory, Karen & McMillan Cottom, Tessie (eds.), *Digital Sociology*. Policy Press, pp. 211–231.

McMorran, Chris (2015) Between fan pilgrimage and dark tourism: Competing agendas in overseas field learning. *Journal of Geography in Higher Education*, 39(4): 568–583.

Meda, Lawrence (2020) Decolonising the curriculum: Students' perspectives. *Africa Education Review*, 17(2): 88–103.

Merleau-Ponty, M. (2013) *Phenomenology of Perception*. Routledge.

Metzgar, Emily T., Kurpius, David D. & Rowley, Karen M. (2011) Defining hyperlocal media: Proposing a framework for discussion. *New Media and Society*, 13(5): 772–787.

Michailova, Snejina, Piekkari, Rebecca, Plakoyiannaki, Emmanuella, Ritvala, Tiina, Mihailova, Irina & Salmi, Asta (2014) Breaking the silence about exiting fieldwork: A relational approach and its implications for theorizing. *Academy of Management Reviews*, 39(2): 138–161.

Middleton, J. (2010) Sense and the city: Exploring the embodied geographies of urban walking. *Social and Cultural Geography*, 11(6): 575–596.

Mieville, China (2009) *The City and The City*. Pan Macmillan.

Miles, Matthew B. & Huberman, A. Michael (1994) *Qualitative Data Analysis: An Expanded Sourcebook*. Sage.

Miller, Daniel & Slater, Don (2000) *The Internet: An Ethnographic Approach*. Berg.

Millora, Chris, Maimunah, Siti & Still, Enid (2020) Reflecting on the ethics of PhD research in the Global South: Reciprocity, reflexivity and situatedness. *Acta Academica*, 52(1): 10–30.

Mistry, Jayalaxshmi, Berardi, Andrea & Simpson, Matthew (2009) Critical reflections on practice: The changing roles of three physical geographers carrying out research in a developing country. *Area*, 41(1): 82–93.

Mitchell, Claudia, de Lange, Naydene & Moletsane, Relebohile (2016) Me and my cellphone: Constructing change from the inside through cellphilms and participatory video in a rural community. *Area*, 48(4): 435–441.

Mitchell, William J. (2003) Wunderkammer to world wide web: Picturing place in the postphotographic era. In Schwarz, J. M. & Ryan, J. R. (eds.), *Picturing Place: Photography and the Geographical Imagination*. Routledge, pp. 283–305.

Moncrieffe, Marlon, Race, R., Harris, R., Chetty, D., Riaz, N., Ayling, P., Arphattananon, T., Nasilbullov, K., Kopylova, N. & Steinburg, S. (2020) Decolonising the curriculum: Transnational perspectives. *Research Intelligence*, 142: 9–27.

Monk, J. (2007) Foreword. In Kingdon, S., Pain, R. & Kesby, M. (eds.), *Participatory Action Research Approaches and Methods*. Routledge, pp. xxiii–xxiv.

Moore, Niamh, Salter, Andrea, Stanley, Liz & Tamboukou, Maria (2016) *The Archive Project: Archival Research in the Social Sciences*. Routledge.

Morrison, Marlene (2012) Reflection on research using diaries and blogs. In Briggs, Ann R. J., Coleman, Marianne & Morrison, Marlene (eds.), *Research Methods in Educational Leadership and Management*. Sage, pp. 323–338.

Morrison, Zachary James, Gregory, David & Thibodeau, Steven (2012) Thanks for using me: An exploration of exit strategy in qualitative research. *International Journal of Qualitative Methods*, 11(4): 416–427.

Mould, Oli (2018) *Against Creativity*. Verso.

Mowforth, M. & Munt, I. (1998) *Tourism and Sustainability: New Tourism in the Third World*. Routledge.

Mulhall, Anne (2003) In the field: Notes on observation in qualitative research. *Journal of Advanced Nursing*, 41(3): 306–313.

Mullings, Beverley (1999) Insider or outsider, both or neither: Some dilemmas of interviewing in a cross-cultural setting. *Geoforum*, 30(4): 337–350.

Munck Petersen, Rikke (2020) The dispatched drone and affective distance in fieldwork. *Senses and Society*, 15(3): 311–328.

Munthali, Alister (2001) Doing fieldwork at home: Some personal experiences among the Tumbuka of Northern Malawi. *African Anthropologist*, 8(2): 114–136.

Murphy, Eileen, Dingwall, Robert, Greatbatch, David, Parker, Sheila & Watson, Pamela (1998) Qualitative research methods in health technology assessment: A review of the literature. *Health Technology Assessment*, 2(16): 1–260.

Murphy, James (2012) Subway symphony: Making the city a slightly nicer place to be. www.subwaysymphony.org/about/. Last accessed 8 September 2022.

Murphy, Kate (2020) *You're Not Listening: What You're Missing and Why it Matters*. Random House.

Murris, Karin (2016) #Rhodes must fall: A posthumanist orientation to decolonising higher education institutions. *South African Journal of Higher Education*, 30(3): 274–294.

Myers, Garth A. (2001) Protecting privacy in foreign fields. *Geographical Review*, 91(1–2): 192–200.

Nadkarni, Ashwini & Hofmann, Stefan G. (2012) Why do people use Facebook? *Personality and Individual Differences*, 52: 243–249.

Nagar, Richa & Ali, Frah (2003) Collaboration across borders: Moving beyond positionality. *Singapore Journal of Tropical Geography*, 24(3): 356–372.

Nairn, K., Higgitt, D. L. and Vanneste, D. (2000) International perspectives in field courses. *Journal of Geography in Higher Education*, 24(2): 246–254.

Nakamura, Lisa (2020) Feeling good about feeling bad: Virtuous virtual reality and the automation of racial empathy. *Journal of Visual Culture*, 19(1): 47–64.

Nast, Heidi J. (1994) Women in the field: Critical feminist methodologies and theoretical perspectives. *Professional Geographer*, 46(1): 54–66.

Nast, Heidi J. & Pile, Steve (eds.) (2005) *Places Through the Body*. Routledge.

Ndlovu-Gatsheni, Sabelo J. (2011) The logic of violence in Africa. Milton Keynes: Ferguson Centre for African and Asian Studies Working Paper 233.

Ndlovu-Gatsheni, Sabelo J. (2018) *Epistemic Freedom in Africa: De-Provincialization and Decolonization*. Routledge.

Neal, Sarah, Mohan, Giles, Cochrane, Alan & Bennett, Katy (2016) 'You can't move in Hackney without bumping into an anthropologist': Why certain places attract research attention. *Qualitative Research*, 16(5): 491–507.

Newing, Helen, Eagle, Christine, Puri, Rajindra & Watson, C. Bill (2010) *Conducting Research in Conservation: Social Science Methods and Practice*. Taylor and Francis.

Nhemachena, Artwell, Mlambo, Nelson & Kaundjua, Maria (2016) The notion of the 'field' and the practices of researching and writing Africa: Towards decolonial praxis. *Africology: The Journal of Pan African Studies*, 9(7): 15–36.

Oliver, Catherine (2021) Mock meat, masculinity, and redemption narratives: Vegan men's negotiations and performances of gender and eating. *Social Movement Studies*, 22(1): 62–79. doi: 10.1080/14742837.2021.1989293

O'Neill, M. E. (2001) Corporeal experience: A haptic way of knowing. *Journal of Architectural Education*, 55(1): 3–12.

Ostuni, J. (2000) The irreplaceable experience of fieldwork in geography. In Gerber, R. & Chuan, G. K. (eds.), *Fieldwork in Geography: Reflections, Perspectives and Actions*. Kluwer Academic, pp. 79–98.

Pánek, Jiří, Pászto, Vit & Perkins, Chris (2018) Flying a kite: Playful mapping in a multidisciplinary field-course. *Journal of Geography in Higher Education*, 42(3): 317–336.

Papacharissi, Zizi (2015) We have always been social. *Social Media + Society*, 1(1): 1–2.

Parker, Steven (2015) Researching the values of participants attending strategic boards in public services: Semi-structured interviews, documentary research and observation. Sage Research Methods Cases Part 1. doi: https://dx.doi.org/10.4135/978144627305014558049

Parr, Hester (1998) Mental health, ethnography and the body. *Area*, 30(1): 28–37.

Parr, Hester (2001) Feeling, reading, and making bodies in space. *Geographical Review*, 91(1–2): 158–167.

Parr, Hester & Stevenson, Olivia (2014) Sophie's story: Writing missing journeys. *Cultural Geographies*, 21(4): 565–582.

Patel, K. (2015) Teaching and learning in the tropics: An epistemic exploration of 'the field' in a development studies field trip. *Journal of Geography in Higher Education*, 39(4): 584–594.

Pawson, Eric, Fournier, Eric, Haigh, Martin, Muniz, Osvaldo, Trafford, Julie & Vajoczki, Susan (2006) Problem-based learning in geography: Towards a critical assessment of its purposes, benefits, and risks. *Journal of Geography in Higher Education*, 30(1): 103–116.

Pawson, Eric & Teather, Elizabeth K. (2002) Geographical expeditions: Assessing the benefits of a student-driven fieldwork method. *Journal of Geography in Higher Education*, 26(3): 275–289.

Payne, Phillip G. (2014) Vagabonding slowly: Ecopedagogy, metaphors, figurations, and nomadic ethics. *Canadian Journal of Environmental Education*, 19: 47–69.

Peeters, David (2020) Bilingual switching between languages and listeners: Insights from immersive virtual reality. *Cognition*, 195: 1–12.

Pegg, Ann, Waldock, Jeff, Hendy-Isaac, Sonia & Lawton, Ruth (2012) *Pedagogy for Employability*. Higher Education Academy.

Perec, Georges (1997) *Species of Spaces and Other Pieces*, trans. J. Sturrock. Penguin.

Perec, Georges (2010) *An Attempt at Exhausting a Place in Paris*, trans. M. Lowenthal. Wakefield Press.

Phillips, Adam (2019) *Attention Seeking*. Penguin.
Phillips, Richard (1997) *Mapping Men and Empire: A Geography of Adventure*. Routledge.
Phillips, Richard (2006) *Sex, Politics and Empire: A Postcolonial Geography*. Manchester University Press.
Phillips, Richard (2007) Histories of sexuality and imperialism: What's the use? *History Workshop Journal*, 63(1): 136–153.
Phillips, Richard (2010) The impact agenda and geographies of curiosity. *Transactions of the Institute of British Geographers*, 35(4): 447–452.
Phillips, Richard (2014) Space for curiosity. *Progress in Human Geography*, 38(4): 493–512.
Phillips, Richard (2015) Playful and multi-sensory fieldwork: Seeing, hearing and touching New York. *Journal of Geography in Higher Education*, 39(4): 617–629.
Phillips, Richard (2016) Curious about others: Relational and empathetic curiosity for diverse societies. *New Formations*, 88: 123–142.
Phillips, Richard (2017) Visual research on changing places: An example from Hackney. *Geography Review*, 30(3): 10–12.
Phillips, Richard (2018) Georges Perec's experimental fieldwork: Perecquian fieldwork. *Social and Cultural Geography*, 19(2): 171–191.
Phillips, Richard, Ali, Nafhesa & Chambers, Claire (2020) Critical collaborative storying: Making an animated film about halal dating. *Cultural Geographies*, 27(1): 37–54.
Phillips, Richard, Chambers, Claire, Ali, Nafhesa, Karmakar, Indrani & Diprose, Kristina (2021) *Storying Relationships: Young British Muslims Speak and Write about Sex and Love*. Bloomsbury.
Phillips, Richard & Evans, Bethan (2018) Friendship, curiosity and the city: Dementia friends and memory walks in Liverpool. *Urban Studies*, 55(3): 639–654.
Phillips, Richard, Evans, Bethan & Muirhead, Stuart (2015) Curiosity, place and wellbeing: Encouraging place-specific curiosity as a way to wellbeing. *Environment and Planning A: Economy and Space*, 47(11): 2339–2354.
Phillips, Richard & Johns, Jennifer (2012) *Fieldwork for Human Geography*. Sage.
Phillips, Richard & Kara, Helen (2021) *Creative Writing for Social Research*. Policy Press.
Phillips, Richard, Seaborne, Katie, Goldsmith, Angus, Curtis, N., Davies, A., Haynes, William, McEnroe, R., Murphy, N., O'Neill, L., Pacey, C. & Walker, E. (2022) Student loneliness through the pandemic: How, why and where? *The Geographical Journal*, 188(2): 277–293.
Pick, Doreén & Zielke, Stephan (2015) How electricity providers communicate price increases: A qualitative analysis of notification letters. *Energy Policy*, 86: 303–314.
Pink, Sarah (2005) *The Future of Visual Anthropology: Engaging the Senses*. Routledge.
Pink, Sarah (ed.) (2012) *Advances in Visual Methodology*. Sage.
Pink, Sarah (2015) *Doing Sensory Ethnography*. Sage.
Pink, Sarah (2020) *Doing Visual Ethnography*, 2nd ed. Sage.
Pink, S., Alfonso, A. I. & Kürti, L. (2004) *Working Images: Visual Research and Representation in Ethnography*. Routledge.
Plaisier, Heleen (2015) Unravelling Lepcha manuscripts. In Kominko, Maja (ed.), *From Dust to Digital: 10 Years of the Endangered Archive Programme*. Open Books, pp. 189–224.
Plummer, Ken (2001) *Documents of Life 2: An Invitation to a Critical Humanism*, 2nd ed. Sage.
Pole, Chris (ed.) (2004) *Seeing is Believing? Approaches to Visual Research*. Emerald.

Pole, Chris & Hillyard, Sam (2016) *Doing Fieldwork*. Sage.

Portelli, Alessandro (1991) *The Death of Luigi Trastulli and Other Essays: Form and Meaning in Oral History*. State University of New York Press.

Posel, Deborah & Ross, Fiona C. (eds.) (2014) *Ethical Quandaries in Social Research*. HSRC Press.

Potter, Jonathan & Hepburn, Alexa (2005) Qualitative interviews in psychology: Problems and possibilities. *Qualitative Research in Psychology*, 2: 281–307.

Powell, Richard C. (2002) The sirens' voices? Field practices and dialogue in geography. *Area*, 34(3): 261–272.

Powell, Richard C. (2008) Becoming a geographical scientist: Oral histories of Arctic fieldwork. *Transactions of the Institute of British Geographers*, 33(4): 548–565.

Pratt, Geraldine (2007) Working with migrant communities: Collaborating with the Kalayaan Centre in Vancouver, Canada. In Kingdon, S., Pain, R. & Kesby, M. (eds.), *Participatory Action Research Approaches and Methods*. Routledge, pp. 95–103.

Pratt, Geraldine (2012) *Families Apart: Migrant Mothers and the Conflicts of Labor and Love*. University of Minnesota Press.

Pratt, Geraldine & Johnston, Caleb (2017) Crossing oceans: Testimonial theatre, Filipina migrant labor, empathy, and engagement. *GeoHumanities*, 3(2): 279–291.

Pratt, Mary Louise (1986) Fieldwork in common places. In Clifford, J. & Marcus, G. (eds.), *Writing Culture*. University of California Press, pp. 27–50.

Prinsloo, Estelle H. (2016) The role of the humanities in decolonising the academy. *Arts and Humanities in Higher Education*, 15(1): 164–168.

Pullen, Alison (2018) Writing as labiaplasty. *Organization*, 25(1): 123–130.

Putnam, Lara (2016) The transnational and the text-searchable: Digitized sources and the shadows they cast. *American Historical Review*, 121: 377–402. https://doi.org/10.1093/ahr/121.2.377

Rabinow, Paul (1996) *Essays on the Anthropology of Reason*. Princeton University Press.

Radley, Alan & Taylor, Diane (2003a) Images of Recovery: A photo-elicitation study on the hospital ward. *Qualitative Health Research*, 13(1): 77–99.

Radley, Alan & Taylor, Diane (2003b) Remembering one's stay in hospital: A study in photography, recovery and forgetting. *Health*, 7(2): 129–159.

Raimbault, Manon & Dubois, Danièle (2005) Urban soundscapes: Experiences and knowledge. *Cities*, 22(5): 339–350.

Ray, Joyce M. (2014) *Research Data Management: Practical Strategies for Information Professionals*. Purdue University Press.

Raynor, Ruth (2017) Dramatising austerity: Holding a story together (and why it falls apart …). *Cultural Geographies*, 24(2): 193–212.

Raynor, Ruth (2019) Speaking, feeling, mattering: Theatre as method and model for practice-based, collaborative, research. *Progress in Human Geography*, 43(4): 691–710.

Reason, P. & Bradbury, H. (eds.) (2005) *Handbook of Action Research*. Sage.

Reeves, Scott, Kuper, Ayelet & Hodges, Brian David (2008) Qualitative research methodologies: Ethnography. *British Medical Journal*, 337(7688): 512–514.

Reis, Arianne C. (2011) Bringing my creative self to the fore: Accounts of a reflexive research endeavour. *Creative Approaches to Research*, 4(1): 2–18.

Riach, Kathleen & Warren, Samantha (2015) Smell organization: Bodies and corporeal porosity in office work. *Human Relations*, 68(5): 789–809.

Richardson, Michael J. (2015) Theatre as safe space? Performing intergenerational narratives with men of Irish descent. *Social and Cultural Geography*, 16(6): 615–633.

Richardson, Pamela (2022) Participatory video (remote, online): Participatory research methods for sustainability-toolkit# 2. *GAIA-Ecological Perspectives for Science and Society*, 31(2): 82–84.

Richardson-Ngwenya, Pamela, Restrepo, Maria, Fernandez, Raúl & Kaufmann, Brigitte (2019) Participatory video proposals: A tool for empowering farmer groups in participatory innovation processes? *Journal of Rural Studies*, 69: 173–185.

Roberts, J. Kessa., Pavlakis, Alexandra E. & Richards, Meredith P. (2021) It's more complicated than it seems: Virtual qualitative research in the Covid-19 era. *International Journal of Qualitative Methods*, 20. https://doi.org/10.1177/16094069211002959

Roberts, Lynne D. (2015) Ethical issues in conducting qualitative research in online communities, *Qualitative Research in Psychology*, 12(3): 314–325, doi: 10.1080/14780887.2015.1008909

Roberts, Margaret (2013) The challenge of enquiry-based learning. *Teaching Geography*, 38(2): 50.

Robson, Colin & McCartan, Kieran (2015) *Real World Research*. John Wiley.

Rodaway, Paul (1994) *Sensuous Geographies: Body, Sense and Place*. Routledge.

Rodrigues, Marta (2019) Putting women in their place: Contributions to a Portuguese historiography of geography (1955 to 1974). University of Sheffield, PhD dissertation.

Rose, D. (1987) *Black American Street Life: South Philadelphia, 1969–71*. University of Pennsylvania Press.

Rose, Gillian (1993) *Feminism and Geography: The Limits of Geographical Knowledge*. Polity.

Rose, G. (1997) Situating knowledges: Positionality, reflexivities and other tactics. *Progress in Human Geography*, 21(3): 305–320.

Rose, G. (2022) *Visual Methodologies: An Introduction to Researching with Visual Materials*, 5th ed. Sage.

Rose, Morag (2020) Pedestrian practices: Walking from the mundane to the marvellous. In Holmes, Helen & Hall, Sarah Marie (eds.), *Mundane Methods: Innovative Ways to Research the Everyday*. Manchester University Press, pp. 211–229.

Rosenblatt, Paul C. (2007) Recovery following bereavement: Metaphor, phenomenology and culture. *Death Studies*, 32(1): 6–16.

Rosenthal, Caitlin (2018) *Accounting for Slavery: Masters and Management*. Harvard University Press.

Roth, Cassia (2018) Kindling for the fire: Why Brazil's lost research archives are irreplaceable. Available from: www.theartnewspaper.com/2018/10/01/kindling-for-the-fire-why-brazils-lost-research-archives-are-irreplaceable. Last accessed 18 January 2022.

Rothe, J. Peter, Ozegovic, Dejan & Carroll, Linda J. (2009) Innovation in qualitative interviewing: 'Sharing circles' in a First Nations community. *Injury Prevention*, 15: 334–340.

Rousseau, Jean Jacques (1762) *Émile: Or, Concerning Education*. DC Heath.

Ruby, Jay (2000) *Picturing Culture: Explorations of Film and Anthropology*. University of Chicago Press.

Runco, Mark A. & Jaeger, Garrett J. (2012) The standard definition of creativity. *Creativity Research Journal*, 24(1): 92–96.

Russolo, Luigi (1986) *The Art of Noises (Futurist Manifesto, 1913)*, trans. Robert Filliou. Pendragon Press.
Sabati, Sheeva (2018) Upholding 'colonial unknowing' through the IRB: Reframing institutional research ethics. *Qualitative Inquiry*, 25(9–10): 1056–1064.
Said, Edward W. (1978) *Orientalism*. Pantheon.
Salinas, Margaret R. (2023) Are your participants real? Dealing with fraud in recruiting older adults online. *Western Journal of Nursing Research*, 45(1): 93–99.
Salmons, Janet E. (2017) Getting to yes: Informed consent in qualitative social media research. In Woodfield, Kandy (eds.), *The Ethics of Online Research*. Emerald, pp. 109–134.
Salmons, Janet E. (2021) *Doing Qualitative Research Online*, 2nd ed. Sage.
Sandoval, Marta, Morgado, Beatriz & Doménech, Ana (2021) University students with disabilities in Spain: Faculty beliefs, practices and support in providing reasonable adjustments. *Disability and Society*, 36(5): 730–749.
Sarmento, J. C. V. & Brito-Henriques, E. (2013) *Tourism in the Global South*. Universidade de Lisboa. Centro de Estudos Geográficos.
Sassatelli, Monica (2007) The arts, the state, and the EU: Cultural policy in the making of Europe. *Social Analysis*, 51(1): 28–41.
Satter, Raphael G. (2008) UK loses data on 84,000 prisoners. NBC News. Available from: www.nbcnews.com/id/wbna26347817. Last accessed 3 May 2022.
Sauer, Carl (1956) The education of a geographer. *Annals of the Association of American Geographers*, 46(3): 287–299.
Saunders, Kristina (2021) 'I think I stick out a bit': The classification of reproductive decision-making. *Sociological Research Online*, 26(1): 75–91.
Scarth, Bonnie J. (2016) Bereaved participants' reasons for wanting their real names used in thanatology research. *Research Ethics*, 12(2): 80–96.
Schaeper, Hildegard (2009) Development of competencies and learning-teaching arrangements in higher education: Findings from Germany. *Studies in Higher Education*, 34(6): 677–697.
Schafer, R. Murray (1977) *The Tuning of the World*. Alfred A. Knopf.
Schartz, Dona (1992) *Waucoma Twilight*. Smithsonian Institution Press.
Schensul, S. L., Schesul, J. J. & LeCompte, M. D. (1999) *Essential Ethnographic Methods: Observations, Interviews and Questionnaires*. Sage.
Scheyvens, Regina (ed.) (2014) *Development Fieldwork: A Practical Guide*, 2nd ed. Sage.
Scheyvens, Regina, Nowak, Barbara & Scheyvens, Henry (2003) Ethical issues. In Scheyvens, Regina (ed.), *Development Fieldwork: A Practical Guide*, 1st ed. Sage, pp. 139–166.
Schmidtpott, Katja & Schölz, Tino (2020) Clever approaches to tricky sources: How to extract information from business archives and war memorials. In Kottmann, Nora & Reiher, Cornelia (eds.), *Studying Japan: Handbook of Research Designs, Fieldwork and Methods*. Nomos, pp. 248–251.
Schofield, John & Rellensmann, Luise (2015) Underground heritage: Berlin techno and the changing city. *Heritage and Society*, 8(2): 111–138.
Schotanus-Dijkstra, Marijke, Havinga, Petra, van Ballegooijen, Wouter, Delfosse, Lynn, Mokkenstorm, Jan & Boon, Brigitte (2014) What do the bereaved by suicide communicate in online support groups? A content analysis. *Crisis: The Journal of Crisis Intervention and Suicide Prevention*, 35: 27–35.

Schrag, Zachary M. (2011) The case against ethics review in the social sciences. *Research Ethics*, 7(4): 120–131.

Schrage, Michael (1999) *Serious Play: How the World's Best Companies Simulate to Innovate*. Harvard Business School Press.

Schroeder, Doris, Chatfield, Kate, Singh, Michelle, Chennells, Roger & Herissone-Kelly, Peter (2019) The San code of research ethics. In Schroeder, D., Chatfield, K., Singh, M., Chennells, R., Herissone-Kelly, P., Schroeder, D. & Herissone-Kelly, P. (eds.), *Equitable Research Partnerships: A Global Code of Conduct to Counter Ethics Dumping*. Springer, pp. 73–87.

Schuermans, Nick & Newton, Caroline (2012) Being a young and foreign researcher in South Africa: Towards a postcolonial dialogue. *Singapore Journal of Tropical Geography*, 33(3): 295–300.

Scott, John (1990) *A Matter of Record: Documentary Sources in Social Research*. Polity Press.

Scott, Steffanie, Miller, Fiona & Lloyd, Kate (2006) Doing fieldwork in development geography: Research culture and research spaces in Vietnam. *Geographical Research*, 44(1): 28–40.

Sennett, Richard (2008) *The Craftsman*. Yale University Press.

Sennett, Richard (2012) *Together: The Rituals, Pleasures and Politics of Cooperation*. Allen Lane.

Sessions, Carrie, Wood, Spencer A., Rabotyagov, Sergey & Fisher, David M. (2016) Measuring recreational visitation at US National Parks with crowd-sourced photographs. *Journal of Environmental Management*, 183: 703–711.

Siegelbaum, Lewis H. & Sokolov, Andrei K. (2000) *Stalinism as a Way of Life: A Narrative in Documents*. Yale University Press.

Silver, Christina & Lewins, Ann (2014) *Using Software in Qualitative Research: A Step-by-Step Guide*, 2nd ed. Sage.

Silverman, David (2020) *Qualitative Research*, 5th ed. Sage.

Silvey, Rachel (2003) Gender and mobility: Critical ethnographies of migration in Indonesia. In Blunt, A., Gruffudd, P., May, J., Ogborn, M. & Pinder, D. (eds.), *Cultural Geography in Practice*. Arnold, pp. 91–105.

Simmons, Deborah A. (1994) Urban children's preferences for nature: Lessons for environmental education. *Children's Environments*, 11(3): 194–203.

Singer, Peter (2016) *Ethics in the Real World*. Princeton University Press.

Skeggs, Beverley & Wood, Helen (2008) The labour of transformation and circuits of value 'around' reality television. *Continuum*, 22(4): 559–572.

Slater, Alison (2020) Listening to dress: Unfolding oral history methods. In Holmes, Helen & Hall, Sarah M. (eds.), *Mundane Methods: Innovative Ways to Research the Everyday*. Manchester University Press, pp. 32–48.

Sloan, Luke & Quan-Haase, Anabel (eds.) (2017) *The Sage Handbook of Social Media Research Methods*. Sage.

Smith, Andrew & Johns, Jennifer (2019) Historicizing modern slavery: Free-grown sugar as an ethics-driven market category in nineteenth-century Britain. *Journal of Business Ethics*, 166: 271–292.

Smith, Keri (2008) *How to be an Explorer of the World*. Penguin.

Smith, Linda Tuhiwai (2021) *Decolonizing Methodologies: Research and Indigenous Peoples*, 3rd ed. Zed/Bloomsbury.

Smith, Louis (2012) Biographical method. In Goodwin, John (Ed.), *Sage Biographical Research*. Sage, pp. 1–36. https://dx.doi.org/10.4135/9781446268537

Smith, Susan (1994) Soundscape. *Area*, 26(3): 232–240.

Smith, Susan (2000) Performing the (sound) world. *Environment and Planning D: Society and Space*, 18(5): 615–637.

Snelson, Chareen L. (2016) Qualitative and mixed methods social media research: A review of the literature. *International Journal of Qualitative Research Methods*, 15(1). https://doi.org/10.1177/1609406915624574

Søderberg, Anne-Marie (2006) Narrative interviewing and narrative analysis in a study of a cross-border merger. *Management International Review*, 46(4): 397–416.

Soja, Edward W. (1989) *Postmodern Geographies: The Reassertion of Space in Critical Social Theory*. Verso.

Sontag, Susan (1973) Freak show. *New York Review of Books*, 15 November.

Soukup, Martin (2014) Photography and drawing in anthropology. *Slovenský Národopis/Slovak Ethnography*, 62(4): 534–546.

South African San Institute (2017) San code of research ethics. Available from: http://trust-project.eu/wp-content/uploads/2017/03/San-Code-of-RESEARCH-Ethics-Booklet-final.pdf

Spronken-Smith, Rachel (2005) Implementing a problem-based learning approach for teaching research methods in geography. *Journal of Geography in Higher Education*, 29(2): 203–221.

Staeheli, Lynn A. & Lawson, Victoria A. (1994) A discussion of 'women in the field': The politics of feminist fieldwork. *Professional Geographer*, 46(1): 96–102.

Stanley, Liz (2016) Archive methodology inside the black box: Noise in the archive! In Moore, Niamh, Salter, Andrea, Stanley, Liz & Tamboukou, Maria (eds.), *The Archive Project: Archival Research in the Social Sciences*. Routledge, pp. 33–68.

Statista Research Department (2022) Leading countries based on Facebook audience size as of January 2022. Statista. Available from: www.statista.com/statistics/268136/top-15-countries-based-on-number-of-facebook-users/. Last accessed 27 May 2022.

Steele, Catherine K. (2021) *Digital Black Feminism*. New York University Press.

Stevens, Stan (2001) Fieldwork as commitment. *Geographical Review*, 91(1–2): 66–73.

Stiglich, Matteo (2021) Unplanning urban transport: Unsolicited urban highways in Lima. *Environment and Planning A: Economy and Space*, 53: 1490–1506.

Stoddart, David R. (1986) *On Geography and its History*. Basil Blackwell.

Stoodley, Lyndsey (2020) Water-based methods: Conducting (self) interviews at sea for a surfer's view of surfing. In Holmes, Helen & Hall, Sarah M. (eds.), *Mundane Methods: Innovative Ways to Research the Everyday*. Manchester University Press, pp. 248–266.

Straughan, Elizabeth R. & Bissell, David (2021) Curious encounters: The social consolations of digital platform work in the gig economy. *Urban Geography*, 43(9): 1–19.

Suchar, Charles (2004) Amsterdam and Chicago: Seeing the macro-characteristics of gentrification. In Knowles, Caroline & Sweetman, Paul (eds.), *Picturing the Social Landscape: Visual Methods and the Sociological Imagination*. Routledge, pp. 147–165.

Sullivan, Tom & Gill, Derek (1975) *If You Could See What I Hear*. Harper and Row.

Sutton-Smith, Brian (1997) *The Ambiguity of Play*. Harvard University Press.

Svensson, Lars (2009) *Collins Bird Guide*, 2nd ed. HarperCollins.

Tarboton, Warwick & Ryan, Peter (2016) *Guide to Birds of the Kruger National Park*. Struik Nature/Penguin-Random House.

Taylor, T. L. (2006) *Play Between Worlds: Exploring Online Gaming Culture*. MIT Press.

TechCrunch (2011) Flick accidentally wipes out account: Five years and 4,000 photos down the drain. Available from: https://techcrunch.com/2011/02/02/flickr-accidentally-wipes-out-account-five-years-and-4000-photos-down-the-drain/?guccounter=1. Last accessed 2 May 2022.

Thanem, Torkild & Knights, David (2019) *Embodied Research Methods*. Sage.

Thompson, Emily (2002) *The Soundscape of Modernity: Architectural Acoustics and the Culture of Listening in America*. MIT Press.

Thomson, P. & Hall, C. (2016) *Place-Based Methods for Researching Schools*. Bloomsbury.

Thorndycraft, Varyl R., Thompson, Don & Tomlinson, Emily (2009) Google Earth, virtual fieldwork and quantitative methods in physical geography. *Planet*, 22(1): 48–51.

Tight, Malcom (2019) *Documentary Research in the Social Sciences*. Sage.

Tiilikainen, Marja (2002) Homes and fields, friends and informants: Fieldwork among Somali refugee women. In Sakaranaho, T., Sjöblom, Utriainen, T. & Pesonen, H. (eds.), *Ethnographic Perspectives in Comparative Religion: Styles and Positions*. University of Helsinki, Department of Comparative Religion, pp. 272–288.

Tilley, Helen (2011) *Africa as a Living Laboratory: Empire, Development, and the Problem of Scientific Knowledge, 1870–1950*. University of Chicago Press.

Tindana, Paulina Onvomaha, Kass, Nancy & Akweongo, Patricia (2006) The informed consent process in a rural African setting: A case study of the Kassena-Nankana district of Northern Ghana. *IRB*, 28(3): 1–6.

Tolia-Kelly, Divya P. (2007) Capturing spatial vocabularies in a collaborative visual methodology with Melanie Carvalho and South Asian women. In Kingdon, S., Pain, R. & Kesby, M. (eds.), *Participatory Action Research Approaches and Methods*. Routledge, pp. 158–166.

Tooth, Stephen & Viles, Heather A. (2021) Equality, diversity, inclusion: Ensuring a resilient future for geomorphology. *Earth Surface Processes and Landforms*, 46(1): 5–11.

Trowell, Ian (2019) Perecquian fieldwork: Photography and the fairground. In Forsdick, C., Leak, A. & Phillips, R. (eds.), *Georges Perec's Geographies: Material, Performative and Textual Spaces*. University College London Press, pp. 200–217.

Tuan, Yi Fu (2001) Life as a field trip. *Geographical Review*, 91(1–2): 41–45.

Tuckman, Bruce W. (1965) Developmental sequence in small groups. *Psychological Bulletin*, 63(6): 384.

Tuckman, Bruce W. & Jensen, Mary Ann C. (1977) Stages of small-group development revisited. *Group and Organization Studies*, 2(4): 419–427.

Uddin, Nasir (2011) Decolonising ethnography in the field: An anthropological account. *International Journal of Social Research Methodology*, 14(6): 455–467.

Udupa, Shana (2016) Archiving as history-making: Religious politics of social media in India. *Communication, Culture and Critique*, 9: 212–230.

United Nations (2006) United Nations Convention on the Rights of Persons with Disabilities. Available at: www.un.org/development/desa/disabilities/convention-on-the-rights-of-persons-with-disabilities/convention-on-the-rights-of-persons-with-disabilities-2.html. Last accessed 5 September 2022.

Urban Sketchers (2022) Homepage. Available at: https://urbansketchers.org/. Last accessed 6 September 2022.

Urry, John (1990) *The Tourist Gaze*. Routledge.

Urry, John & Larsen, Jonas (2011) *The Tourist Gaze*, 3rd ed. Sage.

van Baalen, Sebastian (2018) 'Google wants to know your location': The ethical challenges of fieldwork in the digital age. *Research Ethics*, 14(4): 1–17.

Van Doorn, Niels (2013) Assembling the affective field: How smartphone technology impacts ethnographic research practice. *Qualitative Inquiry*, 19(5): 385–396.

Van Leeuwen, Theo & Jewitt, Carey (2001) *A Handbook of Visual Analysis*. Sage.

Vanderbeck, Robert M. (2005) Masculinities and fieldwork: Widening the discussion. *Gender, Place and Culture*, 12(4): 387–402.

Verne, J. (1867) *Michael Strogoff; or, The Courier of the Czar*. Available at www.gutenberg.org/files/1842/1842-h/1842-h.htm. Last accessed 6 September 2022.

Verran, Helen (1998) Re-imagining land ownership in Australia. *Postcolonial Studies*, 1(2): 237–254.

Vieno, Atte (2021) 'Airport people' in transformation: Vertical disintegration and the reconfiguration of occupational belonging in terminal work at Helsinki Vantaa International Airport. *Sociological Research Online*, 26(1): 108–124.

Visser, Maretha (2012) Participation in community research: Experiences of community researchers undertaking HIV research in South Africa. In Goodson, L. & Phillimore, J. (eds.), *Community Research for Participation: From Theory to Method*. Policy Press, pp. 123–138.

Vitalis, Robert (2006) The past in another country. In Perecman, Ellen & Curran, Sara R. (eds.), *A Handbook for Social Science Field Research: Essays and Bibliographic Sources on Research Design and Methods*. Sage, pp. 5–17.

Volvey, Anne (2012) Fieldwork: How to get in (to) touch – towards a haptic regime of knowledge in geography. In Paterson, M. & Dodge, M. (eds.), *Touching Space, Placing Touch*. Ashgate, pp. 103–130.

von Benzon, Nadia (2019) Informed consent and secondary data: Reflections on the use of mothers' blogs in social media research. *Area*, 51(1): 182–189.

Vosoughi, Soroush, Roy, Deb & Aral, Sinan (2018) The spread of true and false news online. *Science*, 359: 1146–1151.

wa Thiong'o, Ngugi (1992) *Decolonising the Mind: The Politics of Language in African Literature*. East African.

Wacquant, Loïc (2004) *Body and Soul: Notebooks of an Apprentice Boxer*. Oxford University Press.

Wacquant, Loïc (2005) Carnal connections: On embodiment, apprenticeship, and membership. *Qualitative Sociology*, 28: 445–474.

Wacquant, Loïc (2015) For a sociology of flesh and blood. *Qualitative Sociology*, 38(1): 1–11.

Walker, Rob (2019) *The Art of Noticing*. Penguin.

Walter, Maggie & Andersen, Chris (2016) *Indigenous Statistics: A Quantitative Research Methodology*. Routledge.

Walton, Marion & Hassreiter, Silke (2015) Real friends and fake friends: Research relationships in an era of global social media. In Ross, F. & Posel, D. (eds.), *Ethical Quandaries in Social Research*. Human Sciences Research Council, pp. 228–249.

Wang, Di & Liu, Sida (2021) Doing ethnography on social media: A methodological reflection on the study of online groups in China. *Qualitative Inquiry*, 27(8-9): 977–987. doi: 10.1177/10778004211014610

Ward, Catherine, Freiman, Lesley, Jones, Sarah, Molloy, Laura & Snow, Kellie (2011) Making sense: Talking data management with researchers. *The International Journal of Digital Curation*, 2(6): 265–273.

Ward, Richard, Campbell, Sarah & Keady, John (2014) 'Once I had money in my pocket, I was every colour under the sun': Using 'appearance biographies' to explore the meanings of appearance for people with dementia. *Journal of Aging Studies*, 30: 64–72.

Ware, Vron (2006) Info-war and the politics of feminist curiosity: Exploring new frameworks for feminist intercultural studies. *Cultural Studies*, 20(6): 526–551.

Warren, Saskia (2016) Pluralising the walking interview: Researching (im)mobilities with Muslim women. *Social and Cultural Geography*, 18(6): 786–807.

Warren, Saskia (2021) Pluralising (im)mobilities: Anti-Muslim acts and the epistemic politics of mobile methods. *Mobilities*, 16(6): 90–92.

Warwick-Booth, Louise, Bagnall, AnneMarie & Coan, Susan (2021) *Creating Participatory Research: Principles, Practice and Reality*. Policy Press.

Watts, Jacqueline H. (2008) Emotion, empathy and exit: Reflections on doing ethnographic qualitative research on sensitive topics. *Medical Sociology Online*, 3(2): 3–14.

Weale, Sally (2018) London's Black Cultural Archives get £200,000 stopgap funding for survival. *Guardian*. Available from: www.theguardian.com/uk-news/2018/dec/13/london-black-cultural-archives-gets-thousands-stop-gap-funding-for-survival-heritage. Last accessed 8 March 2022.

Webb, Lynne (2017) Online research methods, qualitative. In Matthes, Jörg, Davis, Christine S. & Potter, Robert F. (eds.), *The International Encyclopaedia of Communication Research Methods*. Wiley-Blackwell, pp. 1–9.

Webb, Lynne & Wang, Yan (2013) Techniques for analyzing blogs and micro-blogs. In Sappleton, Natalie (ed.), *Advancing Research Methods with New Technologies*. IGI Global, pp. 183–204.

Weinryb, Noomi, Gustafsson, Nils & Gullberg, Cecilia (2021) Reading and interpreting social media: Exploring positive emotional expressions in organising. In Kostera, Monika & Harding, Nancy (eds.), *Organizational Ethnography*. Edward Elgar, pp. 129–150.

Weller, Wivian & da Silva, Catarina M. (2011) Documentary method and participatory research: Some interfaces. *International Journal of Action Research*, 7(3): 294–318.

Wells, Naomi, Forsdick, Charles, Bradley, Jessica, Burdett, Charles, Burns, Jessica, Demossier, Margaret & Wall, G. (2019) Ethnography and modern languages. *Modern Languages Open*, 1: 1–16.

Welsh, Katherine E., Mauchline, Alice L., Powell, Victoria, France, Derek, Park, Julian R. & Whalley, W. Brian (2015) Student perception of iPads as mobile learning devices for fieldwork. *Journal of Geography in Higher Education*, 39(3): 450–469. doi: 10.1080/03098265.2015.1066315

Wengraf, Tom (2001) *Qualitative Research Interviewing*. Thousand Oaks, CA: Sage.

Wengraf, Tom, Chamberlayne, Prue & Bornat, Joanna (2012) A biographical turn in the social sciences? A British-European view. In Goodwin, John (ed.), *Sage Biographical Research*. Sage, pp. 77–100. https://dx.doi.org/10.4135/9781446268537

West, R. C. (1979) *Carl Sauer's Fieldwork in Latin America*. Department of Geography, Syracuse University.

White, Peter (2004) *With the Jocks: A Soldier's Struggle for Europe 1944–45*. Sutton.

Whiteman, Gail & Cooper, William H. (2011) Ecological sensemaking. *Academy of Management Journal*, 54(50): 889–911.

Wickramasinghe, V. & Perera, L. (2010) Graduates', university lecturers' and employers' perceptions towards employability skills. *Education + Training*, 52(3): 226–244.

Wilk, Richard & Barbosa, Livia (eds.) (2012) *Rice and Beans: A Unique Dish in a Hundred Places*. Berg.

Williams, Raymond (1961) *The Long Revolution*. Chatto & Windus.

Willis, Paul (1977) *Learning to Labour: How Working Class Kids Get Working Class Jobs*. Routledge.

Windchief, Sweeney & San Pedro, Timothy (2019) *Applying Indigenous Research Methods*. Routledge.

Wooldridge, S. W. (1955) The status of geography and the role of fieldwork. *Geography*, 40(2): 73–83.

Wright, John K. (1947) Terrae Incognitae: The place of the imagination in geography. *Annals of the Association of American Geographers*, 37(1): 1–15.

Wu, Di (2022) More than a solo method: Netnography's capacity to enhance offline research methods. *Area*, 54(1): 88–95.

Wulf, Andrea (2015) *The Invention of Nature: The Adventures of Alexander von Humboldt, the Lost Hero of Science*. Knopf.

Yorke, Mantz (2006) *Employability in Higher Education: What it is – What it is Not* (Vol. 1). Higher Education Academy.

Young, Iris Marion (1990) *Throwing like a Girl: Essays in Feminist Philosophy and Social Theory*. Indiana University Press.

Young, Lorraine & Barrett, Hazel (2001) Adapting visual methods: Action research with Kampala street children. *Area*, 33(2): 141–152.

Young, Nathan (2020) Pokémon GO in the field: Digital gaming apps and ethnographic methods. *Journal of Folklore Research*, 57(3): 63–85.

Yow, Valerie R. (2015) *Recording Oral History: A Guide for the Humanities and Social Sciences*, 3rd ed. Rowman & Littlefield.

Zardini, Mirko (2005) *Sense of the City: An Alternative Approach to Urbanism*. Canadian Centre for Architecture and Lars Muller.

Zeitlyn, David (2015) Archiving Cameroonian photographic studio. In Kominko, Maja (ed.), *From Dust to Digital: 10 Years of the Endangered Archive Programme*. Open Books, pp. 531–546.

Ziller, Robert C. (1990) *Auto-photography: Observations from the Inside-out*. Sage.

Zuss, Mark (2012) *The Practice of Theoretical Curiosity*. Springer.

INDEX

Note: Page numbers followed by "*f*" indicate figure and "*t*" indicate table in the text.

A
Aarseth, Espen J., 158
Abbott, Dina, 16, 78, 79
Abdelnour, Samer, 161
ableism, 9, 43
academic identify fieldwork, 8
academic researchers, 188
academic tourism, 16
active learning, 1, 16–17
Adamson, George, 216
Adjaye, David, 142, 143
adventure, 9
Aguinis, Herman, 164
Ahamat, Amiruddin, 99
Akemu, Onajomo, 161
Alberti, Fay Bound, 216
Alder-Nissen, Rebecca, 100
Aldridge, Judith, 236
ambient sounds, 196
Angelo, Anaïs, 217–218, 226
anonymity, 59–60, 168
anti-slavery archive, 209
Aotearoa New Zealand, 14, 41, 146, 239
    Hamilton, 122
appearance biographies, 107
Arbus, Diane, 151
archives, 59, 221
    digital archives, 223
    ecclesiastical archives, 221
    notarial archives, 221
    research, 222*f*
    types of, 221
Argentina, 107
artefacts, 59
The Art of Noticing (Walker), 28
augmented reality (AR), 153, 164
Australia, 110, 160, 181, 246
    Melbourne, 26
Austria, 59–60
    Vienna, 59
auto-photography, 145
Ayrton, Rachel, 58

B
Back, Les, 193, 205
Bahn, Susanne, 110
Bail, Chris, 185
Barratt-Pugh, Llandis, 110
Bates, Jessica, 106
Bendiner-Viani, Gabrielle, 146
Benjamin, Walter, 206
Bennett, Jane, 207, 248
Bennett, Linda, 107
Benzon, Nadia von, 168, 170
Berger, John, 149
big data, 232
Bissell, David, 26
Blanchin, Alice, 100
Boniface, Kevin, 201
Bordessa, Ronald, 206
Botswana, 87
Bozzoli, Belinda, 107
Brace-Govan, Jan, 183
Bruckman, Amy, 168
Bryson, John R., 97, 233–234
Bunge, William (Bill), 206
Burgess, E.W., 19
Burgess, Jaquelin, 119
Burgess, Robert G., 216
Burrell, Jenna, 161
Butler, Judith, 117

C
Calvey, David, 62
Canada, 96, 181, 246
    Alberta, 110
    British Columbia, 12, 81
    Edmonton, 202
    Quebec, 12
Carr, Kate, 196
Carter, Stacy, 169
Castleden, Heather, 124
Central America, 69
Chacko, Elizabeth, 68
Chambers, Megan, 184

Chaplin, Elizabeth, 62, 135, 143
Chapman, Lynne, 62, 136, 137, 139
chicken farm, 10
Child Health Literacy, 62
China, 160
Chinese-Canadian communities, 223, 223*f*
Cleaver, Elizabeth, 145
Cloke, Paul, 145
cloud data storage, 236
Code of Practice for Socio-Economic Research, 58
Coe, Neil, 17
Coffey, Amanda, 69
collaborative fieldwork, 40
collective fieldwork, 51
colonialism, 12, 75, 76
colonisation, 85, 86
computer-aided qualitative data analysis software (CAQDAS), 240
confidentiality, 63
conflict resolution, 246
Cooper, William, 96
corporate social responsibility (CSR), 242
Côté, Isabelle, 177, 179
Cottom, Tressie McMillan, 180
counter-tourism, 148
COVID-19, 105, 154, 187103
Craciun, Catrinel, 106
Crang, Mike, 197
Crang, Phil, 117, 124
Crawley Jackson, Amanda, 137, 138*f*, 139
creative research methods, 13
Crenshaw, Kimberlé Williams, 13
critical visual methodology, 150
Cropper, James, 209
cultural values, 85
cultural work, 30
Cupples, Julie, 69
curiosity, 9, 23–36, 194, 247
　being/becoming, 24–26
　cultivating ways, 26–31
　ethical, 31–35
　and learning, 30–31
　openness and, 31
　scientific, 32
　serendipitous, 26
　value of, 27
curiosity-driven enquiry, 31
curriculum, 77
Cyclogeography (Day), 199

D

dark tourism, 78
data, 2
　analysis, 235, 235*f*, 238
　capturing, 234–235
　challenges, 230

data, *cont.*
　cloud-based data storage, 240
　collection, 157, 210, 230, 235
　critical judgements, 233–234
　digitise, 230
　physical storage, 240
　primary research, 210–212, 214
　processing, 231*t*
　qualitative, 233–234
　quality, 235–238
　recording, 234–235
　research, 230
　secondary research, 15, 210–212, 214–215, 218, 226
　security, 235–238
　storage, 231*t*, 232
　text, 230
　types of, 229–234, 231*t*
　understanding, 229–244
data handling, 229–244
　digital analysis, 240
　insights, 229–230
　sustainable supply chain research, 241–243
data management, 232–233
　recording, 233
　storage, 233
　technologies, 234–235
　volume, 232
data research
　field notes, 239
　through notebook, 238–239
　visual and multisensory methods, 239
data-rich society, 155
Day, Jon, 199
DBS clearance, 57
Dean, Elizabeth, 103
decolonisation, 77
decolonising fieldwork, 72, 75–88, **83**
　form of, 82
　methods, 86
　practical steps, 82–87
　reflexivity, 87–88
Decolonizing Methodologies (Smith), 78
Demsar, Vlad, 183
desk-field, 153
diaries, 142–143
　identifying factors, 216–217
　policy documents, 211
digital data, 236
digital ethnography, 159–160, 188
digital field environments, 160–163
digital fieldwork, 15, 39, 133
　advantages of, 160
　anonymity, 168
　applications, 156–157*t*
　authorship *versus* human research participants, 167–168

digital fieldwork, *cont.*
    challenges of, 166–167
    commercial datasets, 158
    digital spaces, 158–159
    ethics, 167–170
    gaining consent, 168
    immersive, 163–166
    informed consent, 168
    limitations of, 170
    new media, 157–158
    online consent information, 169
    online qualitative methods, 157–158
    pseudonymity, 168
    public/open-source data, 158
    public/private space, 167
    stages, 155
    tools, 156–157*t*, 163–165
digital media, 154
digital spaces, 158–159
digital storytelling, 187–188
digital techniques, 162–163
digital technologies, 153, 154, 162, 229
digitisation, 221
disability, 49, 50–51
disabled people, 50
discrimination, 13
documentary, 210, 212–220
documenting smells, 203–205
Dodman, D. R., 150
Dowling, Robyn, 88
Drakuliæ, Slavenka, 219
drug use, 126–127

E
Edge, Victoria, 146
Egypt, 215
    Cairo, 215
email interviews, 104
emancipatory research, 116
embodied fieldwork, 191, 206
Émile: Or, Concerning Education (Rousseau), 24
employability, 245–246, 247*t*
England. *see* United Kingdom (UK)
England, Kim, 63
environmental researchers, 84
episodic interviewing, 106
epistemic privilege, 84
Esselment, Anna Lennox, 181
ethical fieldwork
    challenges, 55, 56
    clearance, 57, 58
    dilemmas, 68, 69
    ethics screening questions, *58*
    exit strategies, 69–72
    informed consent, 62
    issues, 72, 73, 96

ethical fieldwork, *cont.*
    participant information sheet, 61*f*
    positionalities, 69–72
    printed consent, 62
    proactively, 67–68
    procedures, 57
    relationships, 69–72
    research method, 64–66
    responsibilities, 55
    review, 56, 57–60
    risks, 142
    safeguards, 57
    scrutiny, 72
    tips, 71–72
ethics, 2, 55
    committees, 61
ethnographic research, 214
ethnography, 19, 80, 115–116
eurocentrism, 79
exit strategy, 69
exoticism, 85

F
face-to-face interviews, 103, 105
Feminist Webs, 216
Feneck, Amy, 144
field, 1, 7–21
    class, 1, 7, 16
    course leaders, 17
    interviewing, 93–112
    sites, 79
    trip, 8, 24, 42, 51, 133
    trip leaders, 2, 50
field-based data analysis, 230
field interview
    alternative forms of, 100–103
    email interviews, 104
    episodic, 106
    ethics, 95–96
    face-to-face, 103, 105
    insights, 94–95
    key questions, 95*f*
    limitations of, 110–112
    mobile interviewing, 99
    narrative, 105–106
    one-to-one nature of, 96
    online, 103–105
    oral history, 106–109
    popularity of, 93
    qualitative, 111
    radical critiques of, 111*f*
    reflections on, 110–111
    self-interviewing, 102–103
    semi-structured, 93, 97
    Sharing Circle, 110
    structure, 99–100

field interview, *cont.*
   unstructured, 100
   using artefacts/contemporary objects, 109–110
   virtual world, 103
   walking, 101–102, 109
field research project
   ideas, 32–33, *33*
   methods, 33–35
fieldwork, 1, 7–21
   academics identify, 8
   active learning, 16–17
   affective-focused fieldwork, 248
   challenge of, 249
   collaborative, 40
   collective, 51
   colonial, 78
   creativity, 249
   curiosity, 31, 247
   decolonising, 72
   definition, 11–14
   digital, 39, 133
   emotional experiences, 248
   endotic, 15
   ethics of, 86
   failure, 35
   group, 43
   hallmarks of, 246–247
   hands-on enquiry, 249
   haptic, 197–201
   inclusive, 44, 45
   innovation, 19–20, 249
   methods, 80
   mixed methods research, 211, 212
   normative whiteness, 79
   off-the-peg methods, 249
   participatory, 123
   perspectives on, 11–12*t*
   photographic, 136, 144*f*
   physical, 154
   power of, 8
   problem solving, 249
   qualities, 249
   reflexive, 88
   sensory experiences, 248
   serendipitous, 26
   skills, 247*t*, 249
   student, 7
   students calling for change, 76–77
   tradition of, 19–21, 118, 155
   visions, 24
   willingness, 248
Finland, 70, 93
Flick, Uwe, 106
Foley, Geraldine, 104–105
food, 117–118
   comfort zone, 123

formal ethical reviews, 58
Foucault, Michel, 148
Frazier, Emily, 35
free writing, 27
Freire, Paulo, 77
Fujii, Lee Ann, 237, 238

G
Gambia, 16
Gangneux, Justine, 183
Garland-Thomson, Rosemarie, 135
garment supply chains, 233
Garrett, Bradley, 192
gatekeepers, 124
Geertz, Clifford, 19, 125
Germany, 108
Gerster, Julia, 181
Ghana, 161
Glass, Michael, 43–44
Goldblatt, David, 144
Góralska, Magdalena, 153
greenwashing, 233
Guillet, David, 234
Gullberg, Cecilia, 181
Gustafsson, Nils, 181

H
Haenlein, Michael, 173
Hall, Sarah Marie, 70–71, 99
Hammond, Timur, 224
Hansen, Nancy, 116
haptic fieldwork, 197–201
Haque, Saira, 182
harm, 56
Harper, Sherilee, 146
Harris, Cole, 8, 12–13
Haynes, Will, 64–66, 136
healthcare, 62
Heath, Sue, 139, 145
Heidbrink, Simone, 158, 159
Henshaw, Victoria, 203
Herrera, Yoshiko M., 235
Herrick, Clare, 24
Hine, Christine, 170
Hinton, Sam, 182
Hitchings, Russell, 59–60
Hjorth, Larissa, 182
Hochman, Nadav, 182, 183
Ho, Elsie, 123, 130
Holton, Mark, 101
Hong Kong, 20
hooks, bell, 126
How to be an Explorer of the World (Smith), 28
Hubbard, Timothy D., 164
Hudson, James, 168
Humboldt, Alexander von, 19, 76

I

identities, 84
immersive digital fieldwork, 163–166
immersive technologies, 153
inclusive fieldwork, 44, 45
India, 30–31
    Madurai, 30
    Thiruvananthapuram, 30
Indigenous, 77
Instagram, 160
institutional ethical codes, 57
interpersonal skills, 246
interviewing, 14
Israel, 213
Italy
    Rome, 64

J

Jackson, Peter, 9, 10, 13, 119
Jacobs, Jane, 13, 118, 121, 125
Jalloh, Alusine, 217
Jamerson, Trevor, 183
James, Daniel, 107
Japan, 211, 221
    Tokyo, 111
Javornick, Ana, 165–166
Jazeel, Tariq, 87
Jertfelt, Isa Gustafsson, 100
Johnsen, Sarah, 145
Johns, Jennifer, 108–109, 209, 214, 220f, 233–234
Johnson, Azeezat, 13
Johnson, Max, 121, 126–127
Johnston, Lynda, 123, 130

K

Kaplan, Andreas, 173
Kapur, Devesh, 235
Kara, Helen, 13, 85
Katz, Cindi, 67, 68
Kaul, Vaibhav, 84
Kaundjua, Maria, 80
Kazakhstan, 25
Kearns, Robin, 19, 125
Keikelame, Mpoe Johannah, 17–19, 26, 117
Kerson, Toba, 104
Kim, Minsung, 162–163, 163f
Kozinets, Robert V., 165

L

Lamb, Christopher, 124
LaRocco, Annette Alfina, 87
Larsen, Jonas, 134
Lashua, Brett, 197, 202–203
Latin America, 212
Laurier, Eric, 115
Leeuw, Sarah de, 80–82
Lèvi-Strauss, Claude, 19, 125
LGBT+, 45, 48
life, 246–249
Li, Jun, 34–35, 121–122
Li, Mohan, 147
Li, Sihong, 100
Longhurst, Robyn, 122, 123, 125, 130
Lorimer, Hayden, 224
Lykes, Brinton, 145

M

MacGinty, Roger, 216
Madise, Kentse, 87
Malaysia, 99, 237
    Kuala Lumpur, 43
Malbon, Ben, 124, 126
Maramwidze-Merrison, Efrider, 181
marginalisation, 77
Marland, Alex, 181
Mason, Olivia, 101
Mato, Daniel, 211, 212, 226
May, Jon, 145
McAvity, Katharine, 107
McCartan, Kieran, 32
McCarthy, Lucy, 241–243
McCoyd, Judith, 104
McDowell, Linda, 72, 73, 87, 98, 110
McFarlane, Colin, 87
McFarlane, Hazel, 116
McLafferty, Sarah, 87
McLean, Kate, 203, 204–205
Merleau-Ponty, Maurice, 192
messages, 168
microcomputers, 234
Miller, Daniel, 182
Mitchell, William, 151
mixed reality (MR), 153, 164
Mlambo, Nelson, 80
mobile interviewing, 99
mobility, 49–50
Moore, Niamh, 215, 216
Morgan, Vanessa Sloan, 124
Morrison, Marlene, 216
Mountain, Priest, Son (Kaul), 84
multisensory fieldwork, 191
    describing, 201–203
    documenting smells, 203–205
    interpretation, 205–206
    listening, 193, 194
    noise, 194, 196
    physical contact, 200
    recording, 201–203

multisensory fieldwork, *cont.*
  smell, 204
  sounds, 193, 195, 196
  touch, 198
  voice, 195
Murphy, Kate, 193
Muslims, 45
Myers, Garth, 63

N
narrative interviewing, 105–106
natural environment, 59
Nepal, 67
netnography, 165
neurodiverse, 42, 50
new media, 157–158
New Zealand. *see* Aotearoa New Zealand
Nicaragua, 120
Niezna, Maayan, 212–213
Nkotsoe, Mmantho, 107
non-consenting others, 56
normative whiteness, 79
Northern Ireland, 106

O
official records, 215
Oliver, Catherine, 160
online interviewing, 103–105
online qualitative methods, 157–158
open-ended fieldwork, 30–31
oral history interviewing, 106–109
otherness, 183

P
Pakistan, 115, 119
  Lahore, 119–120
Parker, Simon, 211
Park, Robert E., 19
Parr, Hester, 63, 124, 125, 192
participant observation, 115–130
  ethical challenge, 121
  ethics, 120–122
  insights, 117
  interpreting findings, 125–129
  learning by doing, 117–120
  writing, 125–129
participatory fieldwork, 115–130
participatory research, 116
Pawson, Eric, 14, 40
Pedagogy of the Oppressed (Freire), 77
Perec, Georges, 28
personal documents, 216
personal qualities, 246–249
Phillips, Adam, 27

Phillips, Richard, 139–142, 218, 219*f*
photo-elicitation, 145–146
photography, 147
  fieldwork, 136, 144*f*
  studies, 143–145
  surveys, 142–143
Pick, Doreén, 217
Pink, Sarah, 134, 147
policy documents, 211
positionality, 56, 72, 76, 87
Pottinger, Laura, 99
practicalities, 124–125
proactively ethical fieldwork, 67–68
problem-based learning (PBL), 33, 40
pseudonymity, 168
public policy, 211
Putman, Lara, 223

Q
Qualitative Research (Silverman), 33

R
Radley, Alan, 145
Ramli, Kautsar, 237
're-Africanising African universities' (Mazrui), 31
reciprocal learning processes, 68
reflexivity, 87–88
Reis, Arianne, 239
research
  design, 23–36
  emancipatory, 116
Rhodes, Cecil, 76–77
Richardson, Pamela, 20, 122, 123, 123*f*, 146, 187–188
Riley, Mark, 101
Roberts, J. Kessa, 168–169
Roberts, Lynne, 167, 168
Robson, Colin, 32
Rose, Gillian, 9, 45, 150
Rose, Morag, 49–50
Rosenblatt, Paul, 96
Rothe, Peter, 110
Rousseau, Jean Jacques, 24
Russell, Polly, 9

S
safeguards, 57
Salinas, Margaret, 184
Sassatelli, Monica, 100
Sauer, Carl, 19
Saunders, Kristina, 109–110
Schartz, Dona, 151
Scheyvens, Regina, 61
Schmidtpott, Katja, 221, 223

Schrage, Michael, 9, 248
scientific curiosity, 32
secondary research, 209–227
    accessing, 220–224
    critical challenges of, 225–226
    digital material, 221
    and documentary sources, 214–220
    ethical challenges of, 226–227
    insights, 210–214
    physical material, 221
    practical challenges of, 224–225
self-directed photography, 145
self-interviewing, 102–103
self-reflexive, 147–149
Sennett, Richard, 33
Shinn, Jamie E., 87
Siegelbaum, Lewis, 217
Silverman, David, 33
Silvey, Rachel, 239
Singapore, 20
Skeggs, Bev, 94
skills, 245–246
    soft, 246
    subject-specific, 246
    technical, 246
Slater, Alison, 107
Slater, Don, 182
slavery
    archives, 209
    history of, 78
smellscape research, 203, 207
Smith, Andrew, 209
Smith, Keri, 28
Smith, Linda Tuhiwai, 78, 86
Smith, Matt Baillie, 29–31
Smyth, Fiona, 17
Snelson, Chareen, 174
social change, 122
social context, 180
social media, 68, 158
    accessing research communities, 181–182
    amplify social phenomena, 182
    characteristics of, 180
    definitions of, 174
    ethical considerations, 177–179, 178t
    fake news, 185
    forms of, 173, 174, 176t
    insights, 173–177
    limitations of, 188
    networks, 185
    noise of, 183
    offline methods, 186
    platforms, 177, 181, 183, 186
    research, 174, 182–184

social media, *cont.*
    research challenges, 184–185
    research dissemination tool, 185–188
    technologies, 174
    use of, 180, 184
    users, 185
social phenomena, 180
Søderberg, Anne-Marie, 106
Soja, Ed, 14
Sokolov, Andrei, 217
Sontag, Susan, 151
soundscapes, 197
soundwalk, 197
South Africa, 58, 76, 77, 181
    Cape Town, 17–19, 26, 117
South Korea, 20, 24, 162
Spronken-Smith, Rachel, 41
Sri Lanka, 246
Steele, Catherine Knight, 158
Stevenson, Olivia, 63
Stevens, Stan, 67
Stoddart, David, 9
Stoodley, Lyndsey, 102
Straughan, Elizabeth, 26
student fieldwork, 7
Suchar, Charles, 148
Sudan, 67, 68
Su-Jeong Kim, 24–26
Swicegood, Jodi, 182

T
Taylor, Diane, 145
team, 40–44
teamwork
    challenges, 42
    conflicts, 42
    disability, 50–51
    exclusion, 45–50
    including others, 44
    inclusion, 45–50
    skills, 40
    solutions, 42
    team, 40–44
    team members, roles, 41t
Teather, Elizabeth, 14
Thanem, Torkild, 192
Tiilikainen, Marja, 70
Touboulic, Anne, 241–243
tourism
    academic, 16
    dark, 78
    smacks of, 16
tourist gaze, 148
troubleshooting, 88

U

Udupa, Sahana, 185
Uganda, 58
   Kampala, 145
United Kingdom (UK), 58, 63, 76, 78, 108, 110, 111, 123, 160, 181, 215, 220, 226
   Canterbury, 14
   London, 59, 98, 144
   Manchester, 93, 99
   Sheffield, 121, 139–142
United States (US), 35, 75, 108, 118, 158, 160, 181, 184
   California, 24
   Chicago, 19
   New York, 13, 67, 147, 164, 183, 199
   Texas, 168
   Washington, 215
urban planners, 13
urban sketchers, 137
Urry, John, 134
Uzbekistan, 25

V

values, 246–249
Vanchan, Vida, 233–234
Verran, Helen, 216
video games, 158–159
virtual reality (VR), 153, 164
visual data, 150
visual encounter, 135–136
visual ethnographers, 134
visual ethnography, 146–147
visual fieldwork
   diaries, 142–143
   drawing, 137–142
   ethics, 135–136
   insights, 134
   interpreting findings, 149–151
   limitations of, 133
   methods, 134

visual fieldwork, *cont.*
   observational sketches, 139–142
   photo-elicitation, 145–146
   photographic studies, 143–145
   photographic surveys, 142–143, 143*f*
   sketch, 137–142
   surveillance, 151
   urban sketchers, 137
Vitalis, Robert, 215
Volvey, Anne, 197
Vosoughi, Soroush, 185

W

Wacquant, Loïc, 199
Walker, Rob, 28
walking interviewing, 101–102
Wang, Yan, 157
Ward, Catherine, 232
Webb, Lynne, 157
Weinryb, Noomi, 181
Wells, Naomi, 31
Whiteman, Gail, 96
Wilkins, Lisa Wescott, 174, 175
Williams, Raymond, 134
Willox, Ashlee Cunsolo, 146
Wooldridge, Sidney William, 17
work, 245–246
Wright, John K., 32
Wu, Di, 160

Y

Young, Nathan, 159
Yow, Valerie, 98

Z

Zaidi, Sobia, 119–120, 123
Zielke, Stephan, 217
Zimbabwe, 123, 146, 187
Zuss, Mark, 192